MW00453089

GIDI
One Chasing a Thousand

JOSEPH EVRON

ONE CHASING A THOUSAND

Translated from the Hebrew by
Philip Simpson

MENACHEM BEGIN
HERITAGE CENTER

JERUSALEM ◆ NEW YORK

The Late Amihai Paglin (Gidi) Memorial Society
wishes to thank Menachem Begin Heritage Center
for assistance in the publication of the English edition.

Typesetting: KPS, Jerusalem
Cover Design: S. Kim Glassman

ISBN 978-965-229-441-8

Edition 1   3   5   7   9   8   6   4   2

Gefen Publishing House Ltd.   Gefen Books
6 Hatzvi Street, Jerusalem 94386, Israel   600 Broadway, Lynbrook, NY 11563, USA
972-2-538-0247 • orders@gefenpublishing.com   1-800-477-5257 • orders@gefenpublishing.com

www.gefenpublishing.com

Printed in Israel   *Send for our free catalogue*

CONTENTS

THE STORMING OF ACRE PRISON

THE BATTLE FOR JAFFA

END OF THE JOURNEY

SOURCES

APPENDIX: THE CID REPORT ON HEINRICH REINHOLD (YANAI) AND THE IZL

HISTORICAL BACKGROUND

On February 1, 1944, Menahem Begin, the commander of the Irgun Zvai Leumi, issued a proclamation of revolt against British rule in Palestine. It was a declaration of a war, a war that was not to end until Britain left Palestine over four years later on May 15, 1948.

The Irgun was at the time a small underground military organization that had undergone difficult and turbulent times in the previous four years. With the outbreak of World War II on September 1, 1939, the Irgun was faced with a dilemma: to continue its attacks against the British in Palestine, or to declare a truce and cooperate with Britain in the war against Nazi Germany. What might have been an easy decision, considering Hitler's blatant anti-Jewish policies, was made difficult by Britain's anti-Zionist policies in Palestine. On May 17, 1939, the British government had announced a new policy for Palestine, the MacDonald White Paper, which, if implemented, would have sounded the death knell for the Zionist dream of establishing a Jewish state in Palestine. Moreover, according to this new policy, Jewish immigration to Palestine would be limited to a total of 75,000 for the following five-year period. The Jews of Europe, persecuted by the Germans and desperately seeking a refuge, had the doors to Palestine slammed in their faces by the British government. Would a continuation of the fight against British rule in Palestine by the Irgun force Britain to retreat from this policy? Should the Irgun, rather than aiding Britain in the fight against Germany, continue its attacks against Britain? These were the questions that faced the rank-and-file members of the Irgun in 1940 and led to a split in its ranks.

Zeev Jabotinsky, the supreme commander of the Irgun, had no doubts about the course of action that needed to be taken. He was convinced that the war against Germany must take precedence over everything else – the Jewish people must fight its arch-enemy, and take its place in the ranks of the nations fighting Germany. The fight against British rule in Palestine would have to be suspended in the meantime. The commander of the Irgun, David Raziel, accepted wholeheartedly Jabotinsky's decision, and began preparations for cooperation between the British military and the Irgun. But not all in the Irgun agreed. Avraham Stern ("Yair"), a leading member of the Irgun, disagreed and led a split in the Irgun on this issue and formed a new organization, the Freedom Fighters for Israel (the Stern Group), dedicated to a continuation of the struggle against British rule in Palestine. Both men were to give their lives for the cause they believed in during the following months. Raziel fell in May 1941 while on a mission for the British in Iraq, and Stern was gunned down by British policemen in Tel Aviv in February 1942.

Begin assumed the leadership of the Irgun at the end of 1943, determined to resume the fight against British rule in Palestine. At this time the Germans were in retreat on all fronts. Allied victory was by now only a matter of time. The news of the mass extermination of the Jews of Europe had reached Palestine, but the British still prevented Jewish refugees escaping from Europe from reaching the shores of Palestine. Begin concluded that the time had come to resume military action against the British in Palestine in order to force them to leave. From now on the Irgun, and the smaller Freedom Fighters for Israel (FFI), would battle the British until they eventually were to leave Palestine.

The Irgun at the time numbered no more than a few hundred fighters. It was short of resources and poorly armed. Since it could not expect to defeat the over 100,000 British military and police forces stationed in Palestine, its aim would be to inflict sufficient damage to them, so that with the aid of public opinion in the world, aroused by the Irgun's battle, the British government in London would conclude that it was in the British interest to leave Palestine. The Irgun's success would depend on the courage, daring, and unwavering motivation of its fighters.

The chief of operations of the Irgun at the time was 25-year-old Eitan Livni. Under his command the Irgun began a series of attacks against British installations in Palestine. Livni was apprehended by the British in April 1946 and a replacement had to be found in the ranks of the Irgun fighters. One who had made a name for himself in the many attacks against British installations in the previous two years was Amihai Paglin ("Gidi"), a 22-year-old youngster, born and raised in Palestine. In the following years Irgun fighters, in actions planned and directed by him, made life unbearable for the British in Palestine, and succeeded in drawing the world's attention to the struggle going on in Palestine, while at the same time hundreds of thousands of Jewish survivors of the Holocaust languished in displaced person camps in Europe clamoring for the right to reach the Jewish homeland, and "illegal" immigrant ships were turned back by the British navy as they approached the shores of Palestine . Public relations support in the US for the Irgun's attacks in Palestine was provided by the Irgun's delegation in the US, headed by Hillel Kook (Peter Bergson), under the aegis of the American League for a Free Palestine and the Hebrew Committee for National Liberation.

In July 1946 the Irgun staged its most spectacular operation so far – the blowing up of British headquarters in the King David Hotel in Jerusalem. It was becoming clear that the British government was beginning to have second thoughts about continuing to rule Palestine. In February 1947, after months of almost daily Irgun and FFI attacks against British targets, Ernest Bevin, the British foreign secretary, announced that Britain was going to refer the issue of Palestine's future to the United Nations. It was the first signal that the Irgun's campaign was beginning to bear fruit.

But the ultimate intentions of the British government were as yet in doubt. In April 1947, after rejecting repeated appeals for clemency, four Irgun fighters, who had been sentenced by British military courts to death, were hanged in Acre prison. The Irgun's response, in May 1947, was the Acre prison break, freeing many of the Irgun and FFI fighters held prisoner there. When in July the British hanged three more Irgun fighters, the Irgun retaliated by hanging two British sergeants who had been abducted in the hope of preventing the hangings. The struggle between a small underground organization and the British Empire aroused waves of sympathy for the Jewish cause.

Paglin ("Gidi") had shown himself to be a brilliant and daring commander. His actions, under the supervision of Begin, together with the worldwide protest against Britain's policies in Palestine, had forced the British to decide to abandon their rule in Palestine. On November 29, 1947, the United Nations General Assembly decided on the partition of Palestine into a Jewish state and an Arab state. Britain was now obliged to leave.

But before the departure of the British another task awaited Paglin. Jaffa, the largest Arab city in Palestine, was a constant threat, with Arab snipers shooting at people walking the streets of Tel Aviv. The port of Jaffa was most likely to be a port of debarkation for Arab troops reaching for the heart of the Jewish community in Palestine. In April, a month before Israel's declaration of independence, Paglin led an Irgun attack on Jaffa, which – after heavy fighting and severe losses to the Irgun – was successful and led to the fall of Jaffa. In the battle Irgun fighters had to face British troops who intervened in favor of the Arabs. But Paglin's brilliant leadership won the day.

More than four years passed after Begin's proclamation of revolt until the British departure from Palestine. Their decision to leave was the result of a combination of factors and the result of the combined effort of many. But the battle waged by the Irgun stands out above all others. And the man who commanded that battle in the decisive years was "Gidi," Amihai Paglin.

Moshe Arens
former Defense Minister
and Foreign Minister of the State of Israel

INTRODUCTION

Few knew him by his full name, Amihai Paglin.
Everyone called him "Gidi."
His name became a legend.

He appeared suddenly, like a shooting star, out of the looming storm-clouds of the Jewish war for independence in Palestine – Eretz Israel.

He turned the Irgun Zvai Leumi (IZL[1]) into a formidable fighting machine, striking at the British without pause and without mercy – and 100,000 military and police personnel could find no effective response.

"What this marvelous young man has done – this man whose military expertise is without doubt close to genius – the British will remember all their days on this earth," said Menahem Begin.

He did not exaggerate.

"It was the Irgun Zvai Leumi that caused the British evacuation from Palestine," Winston Churchill admitted. "Members of the Irgun caused us so much trouble that we had to station eighty thousand troops in the country to cope with the situation. The military costs were too high for

---

1.   Irgun Zvai Leumi means "National Military Organization." It is also commonly known by its abbreviation IZL (*aleph, tzadi, lamed*), pronounced in Hebrew as Etzel.

1

our economy to bear, and the Irgun was responsible for driving the costs to such a high level."[2]

"Lean, tall, dark-haired, deep and fiery eyes – a man not knowing the meaning of fear"[3] – was the description of the man who, leading a handful of young men and showing an exceptional grasp of strategic planning, carried out daring and complex operations, which in terms of conventional warfare would have required the deployment of battalions of regular troops, on a scale infinitely beyond the resources available to the underground at that time.

It is hard to come to terms with the fact that the task force that breached the wall of Acre prison numbered just 34 fighters, the youngest 17 years old and the oldest 34. But fact it is.

The concept of impossibility did not exist in the consciousness of Amihai Paglin.

He proved this in the bombing of the King David Hotel, in the raid on Goldschmidt House, and above all, perhaps, in the conquest of Jaffa.

He made the lives of the British in Eretz Israel hell.

In a debate on the subject of "Palestine (Jewish Terrorism)" held in the House of Commons on January 31, 1947, Oliver Stanley, formerly minister for the colonies in Churchill's government, painted a grim picture of the situation on the ground, and the atmosphere of intimidation surrounding the British soldier in Palestine in the war against terrorism:

> Under the conditions of war, as we knew it, we did know who our enemies were, where they were, and the rules permitting us to try to hit them before they hit us. Here, in the circumstances which our troops have to endure, no one knows who their enemy is. It may be the girl who has served one in the café; it may be the man one passes in the street. No one knows where one's enemies are. They may be at one's elbow at any moment and the circumstances are usually such that one has got to let them make their attack before, with safety, one is entitled to reply.... I do not believe that, on these lines, it is possible to carry on

---

2. Winston Churchill, quoted by author and dramatist Ben Hecht, *Perfidy* (New York: Messner, 1961), p. 40.
3. Description of Gidi by Colonel (Res.) Yehuda Naot (Globman), interview with the author, 1997.

the Government of Palestine. No authority can stand up against such blows. No troops, no police can carry out their duties in circumstances such as these.… Frankly, so far as I am concerned, sooner than that this country should have to endure further humiliations of this kind, I would prefer that we should clear out of Palestine and tell the peoples of the world that we are unable to carry out our Mandate there.[4]

"He was a genius in all aspects of military operations, with his ability to think in unorthodox terms," former defense minister Moshe Arens said of him.

"His outstanding technical skill, his inventiveness, and his courageous leadership in battle were renowned, and his reputation reached those of us exiled in Africa,"[5] according to former prime minister and commander of the Lehi (Lohamei Herut Israel) in the underground era Yitzhak Shamir (see page 363).

"Gidi didn't send others into action – he led it himself," said Brigadier (Res.) Mordecai Zipori. "He personally handled every stage of the operation, from preliminary reconnaissance to execution. He was always on the front line, as is typical of our style of warfare. He was someone we could all learn from."[6]

This book deals exclusively with Amihai Paglin's activities during the underground period. Even so, the screen is too small to accommodate the whole, and I have been forced to exercise rigorous selectivity in the choice of material. Furthermore, of all Gidi's operations here I have concentrated on the greatest and most daring of them; those which at the time shook the pillars of an empire and undermined the very foundations of British dominion over the region.

This in no way detracts from the importance of the rest.

On the other hand, it should be stressed that Gidi's activities were not confined to the underground period. A dynamic and vibrant personality such as his could not be constrained by any narrow time frame. Without going into every detail of his activities after the establishment of the

---

4. Hansard, House of Commons Debate (HC Deb), vol. 432, cols. 1302–1306.
5. Yitzhak Shamir was among the underground prisoners exiled by the British to Eritrea.
6. Mordechai Zipori, in a speech marking the fifteenth anniversary of the deaths of Tzipora and Amihai Paglin.

State – some of them still classified – I can refer obliquely, and in general terms, to a few of these topics, as they have arisen from interviews that I conducted with those involved.

Colonel Yosef Yariv relates:

> It was shortly before the outbreak of the Six-Day War. At that time I was commander of the operational unit of the Mossad. One of our plans was to blockade the Suez Canal. We were going to buy a big ship, load it with ballast, and sink it at the entrance to the canal, blocking all traffic. The problem was, how to make sure the ship was going to sink quickly, before the Egyptians got the chance to tow it away. And then someone (I don't remember who) brought up the name of Amihai Paglin and suggested he be consulted "as an expert saboteur."[7] I remember hearing someone say, "He's got a brilliant mind for machines and special operations."
>
> We met. I don't remember who arranged the meeting. He was just suddenly there, in my office at HQ, and he agreed to take the project on. It didn't take him long to find the technical solution that was needed; he constructed several models, demonstrated them to us and then got down straightaway to the operational stages. He did the job in his own workshop and in the Mossad's laboratories. As far as I remember, he did everything himself. He prepared two or three operational machines that worked to our satisfaction, but then the war broke out – we were simply overtaken by events and the project was never implemented.[8]

"Once I had formed a government, I invited Gidi to be my advisor in the campaign against Arab terrorism," Menahem Begin has said. "It was a natural choice. There was no one better suited for the job. In the few months which he spent in this role, he achieved a great deal…. Naturally, I can't make the details public, but we're talking about saving lives."[9]

One aspect of this commitment to the safety of citizens of the State of Israel is revealed by his assistant at the time, Azriel Nevo:

---

7. The recommendation to approach Gidi came from the man then serving as prime minister and minister of defense, Levi Eshkol. Information from Neriel, son of Amihai Paglin, who heard it from his father.
8. Recorded interview with Colonel Yosef Yariv, January 30, 1997.
9. Menahem Begin, in funeral oration for Amihai Paglin and his wife Tzipora.

He arrived full of ideas. The demolitions branch of the Israeli police force had a low priority rating at that time, and was seriously underfinanced. He summoned the chief demolitions officer of the force, Yosi Wartzmann.

"What century are you people living in?" he asked.

"I've got loads of ideas and prospectuses," Wartzmann replied, "but I can't get the funding…"

"Bring me the prospectuses," said Gidi.

That same day he picked up the phone and called a robot manufacturer in Britain. He spoke directly to the manager and then an urgent order was dispatched by telex (fax wasn't yet in use). He personally approached the bureaucrats of the Treasury and, wondrous to relate – funding was approved. It wasn't long before the first bomb-disposal robot began working for the Israeli police force.

Another pet project of his was the protection of civilian aircraft from missile attack. His technical talents and operational abilities were truly amazing. I remember engineers who witnessed his experiments asking me repeatedly, "Which university did he study at?"

The short time I spent working with him was an unforgettable experience. He had a fertile mind, and people who used to dismiss his ideas as "science fiction" suddenly began camping on his doorstep.[10]

Another high-profile product, of a totally different kind, constructed in Paglin's workshop, was the furnace in which the corpse of Adolf Eichmann was cremated.

Fifteen hours was the deadline allotted to Gidi for the completion of the project. "We worked like madmen," he recalled.[11] "It turned out that the government was under intense international pressure to spare Eichmann's life, so it wanted the sentence carried out immediately."

In the agreement whereby the IZL was incorporated into the IDF (Israel Defense Force), there was a clause stipulating that three of its commanders – Meridor, Lenkin, and Paglin – would be recruited with the rank of general.

---

10. Recorded interview, December 17, 1996, with Azriel Nevo, serving at that time as intelligence attache to the Prime Minister's Office.
11. *Yediot Aharonot*, September 16, 1977.

Twice Amihai Paglin presented himself at the recruitment office. Twice he was rejected. "Unfit for service – on grounds of health" was the note attached to his dossier.

Who said that the IDF hierarchy has no sense of humor?

Gidi was not amused. This was a slight that he would not forgive until his dying day.

"If the rulers of Israel had been intelligent, and had exploited the full potential of commitment, sacrifice, and tactical skill, and men like Gidi had played a part in running the War of Independence – the borders of the country would be different today and the character of the State would be different," was the bitter comment of Brigadier (Res.) Mordecai Zipori.[12]

A few words about the origins and content of the book.

Thirty-nine years ago, in January 1969, the late Amihai Paglin (Gidi) approached me, asking if I would record his memories of the underground period, as the basis for the writing of a book. I agreed readily. The man and his activities were not unfamiliar to me.

We met for the first time in the spring of 1946 – shortly after the IZL's attack on the police headquarters in Ramat Gan. I had been recruited into the Palmah, naval section. This was the period of the Hebrew Resistance Movement – and the atmosphere was tense. Like many others, I was full of nervous expectation, when we were summoned one evening for "a friendly chat" with the Palmah's information officer. It's not hard to imagine our astonishment when the lecturer – utterly disregarding the principle of unified struggle against the British – unleashed a furious tirade against the IZL, denouncing the attack on the Ramat Gan police HQ and declaring that the time had come for a new "Saison" (purge). To my surprise, on this occasion there were even cries of protest from the Leftists in the group. For my part, I decided to warn the underground organizations without delay.

I made contact with a girl I knew from my hometown (Safed), the late Tzipora Perl. She set to work and arranged a meeting for me in Petah Tikva, with someone known as Gidi. "You can speak to him freely," she assured me.

Following this meeting, we saw one another a number of times.

"A warning has been passed to those affected," Gidi told me at our

---

12. Mordecai Zipori, speech (see n. 5).

second meeting, but he said we should stay in touch. When tempers had cooled a little, he surprised me with a sudden invitation: "What's keeping you there? Who's keeping you there? Come and join us."

And so I found myself a few months later in the Tel Aviv "combat squad," which would be at the center of some of the most dramatic events of those times.

Twenty-three years later I recorded the events to which I had been an inside witness – as recalled by the man who initiated them, planned them, and sometimes participated in their implementation.

After several taped interviews Gidi changed his mind about writing a book.

"I'm still too young to be bothering with memoirs," he said. "The whole of my future is in front of me. Hold on to the tapes until the time is right." When that would be, he didn't say.

Nine years later he was killed in a road accident, together with his wife, Tzipora Paglin (Perl).

For 31 years the tapes were in my possession. The year 2000 seemed "the right time" to release their contents.

In 1996 the family of the late Amihai Paglin and a group of former comrades-in-arms decided to commission a book to perpetuate his memory. They approached me. As one who had pursued such a project during Amihai's lifetime and conducted a series of personal interviews with him, I gladly accepted the commission.

It soon became clear to me that I had taken on a far from simple task. Describing Gidi's personality and activities amounts to telling the whole story of the IZL's war against the British authorities. You won't find a single major operation in those critical years with which Gidi's name is not associated – in the planning and often in the execution as well. His footsteps are imprinted, as landmarks, on the road of the IZL's campaign in the fateful years 1946–1948. Gidi's story and the IZL's struggle at that time are closely intertwined and inseparable.

I suddenly realized that the project – given the limitations of space and time – might well prove beyond the ability of one individual, possibly even beyond the ability of a professional team.

Three years were spent in research and selection of material, including dozens of interviews with former comrades-in-arms and close friends – and who didn't know Gidi? Who didn't share an experience with him that is "worth recording"? Every publication has been scoured meticulously, every word subjected to keen analysis. The very paucity of written material (the man was naturally modest and shy of publicity) has actually made the task much more difficult; no written source, long or short, could be overlooked. It has been a painstaking job, demanding endless patience.

Furthermore, the number of newspaper interviews given by Gidi throughout his life could be counted on the fingers of one hand. Hence the importance of the tapes that I have kept with me for over 30 years, their contents seeing the light of day here for the first time.

I don't presume to say that I've covered every angle of the subject in exhaustive detail and, owing to limitations of space, not all the interviews have found a place in the book; however, all the interviewees will find their contributions reflected in the spirit and content of the writing – even if they are not quoted verbatim.

I trust that this book will respond to the aspirations of many readers and will add an important additional layer to the monument celebrating the heroes and liberators of this nation.

My sincere thanks to all who have assisted me in this project – with material, research, pictures, advice:

- First to the Paglin family – to Gidi's brother, Yitzhak – who illuminated every facet relating to the deceased and commented constructively on a number of topics requiring clarification; to Gidi's children, Neriel, Galia, and Guy – who spared no effort in helping me with material, recordings, pictures, everything required for completion of the task; I especially would like to thank Neriel Paglin for his intensive support for the publication of this English edition – without his ongoing assistance, it is doubtful that this book would have seen the light of day
- To Shraga Ellis (aka Haim Toyte, comrade-in-arms and close friend of Gidi – for a series of interviews and many comments regarding all aspects of Gidi's activities and personality
- To Baruch Weiner (Konous) – for his willingness to assist in every possible way in perpetuating the memory of the late Gidi

- To Professor David Danon, Amihai's childhood friend, who knew him better than anyone else – from classroom to battlefield – for a series of instructive interviews
- To Nahum Slonim – for breaking his habit of *not* giving personal interviews regarding the underground period and for shedding light on many points regarding the conditions and circumstances that formed the backdrop to Gidi's activities
- To Shula Polak (Slonim) for her efforts to assist me with all the material at her disposal
- To Aryeh Eshel – for his generosity in giving me access to his private archive, including an interview with Gidi
- To Amira Stern, director of the Jabotinsky Archives, and her team of dedicated assistants – for putting at my disposal (for inspection and photocopying) all the relevant documentation and written material, and assisting me to the best of their ability
- To Neri Areli, director of the Haganah Historical Archives, and his team of assistants – for their generosity and willingness to help
- To Yosef Nahmias, Bet-Gidi Museum – for help at all times and a fascinating interview
- To Yosef Kister, director of the IZL museum – for assistance with material and pictures
- To Julia Schwartz (London) – for her efforts to locate and provide historical material relating to the Mandate period, deposited in the Public Record Office
- To Yossi Barnea – for patience and persistence in research
- And last – and by no means least – to my wife Yehudit; were it not for her unconditional support over the four years of work on this book and her technical assistance and moral support, I doubt I would have found the emotional strength to complete this work.

Joseph Evron
Tel Aviv, April 2009

THE FATEFUL TRAIN

On April 18, 1948 – 27 days before the end of the British Mandate over Palestine – a unit of the IZL attacked a military train loaded with ammunition at Kilometer 41 between Hadera and Binyamina, near Pardes Hanna. Over several hours a fierce battle was fought on open ground, between the IZL and British troops armed with mortars and heavy machine guns. The outcome of the battle, in which three IZL fighters fell and a whole platoon of British soldiers, with its commander, was taken prisoner, had decisive implications for the conquest of Jaffa, which took place a week later.

This audacious operation – the full story of which is told here for the first time – was under the direct command of the operations officer of the Irgun Zvai Leumi, Amihai Paglin, known as Gidi.

STAGED AND DIRECTED BY GIDI

THE WARNING

The first indication that something was amiss reached Gidi as he was crouching over the mine underneath the culvert. He straightened up slowly and read again the text of the radio message from the lookout in the hills of Zikhron Yaakov, "It isn't a weapons train, it's a troop train!" The information was worrying, and a contradiction of previous intelligence, which had predicted "a train loaded with military equipment escorted by a handful of soldiers…." The entire operational plan had been based on this. Two weeks of meticulous preparation and continual reconnaissance seemed to have come to nothing. Concerned, he looked along the railway lines to the north, at that point on the horizon at which the train was supposed to appear. Again, he reviewed the combat apparatus on the ground: three attack sections dug in and camouflaged among the trees, to the east of the railway line – constituting the basic assault team; two backup sections, to the north and south, both at a distance of six-tenths of a mile (one kilometer) from the point of attack – to prevent reinforcements reaching the scene. Mentally he went over the plan for the umpteenth time: *when the engine reaches the culvert over the stream, Yuval and Shaika will detonate the mines under the two armored carriages occupied by the escort – the second and the ninth. As the train grinds to a halt the attack units, covered by machine-gun fire, will*

13

launch an assault before the troops have recovered from the shock and mop up any residual resistance. Then the signal will be given and Yehoshua will set the logistical operation in motion: 80 trucks and around 100 "porters" – waiting in readiness – will dash towards the carriages and load up the precious booty. Nothing about the operation seemed complicated, and more dangerous ones had been carried out in the past. Anyway – he reflected – it was too late to change anything. And then his glance fell on Avtalion and he felt a twinge of unease: he saw in him a living reminder of his past. Five and a half years had elapsed since they had carried out together the first assault on the "Steel Brothers," an operation for which Avtalion paid the price of his freedom; he had only recently escaped from jail, and Gidi wondered if he should have ignored his entreaties to take part in the operation.

A light touch on his shoulder broke his thread of thoughts and brought him back to reality. Yehoshua had also read the message. In reply to his questioning glance, Gidi announced, "Proceeding according to plan." Yehoshua nodded his assent.

THE PREPARATION

Konous hoisted the Bren on his shoulder, looked around for the men of the covering section, and signaled to them to follow him.

The trucks pulled up some 500 yards from the objective. The orchards and the eucalyptus trees hindered visibility somewhat, but by this time the commanders had familiarized themselves with the terrain.

A few minutes later one could make out the railway tracks, marked out clearly against the backdrop of hills. His gaze lingered on two tree trunks projecting from a small hill about 50 yards from the line. "There!" he pointed. It wasn't a naturally defensible position, but enough to provide cover from the troops of the train escort. Unconsciously he glanced at his watch; the hands showed nearly nine. He set up the machine gun, hastily wiped the sweat from his brow, and checked the cocking mechanism. The equipment seemed to be in order. From his right he heard the sound of hurried footsteps. Panting and wheezing, Avtalion dropped the bag of spare parts and ammunition. "Machine gunner number 2 reporting!" he announced solemnly. *The boy's okay!* – Konous mused – *Less than two weeks since he broke out of jail, and he insisted on coming along. Five years in prison, hours of interrogation and torture – and his spirit wasn't broken.* For some reason he felt a special affinity towards him, a kind of shared destiny: he himself had escaped from a detention camp two months before, and since then had already participated in two operations (*29 in total since joining the Irgun!* – he reflected proudly). Out of the corner of his eye he continued to watch developments in the sector, and his gaze drifted to the railway lines, scanning them through the sights of the Bren. For a moment the sights locked on the culvert, the point where Avtalion had just planted the mine. From there they moved to the right, to the anticipated attack zone, and it was then that he heard the high-pitched whistle. 10:30 AM.

Some distance away, up ahead, Danny assembled the small assault team that was going to outflank the first guard carriage from the left. Before this, he had helped set up the second mine – about 100 yards north of the culvert. His expertise in sabotage had stood him in good stead this time, he reflected with satisfaction – but for that, he wouldn't be here. His squad was on disciplinary suspension and appeals and entreaties were of no avail. "Punishment is punishment," Gidi declared. Only he, Danny Leibowitz, had succeeded in softening Gidi's firm resolve, and this only on account of his experience as a saboteur.

His thoughts drifted back. Even now he couldn't explain what had induced him yesterday to go out for "a night's entertainment," in blatant contradiction to the iron rule that "no one leaves the camp on the eve of an operation." He dragged along several platoon commanders with him, infected by his enthusiasm for "relaxation" over a cup of coffee at the Goldberg Café. In the end the cup of coffee became a glass of liquor and the mood was merry. In a corner of the room a few British soldiers from Camp 101 were drinking beer. The parties exchanged looks, but nothing more.

He remembered going to the phonograph and putting on a record, a tango that the Tommies liked too, humming the tune and singing the words, "Kiss me again..." The atmosphere warmed up, and in his elation he cried, "Let's all dance with Ruthie!" (the daughter of the café owner). He went moving to the rhythm with her – even after the song had ended, and it was only the laughter in the room that brought him back to reality. "Seems I was slightly drunk...," he admitted.

Before they got up to leave, he suggested they all kiss the girl goodbye. "There's no knowing," he said, "which of us will still be alive tomorrow..." Now, remembering, he smiled to himself over the dramatic tone of the words, but yesterday, holding her in his arms, he had been assailed by a weird sensation that even now he couldn't account for. This very evening, he decided, he'd go back to the Goldberg Café and sort things out.

The echoing whistle of the train was heard, right on cue.

To the right, Yitzhak Friedmann's squad was waiting. Most of his men were immigrants, who had only just arrived from refugee camps in Europe, been put through a brief course of training, and sent on their first mission. Yitzhak communicated with them in Yiddish. He himself was a Holocaust survivor who had arrived in the country alone, two years earlier; his experience of guerrilla warfare and his courage (at the age of 16 he had fought the Nazis with the Polish partisans) had earned him rapid promotion to the rank of squad leader, and this would be his first test as a battlefield commander.

About a hundred yards further north, from behind a row of pines, ten pairs of eyes were looking on tensely. Kneeling in his trench, a few paces east of the line, Shaika repeated to himself, once again, the instructions he had been given. "You must count eight carriages from the engine; the ninth is the objective, the armored carriage where most of the escort force will be." On this basis, the point for planting the second device had been selected – about 90 yards from the culvert. When the explosion would be heard, the attack would begin.

The commander of the support platoon in the north, Menahem Ben-Dor, or Yoska the "Jinji" (Carrot Top) as he was nicknamed, was an old warhorse, one of the escapees from Acre prison, with a string of daring operations behind him. The squad that he headed was manned by young recruits from Netanya, who had yet to smell gunpowder; for most of them this would be their baptism under fire. *If it comes to that* – he reflected, on being told that this time his role would be secondary: to secure the access routes from the north to the site of the action and to identify the train. "Your shot in the air," Gidi slapped his shoulder, "will be the signal for general assault. And if everything goes according to plan," he added, "you'll have nothing more to do."

Ben-Dor shrugged his shoulders and said nothing. Experience had taught him that on the ground things have a tendency to go awry.

When they reached the objective, he was the first to jump from the vehicle. He knew the sector assigned to him from prior reconnaissance and he wasted no time. In the orchard nearby he gave out his instructions: Aharon and Eliyahu were sent to wait close to the track, to get a clear view of the carriage numbers (which they had written on their hands); if the train was the one they were expecting, they were to shout immediately "That's it!" and the fun would begin.

THE ASSAULT

As he lay behind the line of eucalyptus trees, eyes riveted to the curving tracks, Eliyahu remembered the sense of relief he had felt when he was named as one of the participants. For months he had waited for this moment, and here he was, calm and composed, as if this were a vacation trip. Absently he glanced at his hand: the numbers were still there.

An hour passed without anything happening. At 10:15 he thought he heard a distant rumble. He put his ear to the ground and picked up a definite vibration. "It's coming, Aharon," he cried, excited. A long black mass shimmered on the horizon, noisily winding its way towards them. The two of them stared as if hypnotized at the open freight cars, crammed with dozens of soldiers enjoying the warm sunshine, some of them without their shirts. The carriage numbers were clearly visible – they were identical to those on their hands.

"That's it!" Eliyahu yelled to his commander behind the bushes.

"That's it!" Aharon echoed after him.

A single shot pierced the air, sending a flock of ravens fleeing from their perch on the telegraph wires. Yuval hurriedly crawled into the narrow trench, peering cautiously through the branches that masked the opening.

The racket of the approaching train grew louder, its black silhouette now clearly visible. Yuval's hand moved slowly towards the electronic detonator. Even before the wheels of the engine had touched the edge of the culvert, his finger pressed the switch.

The sound of the blast was deafening. The engine rose for a moment in the air, then crashed to the ground, rolled over on its side – and was still.

Shaika's eyes didn't shift for a moment from the tracks, and as the train was still thundering past him, he suddenly saw in front of him the target carriage. Without hesitation he pressed the switch. The air shook to the sound of the second blast.

The two explosions were virtually simultaneous, changing the face of the landscape as if with a magic wand. The tranquil scene of a calm and sleepy spring morning was transformed, in a moment, to a battlefield of fire and inferno.

Even before the cloud of smoke above the engine had dispersed, Danny was charging forward at the head of his men, firing from the hip as he ran. Two bullets pierced his chest. He fell dead on the spot.

Yitzhak Friedmann and his squad opened a frontal assault on the train, using all the weapons at hand. They managed to advance a pace or two before they were hit, every single one of them, by ferocious and accurate fusillades.

Konous cocked the machine gun, took careful aim, and set off a long volley in the direction of the guard carriage – but this was the only volley he managed to fire before a mortar bomb tore the Bren from his grip and smashed it to pieces. For a moment he stared about him, stunned, not understanding what had happened. And then the alarming realization flashed into his mind: *they're using mortars…!*

Confused, he looked around for Avtalion, who a moment before had been lying beside him, and when he saw him, a few paces away – he froze. Avtalion lay on his face, not moving, his clenched fist clutching a handful of grass. One quick glance was enough to tell that he was beyond help. He felt a surge of anger and pain, but most oppressive of all was the sense of helplessness. The cries of the wounded rose from all sides, mingling with the whine of the bombs and creating a new and unfamiliar symphony. *This is a new scenario for us*, he reflected bitterly.

His first rational thought was to go looking for Gidi. While he was still hesitating, he heard another sound – the blast of a trumpet. The signal for retreat had been given, too soon.

His finger still poised on the switch, Yuval was staring transfixed at the first carriage which, its doors now bristling with rifle muzzles and mortars, had turned into a war machine spewing fire and brimstone. And as columns of smoke still rose from the overturned engine, the silence that had followed the blast suddenly gave way to a deafening outburst of gunfire and explosions.

Behind, a nightmare scene played out: Yitzhak's assault team had been checked in mid-attack, men falling one after another as if cut down by an invisible scythe.

Yuval couldn't believe his eyes: *They knew about the attack in advance…*the horrifying thought occurred to him, as he pulled himself out of the trench to hurry back to his men, bullets whistling around him angrily and kicking up clouds of dust and sand. In those moments there was only one thought in his mind: *How do we get out of this inferno?*

Dragging two wounded men with him, he crawled towards the communications vehicle hidden among the trees. There – he hoped – he'd find Gidi or some other senior officer.

The van was abandoned and the radio disconnected. There wasn't a living soul around. The groans of his companions brought him back to bitter reality – and a quick look at their anguished faces persuaded him to get the vehicle started and head for the nearest medical facility. As he drove his way cautiously through the pines, the car was exposed and came under heavy fire; within seconds he lost control of the car and crashed head-on into a tree. The engine died, and all attempts to revive it failed. There was no choice but to drag themselves along on foot. Suddenly he felt a stabbing pain in his back and the breath was knocked out of him. "I've got one," he cursed softly. He had barely recovered from the shock when the whistle of a shell was heard close by, and he flung himself to the ground – just in time.

The three wounded men hobbled slowly towards the road. After two unsuccessful attempts to stop passing cars, Yuval lost what was left of his patience, forcing a taxi driver, at gunpoint, to drive them to Binyamina, where they finally received first aid.

Even before his finger left the detonator switch, Shaika knew something wasn't right. He couldn't yet identify the source of the problem, but deep down he knew things weren't going according to plan. For some reason, it seemed to him the train was lurching and not running smoothly. Also there were more carriages than had been expected and this also worried him, although he wasn't sure why. The significance of this fact he was to find out very soon. In the meantime, events moved quickly. The essential mission – to blast open the central carriage and eliminate all resistance – still rested on his shoulders. Aware of his responsibility, he leapt through the bushes behind which the squad was concealed, and just as a shell exploded thunderously, he rushed forward with a cry of "Follow me!"

He didn't get far. He had hardly set foot outside the cluster of pines when a volley of bullets smashed into his leg. Heavy fire from machine guns and mortars was coming now from the tenth and eleventh carriages, turning the place into an inferno. He crawled back the way he had come, streaming blood, and collapsed among his men as if he'd fallen from the moon. They had remained in their positions, returning fire from behind tree trunks and wondering where their commander had disappeared to. Amid all the noise of gunfire and explosions they hadn't heard his cry of "Follow me!" – and had thus been spared the bitter fate of their comrades in the southern sector.

The sequence of events only confirmed Shaika's earlier impression: the British had outsmarted them, adding armored carriages to the train at the last moment. They had also changed the position of the escort squad; instead of the ninth coach, they had put them in the tenth and eleventh.

"We blew up the wrong coach," Shaika complained sadly to his deputy, Cactus. "There are a lot more of their troops than we expected, and they're armed with heavy weapons." As if to confirm this point, the air was pierced by the shrill whine of a shell, exploding nearby with a deafening blast, sending up clouds of dust and sand.

Outwardly he still put on a pretense of "business as usual," but the wound in his thigh was starting to worry him, and deep down he knew that if the wound wasn't bandaged, loss of blood was liable to blunt his senses, to say nothing of the risk of infection. More than anything else he was anxious about the situation on the ground. The radio was out of order, and they didn't have the faintest idea of what was going on in the other sectors.

"I'm going to look for Gidi and I'm giving temporary command to you," he told Cactus. "Keep on firing at the armored carriage, and don't let them poke their noses out till I get back." He succeeded in covering about 20 paces. Suddenly he felt weak, sat down under a lime tree and tried to bandage his leg. When Gidi arrived, he was still slumped against the tree trunk – and still bleeding.

A few minutes after Shaika's departure the firing eased off a little, and Cactus decided to make an attempt to break into the train. At the head of a team of three he began advancing cautiously towards the track, the other members of the squad covering them. They managed to crawl two or three yards before the lethal fusillades opened up again. In the first lull in the firing they returned the way they had come, having achieved nothing. All they could do now was wait, although they had no idea what to expect.

As time passed, Cactus's anxiety increased: storming the carriage – he knew – was no longer an option; if he'd had any illusions, the failure of the last attempt had shattered them. Quite a while passed and Shaika hadn't returned. Cactus was on his own, responsible for deciding the fate of the squad, without any knowledge of what was going on elsewhere. It was an intolerable situation; he decided to take the initiative and go looking for Gidi. He transferred temporary command to Nehemia Levanon, and set off towards operational headquarters.

The closer he came to his objective, the more military debris he found scattered on the ground: steel helmets, ammunition, magazines, spare machine gun parts. Just then the sound of firing stopped completely and there was an eerie silence. For a moment, he thought that the young men might have succeeded in taking control of the guard carriage, and he hurried towards it, calling out to the commanders by name. No answer came. And then to his surprise he saw the muzzles of rifles and machine guns aimed at him from behind the raised shutters of the carriage. He flung himself to the ground just as a deadly volley was unleashed at him. Bullets whistled around him, raising plumes of sand. There was no cover in the area, not even a dip in the ground. He was caught like an animal exposed in the field, a sitting duck for snipers. With what was left of his strength he crawled toward the nearby grove and collapsed straight into the arms of Nehemia Levanon, who had been alerted by the sound of firing and had come out to look for him.

"What's happened?" Nehemia asked anxiously. "Send the boys home, all the others have gone…," Cactus rasped, barely able to speak, and if they hadn't taken hold of him he'd have fainted then and there. He had taken three bullets and lost a lot of blood.

THE TURNING POINT

While all this was going on, and the attack mounted in the central sector had faltered under the ferocious firepower of the British – about a hundred yards further north a dramatic series of events was unfolding, which was to turn the situation topsy turvy and decide the outcome in a quite unexpected way.

Even before the echoes of the explosions had died away, two panic-stricken soldiers leaped down from the last carriage and took refuge in a ditch at the side of the track. Three of their shell-shocked comrades followed them and opened fire in all directions. Yoav's RKM machine gun began stuttering in reply, and in the confusion Eliyahu and Aharon succeeded in rejoining their unit. And amid all this commotion, Ben-Dor suddenly remembered Gidi's order to cut the telephone wires (to foil any attempt at communicating with police outposts in the vicinity). The job was entrusted to Aharon. "They gave me a big pair of scissors," he recalled. "I climbed up the pole, exposed to gunfire, and did the job as professionally as I could…. To this day I don't know how I did it…. There's a first time for everything, I suppose, even climbing telegraph poles…"

While he was cutting the wires, Eliyahu "Arokh ha-Raglayyim (Long-legs)" suddenly spotted a British soldier standing on the steps of the carriage, aiming his weapon at him. "I didn't hesitate for a moment," he recalled. "I got him in my sights and pulled the trigger; the soldier jerked upright for a moment, dropped his weapon, and fell to the ground with a plaintive cry of 'Oh, Johnny!'"

This was the moment when the tide began to turn.

Suddenly shouting was heard from the direction of the carriage: "Don't shoot! We want to surrender!" When Ben-Dor heard these cries, he ordered his men to stop firing and approach the door of the carriage. "I moved up there myself," he related, "and stood facing them with my tommy gun."

And then something happened which to the youths from Netanya must have seemed like a scene from a fantasy world: three British soldiers, loyal servants of His Majesty, throwing away their weapons, falling on their knees and pleading for their lives. "Please, don't shoot us! We're going home next week!"

One of them pulled out a photograph of his family: "This is my wife, and these are my children…!"

"No one is going to harm you," Ben-Dor assured them. He led the three prisoners – who included a lieutenant and one severely wounded soldier – into the orchard. When they were offered cigarettes and the injured soldier had been given first aid, tension in the northern command post eased, and the sound of gunfire died away, too. All waited anxiously for news of what was happening in the central zone, and this information was slow in coming.

From behind an ancient eucalyptus tree, some 25 yards from the train, Gidi scoured the battlefield with increasing tension: the two mines had been detonated almost simultaneously; the train had been stopped and even before the cloud of dust and smoke had settled, the two assault platoons had attacked the guard carriages. So far – everything according to plan.

What hadn't been expected was the scale of the firepower, from machine guns and mortars (the mortars were the real surprise), turned on them almost immediately from the train. Within less than a minute, three commanders had been killed and another six fighters wounded. Gidi looked on with despair as wave after wave of his soldiers was shot to pieces, his best men cut down as if by an unseen scythe.

"It was a terrible moment," he said later.

Contrary to our expectations, the British had put on extra armored carriages, disguised so they wouldn't be recognized as such and occupied by combat troops, with heavy weapons. They really ripped the attacking force apart. Opposite me, in the windows of the carriage, I could see the muzzles of the rifles moving slowly, to left and right, searching for more targets and blazing again. Suddenly there was a deathly silence and all you could hear were the cries of ravens. It was as if I was the only one left in the sector, but I had no delusions; I knew that dozens of pairs of eyes were staring out from the coaches, and if I moved so much as a couple of inches, I'd be riddled with bullets….

At that time, it seemed to me the operation had failed, and my only concern was for the wounded in the field, and how to help them. But for this, I first needed to extricate myself, and that wasn't going to be easy. I was surrounded by corn stalks, growing about two feet (60 centimeters) high. I decided to risk an old trick. I took off my steel helmet (an Australian helmet, shaped like a flying saucer) and tossed it to my left, in a circular trajectory just above the level of the corn, giving the impression there was someone moving there, bent double. In a fraction of a second the helmet was turned into a sieve – but that was all the time I needed to jump in the other direction, leap over the hedge, and land in the orchard.

As Gidi made his cautious way among the thorny bushes, alert to every slightest sound, he heard a stifled groan. He immediately dropped to the ground and drew his pistol. Three paces away, leaning against the trunk of an orange tree, he saw the figure of a man; a few seconds passed before he recognized Shaika.

"What are you doing here?" he asked, astonished.

"Resting a while," the other replied with a grimace. "I was on my way to you…" He tried to stand, but sank down again with a moan of pain.

It was only then that Gidi saw the bleeding wound to his thigh.

"They fooled us," Shaika mumbled apologetically. "We blew up the wrong carriage."

Gidi nodded his head, showing that he understood: "First of all we've got to get you some medical treatment."

"Out of the question," Shaika protested vigorously. "I must get back. The squad's waiting for orders."

"I'll see to that," said Gidi. "You stay where you are!" and he disappeared into the thick vegetation.

Shaika tried to crawl after him and had managed to cover a couple of yards when he thought he heard faint moans and someone calling his name. He looked around him cautiously, trying to locate the source of the sounds and then, a few paces away, came across the blood-spattered figure of Yitzhak Friedmann. He was sprawled on the ground, writhing in pain and staring at him with entreaty in his eyes, "Help me, Shaika," he whimpered, "I'm going to die!" One close look was enough to confirm that this young man was indeed mortally wounded. He was pale as chalk, with a chest full of bullets and blood streaming from his punctured lungs. Feeling helpless, Shaika tried to stop the holes with his fingers, but to no avail. Suddenly the wounded man rose to his feet, cried out something incomprehensible, and careered away as if possessed. Shaika tried to stop him, in vain. He called to him – but he didn't hear. He wasn't conscious. His spirit had flown far away, to some place in the forests of Poland, in the ranks of the partisans, a 16-year-old Jewish orphan struggling for his life and shouting with the last vestige of his strength: "He-elp me-e!"

He was found later, just a few paces from there, slumped against the trunk of a eucalyptus tree, lifeless.

For some time after Cactus had set out to look for his commander, the squad continued exchanging fire with the guard carriages. Gidi arrived during a lull, and one look was enough to convince him of the futility of carrying on this bizarre duel.

"Collect all the equipment," he told Nehemia Levanon, "the operation's over!"

Shaika he found in the same posture, and almost in the same place as he had left him; for some reason it seemed to him that the condition of the wound had worsened. He held out a hand to help him up. "We're moving!" he said. The pair of them began staggering slowly eastward, towards the road; for most of the time, Gidi was carrying the injured man on his back.

On reaching the orchard they met Yehoshua. He stared at them as if in disbelief, clearly much relieved.

"I came out to look for you," he gazed at Gidi as if mesmerized, but the latter silenced him with a weary gesture of the hand, "The operation's aborted, and we'd better get that into our heads!" His voice was quiet, businesslike, betraying nothing of his inner turmoil. "We have to pull all units out of the sector, disperse the trucks and their drivers, and discharge the auxiliaries recruited for the operation."

Seeing the expression on Yehoshua's face, he gave him an encouraging slap on the shoulder. "Cheer up old friend, it's only one round…"

Shaika had drifted back into consciousness. "I've got to get back to my unit," he mumbled. Gidi signaled to Yehoshua, and without exchanging a word they picked him up and carried him into the orchard. At that very moment – as if this was the sign they were waiting for – the troops on the train unleashed a renewed fusillade, this time targeting the groves as well. This warm reception forced the trio to take refuge in a ditch beside the road. The noise and the confusion in this section of the road were almost intolerable. All the logistical apparatus – prepared well in advance – was concentrated in this area; the order for withdrawal had already been given and dozens of trucks – with their drivers and the auxiliaries who had been there to help with the loading of the looted weapons – began moving back to their bases.

One after another the wounded were arriving here too – some under their own steam, others supported by their mates. A medical team, led by Bobby, improvised a first-aid post and gave them such treatment as they could. Shaika's leg was bandaged, but he was told to wait in the ditch until transport could be found for him.

All this time Gidi, his eyes darting about restlessly, was running to and fro among the men, giving orders, asking questions. Suddenly his gaze fell on Konous, who like many others was wandering about aimlessly, stunned by the weight of events. With two quick paces he was beside him, "Where's Avtalion?" he asked.

Konous, still in shock, spread his hands in a gesture of helplessness. "A mortar bomb got him…killed on the spot."

Gidi's heart missed a beat. For a moment the world stood still. "Oh, for God's sake," he muttered. "Why did I let him join us today?"

Seconds passed, seeming like years. When he finally opened his eyes, Yehoshua was standing beside him. Konous's voice sounded faint, apologetic. "They were using mortars, there was nothing we could do…"

Gradually Gidi regained control of himself, and when he spoke his voice was again that of the lucid, responsible commander. "Has anyone told Ben-Dor about the withdrawal?"

The question hung in the air, unanswered. In the chaos they'd forgotten the northern buffer force.

Konous seemed to come to life. "I'll do that," he volunteered.

Gidi nodded, "Tell them I'm on my way."

When the sound of Konous's footsteps faded, Gidi turned to Yehoshua, his voice sounding strange and detached. "Make sure no bodies are left on the field." For a moment he stood there as if about to add something, then changed his mind, turned on his heel, and disappeared among the trees of the orchard. Resentment gnawed at his heart – failure! *I've never failed before*, he reflected bitterly, *not like this*. He'd always heard the young men say, "If Gidi's here, then all's well." And here he was – and everything had blown up in his face. Weeks of planning gone to waste, and his best men lying out there in the field. *How the hell did that many soldiers get to be on the train – without us knowing? –* he mused angrily. *And why weren't we warned about the mortars?* He quietly cursed his informant, cursed the British who had outsmarted him, cursed his own stupidity for falling into this trap. But none of this mattered now; what he had to do was get his men out of the sector as soon as possible, *those who are still walking, that is*…he thought, as the image of Avtalion again flashed before his eyes. He choked back the tears.

He skirted the orchard to the east of the railway line in a broad arc, reaching Ben-Dor's unit from the north – at almost the same moment as Konous. The first to see them was Yoav (Kushi), whose job was to watch the road from Binyamina, the Polish RKM machine gun ready at hand, and when he identified the figures he hurriedly informed his commander and ran to meet them, obviously excited. Since morning the northern buffer force had scored some significant successes, and the young men were proud and even a little blasé, but contact with the other units had been lost and no one had any idea what was going on. Now everything was quiet here, and the appearance of the two men aroused curiosity and anticipation.

Gidi didn't waste time. "The operation's gone wrong, the order to withdraw has been given," he stated without preamble. "In fact," he admitted, "the other forces have already moved out and you were almost forgotten."

The silence that followed was broken by Yoav, asking indignantly, "So what the hell are we supposed to do with the prisoners?"

"What are you talking about?" asked Gidi, mystified.

"About them!" – he pointed to the corner of the orchard where the three British soldiers sat huddled together, as one of the young men watched over them, pistol in hand.

Gidi tensed, as if an electric current had passed through him. "How did they get here?" he asked.

Ben-Dor recounted the sequence of events, and for the first time that morning the shadow of a smile flitted over Gidi's face. "I came here to order a retreat," he said. "It looks as if I'll be catching the train after all."

Gidi glanced at the Tommies, making an effort to recall all that he knew of their language. "How're you doing, lads?" he asked lightly. Although he wore no insignia, the lieutenant sensed that this was a man of authority. "We're OK, but what's going to happen to him?" he pointed to his wounded comrade, who was moaning faintly. Gidi glanced around him as if making up his mind. "Don't worry, he'll get the treatment he needs," he assured them. "But before that, I've got a little job for one of you…. You there!" he pointed to the third soldier, who was just sitting quietly, not joining in the conversation. "What's your name?" The other stared at him nervously. "Johnny," he murmured, barely audibly. "OK, Johnny, you're to take a message to your commander on the train. What's his rank, by the way?" Gidi asked. "A captain," the other replied mechanically.

"All right, tell him, in the name of the operations commander of the Irgun Zvai Leumi, that if the troops don't surrender within ten minutes from the time this message is delivered – we'll blow up the train and everyone on it. There are charges laid underneath it, and we've got plenty of Fiat antitank guns at our disposal, from the raid on Camp 80. Responsibility for what happens is on the captain's head, absolutely. Tell him this, too," he added. "We're only interested in the weapons on the train. We've nothing against the soldiers and we'll do them no harm."

The private glanced at the lieutenant. "How do we know," the officer intervened, "that you'll keep your word, and not have us shot when it's all over?"

"My word of honor as commander," Gidi replied, peeking impatiently at his watch. "Every passing minute endangers the lives of your mates on the train," he warned.

The officer nodded at his subordinate, "Do it, Johnny. Tell the captain there's no choice."

The latter rose, without much confidence, glancing anxiously at the train. "Don't be afraid," Gidi encouraged him. "They know you. They're not going to shoot you by mistake, not at this range."

The soldier began walking slowly, hesitantly, towards the central carriage – 80 yards along the track. His steps were cautious, measured, as if he were walking through a minefield. He waved his arms desperately, shouting at the top of his voice, "Don't shoot! It's me, Johnny."

Gidi signaled to Konous, and the two began following him a short distance behind, dodging from tree to tree and using the pine trunks as temporary cover, fingers welded to triggers.

The soldier carried on walking like an automaton, still calling out to his comrades. When he reached the carriage that had been knocked on its side by the blast, several pairs of hands were held out to him, and he disappeared behind the sheets of armor plating. Silence fell.

A moment after the soldier's disappearance, doubt began to gnaw at Gidi's heart: *what if he tells his commander not to take the warning seriously, because the force confronting them amounts to just a handful of young men, eight at the most, armed with an antiquated machine gun and a few pistols, and what if on the basis of that information, the captain decides to launch a counterattack?*

It was a big gamble – an even bigger risk. All the anger, frustration, disappointment, and bitterness accumulated in him during the day were now ready to burst out. At moments like this a man loses all sense of time, and of fear. Gidi had such a moment. Suddenly he stood up to his full height, drew his pistol, and began running dementedly towards the stationary train with dozens of rifles poking from every aperture, shouting with all the force he could muster, "Give yourselves up, or we're going to blow up the train. You lost the game!"

When no answer came, Gidi began running in a crouch along the line of carriages, straightening up at intervals to shout wildly, "Are you mad? You've got just three minutes to surrender!"

Years later, recalling this terrifying experience, he admitted he was acting on an impulse that he couldn't control:

> Deep down inside, I knew my chances of getting out of there alive were virtually nil, but this thing was stronger than me. It was as if I were possessed. I was running, knocking on the doors of the carriages, and shouting, "You've got four minutes left…three minutes…," and I see the muzzles of the machine guns moving, trained on me, and I think to myself, any second now they're going to open fire and tear me to pieces. But nothing happens. And then suddenly the door of the carriage swings open, and in the doorway there's an officer with a revolver in his hand. And I'm still sure I'm a goner – and then a bunch of armed British soldiers jump out of the door with their hands up. I couldn't believe what I was seeing, but I pulled myself together straightaway. "Weapons to the left," I commanded, "men to the right." They obeyed. Out of the corner of my eye I saw Konous, looking on in amazement. I beckoned to him, and gave him the job of guarding the prisoners. My heart was beating fast but I went on threatening the ones still hiding in the carriages, "You have two more minutes…one more minute…" and I pretend to be backing off from the train in a hurry, stooping to avoid the shrapnel that's about to start flying…

It seems that the nerves of the British couldn't take any more; the train had been under siege for so long, and no help had arrived. Now the IZL men were threatening to blow up the cars with all their occupants, and experience had taught them they were capable of doing it (memories of the raid on Camp 80 were still fresh in their minds).

A long moment passed, seeming like an eternity – and the unbelievable happened: the first to step down was the captain, his rifle at his shoulder; behind him all the others stood in a line, about a dozen armed men clutching their weapons. A moment of confusion:

> I didn't know if they were going to attack or surrender, but I didn't give them time to think about it. "Put your guns down!" I commanded. First to put his weapon down was the captain. "OK, lads, we lost the game!"

he said. All the others followed his example. Just in time I stifled the sigh of relief that was about to emerge, and I stood there brandishing my revolver while Konous kicked their weapons out of reach, towards the ditch at the side of the track. I told him to get help from the northern command post. Three young men arrived. From then on things happened quickly.

While one small party was gathering up the soldiers' personal weapons, and the prisoners were being assembled near the central carriage, a messenger was dispatched on a motorcycle to call back the trucks and the auxiliary forces. About half of the vehicles were intercepted but most of the "porters," who were supposed to be loading the weapons, were long gone.

Meanwhile, Gidi was breaking open the doors of the carriages. His disappointment was intense: no weapons to be found! All the boxes contained just one type of ammunition – 3-inch mortar bombs. "This wasn't what I had in mind…," he admitted to his boys, but added hastily: "We've already paid the price in blood, and too much of it – let's load it all up anyway!"

But how to do this? The number of men he had succeeded in recalling was far from sufficient. From time to time other individuals joined them, but it was clear that in these circumstances the loading would take hours. And time was pressing: there could be no doubt that British reinforcements were on their way.

Gidi's wandering gaze alighted on the British commander, who was engaged in animated conversation with his platoon sergeant. He approached him with a genial expression: "Captain, please assemble your men," he said. "I need to talk to them."

The officer's face turned as white as chalk. "You're going to have us all killed!" he cried, shaking with emotion. "And you promised…gave your word of honor. I tell you, we'll fight for our lives with our bare hands if we have to, we won't go like lambs to the slaughter…"

Surprised by the intensity of this response, Gidi was quick to reassure him: "Don't be a fool. We don't break promises and we don't kill prisoners – all we want is your men's help loading the bombs. Help us get the job done quickly – and you'll be free all the sooner."

The captain gave Gidi a long look, as if trying to read his mind. "I believe you," he said at last. "Sergeant, give them all the help they need. Carry on!"

The soldiers took up the task with vigor, working in pairs. Each box weighed upwards of 88 pounds (40 kilograms); there were hundreds of boxes and thousands of shells. Nothing easy about this job. Except for the captain and one other wounded soldier, all pitched in, working hard and sweating profusely, the sergeant standing over them and encouraging them; some almost fainted from exhaustion and to revive them, Gidi sent for oranges from the nearby orchard.

Amid all the commotion, he suddenly remembered his promise to the British lieutenant. He looked around and located Konous, running back and forth between the train and the trucks. "Leave all this," he told him: "You're to take that British casualty for treatment. I gave my word."

Konous shrugged. The soldier still lay in the orchard, covered in blood and moaning softly. The bullet wound in his gut was agonizing.

"We put him in the back seat of a private car," he recalled, "and a few minutes later we were knocking on the doctor's door in Pardes Hanna: 'For God's sake, Doc, do everything you can to save him,' I said. For a moment the wounded man opened his eyes and smiled at me faintly as if he understood what I was saying, even though it was a foreign language. He lifted his arm slowly and his fingers closed weakly around my hand."

It was to be a long time before Konous could forget that handshake from a British soldier, whose life was indeed saved on that occasion – but whose name he never knew.

The work of loading and unloading took some two hours. Thirty of His Majesty's soldiers and some 20 IZL men worked shoulder-to-shoulder, gathering "metal" for the underground's arsenals, with the kind of comradeship-in-arms that isn't often found between liberation armies and forces of occupation.

About twenty thousand 3-inch mortar shells were loaded on some 30 trucks, moving constantly between Pardes Hanna and Zikhron Yaakov. The precious "goods" were stashed in the cellars of Baron Rothschild's winery and the houses belonging to the Aaronsohn family, under the noses of the British, who repeatedly searched the area but came up with nothing.

While all this was going on, the captain watched events with interest, but not without a trace of concern. "Your operation was well planned," he said to Gidi.

"And your lads are doing a fine job," Gidi returned the compliment.

"I just hope you don't reward them with gunfire," said the Englishman in an attempt at humor, but with fear showing clearly on his face.

Gidi looked at him with reproof and the captain hurriedly apologized: "Just joking," he said, and forced an awkward laugh.

The moment Gidi had dreaded came sooner than he expected. At 1:00 PM – an hour after the loading work had begun – a messenger on a motorcycle informed him that a military train, crammed with soldiers, was heading towards them at full steam, expected to arrive within half an hour.

Gidi made a quick assessment of the situation: it would take another hour to complete the job, or less, if they speeded up the work rate; by this stage all were racing frantically against the clock and most of the ammunition had already been loaded. He doubted they could be spurred to any extra effort, but he was determined to exploit the little time remaining to the fullest.

First of all, he ordered the small force in the north to deploy against the British reinforcements, and among other things, to mine the railway line again, using the gelignite blocks which had previously been planted on the road to Binyamina but had not been detonated.

The unit commander worked quickly. Two of his men, Yoska Altalena and Eliyahu "Arokh ha-Raglayyim," armed with gelignite blocks and a Bren (from the looted weaponry), were sent across the track to mine the tracks and secure the sector. The team with Kushi's Polish RKM was stationed a few dozen yards from the anticipated detonation point, ready to go into action at any moment. The four remaining fighters, led by Ben-Dor, took up positions among the trees. All waited tensely for whatever lay ahead.

At 1:30 PM a long whistle presaged the arrival of the train. A runner was immediately dispatched to alert Gidi.

"At first we didn't see anything," Ben-Dor recalled.

We only heard the noises. The tracks in our field of vision curved towards the west, and eucalyptus trees had been planted alongside them, obstructing the view. The train came to a halt, brakes squealing, just before the bend, and then after a few minutes moved on again. Suddenly we saw this gigantic, black, intimidating hulk of an engine, moving slowly towards us, pulling behind it a string of dark and silent coaches. It was a scary sight: a great mass of steel bearing down on you, and nothing you can do about it. The explosives went off underneath it with a deafening sound but had no effect at all; the RKM fired volleys of bullets, but they bounced off the armor plating like hailstones. It just kept on coming, and it seemed there was no force on earth that could stop it. Finally it reached our position, stopped for a moment – and then began reversing, back the way it had come.[13]

Later it emerged that this had been a calculated ruse: before the bend a number of carriages filled with soldiers had been uncoupled from the train, and while all eyes were on the engine and its diversionary antics, the soldiers were deploying on the ground and taking up positions to the west of the track.

While this was going on, an unequivocal instruction was received from Gidi: "The British reinforcements have to be kept busy for at least 20 minutes, so that our forces can withdraw in an orderly fashion!"

On the other side of the track, from behind a small sand hill, Yoska Altalena and Eliyahu "Arokh ha-Raglayyim" were watching developments. They looked on aghast as the engine cruised smoothly along, crushing the two blocks of explosive as if they were toy balloons and continuing on its way unperturbed. While they were still staring, perplexed, at this bizarre spectacle, the air was split by volleys of fire from Yoav's Polish machine gun.

Eliyahu didn't wait any longer. He cocked the Bren, aimed at the windows in the engine, and pressed the trigger. A light click was heard and nothing more. He spat out a curse, changed the magazine, pulled back the breech handle again (all according to the book), but the result was the same as before – a dull metallic clang. Furiously he began dismantling the weapon but quickly realized there was nothing to be done; the entire mechanism was clogged with sand.

Meanwhile the engine was slowly moving backwards, and for a moment Yoska was under the impression that the British had been repulsed and were retreating. The RKM had fallen silent, too. In the ensuing silence, Ben-Dor's voice could be clearly heard, from the other side of the track. "Return to the unit – we're pulling out!" Even as he spoke, a ferocious fusillade swept both sides of the track. Dozens of soldiers, who had taken

---

13.   Testimony of Menahem Binder Ben Dor (Yosef), Jabotinsky Archives.

up positions in the field, were unleashing lethal firepower in all directions; even houses in the settlement of Pardes Hanna were hit. Crossing the track in these circumstances would be certain suicide. "We're retreating towards Hadera!" Eliyahu shouted at the top of his voice, and the two of them set off in a frantic sprint westward, as angry bullets whistled around them.

The small covering force fought on to the best of its ability. The barrel of the Polish machine gun was red hot. A runner was sent urgently to Gidi. His reply was, "Hold position for a few more minutes!" Ben-Dor began dismissing his men in stages. By two o'clock, only he and the machine gunner were left, changing positions and burning up what was left of the ammunition.

The British continued "subduing" the area with heavy, sustained fire. This went on for a long time, even after Ben-Dor and Yoav (Kushi) had left the scene.

At 1:45 PM Gidi ordered a halt to the loading. It was time to withdraw.

In the northern sector the sounds of explosions and gunfire continued, but Gidi knew what the British did not: in the covering position there were only two left; the others had already been withdrawn in stages, some of them hitching lifts with the convoys transporting the loads.

The last trucks stood ready to move. All that could be taken from the train had been loaded as well as the personal weapons of the prisoners (eight 2-inch mortars, a dozen Brens, and assorted rifles and submachine guns).

There were still dozens of boxes of shells in the carriages – but time was running out. It was time to go.

They parted from the British on amicable terms – although each side was glad to see the back of the other.

The captain shook hands with Gidi. "All wars are the same," was his philosophical comment, "Sometimes you win…sometimes you lose…this time you came out on top, but you've played fair," and after a moment's hesitation he added in a whisper, "up to now…" Despite all his efforts to appear calm and confident there were still signs of suspicion in his face; he ordered his men not, under any circumstances, to turn their backs on their captors.

Fifty years later, the scene was still vivid in Konous's memory: dozens of British soldiers marching slowly, but smartly and in good order – backwards.

It took them a long time to cover the 50 yards separating them from the train. Eventually they disappeared from view one after the other, first in the ditch alongside the track and then behind the listing coach.

And the curtain fell on another episode in the war of the Jews for their independence – a drama staged and directed by Gidi.

PARTICIPANTS IN THE TRAIN OPERATION

1. Amihai Paglin (Gidi)
2. Avtalion Ayub (Yoav)
3. Menahem Ben-Dor (Yoska the Jinji [Carrot Top])
4. Zvi Barzel (Cactus)
5. Yehoshua Diamant (Amos)
6. Baruch Weiner (Konous)
7. Yosef Haddad (Yoska Altalena)
8. Eliyahu Temler (Yehoshua)
9. Yoav Levi (Kushi [Blackie])
10. Aharale Cohen
11. Nehemia Levanon
12. Shimon Levi (Shimon and a Half)
13. Danny Leibowitz (Aviel)
14. Zvi Pooni (Yuval)
15. Yitzhak Friedmann (Zedekiah)
16. Eliyahu Schwartz (Arokh ha-Raglayyim [Long-legs])
17. Yitzhak Shulman (Shaika)
18. Aharon Shechter

HOW IT BEGAN

What was the source of Amihai's nationalistic fervor, as reflected in reminiscences of his childhood? From where did he derive the strength of mind, the unflagging patriotism, the skills and ingenuity that set him apart and put him atop the pyramid of the active struggle against British rule, at a fateful hour in the Jewish nation's campaign for independence in its homeland?

THE START

It all began with the riots of 1936.[1] Like most of the Tel Aviv teenagers at that time, Amihai, too, was enrolled, at 14, in the ranks of the Haganah; he became attached to the communications unit of the intelligence section. His recruitment into the Haganah was to a considerable extent due to the influence of his brother Neriel, who was two years older and served as his model and mentor. While Amihai was still a seventh-grade student at Balfour High School, Neriel already had an impressive record of security activity, ranging from mobile patrols with the Jewish Guard Force in Galilee to membership in Orde Wingate's Night Squads. Later, he was among the first to join the Palmah's naval section and in 1941 was one of the "Twenty-Three Seafarers"[2] who went on a mission to Syria from which

---

1.   Recorded interview with Amihai Paglin, 1969.
2.   Twenty-three members of the Haganah, including veterans of the Mobile Patrols and the Special Night Squads, set out on May 18, 1941, accompanied by a British officer, Major Anthony Palmer, to carry out a sabotage attack on the oil refineries near Tripoli in Lebanon – and vanished without a trace. The last communication with their boat was at noon on the day of embarkation; from that point on radio-silence was maintained. The disappearance of the "twenty-three" and their British escort has remained a mystery to this day.

     In his book *Et le-saper* [Time to tell] (Tel Aviv: Am Oved, 1974), David Hacohen re-examines the episode and lays serious charges against Yitzhak Sadeh as the one

none returned. This event took place during the first years of World War II, and the tragedy hit the Paglin family hard, leaving an indelible mark on young Amihai.

"Amihai refused to believe his brother was dead, and he wanted to mount an expedition to go out and look for him on the northern coastline," related his friend David Danon.[3] "'If their boat was blown up close to the place where they landed – surely there must be traces there,' he insisted. He was deterred from setting out only by his lack of fluency in Arabic. 'They'd identify us as foreigners straightaway,' he said, and gave up the idea."

But the death of his brother continued to obsess him for many years, and changed the whole course of his life as well as his view of the world. As he was to say in an interview years later:

> This was the period of the "White Paper" and in my class at the Balfour School there were lively and impassioned political arguments. One of the pupils there was Eliyahu Bet-Zuri,[4] who made no secret of his extreme right-wing opinions – while I and most of my friends were members of the Haganah. The debates became still more heated when the IZL began reprisals against the Arabs, and the Haganah adopted a policy of restraint. I have to admit that for a long time I was undecided, unable to choose between the two, the Haganah and the IZL. Arguments took place not only between the organizations but within them too.
>
> In those days, protest marches initiated by the Haganah were a fairly common occurrence. I remember I always avoided taking part in them. I saw no point in them; they were just a waste of time and energy. A spark of hope flared in me, briefly, when a "hawkish" group within the Haganah took charge, temporarily. They sent us out to stick

---

responsible for the disaster – "by consenting to this complex operation without giving us adequate time to prepare." Moreover, Hacohen claims in this book that the operation was entirely unnecessary. "Even while discussions with the British were still in progress, in 1941 – he, Yitzhak Sadeh, and some friendly British officers – were unsure as to the purpose and the logic of the mission."

3. Interview with the author, August 5, 1996.
4. Eliyahu Bet-Zuri was a member of the IZL, before joining the Lehi. He was hanged in Cairo, March 22, 1945, together with his accomplice Eliyahu Hakim, having been convicted of the assassination of Lord Moyne. On June 26, 1975, their remains were taken to Israel and interred on Mount Herzl with full military honors.

up posters in the streets of Tel Aviv – printed in big letters and warning the British: *If the provisions of the White Paper are implemented – the Sword of Israel will be unsheathed!* That day Haganah and IZL factions in the school were united. But disappointment came the day after – when they sent us to tear the posters down again! This was a hard blow for me. I realized then that the Haganah had no serious leadership of its own, knowing what it wanted and how to get it. These were tense and turbulent times – and I was sent to a platoon-commanders' course in Kfar Menahem. Some of the best future commanders of the Haganah were graduates of this course, including my elementary school classmate Zvi Zur (Chera), who went on to be the sixth chief of staff of the IDF.

It was while I was on this course that I made up my mind to join the IZL, whose style of military and political struggle – active response to Arab attacks and defiance of the British authorities – had always appealed to me. Halfway through the course there was an intermission (while the training program was transferred from Lower to Upper Galilee), and I took advantage of the break to apply for discharge, from both the course and the Haganah. The pretext: my family had suffered enough with the death of my brother, and from a personal point of view I didn't believe myself capable of handling the stress, nor did I have the right to inflict this on my parents, who had yet to come to terms with the loss of their firstborn son. This vacation proved to be a turning point in my life.

Among the friends who used to visit me were Eliyahu Bet-Zuri and David Danon. Since high school days, the three of us had seldom been parted. Conversations revolved, as usual, around the political situation and the provisions of the White Paper, which were now in force and fomenting bitterness and anger among the Jewish population of the country.

One day in the spring of 1942, while we were sitting on the balcony of our house in Mikveh Yisrael Street near the railway station – we suddenly heard commotion from the direction of the post office building on Allenby Street. We hurried to the scene, to see what all the noise was about, and it turned out to be a demonstration by young Haganah activists against the policies of the White Paper. The youths carried a national flag and were shouting anti-British slogans and calling for an end to immigration quotas. This was just a few days after the sinking of the *Struma* refugee ship[5] and feelings were running high.

For some time we stood quietly on the pavement, watching the demonstration but taking no part in it. Suddenly a British police officer pounced on the flag bearer and wrested the flag from his hands. At the sight of this Eliyahu Bet-Zuri was livid with rage, his whole body shaking, his face turning red, and before we could stop him he raced towards that officer, punched him, grabbed the flag and fled. The officer and one of his subordinates set out in pursuit, brandishing revolvers and on the point of opening fire. Eliyahu barely managed to evade them, slipping away into the side streets where we caught up with him.

Half an hour later we were sitting on the steps of my father's workshop at 4 Mikveh Yisrael Street, discussing the event and its significance. The unavoidable conclusion was shocking: Eliyahu had nearly gotten himself killed…

I was furious: "What on earth were you thinking of?" I scolded him. "They nearly nailed you – and for what?"

"He pinched the flag," he protested.

"So what?" I laid into him. "If you'd gotten yourself killed – how would that have helped the nationalist cause? If you're going to risk your life," I continued, "then do it for a worthwhile cause, not some pointless impulse." After my brusque words there was an awkward silence. Gradually we cooled down and the conversation returned to its normal pitch. For a long time we deliberated over the best contribution

---

5.   The *Struma* refugee ship sank in the Black Sea, February 24, 1942. All but one of the 770 passengers perished. Having left Romania in December 1941, the ship spent some two months anchored in the port of Istanbul, while Jewish institutions appealed to the British to allow the refugees to enter Eretz Israel, despite the stringent restrictions imposed by the White Paper, or at least to admit the children. The British rejected all these appeals, and on February 23, 1942, the Turkish authorities ordered the captain of the *Struma* to return to the Black Sea, although the ship's engines were defective. A Turkish tug towed the *Struma* out into the open sea and abandoned it there. Just before the ship foundered, some two kilometers off shore, a loud explosion was heard.

This was the worst disaster suffered throughout the years of "illegal" immigration, and the effect on the Jewish community was devastating. For a long time it was believed that a German submarine had sunk the *Struma*, or that the ship had struck a mine. Today, it is known that it was a Soviet submarine that torpedoed the ship, unaware of its identity (*Leksikon koah ha-magen ha-Haganah* [Lexicon of the Haganah defense force] [Tel Aviv: Ministry of Defense, 1992], ed. Mordecai Naor, p. 310).

we could make toward the removal of British domination from our country.

After long and thorough discussion we came to the conclusion that only a real political shock would force the British to change their policies. And what could be more shocking to the government than a blow struck at the senior figure of authority, the High Commissioner? There and then we decided to take this mission on ourselves, even at the risk of our lives.[6]

THE HIGH COMMISSIONER

And so, at the end of a turbulent summer day, on the steps of the house at 4 Mikveh Yisrael Street in Tel Aviv, the audacious plan was hatched: an attempt on the life of the High Commissioner of the time, Sir Harold MacMichael.

"The first plan was simplicity itself," Gidi recalled:

The High Commissioner was in the habit of putting in an appearance at social and diplomatic events. All we had to do was burst in with our revolvers and start shooting. The question of our personal safety was way down the agenda. Even if they finished us off afterwards – we'd have done our bit.

But fate had other ideas: as a result of the tension prevailing in the land, the High Commissioner stopped attending receptions and foundation-stone ceremonies in Tel Aviv.

We worked out an alternative assassination plan, using a mine in the road. We discovered that while His Excellency was avoiding Tel Aviv, he was still a regular visitor to Jaffa. We decided to plant an electrically controlled mine in the region of Mikveh Yisrael, but we soon realized that planting the mine was the easy part – what was much more complicated was stretching the wires over fields where Arab workers were constantly on the move. We developed a mine that could be detonated by means of telephone wires, and after a few successful experiments all we had to do was wait for the High Commissioner's motorcade. But the motorcade never came. It seemed he had stopped visiting the coastal plain altogether.

6.   Author's interview with Amihai Paglin, 1969.

If the mountain won't come to Mohammed, Mohammed will go to the mountain, I reflected. At this stage we'd come to the conclusion that charging in with revolvers in our hands wasn't an option; we'd never get close enough for an effective shot. Incidentally, we had three or four revolvers at our disposal then – although to tell the truth, I can't remember now how we came by them. The important thing is, we began some intensive handgun practice in the sands of Holon....

The material for making bombs was supplied to us by Eliyahu Bet-Zuri. He succeeded in "infiltrating" the Tel Aviv Public Works department and was thus able to filch all the stuff we needed. Eliyahu also volunteered to gather information on the High Commissioner's living conditions and habits. For this purpose, he asked his superiors to transfer him to Jerusalem. He used to spend his leisure time, after his day's work in the capital, strolling around the area of the objective.

On one of his reconnaissance tours, he met a young man he knew, working as a gardener at the residence. To his surprise, at the mere mention of the High Commissioner's name, the other exploded in a torrent of curses. It seemed the treatment he was receiving from His Nibs and the rest of the household was humiliating, bordering on persecution. "They call me *donkey*," he complained bitterly – "and they call the donkey *Jew-boy*." ...It wasn't hard for Eliyahu to translate his friend's hostility into fluent information. That was how we discovered the residence was surrounded by many acres of garden, and security over this very large whole area was entrusted to just three policemen – one of them confined to the guard hut and the other two patrolling once every two or three hours; this interval of time was more than enough to allow access to the residence and a safe exit once the job was done.

While the planning was still in progress, Eliyahu suggested it was time we joined the Irgun Zvai Leumi. He himself had been a member in the past, and for David Danon, too, this was a "homecoming" (he'd been in the IZL until the rift with Stern's faction). As for me, this was a real ideological reversal.[7]

7.　Ibid.

"He was introduced to me, if I'm not mistaken, by Meridor," Eitan Livni recalled.

> A tall, impressive young man, he came to us from the Haganah. He didn't arrive as a raw recruit, needing to go through all the normal training procedures. He arrived bursting with ideas, which he used to raise in regular meetings with Meridor. How he got in touch with Meridor, then the commander of the IZL, I don't know. His ideas were mainly to do with technical issues: how to make mines, how to detonate them, and how to make them impossible to defuse. He went through a fast-track lieutenant's course and climbed the ladder of command quickly. The combat squad of the IZL in Tel Aviv had a strength of several dozen at that time, and Amihai was among the outstanding ones. He was popular with his subordinates and gained their trust.[8]

Of his first days in the IZL, Gidi recalled:

> The swearing-in ceremony didn't make much impression on me. I'd gotten used to things like that in my schooldays...but it's imprinted in my memory for another reason: I knew that by this act I was breaking all my social links as part of the Haganah, severing ties with many friends of my youth, and actually turning over a new page in my life. This wasn't an easy concept to digest. I remember I asked one favor of my new bosses: they should never try to extract from me any information regarding the Haganah and the period of my service in it. This they promised, and they kept their word. Soon after I was sent on a command course, which was nothing like the course in Kfar Menahem; there were differences in the training materials and in the degree of professionalism. While in Kfar Menahem the emphasis was on field training, here ideology and the use of small arms occupied most of the time.
>
> Though I admit I was sometimes saddened by the sense of separation from the past...when I think of this, today I reckon what kept me going at that time was the obsessive idea that was constantly in my mind: the assault on the High Commissioner.

---

8. Eitan Livni, at a memorial evening for Gidi, 1978.

In time we co-opted a fourth member, the course commander, Yehuda Borochov. Even though the training was still in progress, we decided to reconnoiter the scene of the operation. This was an experience I'm never likely to forget.

We approached the High Commissioner's residence from the south, slipping through the trees near the fence. When the sentry had passed in front of us, I started forward and crawled toward the residence. To my surprise I caught sight of the profile of the High Commissioner himself, just a few yards from me, through the window of the bathroom. I couldn't believe what I was seeing: all I'd need to do was climb the drainpipe to the second floor, and I'd be inside. Within minutes I could do the job and get out safely. I crawled back to my comrades and told them what I had discovered. We decided to stay in our hiding place a little longer, to get a reliable picture of activity in the area. To our surprise, three hours passed before the guard made its second patrol. We returned to Tel Aviv and throughout the journey I was too excited to relax: no need for explosives or even accomplices; one man could shin up the drainpipe, sneak into his bedroom, stick a knife in him and get out. It wouldn't even be discovered until the morning.

I knew from the start that responsibility for carrying out the attack would be laid on me – if only because in physical ability I was the best fitted for the task; climbing drainpipes was something I could do then with the agility of a cat.

If you ask, was I prepared to do the job with my own hands – the answer is yes. I wasn't sure I'd be capable of stabbing him with a knife. My personal preference would be to use an axe on him. I was confident I could handle that.

We got together again, Eliyahu Bet-Zuri, David Danon and I – and decided the time had come to carry out the attack. We passed this on to the fourth member, Borochov. He was a little surprised but raised no objection. He just asked our permission to inform the commander of the Irgun, "because of the serious repercussions this action will cause in all aspects of life in this country, including the underground organizations." Unfortunately [Gidi sighed] he succeeded in persuading us that this was our duty to the organization we belonged to.

A meeting was arranged with the commander of the IZL at the time, Yaakov Meridor. It was held in a hut behind the old municipal offices in Bialik Street. The three of us arrived, and without wasting time on pleasantries I told him the substance of the operation that we intended to carry out. "Speaking for myself," I added, "I don't see that I'm obliged to inform you about this (as it isn't an Irgun operation), but at the request of my colleagues, I am doing so."

Meridor's answer still echoes in my ears, and it gave me a hint as to why the Irgun had fallen into a state of inertia since the rift with Stern's faction.

I shall try to reproduce the precise words that he used: "You have to understand," he said, "that no organization has the right to carry out an operation such as this. The repercussions are likely to be catastrophic, leading to the elimination of the entire Jewish presence in this land. The scale of the disaster in Europe is such that the remnant surviving here is the last hope of the Jewish people, and if this too is destroyed – the people of Israel will vanish forever from the map of history. No group – least of all the IZL – can afford to take responsibility for an operation that is likely to have such extreme effects from a historical perspective. On the other hand," he added, "if you, as individuals, are intent on going through with this, on your own initiative and your personal responsibility – I see no reason to interfere or stand in your way."

Yaakov's final words led me to hope that maybe he'd be prepared to help us from a technical or logistical point of view, such as supplying explosives if attacking with cold steel were to be rejected as impractical. To this he replied he would willingly supply us with explosives if we approached him a few days before the operation.

A week later I sent Yehuda to him to collect the equipment. He returned empty-handed and out of breath, telling me Meridor had surprising news for me and wanted to see me without delay. The news was indeed surprising, and of far-reaching significance: we were getting not a sack of dynamite but full support for our operation.

"Recently," Meridor told me, not without a hint of pride, "I've been in touch with certain circles in the Haganah and it's been decided to set up a joint front known as Am Lohem[9] to cover all the underground

9.   *Am Lohem* (Fighting Nation) – towards the end of 1943, individual members of the nationalist movement, including Haganah activists and deserters from the British

organizations involved in hostilities against the British, and as a first step your scheme is to be adopted, with one small amendment: instead of killing the High Commissioner, he's to be abducted and put on trial, as responsible for the deportation of Holocaust survivors." Kidnapping the High Commissioner, Meridor explained, "won't lead to such drastic repercussions as would be the case with his murder, but the impact on public opinion here and worldwide will be no less, if not more."

The Am Lohem plan was based on our original scheme, but involved a large-scale diversionary exercise: 100 fighters were to be assembled in Jerusalem, and they were to launch simultaneous attacks on all the police stations in the capital. A light aircraft belonging to the Irgun would be waiting on the airstrip at Atarot, ready to move the High Commissioner to a site near Petah Tikva; the final stage of the journey would transport him in a car with blacked-out windows, under armed guard and by minor roads, to an underground bunker.

I didn't oppose the plan but I made it clear that my agreement was conditional on operational responsibility for the kidnap being mine, and mine alone.

Yaakov assured me that this was understood and asked me to see that the bunker was fitted with suitable amenities for our distinguished guest, "including a flush toilet." I remember that this last item injected a note of levity into the proceedings, easing the tension that we all felt. When I was negotiating over the price of a toilet seat in the plumbing supply store in Herzl Street, pointing out that the one on offer was of less than perfect workmanship – the shopkeeper replied indignantly:

---

army, decided to set up a new framework for coordinated struggle against the British. The name of the organization was suggested by Yigal Hurwitz, a member of the national center of Ha-No'ar ha-Oved (the youth movement, Working Youth). Another cofounder was a leading Revisionist activist, Dr. Binyamin Lubotsky-Eliav.

On November 6, 1943, IZL's radio station announced the inauguration of Am Lohem and outlined its program for action – renewal of the anti-British campaign on a broad base. The first (and last) issue of its periodical, *Am lohem* (November 1, 1943) described the new body as "a coalition of youth groups who have had enough of inaction."

The Am Lohem organization disintegrated within a short period of time as a result of heavy pressure exerted by the Haganah hierarchy on Irgun members who had joined this group. The only positive outcome of this episode was, perhaps, Aharon Kadishman's decision to join the IZL.

"What's all the fuss about? The High Commissioner isn't going to sit on that!" I was so astonished that for a moment I was speechless.

The bunker was ready, down to the smallest detail – and then nothing happened. Something about all this preparation made me uneasy: too many people involved in it, and a secret known to more than three is no longer a secret. I was afraid there would be a leak, and information slip out. And sure enough, in the end, it all fell apart.

After some deliberation, the operation was scheduled for the evening of November 29, 1943. We assembled in Jerusalem, and Meridor kept his promise and appointed me to lead the team that was going to invade the High Commissioner's bedroom. I was ready and confident that, whatever the outcome, I would do the job assigned to me.

We waited hour after hour in some cellar in the center of Jerusalem. At two in the morning we were informed that the operation had been postponed and we were to return to Tel Aviv. From snippets of conversation that I overheard, between Meridor and other commanders, it became clear that my fears had been justified and details of the operation had been leaked in advance to the Haganah, and with the connivance of some IZL commanders in Jerusalem, the whole scheme had been aborted. When zero hour arrived, G. Mali, Jerusalem district commander – acting on orders from the New Zionist Federation leaders in the capital – refused to supply the weapons and the manpower.[10] All those long hours we had been waiting in the cellar, feverish negotiations had been in progress between Meridor and Yunitzman (of the NZF leadership), but to no avail.

I also heard that at one point, when Yunitzman was afraid the operation would go ahead in spite of everything, he alerted the Haganah and two men were sent to throw thunderflash grenades over the fence of the residence. As a result, some 15 policemen were sent to the scene (a force which in normal circumstances would not have induced us to abort an operation).

---

10. Mali was placed on a disciplinary charge for disobeying the Irgun commander's order and refusing to supply men and weapons on the day of the operation, and on December 29, 1943, he was dismissed from his post and suspended for a year from membership of the Irgun.

When we arrived back in Tel Aviv it was already four in the morning. Meridor, unhappy at the turn of events, assembled us at the Kalischer School on Tabor Street to explain what had happened, and what he said only confirmed the rumors I had heard. When he had finished, I asked for the opportunity to speak. "All you have to do," I said, "is give the order to act, and I guarantee that within 24 hours the whole job will be done as originally planned, including the supply of weapons from the IZL arsenals in Jerusalem. If you don't do this," I warned him, "you'll have no weapons and no Irgun." There was silence.

Meridor took up the challenge: "I agree with you," he said, "but this isn't something that can be done today or tomorrow. Give me a few days to sort things out, and you'll hear from me."

And sure enough, a week later he solemnly informed us that the operation was to go ahead, but in a more secretive manner than before and with fewer participants. So once more we set out for Jerusalem, a pared-down squad of just 20 men – and once more nothing came of it.

The Irgun that I had joined, I realized then to my dismay, was proving to be as impotent and indecisive as the Haganah that I had left behind. I felt cheated and hurt: was it for this that I severed all links with my past? The lesson was clear: we should never, from the start, involve outside elements in projects that we initiated; if we hadn't turned to Meridor, that operation would already have been behind us.

But the disappointment wasn't mine alone – the failure of the operation had repercussions at the highest echelons of the organization, and a fundamental restructuring of forces was set in motion. The IZL was split into two: alongside the regular corps, comprising most of the membership – special units were set up, known as "Red Sections." In the initial phase four units were established – in Tel Aviv, Jerusalem, Petah Tikva, and Haifa. Each unit numbered between 10 and 15 fighters, constituting a kind of Irgun commando force, and as their identities were concealed from the regulars, they were effectively an underground within an underground. It seems I had gained Meridor's trust, and he appointed me commander of the Tel Aviv "Red Section." This was a force of 15 men, the largest such unit in the country.

We had separate arms caches and we even rented a small apartment in the Shapira district for our use. We became an independent unit within the framework of the Irgun, with equipment and weapons of our own (perhaps the only viable weapons in the hands of the IZL at that time).

Now we were only waiting for a sign.

STEEL BROTHERS

Gidi went on, describing those unnerving days:

> Days passed, weeks and months. The atmosphere was tense as people waited impatiently for orders that were slow to come. There was unrest, and I admit I helped to fan it.
>
> And then, as nothing was moving and inertia had set in, we decided the time had come to do something. When I say "we decided," I mean myself and a few of my subordinates. The vehicle known as the "Irgun Zvai Leumi" needed a push-start; if we couldn't get it into third gear, we might at least manage first gear. We had to prove ourselves capable of initiating a project and carrying it through.
>
> In the end we decided – David Danon, Avtalion Ayub and I – to hit Steel Brothers in Jaffa. Steel Brothers was a British construction monopoly that had taken over all available public works and at that time was also supplying transport and logistics to the British army. Every evening, between 50 and 100 trucks were parked at their main site in Jaffa. They were our target.[11]

David Danon continued:

> One day Amihai's patience snapped, and he decided to mount a symbolic attack on the British establishment, blowing up the Steel Brothers trucks. I can't say I was 100 per cent in favor. I didn't see it as a particularly significant objective, but Amihai convinced me that we had to do something because otherwise nothing would ever be done. "Somehow," he said, "we have to prove that action is possible, and it doesn't mean the end of the world – not everyone will be imprisoned, not everyone will be killed, and the streets won't be sealed off. Until they realize that things can be done without inviting catastrophic results, they're always

---

11.   Author's interview with Amihai Paglin, 1969.

going to hesitate." Personally, I wasn't convinced that hesitation was an expression of fear – but I let him talk me into going along.

The activation and delay mechanisms we put together ourselves, in a fairly primitive way. In Amihai's house there was a wall panel and all the gadgets were mounted on this to test the interval between activation and explosion. I don't know how we came through these experiments unscathed, but I'm sure that once or twice we came close to killing ourselves.[12]

It was the delay mechanism that was the real proof of Gidi's ingenuity. Being unable to afford timers or electrical detonators, he and his associates devised a simple chemical reaction. David Danon and Shraga Ellis have both described how tiny eye-drop bottles were filled with sulfuric acid, and each bottle sealed with a cork and a metallic disc. The discs were of varying thickness: from a tenth of a millimeter to a millimeter, depending on the length of delay required. The corks were fitted with a condom containing a little potash and saltpeter, and the assembly was completed with the addition of a detonator and a short fuse. The chain reaction started when the bottle was inverted. The acid would burn its way through the barrier of the metallic disc, reacting with the potash and saltpeter to start a fire igniting the fuse and activating the detonator, leading to the explosion.

"We combined the attack on Steel Brothers with a poster campaign," Gidi recalled, "calling on the British authorities to get out of the country, wind up their businesses here, and close their institutions. *Blowing up transport tonight,* we warned, *is only the first step, to show that we mean business.*"

According to Danon:

The posters were printed on the Paglin family's printing press on Mikveh Yisrael Street. It was a slow job, because it was a small, antiquated machine that couldn't handle more than three sheets at a time. We had to keep feeding it manually.

…I remember going out to do the job wearing the best clothes I had, thinking that way I'd look less suspicious…. In the end, this only slowed me down when I was running from the police.[13]

---

12. Author's interview with David Danon, 1996.
13. Ibid.

Gidi takes up the story:

> One of the subjects we discussed was the choice of a signature, for use on the posters. As the three of us – Danon, Avtalion, and I – constituted a new group – we wanted an impressive title, and we finally came up with the name "Warriors." It didn't occur to us how much trouble we were going to cause ourselves with this signature; it suggested a connection with "Warriors for the Freedom of Israel" (Lehi) – of all the underground groups the one most hounded by the British police at that time.
>
> On Friday, June 29, 1944, at 10:00 PM, we – Avtalion Ayub and I – slipped into the parking lot of Steel Brothers, each of us carrying 20 bundles of explosives (weighing a couple of pounds [1 kilogram] apiece) plus the delay gadgets, our own invention and manufacture.
>
> It was a dark night and we had no difficulty breaking through the wire fence and getting inside, unseen by the Arab watchmen. We crept from truck to truck, planting packs of explosives in the cabs. Within 20 minutes we were already clear of the site, leaving behind us at least 20 trucks about to blow.
>
> We didn't take weapons and explosives from the Irgun's armories, because we saw this as "private enterprise." We used the gear we'd been given for the High Commissioner operation, plus a couple of pistols that were our own property. We didn't ask for clearance for the action or even tell anyone what we were planning. We'd learned from experience, and anyway one of our objectives was to jolt the Irgun out of its comatose state.
>
> When the job was done we made our way to Sharon Park, where we'd arranged to meet Danon for the next phase of the operation – sticking up the posters. As we were talking the sound of an explosion shook the air – followed by a succession of blasts, one after another. There couldn't be any doubt: the operation had succeeded. All the explosives had gone off. Two minutes after midnight – time to get the posters up.
>
> We started in south Tel Aviv and worked our way northward, then to the center of town. We didn't yet know how seriously the British police were going to take our escapade, or what kind of repercussions we were going to cause, styling ourselves "Warriors." As we were

calmly putting up posters in the side streets off Allenby, a large police contingent, backed up by troops and armored cars, arrived and began scouring the area.

At the corner of Balfour Street a Bren carrier pulled up beside us with a squeal of brakes. There was a shout of "Hey, you!" In our naïveté we thought the grunts were just asking for directions, but suddenly a dozen armed soldiers leaped down from the vehicle, with a big Alsatian dog. "Scatter, boys!" I shouted to my pals, diving into the nearest courtyard with two uniforms on my heels. I jumped the fence and took refuge in the maze of buildings beyond it. My pursuers hesitated for a moment and that gave me the time I needed to disappear. Danon went in the other direction and succeeded in getting away in the darkness. Only Avtalion was unlucky: the dog caught up with him and he was arrested.

Avtalion's arrest was a severe shock to me, and it troubled my conscience, too. Given the circumstances of his arrest, he could be facing life imprisonment or even the death penalty. If the action had been carried out on behalf of any organization, he would at least have had some support and legal representation. But as things stood then, he had no backup at all. We were a trio of powerless youths without the resources to hire an attorney. As the one who had instigated the operation, I felt the full responsibility for his fate resting on my shoulders, and I had no idea what to do.

The next evening, I was told to report to Eitan Livni, the man responsible for the Irgun's "Red Sections" and my direct superior at that time. He demanded to know if I had any connection with the operation. I admitted that the planning and the execution were entirely mine, and Avtalion had just been there to help. I didn't mention Danon. I said I was prepared to accept all the personal consequences arising from my responsibility for the operation, and I had only one request: "Please, help Avtalion!"

Eitan listened to what I had to say with a stony face and made no direct response. "I'll be in touch," he said. The day after, he had news for me: "Irgun Command has decided to adopt your operation and accept full responsibility for it. Avtalion will get all the moral and material support he needs."

My relief was overwhelming, but I wasn't out of the woods yet.

Eitan gave me a stern look: "I hope you're not planning any more solo efforts…"

He looked around cautiously. "We're on the threshold of a new era," he added. "Very soon there's to be an announcement on behalf of the Irgun, regarding resumption of hostilities against the British authorities."

He paused for a moment as if weighing his words: "Your operation made a crucial contribution to that decision," he said, and for the first time the shadow of a smile crossed his face.

And sure enough a few days later, February 1, 1944, posters were pasted up throughout the land, a historic declaration of revolt against the British occupation of Palestine.

Gidi recalled:

Today I'm convinced that this was a direct result of the attack on Steel Brothers. The operation we initiated may have been small-scale, but it jolted the IZL out of its paralyzed state and speeded up the decision to go out and fight the British. It was made clear to the new leadership, under Menahem Begin, that there was a lot of impatience in the ranks, and if the Irgun didn't act as a body, its members would act as individuals. A paralyzed body is doomed to degenerate and the structure, which had been tottering for years (the failure of the High Commissioner project only accentuated this) – was threatening to collapse altogether. Two sentences in the declaration particularly impressed me: *There is no longer a cease-fire in force between ourselves and the British authorities* and *war will continue until a Hebrew government has been established in Eretz Israel.*

The first targets selected for attack were the immigration offices in the three major towns – Tel Aviv, Jerusalem, and Haifa. The operation was entrusted to the "Red Sections" and the Haifa office was allocated to me. I approached the task energetically, doing everything from assembling the explosives to prior reconnaissance on the ground. My accomplices were Yedidia Mizrahi and one of the girls from the women's corps of the IZL. At the end of the Sabbath, February 12, 1944, we packed the explosives in a suitcase and set out for the building. There were no tenants in residence, and according to our estimate, 25 pounds (12 kilograms) of gelignite in the basement would be enough to shake the whole building.

The only problem was how to get the Arab watchman out of the building and out of harm's way. I asked my two companions to distract his attention somehow. So the two moved to the end of the building and sank into a passionate embrace.... The watchman's curiosity got the better of him and he left his post to take a closer look. At the same time I slipped into the basement of the building with the suitcase, set the mechanism, and left. When the "couple" saw me leaving they followed suit.

The tensions and exertions of the last few days had taken their toll, and I went to my hotel room and fell into a deep sleep. Next morning the landlord was most surprised that I hadn't heard the explosion "which rocked the city of Haifa and reduced the immigration office to a heap of ruins." To tell the truth, I couldn't be bothered to go and inspect the damage; I caught the first train back to Tel Aviv.

THE INCOME TAX OFFICES

Two weeks later Irgun units once again set out for synchronized action in the three major cities. On the hit list this time were the income tax offices – *the chief tool for the exploitation of the Hebrew worker and citizen by a treacherous government*, in the words of the IZL communiqué.

The operation was scheduled for the end of the Sabbath, February 27.

The income tax offices were located at 69 Nahalat Binyamin Street. The building had formerly been occupied by the Credit Bank, and it was still known to the locals by this name, although the bank had long since gone out of business and the premises had been taken over by the Treasury Department of the government of Palestine. The tax section was situated on the ground floor of the building, and there were two entrances: the main entrance on Lilienblum Street and a side door on Nahalat Benyamin.

Gidi took part in the Tel Aviv operation. "The job," he recalled, "was ridiculously easy. We divided into three groups, two for security and the third – of which I was a member – for the business itself. While two of our number waited with weapons ready on the pavement in front of the building, the other four got into the courtyard, broke windows, and got the explosives into the building."

Four loud explosions, between the hours of 8:00 and 9:30 PM, destroyed inner walls, obliterated files and documents, and reduced the ground floor to rubble – without injury to anyone.

The destruction of the tax offices roused the British from their complacency. They decided on a strong-arm approach and launched a series of arrests aimed at members of the Irgun. But the list of names at their disposal dated from before the outbreak of the World War and consisted mainly of the names of Revisionist operatives who had had no contact with the Irgun for years. They picked them up easily enough, but the current activists, most of them young and newcomers to the ranks of the Irgun, remained at large.

In the wake of the mass arrests and searches, commanders of the Irgun decided to retaliate directly, to strike a blow at the intelligence branch of the government, the arm directly responsible for the wave of harassment and arrests: the Mandatory detective service, the CID.[14] As before, the decision was made to hit simultaneously in the three major cities. The operation was scheduled for March 24, 1944.

Gidi relates:

> My task was to prepare the "goodies" and supply them to the attack units, also to command the operation in the Tel Aviv area. Compared with the big projects that we undertook at a later stage, those first operations seem now like children's games, but back then they were reckoned an outstanding success: the British weren't prepared and we seized the opportunity to hit them where it hurt.
>
> As a result of reconnaissance in the target area, it turned out that in the same alley where the CID offices were located, a brothel was in business. Officers and soldiers visited the place regularly, and the sight of drunken men in uniform staggering out the door buttoning their trousers was not uncommon.
>
> We decided to exploit this fact as a way of getting the explosives into the bomb shelter under the CID building: a squad of saboteurs, disguised as soldiers, was to arrive in a taxi as if heading for the "funhouse" and then proceed on foot (unsteadily) to the entrance to the shelter. One of the group had to suggest, drunkenly, going in there

---

14. CID – the Criminal Investigation Department of the Mandatory Police.

"for a piss" and use this as an opportunity to plant the bombs. One backup section was stationed opposite the building and another on the Jaffa–Tel Aviv road.[15]

Eitan Livni relates the sequence of events:

At the appointed time the sabotage squad arrived in a taxi, wearing uniforms of the Polish army (units of the Polish Anders Army were still based in the country at that time). The infiltration was accomplished in total silence and without attracting any attention. They piled the explosives in a corner, turned over the bottles of acid to start the detonation process and left. The delay was set at 20 minutes.

Two girls were given the job of phoning police HQ to warn of the imminent explosion…. Gidi and the other members of the backup team waited across the street, right opposite the main entrance. Although only the width of the street separated the sabotage squad from the backup, for some reason the leader of the saboteurs forgot to notify Gidi that the job had been done. Members of the squad withdrew along the Jaffa–Tel Aviv road, pausing only to contact the girls and tell them to start sending the warnings.

The backup and command team, headed by Gidi, went on waiting opposite the entrance. Not only had they not been informed the bombs were in place – in the darkness they hadn't seen the sabotage squad leaving the scene.[16]

Gidi recalled:

The hands of the clock were moving. More than half an hour had passed and there was no sign of the saboteurs. It was obvious that if by now they hadn't set the explosives, the operation was a dud, and if the explosives had been set, the building could blow up at any moment, with us just across the street…. Suddenly I noticed a lot of commotion at the front of the building, with constables and officers streaming out the

---

15. Ibid.
16. Eitan Livni, *Ha-Ma'amad* [The Stand (internal name for Etzel)] (Tel Aviv: Idanim, 1987), pp. 78–79.

door in a state of high anxiety. There could be no doubt: the bombs had been planted and the warning given. A British police sergeant spotted us across the street and opened fire. One of my men, Zvi Millstein, was hit in the hand but managed to get way with the rest of us, following an exchange of fire. When we reached our base, a mighty explosion was heard. Next day it turned out half the building had collapsed, as if a sharp knife had cut it in two.[17]

THE WEAPONS SEIZURE IN REHOVOT

On October 11, 1945, a unit of the IZL, commanded by Amihai Paglin, carried out a weapons "confiscation" exercise at the British army camp in Rehovot. This was a training center and at the time it also comprised a contingent of Jewish soldiers recently liberated from German POW camps.[18]

Shortly after midnight members of the unit got into the guardroom, overpowered the guards at gunpoint,[19] and got away with 218 rifles, 15 Brens, and assorted items of military hardware. The booty was driven away in army trucks, commandeered for the purpose, and the entire operation was over within a quarter of an hour. No problems.

"This was the biggest seizure of weapons ever carried out by the IZL," Amihai Paglin was to say, recalling these events 20 years later:

> They called it the "private haul" and it comprised more than 400 units of weapons with all their appurtenances. Unfortunately, the Haganah got its hands on the loot, and in the end, we were left with just 60 items....
>
> The raid was carried out against the background of a serious arms shortage, which was a major problem for the Irgun at that time. I reckon we didn't have more than 50 weapons back then, which meant we couldn't send more than 50 men into action. The Haganah, in spite of the negotiations we were engaged in over establishing a united insurgency movement, was continually nibbling away at our arms stocks.

---

17. Author's interview with Amihai Paglin, 1969.
18. David Niv, *Ma'arakhot ha-Irgun ha-Tzeva'i ha-Le'umi 1944–1946* [The battles of the Irgun Zvai Leumi] (Tel Aviv: Hadar, 1976), p. 173.
19. "In this operation most of the combat squad commanders took part," according to Nahum Slonim, one of the organizers and participants. "Most of us arrived at the place unarmed, the only weapons at our disposal...being a couple of revolvers" (author's interview with Nahum Slonim, December 25, 1996).

The last straw, at least for some of the commanders who took part in the operation – was the cavalier behavior of the Haganah in this context and the way they insisted on provoking us: just when the leadership of the Irgun had complied with a request from the Haganah and abandoned the idea of a weapons "confiscation" at Rehovot, Haganah members broke into our arsenal at Petah Tikva, seized all the weapons that were there (about 15 items) and left a broom behind – as a symbol of the way they had cleaned us out....

This incensed some of our commanders, though they still hesitated to take action. In a closed and secret meeting, it was decided to go ahead with the Rehovot raid. In this debate I expressed my feeling in simple terms: "For the Irgun the issue of arms is a matter of life and death. If we don't get arms the Irgun will cease to exist as a fighting force, it will be an army of posters and pamphlets. The hands of our leadership are tied," I explained, "by some promise they gave to the Haganah. That's why there'll be no official approval of the action. Better to spare our leaders any unpleasantness and act on our own judgment. That way the leadership's obligations to the Haganah won't be tainted. Once the weapons are in our arsenals, we can even compromise and offer to share them with the Haganah and Lehi, but most of them will stay in our hands." Personally, I was convinced that our leader – had his hands not been tied – would have given the project his blessing.[20]

"The arms raid at Rehovot was carried out at a time when negotiations over setting up a united insurgency movement were in progress," Begin related,

but before signing of the operative agreement. It was not a pleasant situation for us.... We couldn't reveal the truth, which was that the business took us completely by surprise. It wasn't done in accordance with a decision of the leadership, but on the initiative of the perpetrators alone – a group of young commanders, some of the best and most dedicated men we had. I stood behind a screen and reprimanded them soundly, but my personal feelings were mixed....[21]

---

20. S. Lev-Ami's interview with Amihai Paglin, November 27, 1970, Hebrew University, Institute of Contemporary Judaism.
21. Menahem Begin, *The Revolt* (New York: Nash, 1977), pp. 187–88.

Mark Kahan (Alex), who was also present at this "session," maintains that Gidi never wavered in his conviction that the action was justified. "He insisted that the Irgun needed weapons and couldn't survive without them…. We had to get hold of them wherever we could."[22] Sure enough, concern for equipment and logistics continued to head Gidi's list of priorities throughout his career as an Irgun activist.

THE ARMS RAID ON THE EXHIBITION SITE

On December 27, 1945, the IZL again attacked police as well as secret police headquarters in Jaffa and Jerusalem, and at the same time a unit commanded by Gidi conducted a raid on the exhibition site in Tel Aviv, a place where the British were believed to be holding substantial quantities of arms and equipment. The objective this time was the 200 tommy guns, which according to information received were stored in one of the arsenals.

This was the IZL's first "naval exercise" as some of the attacking force arrived in motor launches on the Yarkon.

The assailants numbered 40 men. They were divided into two groups, one operating from the direction of the city and the other from the Yarkon. Roles were allocated: attack and control squads, a "pin-down" squad, back-up, "porters." According to informants, many hands would be needed to shift the stock of weapons stored there.

Once the wire fences surrounding the camp had been breached, the signal was given and the combat units began taking up field positions. They advanced in two columns and took control of the central building. At the gate Gidi called on the British to surrender and lay down their arms: "You are completely surrounded. If you surrender and put your hands up, none of you will be hurt. We're only after the weapons."

Some 40 soldiers raised their hands and were confined to one of the rooms, under guard. Their personal weapons were confiscated. One of the soldiers, a corporal, tried to resist; he was severely wounded in an exchange of fire and later died in the hospital of his injuries. A solitary British sniper took up position and kept up a steady rate of fire against the insurgents. A number of them were hit, but they continued to advance.

Pesah Zissin (Ehud), who was acting as deputy commander of the

---

22. Testimony of Mark Kahan (Alex), Collected Testimonies of the Underground Period, Tape 5, Jabotinsky Archives.

operation, advanced at the head of his unit toward the building which served as an armory and blew down the door with an explosive charge. The blast caused panic among the soldiers, and this was only increased when another squad opened fire on their barrack block. Guard towers were manned by IZL personnel in British army uniforms, so no one outside would suspect there was anything amiss on the inside.

Following the destruction of the armory door Ehud's squad rushed in and when they switched on the light, were stunned by what they saw. Besides three tommy guns and a few belts of ammunition on a shelf, there were no weapons there. The storehouse was empty.

The disappointment was intense. There was no point staying here any longer. But the way out was exposed to fire from the sniper, who was blocking their retreat.

Ehud threw a grenade towards the source of the firing, but before he was even across the threshold of the armory, a volley of shots hit him, and he collapsed in a pool of blood. He just had time to shout "I'm hit!" before passing out.

Gidi heard his cry. "Stay where you are, I'm coming to you," he replied. He crawled cautiously towards the armory, yard by yard; reaching the door, he leaped inside. Ehud was on the floor, groaning, losing blood rapidly. He had serious wounds to the stomach, hand, and leg.

Gidi lifted him gently onto his back and began crawling out with him. A hail of bullets greeted him and he was forced to go back inside.

"Throw a stun grenade," he shouted to Dov Sternglass and Motka, who had taken refuge behind a nearby wall. Dov took a stun grenade, primed it and just as he was raising his arm to throw – a bullet pierced his chest. He stumbled and fell and the grenade exploded with a deafening roar, shattering his right cheek and hand.

At that moment Gidi succeeded in getting clear, the wounded Ehud still hoisted on his back. Panting, exhausted, he ordered the bugler to sound the retreat.

In ferocious exchanges of fire the young men succeeded in fighting their way back to the boats, dragging the wounded with them – five severely wounded and a number of minor casualties.

At "Seven Mills," Shmulik, the chief armorer, was waiting for them and he took whatever equipment they had. The wounded were transferred to the Paulin Hospital in Ramat Gan. The IZL physician, Dr. Matan, was summoned, and soon after Professor Marcos arrived too, declaring immediately that three were in critical condition and required surgery without delay. He personally phoned Hadassah Hospital and demanded the dispatch of two ambulances at once. Until the operations were complete he stayed by their side, and when a British policeman tried to stop them at a roadblock, the professor explained drily, "I've got typhus patients on board," and the policeman beat a hasty retreat.

At five in the morning Dov Sternglass (Sergeant Avner) lost his fight for life. All the others recovered, eventually, and returned to active service, including Pesah Zissin (Ehud). He owed his life to Gidi, who at great personal risk had extricated him from the fire trap.

The haul of weapons on this occasion was paltry, amounting to a number of tommy guns, taken from the guards at the gate, and a few rifles and grenades. On the other hand, the blow to the prestige of the British army was considerable: 40 professional soldiers had surrendered to a handful of underground irregulars.

THE RAID ON THE AIRFIELDS

On the night of February 27–28, 1946, units of the IZL and Lehi (under the auspices of the "insurgency movement") attacked three British airfields, at Kastina (Hatzor), Kfar Sirkin, and Lod. According to official reports, 22 aircraft were damaged that night, at a cost of some 750,000 Palestine pounds.[23]

The attack on Kastina was commanded by Amihai Paglin.

Reconnaissance had revealed that the airfield at Kastina covered an area of hundreds of dunams. There was paved parking space for 44 heavy bombers of the "Halifax" type, a big hangar, stores, and workshops. Close to these were the takeoff and landing runways, and taxiing strips leading to the parking space. Further to the west were the billets occupied by RAF personnel. The whole area was fenced in with coils of barbed wire. Next to the airfield was the Arab village of Kastina, where various military installations were situated.

The attackers were divided into two: one group, its members disguised as Arabs, climbed aboard a pickup truck laden with straw, under which the weapons and explosives were stowed; members of the other group, in blue

---

23. More than two and a half million dollars at the exchange rate of the time.

shirts and "tembel" hats,[24] set out in a tarpaulin-sided truck, supposedly heading for "a congress of moshav members" in Kfar Warburg. On the way they were joined by three scouts. In an abandoned camp not far from the objective, all the transport was halted and the party continued on foot carrying with them, besides conventional gear, ladders and stretchers. Heavy rain impeded the progress of the unit, which numbered some 40 fighters in all, including two nurses – Mitzi Tau and Tzipora.[25]

According to one of the participants,

> The road we were on wasn't really a road at all, and we kept sinking into the mud up to our knees, which didn't make things any easier. We crossed a swollen wadi, and we had to hold hands to avoid getting swept away. It took us three hours to get to the airfield and we were soaked to the skin. We crossed the first fence, and the second 200 yards further on, and there we were on the landing runway. Suddenly there was an almighty racket and all the floodlights came on. One of the planes had chosen this moment to take off! We threw ourselves down on the tarmac and hardly dared breathe. Gradually things quieted down, and it was pitch dark again. You couldn't see a thing. Gidi told one of the squad commanders to feel his way to the nearest plane – and set it afire. A few minutes passed, seeming like an eternity to us – and then came the explosion, along with a blinding flash. The plane went up in flames and we saw dozens of aircraft just parked there on the ground. The demolition squads set to work right away: plane after plane exploded in flames. The whole sector was lit up, it was bright as daylight. Suddenly we ran out of explosives (we hadn't expected that many "flying targets"). "Shoot straight at the fuel-tanks," Gidi ordered. The steel birds rapidly turned into huge fireballs.[26]

The series of explosions – leading to the destruction of 12 Halifax aircraft – roused the British sentries from their slumber, and they opened up with small arms fire. The backup squads fired in turn and pinned the reinforcements down in their bunkers. A bugle call gave the signal to retreat.

---

24. The tembel hat, a practical work hat for kibbutzniks fashioned of blue or khaki linen with a narrow brim, was ubiquitous apparel among native Israelis of the period.
25. Tzipora Perl from Safed, future wife of Amihai Paglin.
26. Testimony of Baruch Weiner (Konous), "Operation Kastina," Jabotinsky Archives.

The three scouts led the way. Near one of the Arab villages, they came under fire from an orchard. Nazim Ezra Ajami (Yonatan) fell to the ground, blood spurting from a wound in his thigh. The two nurses – Mitzi and Tzipora – cared for him as best they could. "We were sure the British had cut us off," Haim Shafir recalled, "We lay flat, cocked our weapons, and prepared for a long fight."[27] Gidi ordered the machine gunner to "sweep" the orchard with a few bursts from the Bren, but the firing stopped as suddenly as it had started. The fighters carried on through the heavy mud, carrying their wounded comrade on a stretcher made of two battle-dress tunics with rifles inserted in the sleeves. Yonatan died of his wounds soon after. There was no choice but to leave him there, because "by then the British would have had time to block the roads, and cut off all our lines of retreat."[28] "Yosef (Simhon) took off his steel helmet and laid it on the chest of the slain warrior; others took off items of clothing – a coat or a sweater – to cover the body, and having paid their respects to their fallen comrade, took their leave of him."[29]

That very morning, the General Officer Commanding (GOC) British Forces (Middle East), General Bernard Padget, had inspected installations at the Kastina airfield. On hearing of the damage inflicted there, he ordered the immediate removal from Palestine of all British bombers, and their relocation to airfields in Egypt.

Absurd as it may seem, the outstanding achievement of IZL fighters in the airfields operation caused great annoyance to the leaders of the insurgency movement, despite the fact that the operations had been planned, and authorized, under the joint framework. Most enraged of all were Palmah activists, as Yigal Allon testified: "It was my proposal that our 2nd Brigade would destroy military aircraft at Tel Nof, or Lod…. The Brigade scouted, planned, and prepared everything. But Sneh gave the operation to the IZL or Lehi. For my part, I could never forgive him for that."[30]

---

27. *Yediot Aharonot*, January 10, 1969.
28. Iggud le-ma'an Shikum Lohamei Hofesh, *Zikhram Netzah* [Their memory lives] (Tel Aviv, 1959), p. 109.
29. Yosef Nedava, *Darko shel lohem Ivri: Sipur hayav shel Yosef Simhon* [Way of a Hebrew fighter: The life story of Yosef Simhon] (Jerusalem: Merhav, 1965), p. 29.
30. Testimony of Yigal Allon on the "Insurgency Period," March 26, 1970, Haganah Historical Archives (hereafter HHA).

In this context, Eitan Livni tells of an instructive conversation between himself and Yitzhak Sadeh:[31]

> Two days after the successful action carried out by us and by the Lehi, I had a meeting with Sadeh. Sadeh could hardly have missed the look of satisfaction on my face and, indeed, I had good reasons for this.... The attacks had all been successful. A lot of damage had been caused to British military aviation, and the message we wanted to convey had been delivered, loud and clear.... Maybe I expected some words of approval from Sadeh. Instead, he glared at me and said: "Listen, we decided you were to attack Kfar Sirkin and Kastina, but we didn't authorize an attack on Lod."
>
> I couldn't believe what I was hearing. "That just isn't right," I said. "Didn't we sit down together two or three times and discuss it? I remember showing you the routes to and from Lod on the map, and I even spelled out the types of aircraft stationed there." I told Sadeh: "We've struck a blow at every branch of British aviation – fighters, spotter planes, medium and heavy bombers – and instead of congratulations all I'm getting from you are harsh and incomprehensible accusations. Anyone would think I'd deceived you." I reminded Sadeh I'd even passed on to him the code names for each operation, so he could alert his regional commanders if he saw fit....
>
> This unexpected argument left behind a bitter taste. I told Sadeh: "You know what? In the future everything that's agreed is going to be put into writing, so there'll be no argument afterwards." I admit, my disappointment took a lot of getting over.[32]

---

31. Livni, *Ha-Maʼamad*, p. 187.
32. On February 28, 1946, Eitan Livni could not have imagined that five months later (in July 1946) his successor Amihai Paglin would be engaged in a similarly acrimonious dispute with the chief of staff of the insurgency movement, Yitzhak Sadeh, over the date of the King David Hotel operation, with the latter publicly repudiating agreements that he had previously supported.

    With the passage of time it has become clearer that disowning controversial actions, after the fact, was a way of life for Sadeh. It seems there was, indeed, an agreement between him and Allon authorizing the Palmah to attack the airfield at Lod; it is inconceivable that the 2nd Brigade could have "scouted, planned, and prepared everything" as Allon claimed (see above) without the chief of staff of the insurgency movement (Yitzhak Sadeh) giving him the green light. But for some reason or another,

MEETING TZIPORA

One warm summer night in June 1944, in the Jerusalem neighborhood of Nahalat Shiva, a courting couple were to be seen, walking to and fro, arm-in-arm. The young man of 22 and the young lady of 19 were engrossed in their private world and oblivious to their surroundings.

Or so it appeared; in fact they were tense and alert to every sound and movement in their vicinity. Amihai Paglin from Tel Aviv and Tzipora Perl from Safed knew each other by their code names only: Gidi and Yael. They had met that evening for the first time and there was nothing romantic about their "courtship." The two were engaged in a clandestine operation on behalf of the IZL.

The circumstances leading to the first encounter between them is related by the commander of that operation, Eliyahu Lankin:

> That evening we were preparing simultaneous attacks on three central targets in the capital: police headquarters in the Russian Compound, regional government offices on the corner of Jaffa Street and Queen Helena Street, and CID headquarters in Mamilla. For this purpose we'd amassed large quantities of arms (by the standards of those times) in Nahalat Shiva. Because of the scale of the operation, we were sent some combat teams from other sectors. Amihai (Gidi) headed one of these, and he'd been allocated a crucial role in the action. The operation was complicated and not without risk. So we prepared, among other things, a first aid station staffed by a large contingent of girls, and a doctor. The arms were stashed in a courtyard in the neighborhood.

> And then, when all the preparations were complete, suddenly there was a police cordon around the district; one of the local residents had seen unusual movements near her house, suspected a robbery was being planned – and alerted the police. The area was swarming with policemen and soldiers, and there was no way of getting near the cache of arms. We were forced to postpone the operation and send the boys

---

he was forced to give the operation to the IZL and Lehi – almost certainly at the insistence of Sneh. The easiest way to evade responsibility for breaking the deal with Allon was to lay the blame on the IZL, in this instance on Eitan Livni, accusing him of attacking the airfield at Lod without authority. He was to employ precisely the same tactic five months later with Amihai Paglin (see the chapter "The King David Hotel Episode and Its Aftermath").

home. But our biggest worry was the fate of the weapons. If the police managed to get their hands on them, the Irgun would be paralyzed for years. Of all of us, the one who felt most strongly about this was Amihai: "We've got to get the stuff out of there, come what may," he said. "Hell's going to freeze over before those weapons fall into the hands of the British."

I must admit, the vehemence of his words took me aback. I saw before me a lean young man with fiery eyes, declaring boldly, "I'm not going to let the arms and the equipment that we've worked so hard to put together go to waste. I'm appealing to you, as regional commander, to give me responsibility for this."

I said, "Okay, then, let's make some plans. Intelligence is the first priority – we have to assess the situation on the ground, find out where the cops are stationed, how the cache can be approached."

I added, "It's too dangerous for you to do the reconnaissance alone. I'm going to give you a partner and you'll have to act like a courting couple; that way it'll be easier for you to move around and get close to the objective."

I went to the first aid station and asked for a volunteer. All the girls immediately offered their services, in unison. I pointed to Tzipora, a charming, studious type with an air of innocence about her. *That's the girl for this job* – I told myself – and I asked her to follow me. "You've got to act like a pair of lovers," I told Amihai, "so give her a kiss and be on your way." They both blushed to the tips of their ears, looking everywhere but at each other. "It's supposed to look natural," I reminded them, "so any cop who sees you will just wink at you and let you pass."

They did their duty, and did it well. The proof is – three years later they were married. And after that, whenever we met they used to call out to me, "There's our matchmaker!" Over the course of time we became good friends.

But that night, Amihai's stubbornness paid off, and the arms were "liberated." He chose a neglected side road for the approach to the objective, returned with three fellows, and a closed van (commandeered on the spot), and the weapons were loaded and returned intact to the Irgun's armories.

That night Gidi really proved himself a fearless leader prepared for anything. The truth is, we were scared stiff: the British were tense and on edge – liable to shoot first and ask questions afterwards.... It took a lot of nerve and determination to go into the lion's mouth (the whole area was swarming with cops) and get the weapons away under the noses of the British. And he did it.

He could have sent his subordinates to do the job, but it wasn't like Gidi to hide behind the hierarchy of command in times of emergency. He always led from the front. *Follow me!* was his trademark long before it became symbolic of the IDF – and remained so throughout the underground years.

Next morning, I went to headquarters to report to Begin on the circumstances that had led to cancellation of the operation. I concluded: "Despite the setback that we suffered yesterday, I'm proud to announce that a new combat commander has emerged among us, a brave and resourceful leader with a talent for decision making – a man fit in the future for the highest echelons of command."[33]

And so it was that in April 1946 – when the national operations officer, Eitan Livni, was arrested along with 31 others in Bat-Yam – Menahem Begin summoned Amihai Paglin at a late hour of the night, and there and then appointed him the new operations commander of the Irgun Zvai Leumi.

33. Testimony of Eliyahu Lankin, Jabotinsky Institute, Tel Aviv.

ROOTS AND SOURCES

"**M**y earliest memory of Amihai goes back to the time when he was just three years old," says his brother, Yitzhak.

> Even then he showed signs of interest in technical things. We were a family of seven, living in a two-room apartment plus a kitchen and a bathroom. At that time the municipality of Tel Aviv used to freshen the streets with a water tank and sprinkler mounted on a truck. Amihai, at three, was fascinated by this mechanism, and every morning at the regular time he'd be standing on the balcony, clutching the wooden lattice with his little hands and waiting for the truck to appear. And when it arrived, he would chortle with glee, shouting, "Water coming, water coming!"[1]

Amihai was born in 1922. A year earlier, in May 1921, the Arabs had rioted: 47 Jews were murdered and 116 injured. The center of the violence was Jaffa.

"Our family lived at that time in the heart of Arab Jaffa, and my father worked for Litvinsky Brothers in Jaffa," Yitzhak relates.

---

1.   Author's interview with Yitzhak Paglin, December 8, 1996.

Nothing was left in our house. Everything was looted by the rioters and at the end of that day our family found itself with nothing in a hastily improvised refugee camp, in an immigration center on Aliyah Street. We ended up in a basement flat in Shenkin Street in Tel Aviv. These traumatic events affected my parents deeply and naturally they talked about them a lot, so from his earliest childhood Amihai heard about the riots of 1921. There can be no doubt that all this left a deep impression on him and made him apprehensive.[2]

So when the riots of 1936 erupted (he was then in his fourteenth year), alarming stories of the bloody events of the past were still fresh in his mind. By this time his parents were living on Hayarkon Street, Tel Aviv, on the site occupied today by the Dan Hotel, and almost every day Arab funeral processions would pass by, on the way from Jaffa to the Muslim cemetery (now Independence Park). These were dramatic processions, with drums and cymbals and sonorous chanting – intimidating spectacles that remained engraved in his consciousness for a very long time.

In 1938 his brother Neriel joined the Notrim (a Jewish police force) and was sent to Lower Galilee attached to the mobile guard commanded by Yigal Allon. Neriel's military career continued with his transfer to Orde Wingate's "Night Squads," and later to the naval section of the Palmah.

Through contacts with his brother, Amihai became convinced that a new generation was coming of age in the land, a generation with military skills and the imagination to approach things differently. Wingate taught the techniques of ambush and night attack, and he heard about all this from Neriel. His imagination was fired and his eagerness for action aroused.

At the same time, the imposition of stringent immigration quotas angered and embittered him and led him to the conclusion that British authority, perceived as hostile toward the Jews and pro-Arab, was the greatest single problem facing his people. The British had to be fought and expelled from this land, he resolved.

Disillusionment with the institutional leadership of the Jewish community, which was doing nothing to alter the situation, only deepened his sense of frustration. It is not hard to understand his feelings: he was a youth who had grown up in an environment where one security crisis followed

---

2. Ibid.

another, the Jewish community had a hangman's noose around its neck, and no action was forthcoming from the leadership other than the issuing of hollow political declarations. Gradually, he became convinced that the only viable option was to join the underground organizations.

"It's possible that what finally led him to the decision to join the IZL, the last straw," according to his brother Yitzhak, "was the disaster of the Twenty-Three Seafarers. Amihai and the rest of the family believed – and still believe – that that entire operation was pointless and ill-conceived, leading as it did to the loss of some of the finest youths of that time, the Haganah's most talented commanders. And all this, just to curry favor with the British and demonstrate our willingness to collaborate with them."

Amihai's technical aptitudes were revealed at an early age. "He had golden hands from the age of nine onward," Yitzhak relates.

> To earn pocket money he used to make kites and sell them to toy shops. While his friends were spending their time playing, he was tinkering with the machines that Dad imported, dismantling and lubricating them.
>
> Once there was a problem with an imported baking machine. The machine consisted of two parts: the mechanical section, with an arm, and a big bowl. The arm was supposed to knead the dough while the bowl rotated. Sometimes the arm scraped against the bottom of the bowl, and the whole thing would grind to a halt. All the technicians who were called in sang the same tune: something wrong with the mechanism. They would adjust the arm, to shorten it and prevent friction, pocket their fee and leave. Fourteen-year-old Amihai was unimpressed. He wouldn't rest until he found the source of the problem: no one had thought to remove the wax paper wrapped around the base of the mechanism, which was creating an imbalance and affecting the position of the arm. The moment the paper was removed, the problem ceased.
>
> He had a keen eye for anything technical. He was always like that, to the end of his life. He'd go to a machine, glance at it for a few seconds and identify the source of the problem. There wasn't any mechanical problem that he couldn't solve.

The first experiments with explosives and detonation devices Gidi began at 4 Railway Street, before he turned 20. His involvement with the IZL was no secret within the family circle, so there was no reason to make excuses for what he was doing. The experiments were in the design of delay mechanisms for explosives, and the device used was a compressed copper spring, inserted in a test tube of acid. As the acid began consuming the spring, it would be released, setting off the charge. The length of the delay was determined, naturally, by the thickness of the wire used to make the spring, and Amihai set up a long line of test tubes, full of acid and containing springs of varying thickness. He observed the test tubes closely and compared the interval of time it took to release the spring in each case. When he was away from home, the task of observation and recording was entrusted to his mother, Sima, who did the job with meticulous care and was sometimes criticized for this by his father. Her reply was that after what had happened to Neriel, she preferred Amihai's underground activities to be carried on as far as possible under her supervision and control; otherwise he would go ahead and do it anyway, and she would know nothing about it.

Amihai trusted his mother to such an extent that he didn't hesitate to invite his friends and subordinates in the IZL to stay over, and – while she cooked meals for them – they used to talk freely about all kinds of secret and sensitive issues, and nothing ever leaked out beyond the walls of the house.

Amihai felt especially close to his father, Gershon Paglin, and used to spend every spare moment in his workshop. Gershon dealt with the importation of baking machinery and components, and at first Amihai was kept busy unpacking the cases of instruments and equipment; however, his curiosity, technical aptitude, and self-taught expertise were such that he soon became his father's right-hand man, replacing the professional mechanics and technicians and solving problems that others found insoluble.

With the outbreak of World War II, the supply of imported machinery dried up, and there was no choice but to manufacture the equipment themselves. The father was a talented salesman but lacked technical skills; he was incapable of making the switch from retail to manufacture and tended to rely for this on subcontractors. But they weren't familiar with the kind of apparatus he was dealing in, and at times it seemed that the whole business was about to fold – until Amihai came into the picture. As a boy of 18, with his own hands he began putting machinery together, achieving results that previously had been thought attainable only abroad.

To the father, Amihai's successes seemed nothing short of miraculous. In spite of the differences in their personalities – perhaps because of them – unusually close ties developed between father and son, nourished by mutual respect. They became business partners. This warm and intimate partnership continued for 25 years, until Gershon Paglin's death in 1965.

The atmosphere in Gidi's parents' house has been described by Colonel (Res.) Yehuda Naot (Globman):

> An affluent Russian home. A house with culture, with a piano, a big kitchen and an elegant matron with hair styled in the Russian fashion. I'm talking of course about the mother, Sima. We used to meet there, talking quite freely about acts of sabotage, and nothing ever slipped out. The mother used to offer us tea with milk or lemon, according to our preferences. It was an atmosphere quite different from what I was used to at home in Petah Tikva – a typical farmer's household.

Another source of inspiration absorbed by Amihai is described by his childhood friend, David Danon:

> One of our teachers, the late Mr. Keller, had a particularly strong influence on us. Strange as it may seem, he was actually the gym teacher, but he always made sure we were properly dressed, and at recess we used to sit with him in the playground of the Ahad Ha-Am School in Tel Aviv, while he told us stories of Bar-Kochba, of the Hashomer period, of Bar-Giora. He fired our imaginations, entranced the whole class. I'm convinced that if we hadn't met this man, the course of our lives would have been somewhat different…. Amihai never forgot Keller to his dying day, and often mentioned him.[3]

"Dad never stopped taking an interest in what was going on in the country," says his daughter, Galia.

---

3.   Author's interview with David Danon, August 5, 1996.

He always wanted to be kept up to date, in the thick of the action. He always looked forward, to the future. He didn't dwell on the past; the past was gone, he used to say. He had ideas about the way things should be done, and he used to talk passionately about these issues. There was always a group of people around him, treating him with admiration, but Dad was cool-headed about that kind of thing. He stayed away from meetings where people told stories about the heroic days of the underground. His eyes were fixed firmly on the future.

To me, he was first and foremost a wonderfully warm dad. When I got home from some trip or other, and he came in and saw my things scattered all over the place, he'd smile and say, "Gali's home – what a treat!" and I'd feel a great wave of warmth wash over me. When I came home after the accident, I expected at any moment to hear his voice, with that note of gentle mockery, and I felt a cold shudder instead.[4]

His son Guy says:

I was six years old when father died. In my childhood memories he will always be remembered as a diligent, warm father who made me feel safe and spent lots of quality time with me. As a father, he never let me down – he always ate breakfasts and dinners with me, and always finished the day with a story, holding my hand until I fell asleep. I remember in particular his need to demonstrate the stories, and I can still imagine him, kneeling on all fours with socks on his hands, playing the big bad wolf....

At that time, I was still unfamiliar with his great courage and fortitude, of which I learned from his friends long after he died. I was also unaware then of the values he believed in so much: friendship and loyalty to the Israeli nation and land. These values he managed to pass on to me somehow and I will carry them for life.

Father always kept his promises, even those he didn't make himself.... I remember when I was in kindergarten every child was asked to bring a jelly doughnut for the Hanukkah party. Remembering that my father owned a bakery oven factory, I volunteered (without consulting) to bring doughnuts for everyone. Father, after a good laugh,

---

4. Author's interview with Galia Giladi, 1997.

conscientiously kept my promise and brought the doughnuts for all the kindergarten children....

One promise, though, he didn't keep: to come back home from hospital.

The evening of his death I visited him at the hospital. He then promised me, with sheer happiness in his eyes, that tomorrow he'd be home...

The next day, instead of father, came the terrifying news of his death.[5]

---

5.   Letter from Guy Paglin to author, January 2009.

THE RAID ON THE TEL NOF CAMP

"The operation that I consider the most audacious one we ever carried out – in the course of which we were forced to confront a lot of unforeseen surprises – was our attack on the British camp at Akir, known today as Tel Nof," said Amihai Paglin.

This was a vast British airfield, where more than ten thousand soldiers were stationed, including some five thousand Jordanian legionnaires and four thousand British paratroopers, plus around two thousand RAF personnel. The objective was to seize arms, which we needed like air to breathe.

According to information received, in the center of the Akir complex there was a massive arms store – a "supermarket," enough to supply our needs for a long time. We imagined ourselves strolling along the aisles picking up whatever we fancied: revolvers, rifles, ammunition, submachine guns, Brens… A dream supermarket! Just go in and help yourself!

I took two guys with me, Eliyahu Spector (Eli Dam) and Yitzhak Friedmann (Elitzur), and we set out to check the terrain. This was in 1946, after World War II, and I was 24 years old. The main gate was locked, obviously, and flanked by armed guards and fortified bunkers.

No chance of getting in that way. We started walking in the direction of the fields on the other side of the camp, but before we had the chance to carry out any reconnaissance, we were suddenly surrounded by armored cars. Our treatment at the hands of the guard detachment was somewhat peremptory. They locked us in a detention cell and within minutes there were hundreds of Tommies crowding around the windows, eager to catch a glimpse of the "terrorists." It was the first time I was ever arrested by the British – and the last.

Meanwhile Eliyahu Spector (who happened to one of the biggest suppliers of meat to the British army) was indignantly demanding our release. He said we were on our way to buy cattle in the neighborhood, and our detention would only disrupt regular deliveries to the camp. This ploy was unsuccessful – not that I'd pinned much hope on it myself, for the simple reason that the portrait of the third member of the team, Yitzhak Friedmann, was on prominent display in every local police station, bearing the caption "Wanted for Terrorist Offences."

The Brits were waiting for officers to arrive from Jerusalem, and as time passed and there was no sign of them, they transferred us to the police station in Nes Ziona. "I'll get us out of here, trust me!" Spector assured us cheerfully, and we soon discovered the reasons for his confidence: it turned out the station commander was a regular recipient of bribes from him, and the trade in illicit consignments of beef did indeed pave the way for our exit. The commander was summoned and Spector swooped on him: "Do we look like dangerous terrorists?" he asked him with a laugh. "You know me and you know what I like – money, wine, and women!" The Englishman nodded; maybe he wasn't convinced those were Spector's only interests, but he had his own skin to consider, and if the other was to open his mouth…. Anyway, when the detectives arrived we were no longer there.

"Our failure actually worked to our advantage; the journey, as a prisoner, through the camp at Akir taught me a number of things I hadn't known before," Gidi commented, before resuming his account.

We hired a civilian jeep, the only one available in the country at that time, and painted it in British army style, including emblems and numbers, everything completely accurate. Two of the fellows and I, in officers' uniforms, set out on the road between Yahud and Bet-Dagan, to "borrow" the trucks we were going to need to transport the loot. Two army vehicles approached us: we pretended the jeep had a dead battery and we were trying to push-start it. The Brits stopped and kindly offered us their help, and when the officer stepped forward to look inside the jeep, I held my pistol to his head. He didn't try to resist and obeyed my instructions, ordering his men to surrender. We took control of the vehicles and transported the officer and his men to a room in a house belonging to one of our people in Kerem ha-Teimanim. The furniture consisted of a threadbare sofa and a large picture of a nude woman. When visitors came, the picture was turned round, to reveal on the other side a portrait of...Stalin. The officer and his men were held, under guard, in this room until after the raid at Akir. When the British authorities later claimed that "the IZL had carried out the operation with Soviet support," we at least knew how this rumor originated.

After exhaustive discussion, the raid had been scheduled for January 28, 1946.

Shortly before departure, Gidi briefed his team: "Jackson, in the uniform of an RAF sergeant, will drive the jeep. I'll be beside him, in an officer's uniform. The truck driver will be Yosef (Nachmias), with Naftali beside him as co-driver. My deputy, Gad, will be in charge of the other truck, with all the rest of the team on board. There's no reason," he added, "why the operation shouldn't go smoothly and as planned, just so long as everyone does his job, and gets it right. Any questions?"

"What if there's a hitch and they identify us?" asked Baruch Weiner (Konous). All eyes turned to Gidi.

For a moment he scanned the 15 young men, thinking, and then replied grimly, "If that happens, we'll barricade ourselves into the armory. We can hold out there for hours. We'll have all the weapons and ammunition we need," he smiled, "and hostages too...," he added with a wink. "So there's no need to worry. Most likely they'll negotiate with us, and let us go eventually.... The important thing," he stressed, "is not to lose control. Just keep calm, get the job done, and obey orders."

All hurried to the pile of "costumes" and began putting on the uniforms over their civilian clothes, ready to be stripped off quickly should the need arise.

In the middle of the room stood Gidi in an officer's uniform, his chest emblazoned with all the medal ribbons he could find. He waved a jar of Brill Cream. "You've all got to grease your hair till it shines like the sergeant-major's boots!" he ordered, to howls of laughter.

As Gidi tells the story:

At 12:30 PM we arrived on the runway. So far everything had gone like clockwork. My hair was dyed blond and I looked thoroughly respectable, in a manner befitting a wing commander in the Royal Air Force. With me, in the jeep, were four more "British officers." Behind us were the two trucks, containing 13 "soldiers" in labor fatigues. All held mess kits that they rattled in British army style, chanting: "Food, food!"

We arrived at the gate separating the runways from the camp – fortified bunkers and heavy machine guns all around. We knew everything depended on the next few seconds. I behaved in the confident manner of a British officer, ordering the immediate raising of the barrier, and adding a juicy curse for good measure. An Arab Legion officer approached our vehicle, but stepped back hurriedly on finding himself confronted by an officer of the "master race."

"Jacky," I whispered, "that's the armory over there. There must be a door, but I can't see it. Yehuda, get down and do a circuit of the building. Try to find the way in to the weapons storehouse. When you find the door, stand beside it and button up your flies."

While Yehuda was strolling toward the complex, the rest of us waited, hardly daring to breathe, looking around curiously. And suddenly...suddenly walking toward us there were four officers of the British WRAC, smiling pleasantly. I was stunned. My English was still in its infancy, best understood when accompanied by a drawn revolver... and if those four girls started talking to me, we'd all be done for. I was reassured to have Jackson sitting beside me; as a former British soldier, there was nothing wrong with *his* English. "You handle this, Jacky," I whispered to him. Instead of which he pulled the peak of his cap down over his eyes and buried his face in a newspaper. I couldn't believe this was happening. With an impatient gesture, I motioned the women away – conduct unbecoming a British officer, I have to confess. Immediately the smiles were wiped from their faces and they fled, obviously taken aback by my brusqueness. It wasn't till the day after that

I had time to ask Jackson why he'd acted that way. He looked at me in astonishment: "Are you kidding? I was scared stiff! In the Western Desert I got to know two of those four officers *very* well, if you see what I mean. They'd have fingered me straightaway!"

I mention this curious incident, which could have had tragic results, as an example of the "little nail" that can bring the biggest schemes crashing down. These thoughts occurred to me later. At the time, I had no leisure for philosophizing.

I glanced at my watch: 12:40 PM already. By 1:30 PM we should be finished and on our way. Outside one of the buildings, Yehuda was frantically buttoning and unbuttoning his fly…

"Let's go!" I called to my men.

At that moment a British officer appeared, sauntering toward the armory; a moment later another officer followed. *Traffic even in the afternoon?* I wondered.

"There's no way of knowing how many are inside," I said. "I'll go in first and check. If there's too many in there, I'll make some excuse and leave. If I haven't come out in two minutes, it means it's okay and you can join me."[1]

Gidi took off his cap and concealed his revolver underneath it. He opened the door casually. At the desk sat a sergeant, at ease, engrossed in a book. He showed no interest in the new arrival; midday was, after all, a time for relaxing. Two officers were inspecting a machine gun, while three Arab civilian workers were whispering among themselves in a corner. He closed the door behind him, scanned the room and its occupants for a moment, glanced briefly at the stacks of weapons on the shelves, then took his revolver from its hiding place and aimed it at the sergeant, "Hands up!"

All stared in astonishment at the "officer" standing there with legs wide apart, threatening them with drawn weapon. No one raised his hands. They were all too stunned to move.

"Hands up!" he repeated the command.

Very slowly, hesitantly, a few hands were raised. Best way to handle a drunk is to humor him, they were probably thinking. The Arabs copied their masters, looking terrified.

---

1. Dov Goldstein's interview with Amihai Paglin, *Ma'ariv*, September 29, 1972.

"Hands up, I said! I'm not a bloody flying officer, I'm a Jewish terrorist from the Irgun Zvai Leumi!"

All hands were raised now, but the expressions on their faces showed that they still didn't believe a "terrorist" could get into this well-defended place.

"This isn't a joke," Gidi's voice was heard again. "All of you, together in that corner!" he pointed.

Now the men from the jeep joined him. "Tie them up," Gidi commanded.

"I advise you not to try anything stupid," Jackson warned them.

The big trucks were maneuvering noisily outside the doors of the armory. The young men rushed inside eagerly.

"Quick, grab as much as you can and get it loaded," the order was heard.

Jackson, Moshe, and Boris were still busy tying the hands of the captives.

The armory now resembled an ants' nest, with everyone running back and forth and hands working frantically. Nothing was too heavy. The priority was to get the job done – and get out.

"Hands up!" Boris threatened a sergeant who had just wandered in and was now standing like a statue, not believing his eyes. "What's…going on here?" he asked.

Outside, soldiers were strolling about casually. No one suspected that the central armory was being looted under their very noses.

"We spent a long time in that armory," Gidi recalled.

We collected weapons and ammunition of all kinds. It was like we were dreaming. During that time dozens of soldiers and officers came in – and we tied them all up with rope. When we ran out of rope, we tied them up symbolically, with sewing thread…. Not one of them opened his mouth or tried to raise an alarm, and all this time life went on outside as if everything was normal. The trucks were positioned so that the tailgates were aligned with the armory doors. We made the prisoners lie on the floor, close together, and they gave us no trouble.

From the driver's seat, Yosef Nachmias watched with mounting anxiety as the stocks of weapons piled up on the trucks. *Someone should warn Gidi we're getting over-loaded…*, he thought, but it was a vain hope. Everyone was far too busy to pay any attention to him.

"The treasure trove of weapons went to our heads," Gidi sighed.

We'd brought a list with us, but I had a tough job trying to control the lads, who were almost in tears and pleading to be allowed to take more and more…. We went from shelf to shelf, helping ourselves…. Only fighters as hungry for weapons as we were could have gotten that excited in this gigantic "arms bazaar." There were some items we didn't know how to use, and we had to turn to our "guests" for guidance. That way we matched shells to mortars, ammunition to machine guns – an incredible haul.

We loaded 400 submachine guns, 200 machine guns, dozens of mortars, hundreds of grenades and thousands of shells and bullets. I ordered the truck drivers to set off in the direction of Rehovot, only to discover that one of the two vehicles had been so overloaded the suspension was shot. It couldn't be moved and we just had to leave it. I told the men that we, the five of us in the jeep, would follow them 20 minutes later. Our "prisoners" were convinced it must have been a substantial force that took over their camp.

"Listen carefully," I told them. "We're planting mines at the doors and windows. Don't any of you try to move or look up. First to do that will get shot by our backup team. Stay where you are for a quarter of an hour, and then you're free to contact anyone you like, but don't try to leave until your people have defused the mines we've planted… You've been warned!"

The party in the jeep was the last to leave. The prisoners remained in the armory, glancing anxiously at their watches.[2]

The truck was lurching like a drunkard, the engine straining and groaning. But the fellows were in high spirits; they couldn't get enough of feasting their eyes on the piles of weapons and ammunition.

And suddenly…the truck ground to a halt, back wheels spinning, but the vehicle not budging. It was sinking…

Everyone jumped down and began pushing, their cries of "Hey-yup!" mingling with the whine of the engine. But in vain; the truck went on

2. Ibid.

sinking. A group of Arabs were looking on from a distance and the men began shouting at them, "Why are you standing there like dummies?"

The Arabs joined in, without enthusiasm. "Hey-yup! Hey-yup!" The engine howled like a wounded beast but the wheels just sunk deeper and deeper.

"This isn't going to work," cried one of the boys in despair.

Gidi arrived with the jeep, saw what was happening and told them to fetch the steel cable. "We'll try to haul it out with the jeep."

"Where's the steel cable?" came the chorus from all sides. It turned out the cable had been left on the floor of the truck, and was under a huge pile of weapons. No chance of getting to it now.

"Push as hard as you can," Gidi commanded. But still this had no effect.

"They've set off the siren!" one of the boys shouted. All turned, to stare anxiously in the direction of the army camp. On the runways vehicles were racing backward and forward and the siren went on blaring. The boys stood there, unable to move, until Gidi's voice roused them from their paralysis: "Everyone grab a few stens and get on the jeep," he ordered.

Seventeen men clambered onto the jeep – on the wings, on the bonnet, wherever they could find a foothold. The jeep lurched forward. All eyes were turned, gazing at the truck with its precious cargo – left behind.

"I can't see the road," Jackson complained. "You're blocking my vision."

"We'll guide you," said one of the youths perched on the hood.

Jackson accelerated. A team of Jewish laborers, employees of the electricity company repairing overhead cables, stopped working for a moment and stared as the jeep raced by.

"Those RAF guys must be off their heads!" was the consensus.

"We were unlucky this time," Gidi summed up, before sending his men home. And seeing the look of disappointment and despair in their eyes he added, with an effort at a smile: "It's not the end of the world. There will be other opportunities."

Outwardly he maintained his air of composure, but inwardly he could have wept. To have gained such a treasure and then lost it – what could be more heartbreaking?

In the wake of the raid on the airfield at Akir (Tel Nof), British army top brass issued a warning against "terrorists" in disguise, stressing that if these arms-acquisition forays were not foiled, the weapons could in the future be used against the British army itself.

The warning was as follows:

The attempt by the Irgun (otherwise known as the IZL) to steal large quantities of automatic weapons from the Royal Air Force base at Akir obliges all units to take stringent security measures.

The Irgun is suffering from a shortage of arms, and it is our belief that attempts to seize supplies of arms will be repeated. If they succeed, these weapons will be used to kill British servicemen and police personnel.

The terrorists' attacks are carefully planned and executed with vigor. Army uniforms are not proof of the identity of soldiers, and military vehicles are not necessarily transporting Army personnel. Only extreme vigilance will foil their efforts.

This was followed by a brief account of the operation:

On 28 January 1936 at 1215 hours, an army lorry and a jeep stopped by the entrance to the armory of the Akir airfield. The occupants, wearing RAF uniforms, entered the armory, threatened all those present, tied up the British soldiers and forced the Arab civilian staff to load the lorry with a large number of "Sten"-guns, also "Vickers" heavy machine-guns and considerable quantities of ammunition. The terrorists spent a whole hour in the armory, and when leaving they warned all those present to wait at least ten minutes before attempting to leave the building. At 1320 the alarm was raised, and patrols sent out to search the area found the lorry abandoned less than half a mile from the camp, with all the looted weapons still on board, except for 12 "Stens" and a small quantity of ammunition.

A group of Arabs reported seeing 12 men fleeing the scene in a jeep. It later emerged that the lorry had been stolen a week earlier from an RASC unit and painted in RAF livery. The jeep has not been traced.

British sentries at the camp entrance reported no apparent irregularities relating to the arrival and departure of the vehicles.

ROOTS AND SOURCES

*Back row: on the right, the father,
Gershon Paglin; on the left, his son
Yaakov (from a previous marriage).
Front row: the mother, Sima, with
Amihai on her lap; Neri (seated) on the
right; and Yitzhak (standing), on the left*

Amihai Paglin as a youth

THE UNDERGROUND UNITED THEM, AS DID TRAGIC FATE

Tzipora – wife and comrade in arms

Amihai – whom no bullet could best

Southern district police headquarters and CID offices in Jaffa, attacked by the IZL on April 23, 1944, August 23, 1944, and December 27, 1945

THE THREE WHO PLANNED TO ASSASSINATE THE HIGH COMMISSIONER

Amihai (Gidi) in
underground days

David Danon

Eliyahu Bet-Zuri

Part of a poster declaring the revolt by the IZL on February 1, 1944

רצח !

סיר הארולד מק מייכל,
הידוע כנציב העליון לפלשתינה (א"י).

מבוקש עבור רצח

80 פליטים יהודים במימי הים השחור באניה "סטרומה".

MURDER!
SIR HAROLD MAC MICHAEL
Known as High Commissioner for Palestine
WANTED for MURDER
OF 800 REFUGEES DROWNED IN THE
BLACK SEA ON THE BOAT „STRUMA"

This wanted poster was produced by the IZL after the tragedy of the Struma refugee ship and the drowning of 768 "illegal" immigrants in the Black Sea (7 Adar 5702; February 24, 1942).

The Mandate government, headed by the High Commissioner, Sir Harold MacMichael, refused to authorize entry into Eretz Israel of the "illegal" immigrants on the Struma, who had fled from Romania and were returned to the Black Sea, where the catastrophe occurred.

The sinking of the ship and the loss of several hundred women, men, and children led to demonstrations and protests and heightened the tense relations between the Yishuv and the Mandate authorities in early 1942.

One of the expressions of this was the establishment of "Am Lohem," which set as its goal the kidnapping of the High Commissioner and putting him on trial.

KING DAVID HOTEL BEFORE IT EXPLODED ON JULY 22, 1946

The British flag proudly flying over the British Headquarters for the Middle East situated in the King David Hotel building

The instant of the explosion

The minute after, the headquarters are destroyed while the hotel is unharmed

בני ישראל, נער עברי!

שביתת המשק, אשר הוכרזה בראשית המלחמה, הוברה ע'השלטון הבריטי.

יסוד הציונות הממלכתית.

השלטון על ארץ-ישראל ימסר מיד ליד' ממשלה עברית זמנית!

Part of a poster declaring the revolt by the IZL on February 1, 1944

Generations. The truce declared at the start of the war was breached by the british government. The rulers of the country considered neither loyalty nor concessions, nor even victims. They realized and continue to realize their goal: The destruction of National Zionism. Four years have passed and all the hopes pulsing in your hearts in 1939 have come to naught, leaving no trace. We received no international standing, a Hebrew army was not established, the gates of the country were not opened, the British authority completed its shameless treachery against the Hebrew nation we will draw conclusions unflinchingly. There is no longer any truce between the people including the Hebrew youth and the British administration in Eretz Israel, which hands our brethren over to Hitler. The people must wage a war against this government, a war to the finish. This war will demand many painful victims, but we will enter it in full consciousness, for we are faithful to our brothers who were slaughtered and are still being slaughtered, for we are fighting on their behalf and we have remained steadfast to the charge they left us in their wills upon their deaths. And there is no moral foundation for its existence in Eretz Israel and this is our demand: Rule over Eretz Israel should immediately be turned over to a temporary Hebrew government.

From the right: Menahem Begin with Sarah Agassi (Goldschmid) and Israel Levi (Gideon), commander of the King David Hotel operation

Model of a "milk churn" bomb (with a cutaway view of the mechanism) that blew up the main administration building of the Mandate government (in the King David Hotel) in Jerusalem, displayed at the Museum of the IZL

Adina Hai Nisan, the telephone operator who gave the warning, next to the entrance to the hotel's basement

ACRE PRISON

Prison entrance gate

*Storming of the fortress of Acre prison – British soldiers
stand thunderstruck near the breached wall*

Dov Cohen (Shimshon) –
commander of those who
broke into the Acre prison

Michael Ashbel (Mike)
called out toward an
Egged bus that passed
by, "See, Jews, how we
are dying here for you ..."

Monument commemorating the Acre prison break –
silent testimony to that heroic operation

Moshe Horovitz (left) and Meir Feinstein on their way to court. The seriously wounded IZL fighter Meir Feinstein was captured and sentenced to death following the attack on the Jerusalem railway station on October 30, 1946. He blew himself up in his cell on April 21, 1947, on the eve of his scheduled execution, together with his comrade in fate, Moshe Barazani, a member of Lehi who had been sentenced to death after being caught with a hand grenade in his possession during the period of martial law

Explosion at the central Jerusalem railway station

The traitor Yanai (Yehiel Reinhold) in British army uniform

Schneller Camp, attacked on March 12, 1947

Goldschmidt House – British Officers Club, blown up on March 1, 1947

Barrel bomb – Amihai Paglin helps load the barrel bomb onto the truck crane, on its way to police headquarters

The truck onto which the bomb was loaded before setting out for action; on the first day of Sukkot 5708 (September 29, 1947), the "barrel" was dropped as planned on police headquarters in Haifa, causing serious damage

IZL FIGHTERS STORM JAFFA

The British setting up positions to protect the Arabs of Jaffa

Right: Zvi Pooni; middle: Baruch Weiner (Konous); left: Imanuel Dukman (Dukie)

Yehoshua Gal – one of the best IZL commanders – fell on May 19, 1948, at the Police School in Jerusalem. Gidi named his daughter Galia after him.

Yitzhak Avinoam-Yagnes – Jerusalem district commander during the critical years of the struggle, 1946–47

Eliyahu Lankin – the commander who was the "matchmaker" between Tzipora and Amihai in 1944

Avtalion Ayub – joined Gidi in the Steel Brothers operation; he fell on April 18, 1948, in the action against the munition shell train

Elimelech Spiegel – builder of the "milk churn" bombs in 1946

Shraga Ellis (Haim Toyte) – Gidi's deputy, member of the planning division and commander of the Jerusalem combat unit

Eliezer Sudit-Sharon (Kabtzan) in the conquest of Jaffa

Aharon Shani

Amihai's brother Neriel

Shmuel Tamir (right) and Amihai Paglin

*Beit Gidi, the Etzel Museum 1947–1948, named after
Amihai "Gidi" Paglin in memory of the Jaffa liberators, Tel Aviv*

THE KING DAVID HOTEL EPISODE AND ITS AFTERMATH

The idea of striking at the heart of the Mandatory admin-istration was first broached in IZL circles toward the end of 1945. This was the twilight period between the end of the "Saison" and the resumption of Irgun activity (albeit in low gear), on the one hand, and the inauguration of Hebrew Resistance, on the other. "This in-between period isn't going to last forever," Amihai Paglin, then operations officer of the IZL, said to Shraga Ellis (aka Haim Toyte), newly appointed commander of the IZL combat squad in the capital. "We have to prepare for the future, iden-tify objectives of strategic or political importance to the British." The King David Hotel – home of the Mandatory Secretariat and Army HQ – was undoubtedly the most important of them all.

THE EXPLOSION

Monday, July 22, 1946, was a typical, sultry summer day. Heat hung heavy in the streets of Jerusalem. The air seemed to be standing still. People moved about in desultory fashion, searching in vain for a sheltered spot, a refuge from the relentless rays of the sun.

In the region of the King David Hotel, nerve center of the British Mandatory Administration – headed by High Commissioner Sir Alan Cunningham, Chief Secretary John Shaw, and GOC Armed Forces Sir Evelyn Barker – routine life continued as normal. Security forces had built high fences to forestall any attempt by terrorists to lob hand grenades into the complex. The hotel, the Secretariat, and the police detachment were connected by a central alarm system; in the event of any incident, a loud siren would be activated and military and police personnel dispatched immediately to the scene. Surrounded by wire fences and substantial military forces, it was a place where all felt secure and protected.

The civilian wing of the King David Hotel continued to serve as the social center of Mandatory Palestine, an awesome imperial institution comparable to the Paradise in Cairo, or Raffles in Singapore. Behind the uniformed sentries, the armored cars, and the interminable wire fences, cocktails were still being shaken, Swiss chefs and Sudanese waiters continued to cook and serve as usual, and elegant ladies shared the gossip over the tinkling teacups.

The bundles of documents seized three weeks earlier from the Jewish Agency and now stacked in the offices of the Secretariat represented a world far removed from the opulent splendor of the hotel lobby.[1]

During that morning a number of unusual events had been recorded in the vicinity: a container of explosives had blown up not far away, shots had been heard, and there had been some unexplained commotion in the hotel basement. But none of this was enough to disrupt British composure and *sang-froid*, not even the telephoned warning of "bombs in the basement," and besides a few junior officials glancing down casually from their windows at the street below, nobody seemed to be taking any of it seriously.

This was later confirmed by the architect Dan Ben-Dor, at that time an officer in the Royal Engineers. "That morning I was in the hotel in the company of a British brigadier with whom I had professional connections. At about 11:30 A M we heard what sounded like in an explosion in the street. I went down with the brigadier to investigate and outside a little shop we found a blackened square tin that had contained some kind of explosive material. We decided it was nothing serious.... We returned to the hotel and resumed our conversation."[2]

Although the hotel lobby was full of guests and most of the civilian clerical staff was on the point of leaving for lunch, there was no undue congestion. Everything was normal, as it had been yesterday and, so it seemed then, as it would be tomorrow.

At 12:37 precisely a massive explosion was heard, shaking the whole of Jerusalem, sending shock waves as far as London, and rocking the foundations of British domination in the land.

Ears were ringing and the whole street was hidden by a cloud of black smoke. An entire wing of the hotel building had seemed to rise up in the air, then crumble as it collapsed in a hail of masonry and clouds of dust. For a moment all were stunned, unable to move, barely breathing. It was as if a suspense film had jammed at a crucial point, leaving a horrific image

---

1. J. Bowyer Bell, *Terror Out of Zion: Irgun Zvai Leumi,* LEHI, *and the Palestine underground, 1929–1949* (New York: St. Martin's, 1977), p. 170.
2. *Kol ha-Ir – Jerusalem*, September 25, 1981.

flickering on the screen, but no sound; as if human beings had been turned to stone and all movement had ceased.[3]

All the electronic clocks in the hotel had stopped. The walls in the southwest wing had been blown outward. A pall of gray-brown smoke rose to a height of some 200 yards and cast a shadow over the whole of the sector that sun-drenched day. And then, before the thick smoke had cleared, the southwest wing began to disintegrate, the one floor crumpling into the next to the sound of concrete shattering, wood breaking, and steel girders buckling.

Sir John Shaw's office was only a short corridor's distance from the corner sheered off by the blast. If his office had been just a little further down the corridor, he too would have been lying under a heap of smoking rubble.

Customers in the hotel bar, still clutching their pink gins, stared open-mouthed at the counter – or rather at the pile of wood shavings that was all that remained of it. The floor was strewn with shattered mirrors and bottles. In the lobby the floor had been raised and clouds of sand swirled in the air. Only a few hotel guests had been hurt; the Secretariat wing, on the other hand, was now nothing more than a gigantic mound of rubble under a cloud of smoke and dust.[4]

In or around the hotel at the time of the blast were the journalists Gavriel Tzifroni, Ted Lurie,[5] and Julian Meltzer.[6]

Meltzer recalled:

I was sitting in my office in the Reuters building in Jerusalem in what was then Princess Mary Avenue – now Shlomzion ha-Malkah. I was sitting there working away. I can't remember what I was working on but compared with what was about to happen, it can't have been that important. At around 12:30 I heard a tremendous explosion.… I went up on the flat roof and saw a pillar of thick gray smoke rising, and the whole southwest wing of the King David Hotel was in ruins.

Of course, at the time we were all convinced there must have been heavy loss of life. That was the big worry.

---

3.   *Yediot Aharonot*, July 23, 1946.
4.   Bell, *Terror Out of Zion*, pp. 172–73.
5.   Editor of the *Palestine Post* and later of the *Jerusalem Post*.
6.   Julian Meltzer was then the local correspondent of the *New York Times*, also working for Reuters and the *Palestine Post*.

About a year later I was on my way to do a lecture tour in the USA and I made a stop-over in London. I met up with a bunch of journalists, and the conversation turned to what was going on here. Both the IZL and Lehi were very active at that time, and I have to admit that most of the pressmen expressed a lot of solidarity with what they called "the guerilla war" of the Jewish underground. Some of them reckoned that bombs were the only possible response to tyranny.... The prevailing view was that no matter how many millions of words are preached by the Jewish leadership, that's nothing compared with one act of sabotage, something that's going to grab the next day's headlines all over the world.[7]

Lawrence Durrell, author of *The Alexandria Quartet*, happened to be staying in Jerusalem on the day of the explosion. Standing with a group of foreign correspondents watching the sappers clearing away the rubble, he heard one of them say, "After this, the King David won't ever be the same." Durrell retorted, "After this, the whole country won't ever be the same."[8]

Ted Lurie remembered for years afterward a remark made by a *News Chronicle* correspondent, Geoffrey Hoare, as they stood together looking on in silence at the scenes of destruction and the rescue teams at work. Suddenly Hoare turned to him and whispered in his ear, "Here goes your Jewish state, Ted!"[9]

---

7. "Voice of Israel" radio program, Channel Aleph, "The Milk Churns That Roared," June 20, 1969 (Hereafter: Radio program).

8. Avraham Shai, *Kadei ha-halav she-ra'amu* [The milk churns that roared] (Tel Aviv: Hadar, 1977), p. 55.

9. Radio program, n. 7 above.

PLANS, DELAYS, AND OBSTACLES

While the IZL was recovering from the "Saison"[1] and Paglin was cautiously planning future operations, events in the world began to flow at an accelerated pace: on May 7, 1945, Germany surrendered unconditionally to Allied forces, and the war on European soil came to an end.

Two months later, on July 5, 1945, there was a political upheaval in Britain which was to make a deep impression on the whole of the Empire: the Labour Party won a surprise victory in the elections and Winston Churchill – acclaimed as the victorious leader of the Western world – was replaced as prime minister by Clement Atlee.

In Palestine the change of government was greeted with jubilation. Leaders of the socialist parties and senior figures in the Zionist movement were beside themselves with joy. It seemed that the restraint they

---

1.   From December 1944 to April 1945, the Haganah, supported by members of the Palmah, conducted a systematic campaign against the IZL, with the aim of suppressing its activities. This campaign came to be known as the "Saison," i.e., the hunting season, during which IZL members were fair game. To avoid civil war, IZL members obeyed Begin's instructions and did not resist. Not content with kidnapping and harassing IZL activists, the Haganah also betrayed them to the British authorities, who "rewarded" the Haganah for its cooperation, with "Operation Agatha" on "Black Sabbath" (see below).

had preached, and their efforts to stifle protest against the oppressive measures imposed by the White Paper, had finally been vindicated. "Prospects
for progress toward independence and the material development of our
country have never been better," declared *Davar* in an editorial, and eu-
phoria among the institutional leadership of the Jewish community knew
no bounds.

But high expectations were matched by deep disappointment: the new
Labour government, influenced by the conservative permanent staff of the
Foreign and Colonial Offices, was quick to embrace the old and much-
loved dictum, according to which "the vital interests of Great Britain in
the Middle East will be guaranteed only on the basis of an understanding
with the Arab nations, and this requires the continued implementation of
the White Paper." On August 25, 1945, the British government's decision
was communicated to Dr. Chaim Weizmann.

The patience of the Jewish community began to crack. After many
months of virtual inertia, the activists took the lead. Following exhaustive
discussions it was decided at the highest level of the Jewish Agency that
hostilities would be initiated against the British under the name of the "Hebrew Resistance Movement." A coded telegram sent on September 23, 1945,
by Moshe Sneh (at that time national commander of the Haganah) to David
Ben-Gurion in London stated, "It's suggested we cause one major incident,
then announce this is just a warning and a foretaste of much more serious
incidents in the future…if the government decides against us."

Ben-Gurion's reply on October 1, 1945, was trenchant, displaying all
the anger, frustration, disappointment, and bitterness of one who felt betrayed by his socialist colleagues in Britain: "The existence of the White
Paper is a declaration of war on the Jewish people. It is the duty of our
people, powerless and downtrodden as we are, to fight with all available
means…. The response is not to be confined to issues of immigration and
settlement alone, it is essential to embrace sabotage and reprisal…. Any
act of sabotage needs to be significant and impressive."[2]

With his instructions to the Haganah leadership Ben-Gurion surprised
many of his party colleagues: "The two rival factions are to be invited to

---

2.   Ben-Gurion worded his reply carefully, not wanting it to be interpreted as an instruction to act rather than the expression of an opinion, but as far as Sneh was concerned
this was the green light, giving him authority to go on the offensive.

collaborate fully, on terms of unified leadership and absolute discipline. Constant effort is required to ensure unity in the community and, first and foremost, among the fighters."

In this spirit, contacts began between the three underground organizations – the Haganah, the IZL, and the Lehi. At the end of October 1945, after long and detailed discussions, a contract for collaboration between the parties under unified leadership was signed.[3] The Hebrew Resistance Movement was a reality.[4]

FINDING THE ACHILLES HEEL

In Jerusalem Shraga Ellis went on looking for the Achilles heel of the King David Hotel fortress. "Fortunately, I had time on my hands," he recalls with more than a hint of nostalgia.

> I used to wander for hours around the sector, watching army and police movements, noting in my memory every weakness in the fortified structure and making all kinds of plans for whenever they might be needed. The hotel was surrounded by a triple wire fence, hooked into an electrical alarm system. Any contact with the wire would alert the military guard detachments. Camouflaged army and police emplacements were located on the roof of the building and around it, and as if

---

3.   The following are the terms of the agreement (see Menahem Begin, interview in *Ma'ariv*, July 16, 1976; "United Resistance," on Etzel website):

   The Haganah organization will join the armed campaign against British rule.

   IZL and Lehi are not to implement aggressive action without consent of the United Resistance command.

   The United Resistance will require IZL and Lehi to implement certain actions.

   Representatives of the three organizations will meet regularly or as required, to review all plans from political and operational perspectives.

   When consent in principle has been given to operations, operations officers of the three organizations will meet to discuss details.

   Consent of the United Resistance leadership is not required for operations involving confiscation of weapons from the British. The organizations are free to act on their own discretion.

   Agreement between the three organizations is based on "positive obligations."

   If at any time in the future the Haganah is ordered to leave the military campaign, IZL and Lehi will continue the struggle against British rule.

4.   *Haganah Chronicles*, "From Conflict to War," part 2, pp. 804, 805, 808, 841, 853.

all that wasn't enough, there was even a troop of cavalry there, putting on regular mounted patrols.[5]

While Shraga was wandering around the hotel, scouring the terrain for any potential breach in the defensive system, Gidi's fertile brain was working away feverishly, devising innumerable plans for entering the building without attracting attention. His unconventional mode of thinking always sought out the simplest way, the one least expected by the enemy: *a group of tourists with suitcases full of explosives, taking over the hotel lobby and the corridor, could be the simplest and smoothest solution for this complicated case,* he reflected, *if it weren't for all those armed soldiers going in and out of the lobby... One little slip,* he concluded, *could wreck the whole thing.*

Someone suggested a frontal assault through the main entrance; Gidi dismissed this out of hand. "Guaranteed suicide," he said. "Depending on the efficiency of the guards and the electronic alarm systems we might, maybe, succeed in getting in – but no one would get out." (According to information received, aircraft machine guns were in place in the corridors and could be activated remotely from a central control point, strafing the corridors with lethal firepower.)[6]

"Go on digging," he told Shraga, "something will turn up yet."

"There were three of us on stakeout and surveillance duty," according to Israel Levi (code-named Gideon, commander of the King David Hotel operation):

> my brother Eliyahu (Gundar [Warder] Aviel, a senior IZL commander in Jerusalem), Shraga Ellis, commander of the Jerusalem combat-squad, and me. Most of the information we collected had to do with the building itself, its architectonic structure, number of entrances and exits, residents, visitors, strength and deployment of security personnel, the army camp to the south of the building, access routes from the camp to the main Secretariat wing. We also carried out internal surveillance, including night visits to La Regence café; I took part in one

---

5. Author's interview with Shraga Ellis, October 1996.
6. Bell, *Terror Out of Zion*, p. 170; testimony of Israel Levi, "The Bombing of the King David Hotel," Jabotinsky Archives.

of these myself, disguised as a young Arab reveler. I checked the place out close up and got a good look at the gigantic supporting pillars in the middle of the café which held up the entire structure. The biggest of them, I reckoned, would be the best bet for planting explosives."[7]

While conducting their surveillance, the IZL men made an important discovery, which was going to prove crucial in the future in planning the break-in to the hotel: the official responsible for the security of government institutions and offices had decided to build a small extra edifice in the northern wing of the King David Hotel for the use of sentries and security staff. While building work was in progress, a big gap was cleared in the wire fence, giving access to the trucks delivering construction materials, and there was just one Arab watchman supervising the entrance. Suppliers of all kinds of services seized the opportunity to take short cuts to the hotel's storerooms and kitchens, bypassing the main entrance with all its security apparatus.

"This is the key," Gidi declared, "that will unlock this operation." And sure enough, it was this entrance that was to be used by the green van laden with "milk churns."[8]

INTERNECINE POLITICS

When all the data had been gathered and an initial plan elaborated by Gidi, it was presented to the leadership. But weeks passed, and there was no endorsement of the operation. On the reasons for the delay, Menahem Begin relates:

> This was, it will be recalled, the period of the United Resistance Movement, and according to the agreement, we had to submit all our operational plans for approval by the combined leadership. Among other issues, in the spring of 1946 we submitted the plan for an attack on the King David Hotel, the site of two central institutions of British power: Army staff headquarters and the Chief Secretariat of the Mandatory Government.

---

7. Avinoam's recorded interview with Israel Levi, November 15, 1968, Jabotinsky Archives; *Yediot Aharonot*, July 22, 1966.
8. Testimony of Israel Levi, "The Bombing of the King David Hotel," Jabotinsky Archives.

I informed Sneh and Galili that we were taking it upon ourselves to penetrate the administrative wing of the King David Hotel and carry out a comprehensive sabotage operation. Without going into details, I stressed that the explosives we were going to use for this action would be distinguished by two features: first, the British would be unable to move or defuse them, since the slightest touch would set them off; second, they wouldn't be detonated immediately after they had been set, but after half an hour, or an hour – whatever was considered appropriate – to allow time for the evacuation from the hotel of its residents, workers, and clerks. Early evacuation of the hotel was essential according to the rules of warfare we had determined for ourselves; there were many civilians there and it was not our intention to hurt them.

The leadership of the Haganah didn't immediately endorse our plan. Attacking the center of British power seemed to them too ambitious. Their objection wasn't one of principle. Haganah representatives insisted that the time was not yet ripe for an operation of this kind, liable to inflame British anger and bring it to a head. We thought otherwise, but we were bound by the agreement and had to abide by the decision. In spite of this we didn't shelve the plan…. From time to time we would raise it again with the Haganah chiefs, we spoke about it in our private meetings, we wrote about it in coded messages to "Jeremiah"; for camouflage purposes we called the King David Hotel operation "Malonchick" (later simplified to "Chick"). Meanwhile, the Lehi had come up with a scheme to blow up another building used by the government, the premises of David Brothers, and for purposes of distinction Haganah representatives referred to this by the codename "Your slave and redeemer."

These two plans were left hanging in the air for some time.

Thirty-seven years later, in introducing his lecture on "the power of the shield" in a college of journalism, May 25, 1981, Galili, formerly one of the Haganah's most senior commanders, revealed that it was he who dissuaded Sneh from endorsing the action until after "Black Sabbath":[9]

---

9. Black Sabbath – the name given to the wide-ranging search operation conducted by the British throughout the land on Sabbath, June 29, 1946, in response to the "Night of the Bridges," June 17, when Palmah units demolished eleven road and rail bridges on all the inland frontiers of western Eretz Israel. This was the most comprehensive

The idea of blowing up the building where British army HQ was located came up in a meeting with the IZL and the Lehi, attended by Yellin-Mor (the commander of Lehi and its representative in the Resistance Movement), Begin, Sneh, and myself – even before Black Sabbath. Sneh seemed sympathetic to the idea. When the IZL and Lehi representatives had left, I told him, 'Don't be in too much of a hurry to agree to this. You need the support of the leadership in Jerusalem and the Agency for something like this. The King David is no ordinary operation...'

But soon after Black Sabbath the issue was debated by the x Committee,[10] the usual way that things like this were decided (without details of the operation being given, just the general guidelines). Sneh brought for the x Committee's endorsement a proposal to sabotage two "central government buildings" in Jerusalem. The proposal was approved by the x, without its members being aware which buildings were to be targeted.

Although approval had been given, a date for the operation had not yet been agreed with us and we preferred not to give the IZL and the Lehi the go-ahead until a later stage. We didn't want them forcing our hand...

The Haganah decided to entrust execution of the mission to the IZL

---

action ever undertaken under the aegis of the Resistance Movement – and the British decided on a drastic response, with an operation code-named "Agatha." Thousands of British soldiers and police personnel were involved. In Jerusalem the premises of the Jewish Agency were raided, its leaders arrested, and important documents confiscated. In Kibbutz Yagur the Haganah's central armory was uncovered and impounded, and throughout the country some 2,700 persons were imprisoned.

10. As operations broadened and the struggle acquired international political significance – demands were heard in the Executive of the Jewish Agency for the establishment of a public-political-representative body for overall endorsement of courses of action. Pending the constitution of such a body, a three-member committee was set up within the Executive of the Agency, consisting of the chairman of the Executive, David Ben-Gurion, Moshe Sneh, and Moshe Shapira. Meanwhile, the inter-party body had come into being, and this was known as the x Committee. The committee numbered six members: Rabbi Fishman-Maimon, chairman; Moshe Sneh, deputy chairman; Dr. Peretz Bernstein; Levi Skolnik (Eshkol); Israel Edelson (Bar-Yehuda); and Yaakov Riftin. An additional member in a consultative capacity was D. Remez, chairman of the National Committee. (From testimony of Moshe Sneh, Haganah Historical Archives 4681.)

on the grounds that it had been their initiative; they were thus entitled to it, and they also had more experience of operations such as this.[11]

Menahem Begin never received any explanation of the reasons behind the delay. "They gave their endorsement on July 1, 1946 – two days after General Barker launched his major assault on the Haganah, the Palmah, the Jewish community and its official institutions," he writes in *The Revolt*. "Haganah chiefs did not explain to us why the 'Hotel' scheme only became feasible after June 29."[12]

Twenty years later, Amihai Paglin, who at that time had been operations officer of the IZL, was to comment cynically:

> The Resistance Movement was obsessed with "matched operations": for the deportation of immigrants – destruction of a radar installation; for a wave of arrests – attack on a police station. There was nothing that could be "paired" with an assault on the center of power in the country until the British raided the Agency premises on June 29. This was the "pair" to Operation Chick, and the famous note was sent to Menahem Begin: *Time to get to work.*[13]

And sure enough, the day after Black Sabbath, June 30, 1946, the decision was made by Resistance Movement commanders, and the following day confirmation was sent in writing to Menahem Begin.

On the circumstances surrounding the confirmation, Moshe Sneh, at that time Chief of the Haganah General Headquarters, says the following:

> Two days after Black Sabbath, the High Command met in plenary session, and it was decided that our operational capacity had not been impaired.... We moved on to consideration of a series of operations intended to prove we were still in business.
>
> The essential action, entrusted to the Palmah, was to be a raid on

---

11. Israel Galili, "Address to journalism seminar," May 25, 1981 (hereafter: Galili, "Address"); "Clarification of remarks to journalism seminar," August 9, 1983 (hereafter: Galili, "Clarification") – Yad Tabenkin Archives, Unit 15, Box 172, File 5 (Docs. 1, 9).
12. Menahem Begin, *The Revolt*, p. 213.
13. *Yediot Aharonot*, July 22, 1966.

the British military arsenal where, according to reliable information, our weapons confiscated from Yagur were being stored....

The two dissident organizations were entrusted – in instructions communicated in writing to the commander of the IZL and the commander of the Lehi – with operations of a different type: IZL to blow up the offices of the government's Chief Secretariat in the King David Hotel building, and Lehi to destroy the administrative offices in the David Brothers building, both in Jerusalem.

In giving the order for the three operations, I was acting on the basis of appropriate decisions taken by x Committee even before Black Sabbath.... Despite this I convened a meeting of x Committee in my capacity as deputy chairman (the chairman, Rabbi Fishman-Maimon, was at that time imprisoned in Latrun). I delivered a report on the attacks of June 29 and asked for approval of guidelines for further action. I described in general terms the operations being planned...and the Committee's endorsement was given. The ball was rolling.[14]

THE GO-AHEAD

At midday on July 1, 1946, a blond-haired, blue-eyed youth slipped into a building on Ben-Yehuda Street in Tel Aviv. After carefully checking that the coast was clear, he went to the mailboxes, took a sealed envelope from one of them, and quickly withdrew.

The house on Ben-Yehuda served as a communications conduit between the two underground organizations, IZL and Lehi. Letters were delivered first to Lehi headquarters and from there passed on to IZL command. The Lehi member, Avraham Lieberman, then known as Gideon, was the "postman." He handed over the sealed envelope to Yitzhak Shamir, then known by the code name Michael, and he ordered its delivery to IZL headquarters.[15] Later that afternoon an IZL envoy took the letter from a mailbox on Dizengoff Street and handed it to Menahem Begin.

It was the endorsement that they had been waiting for – but this was more than approval; rather, it was expressed in terms of a command. The

14. Moshe Sneh's answers to questions put by Slutsky (editor of *History of the Haganah*), HHA 4681 – 2/158H/80.

15. *Yediot Aharonot*, January 16, 1959.

letter was typed and signed with the single letter M. The addressee was not named. The full text was as follows:

Shalom!

a) You are to execute Malonchick and Your Slave and Redeemer as soon as possible. Inform us of the date. Preferably simultaneously. Identity of those responsible is not to be publicized – explicitly or implicitly.

b) We too are planning something. Will inform you of details nearer the time.

c) Tel Aviv and its environs are to be excluded from any planned operation. It is in the interests of us all to preserve Tel Aviv as the center of Jewish communal life and the center of our activity. If as the result of an operation Tel Aviv is paralyzed (curfew, arrests, etc.), we shall be paralyzed too. Incidentally, the opposition has no vital strategic installations located here. Therefore, Tel Aviv is "off-limits" as regards any action on behalf of the armies of Israel!

d) Recent events have not changed our opinion regarding release of the "three gentlemen."[16] Their continued detention is neither a plus nor a minus, but on the other hand, their release today will underline the difference in battle ethics between the two sides. To cement relations between the three of us, immediate release is vital. We await your response.

e) I have sent to the meeting of the national institutions currently in session in Jerusalem a proposal that all links between the Jewish Community and the authorities be severed, as a prelude to general civil disobedience. Naturally I cannot be seen personally defending the proposal, and its outcome is not yet known.

For God's sake – no personal calls!

We'll meet in a few days.

– M

July 1, 1946

11:00[17]

---

16. The "three gentlemen" were the three British officers kidnapped by the IZL as hostages to prevent the hanging of Simhon and Ashbel, who had been sentenced to death (they were reprieved following the kidnap of the officers).

17. Photocopy of the original document sent to IZL Command by the chief of staff of the Haganah, Moshe Sneh – signing himself "M."

Begin was astonished, not by the endorsement of action (which was only to be expected following the events of Black Sabbath) but by the air of panic that the message conveyed. The demand (virtually an order) – "You are to execute…as soon as possible" – was not to his liking. It was also a departure from the standard form of operational authorization. "The instruction to attack the King David Hotel reached us some weeks after the latest deferment of our scheme," he writes in *The Revolt*. "In the meantime, some of the threads we had held in our hands were severed. We had to resume reconnaissance activities and review all the details again." Begin called in Paglin for urgent consultation, and the latter calmed his anxieties, "Give me a few days and the plan will be complete," he said.

That same evening Gidi arranged a meeting with Shraga Ellis, then serving in the Tel Aviv planning unit.

"You're to go to Jerusalem at once and reconnoiter the King David Hotel again," he said. Shraga had learned long ago not to be surprised by anything Gidi told him. Nevertheless, he was taken aback. "I don't understand," he said, "why the hurry?"

Gidi shrugged, "The commanders of the Resistance Movement seem to have good reasons for it: piles of documents confiscated from the Agency offices are sitting on CID (Criminal Investigation Department) desks in the King David, some of them proving direct links between community leaders and the underground – is it any wonder they're feeling nervous?"

Shraga Ellis nodded. That night he packed his small suitcase. "Luckily I still had use of the room I'd rented in Jerusalem before. But apart from that," he stressed,

> everything had to be done all over again: it had been months since the original plan was put together and although the basic data was unchanged – a long corridor in the basement linking La Regence café to the north wing – all the rest, i.e., security units, inspection points, times of deliveries – had to be reassessed. Then there were the practical preparations for the operation – collecting and packing the milk churns, preparing delay mechanisms, getting weapons and equipment, and most important of all, choosing the right people for the job.[18]

---

18. Author's interview with Shraga Ellis, October 1996.

The next morning Gidi's message reached the Jerusalem regional commander, Yitzhak Avinoam: "Prepare for immediate action."

Operation Chick had moved into high gear.

On Tuesday, July 2, 1946, Gidi arrived early at the little workshop in Feierberg Street. "We need to prepare three milk churns packed with explosives, which will be detonated after a set time, but also to booby-trap them against moving or defusing," he told his assistant Elimelech Spiegel, himself a professional technician. The two of them didn't need lengthy dialogues to know what the other was thinking; over the course of time a deep professional understanding had developed between them, "When Gidi lifted a finger, I knew immediately what he meant," said Elimelech proudly.[19]

The principle of the anti-handling mechanism (whereby any movement dislodged a spring, which in turn completed an electrical circuit setting off the charge) was an old idea of Gidi's; he had already used it successfully to booby-trap two packs of explosives in the government employment office in the capital. But the quantities to be used this time were massive and unprecedented – seven milk churns each containing 110 pounds (50 kilograms) of TNT, three of them fitted with delay and anti-handling devices. That very evening, the churns were "commandeered" from the Tnuva café in Lilienblum Street.

That same morning, Adina Hai Nisan (aka "Tehiyya," serving in Jerusalem area communications) visited the New British Drug Company pharmacy on Jaffa Street in Jerusalem, workplace of Israel Levi ("Gideon") and while apparently fumbling for the prescription in her purse, she whispered softly in his ear, "Avinoam is waiting for you at the corner."

"I don't feel well," he told his employer, and left the shop hurriedly.

Avinoam gave the young man a long look.

"We're planning an operation of the utmost importance," he began, "and you've been chosen to lead it." He didn't care to waste time on preliminaries. "Are you prepared to take on the job?"

Levi's heart was beating fast. He hadn't the faintest idea what was being discussed, and he heard his own voice as if coming from far away. "At your disposal, commander!"

The Jerusalem district commander was satisfied. Only that morning he had received Gidi's note telling him to go ahead and the priority now

---

19. Author's recorded interview with Elimelech Spiegel, October 1996.

was to find a man fit to lead such a daring and significant enterprise. From a list of recommended candidates supplied to him by Shraga Ellis, he had chosen Israel Levi, a youth whom he believed to be endowed with nerves of steel, leadership qualities, inventiveness, and what was most vital for this particular operation – command of the Arabic language. The resolute response of his subordinate confirmed his judgment, but he kept his face blank and showed nothing of what he was thinking. "You're to go to Tel Aviv today and report to the national operations officer," he continued in a practical tone.

In response to his appeal for further information, all Levi got was a warm handshake and a broad smile.[20]

Gidi glanced briefly at the face of the swarthy, solid young man who had been chosen to command one of the most audacious and sensitive operations in the history of the Irgun: dark curly hair, soft and dreamy eyes, an innocent cast of features. But Gidi wasn't one to be misled by outward appearances; he was aware of the man's record as a fighter and knew it wasn't for nothing that Avinoam had recommended him so warmly: the youth had helped in the planning of most of the IZL's operations in Jerusalem, had participated in the attack on CID headquarters in the Russian Compound, and successfully led a raid on the vaults of Barclays Bank in Shechem. But all of these, Gidi knew, were as nothing compared with the operation being planned now. He chose his words carefully. "The objective we have in mind is the center of British power in this land." And after a brief pause, staring intently at the younger man, he added, "We're talking about the King David Hotel..."

Long afterward, on his way back to Jerusalem, Levi hadn't yet recovered from the shock and Gidi's voice still echoed in his ears: "The mission is to blow up the southern wing of the hotel, with all the police files and documents that are stored there. Execution of the scheme is in your hands..." The slap on his shoulder had seemed to accentuate the weight of the responsibility laid upon him.

And he hadn't yet turned 20.

20. Amrami's interview with Avinoam, July 1968, Jabotinsky Archives; radio prog. (see n. 7).

Twenty-four hours later reconnaissance in the region of the hotel was resumed.

Equipped with an official entry pass, identifying him as an accredited employee of the electricity company, Levi accompanied the company's (official) maintenance specialist, a man with links to the IZL, on a leisurely tour of the ground floor of the hotel, carefully checking the electricity cables…

After two days Levi had a detailed picture of all the entrances and exits, passages between floors and corridors linking the extremities of the building. What drew his attention especially was the basement, where all the services were concentrated, and he discovered a significant detail which was to be of crucial importance to the plan: all deliveries – including food supplies – came in via a side door at the northern end of the hotel, and what was no less significant, there were no British soldiers stationed at this point, just a solitary Arab watchman.

With his fluent Arabic and his command of oriental manners, Levi rapidly gained the trust of the young Arab, who was soon confiding in his "new friend," complaining about the arrogant attitude of his employers and his heavy workload: every time there was a delivery, he said, he had to sort everything out and keep detailed records. And once he had begun talking, the vital information flowed unchecked. "It's lucky for me," he sighed, "that the deliveries don't all drop on me at once: vegetables come at 9:00 AM, bread at 10:00, milk at 12:00…" Levi had difficulty hiding his excitement: *If the fool only knew what was being planned here and what vital information he's given me!* he thought. But outwardly he maintained an expression of understanding and sympathy, telling the young Arab of troubles of his own, the hazards of electrical maintenance… The conversation continued smoothly and amicably, until the last nugget of information had been extracted.

The data accumulated over two days of reconnaissance was to serve as a vital element in the operational plan, but still the essential component was lacking: finding the optimum site for placing the explosives. The part of the basement which had been reconnoitered housed the supports of the hotel at the northern end of the building; the objective of the attack, however, was on the southern side. The two parts of the building were separated by a corridor 150 yards long, and at one end, above La Regence café, all the central institutions of government were located: Chief Secretariat, Army

HQ, CID, etc., etc. It was impossible for the "electrician" to infiltrate this sector, since all the electrical work there had been completed long before.[21]

"Nothing's impossible," declared Shraga Ellis when he heard the report. "All we need is a change of disguise: instead of overalls – evening dress…"

Next day Shraga Ellis and Eliyahu Levi arrived at La Regence, reputedly the most expensive restaurant in Jerusalem, in tuxedos and black ties, obviously a pair of well-heeled Christian Arabs. They made their entrance cautiously, accompanied by their escorts, Sarah and Tzipora.

Of all the foursome Tzipora was the only one walking with confidence. As a girl-about-town she had visited this place a number of times and some of the guests even waved at her. Shraga was pleased to see this; her obvious popularity was good for their cover and he was glad he'd had the forethought to hire the services of a professional.

This was Sarah's first experience of glittering nightlife. She stared at the grandeur all around, feeling as if she had been transported to a fantasy world. Soft lamplight was reflected on brass cocktail tables, the orchestra played soothing music, the stage lights changed colors, the atmosphere was intoxicating – so different from anything she had known before. Most of all she was enchanted by the tall Sudanese waiters, immaculate in their white robes and scarlet tarbooshes.

"You're to look your best tonight," Levi had told her. They moved slowly to the rhythm of the waltz, eyes peeled for any significant detail. Suddenly she felt herself being propelled toward the screen behind the orchestra, and in the process of disentangling themselves from the heavy velvet curtain, they discovered behind it a locked iron door facing the front of the hotel. "Worth knowing…," Levi muttered, drawing her back onto the dance floor.

Among the guests it was easy to pick out the British servicemen, some of them in the company of Jewish girls. As if through a mist Sarah became aware that somebody was bowing to her; one of the officers was inviting her to dance. Levi smiled cheerfully and nodded, but she felt a sudden surge of anger and shrugged her refusal. "Sorry," she heard herself say, "I don't dance…" She almost added "with Englishmen…" The officer muttered

---

21. Testimony of Israel Levi, "The Bombing of the King David Hotel", Jabotinsky Archives.

something unintelligible and withdrew politely, but he had his eye on her all evening. She didn't dare dance anymore.[22]

Eliyahu Levi on the other hand, he's got all the manners and rituals down pat, an Effendi to the manner born, he knows what drinks to order and even makes the waiters laugh with his witty remarks....

Around midnight, Shraga suggested that the girls pay a visit to the Ladies. "Stay there as long as you can," he whispered. "Of course, we waited for them politely, like gentlemen," he recalled with a smile, "and when they took some time I started pacing anxiously up and down the corridor. I must have been distracted because suddenly I found myself at the kitchen door – the kitchen that was supplied via the alleyway running between the hotel and the French Consulate. My heart beat fast, and I could hardly contain my joy: my hunch had been proved right – the long corridor did indeed connect the hotel kitchen with La Regence and could be used to transport the charges to a point directly underneath the government offices.[23] "Next day," he continued, "we made a full-scale reconnaissance of the hotel exterior and noticed that around twelve noon a van arrived with provisions for La Regence and Arab workers were unloading crates of vegetables and milk churns at the northern entrance to the hotel. We decided this was the route to be used for the delivery of the explosives."

All the data thus gathered was presented to Gidi and carefully evaluated by him. Not all of the picture was rosy: the area around the hotel was crammed with military emplacements, and the entire district was strewn with army barracks and police stations. These were the facts distilled from the data:

- Backup squads would be needed to block – with fire – access from the army camp to the hotel garden, and from there to the hotel itself. A survey of the local topography led to the conclusion that a machine-gun post should be positioned between the hotel complex and the Yemin Moshe district to the east, severing communications between the hotel and the camp.
- The front of the hotel faced the main entrance of the YMCA building, and between the two buildings was St. Julian Street, stretching away

---

22. Avinoam's interview with Sarah Goldschmid, October 20, 1968, Jabotinsky Archives.
23. Author's interview with Shraga Ellis, October 1996.

toward the south of the city and the German Colony, site of the regional police headquarters and a large army camp. An alarm from the hotel was liable to produce the immediate dispatch of military reinforcements in motorized transport and armored cars. It was decided that this road could be blocked by a wall of fire – a mixture of petrol and paraffin. A blockage of this order could delay the movement of vehicles for some ten minutes, and two men with submachine guns and hand grenades could delay advancing infantry for a while longer.

- About 100 yards north of the hotel in St. Julian Street were three barrack blocks and on the other side of the road was a military garage. Access to the hotel from these two points also had to be denied, with the use of inflammable liquids and an extra backup unit.

Gradually a plan of action was taking shape in Gidi's mind, a plan destined to be laid before Yitzhak Sadeh, chief of staff of the Haganah, and to earn his endorsement[24] and a rare compliment on his part, "A simple and beautiful plan," was how he described it to Yigal Allon (see below).

A TECHNICAL MEETING

"Between July 1, the day we received the instruction from Haganah command to 'execute Chick as soon as possible' and the day of the actual attack," Begin writes in *The Revolt*, "there was an interval of more than three weeks. During this time there was a 'technical meeting' between the operations officer of the Haganah, Yitzhak Sadeh, and Gidi, the operations officer of the Irgun Zvai Leumi."

The two men eyed one another warily.

Sadeh was a big man with full, fleshy face and graying beard, balding with curly gray hair at the temples, and showing the beginnings of a paunch. Since Black Sabbath he had gone underground and adopted the disguise of a professor. "The disguise amused him so much, he did everything he could to make it ineffective," his daughter, Izah, recalled.[25]

Gidi, by contrast, was boyish, tall and lean, his brown eyes looking straight at the chief of staff of the United Resistance Movement.

24. Avraham Shai (n. 8 above); Avinoam's interview with Israel Levi, November 16, 1968, Jabotinsky Archives.
25. *Yediot Aharonot*, "Seven Days," August 17, 1980.

This was their first meeting.

Here is the man who sent the Twenty-Three Seafarers to their doom, the thought flashed through Paglin's mind. The image of his brother Neriel rose again before his eyes and his heart missed a beat.

Sadeh was well aware of this unhappy chapter in the history of the Paglin family. The fact that he was now standing face to face with the brother of Neriel, the young man sent by him on that ill-fated mission from which no one returned, raised painful memories and for a moment he almost forgot the purpose of this meeting.

Gidi was the first to collect himself. He held out his hand.

Sadeh shook it without enthusiasm and without rising from his seat. The gap of years between the two spanned more than a generation, but this was not all that divided them. From the start there was no chemistry here.[26]

Paglin describes the meeting thus:

I turned up at Yitzhak Sadeh's apartment at the time agreed. He was alone, but I got the distinct impression there were others in the room next door, listening to our conversation. I gave him all the details of our plan, except for the mustering and jump-off locations, and Sadeh queried three points:

He insisted that the quantity of TNT we planned to use (770 pounds; 350 kilos) was insufficient and wouldn't destroy the wing.

My reply was that a bigger charge would bring down the whole building, including the part that served as a civilian hotel.

He had reservations about the place we'd chosen to place the explosives – La Regence café – and expressed concern lest the British find them and defuse them.

I explained that we were going to add anti-handling devices that would set off the charges if there was any attempt to tamper with them.

Finally he queried the interval of time we had decided on between the warning and the explosion – 45 minutes. In his opinion this was too long and would enable the British to locate the explosives.

I repeated my assurance that the milk churns, once in place, could not be moved by anyone, not even the saboteurs themselves, and this was one of the subtleties of our bombs. I explained we were also going

---

26. Author's interview with Amihai Paglin, 1969.

to fix warning notices to the churns, making it clear that any attempt to move them would cause immediate explosion. British bomb disposal experts, in my judgment, would have the common sense to take these warnings seriously.

Sadeh stood his ground, insisting that the warning period had to be shortened. None of my arguments made the slightest impression on him…. I suggested a compromise: 30 minutes, but he still wasn't satisfied, and raised objection after objection. To put an end to the argument, I insisted we didn't have delay mechanisms for a shorter interval, but he wasn't giving up. "We'll supply you with British 'pencils' from the Haganah arsenal," he said. I replied that if there was a hitch and the charges didn't work – or worked prematurely – members of the IZL would be convinced that the Haganah had "shafted" them deliberately, and relations between the organizations would be poisoned.

This final argument persuaded him, and he agreed to an interval of 30 minutes.[27]

Throughout this conversation, the timing of the operation was never mentioned. Sadeh was interested in the technical principles of the operational plan; he couldn't be bothered with details. Once, he suggested that the action be carried out at night. "Have you forgotten that half the building is still a hotel?" Gidi reminded him. "It's true that we're experts in these things and have a lot of experience, but what if it turns out there's been a miscalculation, and instead of just the southern wing the whole building comes down, including the civilian hotel section?" The idea was dropped there and then.[28]

Yitzhak Sadeh was no friend of the IZL. "He preferred Lehi, and resented the IZL."[29] At the time of the resistance he was staying with Galili and would occasionally unburden himself to him. Even Ben-Gurion wasn't immune from his tongue-lashings.

When Gidi had left the room, Sadeh turned over in his mind the scheme to blow up the Chief Secretariat in the King David Hotel – and marveled at it. "A simple and beautiful plan," he told Yigal Allon. "I admit

27. *Yediot Aharonot*, July 22, 1966; Radio prog., n. 7 above.
28. Israel Galili, Yad Tabenkin Archives, Unit 15, Box 172, File 4, Docs. 14–15; "Caged Lion," Radio prog., IDF channel.
29. Galili, "Address," n. 20 above.

I was green with envy," said the commander of the Palmah. "Why wasn't this operation given to us?" he asked. "It was their idea," Sadeh replied and after a moment's thought added, "It's going to be a beauty."[30]

Dov Tsisis, operations officer of the Palmah, was also Sadeh's personal assistant and bodyguard. From time to time, the chief of staff of the Hebrew Resistance Movement gave him the job of checking and evaluating schemes that had been proposed.

The day following the meeting with Gidi, Sadeh called him in. "He sent me to Jerusalem to verify certain details about the building itself and its surroundings – apparently with the idea of checking out what the IZL was suggesting," Tsisis said in 1970. "My uncle, Yerah Etzion, gave me some information, as he used to work in the building. I got inside the hotel and wandered around, and got the data that Yitzhak wanted – about entrances, exits and so on. Yohai Ben-Nun was with me on one of these trips to Jerusalem. I knew from this mission that something was being planned, but I wasn't involved in the operation."[31]

Eighteen years later, August 19, 1988, in an interview with the weekly *Tel Aviv*, Tsisis confirmed the statement that he had reconnoitered the King David Hotel at Sadeh's behest. He added, "After the hotel was blown up, it was said the Haganah knew nothing about it. That is absolutely untrue. The IZL prepared an operational plan and Yitzhak Sadeh, who was also a close friend of mine, sent me to check it out. The IZL didn't blow up the hotel until Sadeh gave them the all clear, following my reconnaissance."

TIMING AND DELAYS

Two proposals were put before the IZL planners regarding timing of the attack: one, at eleven in the morning and the other, between four and five in the afternoon. Begin analyzed the options:

> Both these times had the same reasoning behind them: the milk churns could only be taken into the government section of the hotel via La Regence café, in the basement of the building. During the morning and the early evening the café was deserted but at lunchtime it would be crowded with guests, including army officers, civilians, and women.

30. Testimony of Yigal Allon, Yad Tabenkin Archives, Unit 15, Box 172, File 6, Doc. 7.
31. Testimony of Dov Tsisis, Yad Tabenkin Archives, Box 172, File 6, Doc. 5.

British officers were under orders to carry arms at all time, and technical and moral considerations demanded avoidance of confrontation; a premature exchange of fire was liable to lead to civilian casualties as well as give the enemy time to call up reinforcements…. For these reasons, the choice was between two times at which the café would be empty, and of the two we chose the earlier – eleven o'clock. An additional consideration was the need to coordinate our attack with that of the Lehi on the David Brothers building. We were all agreed that the two operations should be executed simultaneously. When the basics had been settled, we also fixed details of the warnings."[32]

Once the plans were complete and everything was ready for the operation, a series of delays began – some of them instigated by the Haganah, for all kinds of weird reasons, and some of them requested by members of Lehi, who needed more time to organize their attack on David Brothers (codenamed Your Slave and Redeemer).

"We were ready to take on Barker and his staff early in July," Begin reveals in *The Revolt*:

but once we postponed the operation at the request of Lehi, whose preparations weren't complete, and two or three times at the Haganah's request. The delays were very dangerous. Every change of date meant there were more people knowing about it. As a rule, detailed information about an imminent operation wasn't distributed until the last moment, to reduce the risk of leaks, but in the case of the King David Hotel, a relatively large number of people had already been briefed, and every additional delay was liable to endanger not only the scheme but the perpetrators, too. So we protested against the delays but we went along with them, rather than defy the authority of the United Resistance Movement, and we accepted the explanation that time was needed for the transfer of weapons to secure locations, in advance of further searches on the part of the British.

"For political and technical reasons we didn't endorse the dates of the

---

32. Begin, *The Revolt*, p. 217.

operation given to us initially by the IZL," says Galili. He further admitted and then explained:

> They weren't happy with this, and insisted that delay would endanger secrecy. They had a point, plus the fact that a lot of the planning that had gone into it, like reconnaissance and stake-outs, would be invalidated by delay. At the same time, we made it clear that one of the conditions for our participation was absolutely secret planning that does not set fixed dates for implementation....[33]
>
> The first delays came as a result of operational factors or the need for coordination between the IZL and Lehi, and then came the unexpected intervention of Weizmann, who demanded we suspend all military operations until the meeting of the Zionist Executive in August in Paris. This was an unprecedented intervention, bypassing the usual chain of command (the political leadership was interned in Latrun, in the wake of Black Sabbath, and Ben-Gurion was abroad).[34]

After the confirmations had been sent to the IZL and Lehi, Moshe Sneh received a message at his temporary housing ("I was deep underground at the time") that Meir Weisgal wanted to meet him urgently, on Weizmann's behalf. Weisgal gave him a letter containing the following message, in the name of the president of the Zionist Federation:

> Recent events have shocked me deeply. We are standing on the edge of an abyss. Everything could be ruined if you continue with these actions. It will be seen as a declaration of war on Britain, and the British will respond forcefully. It is the convention in most states that the president is also the commander-in-chief of the armed forces...and I invoke this prerogative in appealing to you to halt all operations... until the Zionist leadership has met in plenary session, insofar as that is possible. I am asking you for an unequivocal reply – if your reply is negative, I shall resign immediately and make the reasons for my resignation public...

---

33. Israel Galili, Yad Tabenkin Archives, Box 172, File 5, Doc. 1.
34. Galili, "Address," n. 20 above.

Weisgal waited patiently until Sneh had finished reading the letter and then added, "The president is asking for your reply here and now, so he can decide how to proceed."

Sneh couldn't believe what he was hearing. "I have colleagues who share the responsibility and authority," he said, struggling to control his anger. "I can't give an answer on the spot. I shall consider this, consult the others, and give you my answer soon, as soon as possible."

After consulting his fellow commanders, Sneh replied that he wasn't entitled to cancel an operation that had been approved by the x Committee; only they had the authority to do this. "There was an element of evasiveness here," Galili explains, "a protest against Weizmann's way of doing things. But we were also taking a risk referring it back to the x Committee, as there was no way of knowing what the decision would be."

And sure enough, when the issue was debated in this forum, a majority voted to comply with Weizmann's directive.

"I put forward President Weizmann's ultimatum," Sneh relates, "and expressed my opinion that the x Committee, embodying the authority of the Zionist leadership and the Va'ad ha-Le'umi (National Council) on issues of the [national] struggle, was the only democratic agency entitled to decide on operations and their timing, and it was not within the prerogative of the president to set conditions challenging its authority, responsibility, and freedom of judgment."[35]

Sneh was an accomplished speaker and his words should have flattered the self-importance of committee members, but neither he nor Galili appreciated the scale of the demoralization inflicted on the leaders and administrators of the Yishuv (the Jewish community in Palestine) by the trauma of Black Sabbath. The fear and trepidation expressed by Weizmann reflected their own feelings, and by a majority of four to two (the two being Sneh and Israel Bar-Yehuda) they decided to accept Weizmann's instructions. According to Sneh, "Bar-Yehuda was incandescent with rage, and told me he feared this was the beginning of the end of the struggle."

There and then Sneh presented his resignation from the post of Haganah chief, although he remained a member of the national command. As his replacement he appointed Zev Shefer, thereby upsetting Galili who had wanted the job himself and didn't hide his disappointment. "This was

---

35. Testimony of Sneh, A.T.H./4681 2/H 158/80.

a demonstration of lack of confidence in me, and it had more to do with party politics than with the best interests of the Haganah."[36] Sneh decided to go to Paris to attend the plenary session of the Jewish Agency leadership, also hoping to enlist Ben-Gurion's support for the continuation of the campaign.

Moshe Sneh took no pleasure in implementing the decision of the x Committee:[37]

> I told the chief of staff and the Palmah leadership to cancel the planned raid on the arms store, and sent notes to the commander of the IZL and the commander of Lehi telling them to postpone the bombings in Jerusalem. I didn't tell them of the x Committee decision – first, because it was an internal matter, and second, because I feared they would see this as an abrogation of the agreement and take it upon themselves to act freely without the supervision of the United Resistance Movement Command; this would result in anarchy. I sent an additional personal note to Menahem Begin, asking him to call off the King David Hotel action. When the bombs went off in the hotel, I was no longer Haganah chief. I'd resigned and that day I was in Haifa, about to board a ship for France.[38]

"I think that the wording of the directive to the IZL was misleading. It should have been put more clearly. There were some of us who thought Sneh wanted them to go ahead. I reckon Sneh was trying to be subtle, so the IZL wouldn't suspect the business had really been cancelled," declares Galili.[39]

Yaakov Yanai (Yan), who was deputy Haganah chief and a close friend of Moshe Sneh, accompanied him to Haifa on the first leg of his journey to Paris and handled all the travel arrangements. "I was with him when news of the King David Hotel blast reached us," he said.[40] "He was put into a bit

---

36. Yad Tebenkin Archives, Box 172, File 6, Doc. 18.
37. Twenty years later, in a symposium sponsored by *Ma'ariv* and featuring three former underground leaders – Menahem Begin, Natan Yellin-Mor and Moshe Sneh – Sneh said: "It could be that today I regret having consulted the x Committee."
38. Testimony of Sneh, HHA 2/H 158/80.
39. Galili, "Address"; "Clarification," n. 20 above.
40. Testimony of Yaakov Yani (Yan), Yad Tabenkin Archives, Box 172, File 6, Doc. 14.

of a panic when he heard of the scale of the explosion and the casualties and was afraid it might impede his journey, as his passport was in his real name. I don't remember him cursing the IZL or expressing any particular indignation."

Yanai raises doubts as to whether the cancellation messages were in fact sent to the IZL. "I don't know anything about cancellation notes, but I do know that Sneh himself wasn't in favor of canceling the operation. Maybe he was afraid to tell them to cancel – so he asked for a delay. As for Lehi, I remember an instruction to cancel. There was talk of calling off the King David job, but it wasn't passed on to them."

"It was believed Sneh's letter reached its destination, but there was no response from the addressee to Haganah command," according to Israel Galili.[41]

"Contact was through mailboxes in some house. Whether their man turned up or not wasn't at all certain. There were meetings that were canceled because messages didn't get through. Once or twice Natan Yellin had to stay overnight at my place, because I hadn't been notified of a cancellation," explains Yaakov Yanai, whose house was used for meetings between Hebrew Resistance Movement chiefs and the IZL.

"After Weizmann's intervention," Galili continues, "Sneh told me he had informed the dissidents of the cancellation, and I had no idea he was only asking them for a delay of a few days... I don't think that's the way to settle an issue like this, leaving it as a request for a few more days... The initiative for contacts and meetings was in Sneh's hands," he adds, pointing the finger of blame at the Haganah chief and absolving himself of responsibility for the breakdown of communications with the IZL.

Somewhat defensively he goes on, still intent on laying all the responsibility on Sneh:

I don't know of any meeting with the dissidents to discuss cancellation of the King David Hotel action, between the x Committee's deliberations and the execution of the operation. I certainly wasn't present at such a meeting.... Until July 19, three days before the blast I had nothing to do, because it was all up to Sneh (not Shefer). Sneh told me to

---

41. Testimony of Galili, October 30, 1970, Yad Tabenkin Archives, Box 172, File 6, Doc. 18.

inform them Shefer had been appointed Haganah chief – and where did that leave me? Moshe Sneh isn't saying now that he told Shepher or Galili to set up a meeting with the IZL to discuss what was going on. Moshe Sneh isn't pretending any longer that he made arrangements for such a meeting, before going off on his travels."[42]

According to Begin, the operation was postponed for the last time on July 19.[43]

The previous day, July 18, 1946, the IZL men detailed to take part in the operation had been ordered to report the following morning at the assembly points assigned to them from the start. Those of the Jerusalem commanders who weren't involved in the operation were advised to leave the capital for a while.

On Friday, July 19, 1946, Yehoshua Gal met Zvi Barzel and three other members of the combat unit in the cellar of a building in the Bukharan quarter. He had barely begun briefing them on their role in the forthcoming operation when a messenger arrived on a motorcycle and handed him a sealed letter. He glanced at the contents and said with a sigh of disappointment, "The operation's been postponed. You're free to go, but don't breathe a word of what's been said here. I'll be in touch."[44]

That morning, Sneh's note had reached Begin:

> Shalom,
>   I've heard from my colleagues about the most recent conversation. If you attach any importance to my personal appeal, I'm asking you as forcefully as I can to delay the planned operation for a few more days.

When Begin received the "personal appeal" from Sneh on July 19, 1946, he didn't know it was invalid, having been written after Sneh's resignation from the post of Haganah chief. Nor had Sneh deigned to keep him abreast of recent dramatic developments, on the grounds that he saw it as "an internal matter" as he later explained. Twenty years later, in a *Ma'ariv*

---

42. Israel Galili, Yad Tabenkin Archives, Unit 15, Box 172, File 4.
43. Begin, *The Revolt*, p. 218.
44. Author's interview with Zvi Barzel, September 26, 1999.

symposium,[45] he attempted to justify himself, explaining the sequence of events as follows, "I wrote a note to Mr. Begin – this was after my resignation – addressing a personal appeal to him (I couldn't tell him why it had to be a personal appeal, because my resignation was a secret)."

"We went along with this request too" – said Begin – "and the final date was set for July 22, 1946."[46]

YANAI

Shortly before Shraga left Jerusalem, Avinoam introduced him to Yanai (aka Heinrich Reinhold). "Tall, strong, and apparently a courageous fighter," was Shraga's first impression.

Once they had become acquainted, Shraga invited Yanai to join him for a stroll around the streets of the city, occasionally pointing out to him possible objectives for future attack. "What I remember most," he said later, "were the questions he bombarded me with whenever I showed him any objective. He was particularly insistent on knowing the dates of future operations, if they'd been decided. I told him I didn't know and that was the truth. Questions like that were Gidi's department. Of course, I didn't tell him that."[47]

On the morning of the operation Avinoam arrived at Yanai's room.

Yanai's heart was beating fast. Since yesterday he'd been ordered not to leave the apartment. He hadn't been told anything explicitly; from the little he'd been able to glean with his acute senses, he understood that the King David Hotel was on the hit list. He glanced at Avinoam – broad-shouldered, smartly dressed, neatly shaved, an alert look in his eyes.[48]

"Going to work?" he asked casually.

"You'll find out soon enough," was the laconic reply.

Yanai shrugged. "I've got some documents,[49] I'd like to give them to a friend for safekeeping…"

---

45. Symposium of underground leaders sponsored by *Ma'ariv* in 1966, chaired by Geulah Cohen.
46. Begin, *The Revolt*, p. 218.
47. Author's interview with Shraga Ellis, October 1996.
48. Description of Avinoam as passed to the CID by Reinhold, who did not know his real name (see the chapter "The Jerusalem Railway Station Bombing").
49. Y. Amrami's interview with Avinoam, 1968, Jabotinsky Archives.

Avinoam nodded his agreement and led him to the taxi.

A few minutes later Yanai pointed to a building. "That's the house."

Avinoam looked at his watch, "Just be quick about it."

He ran up the steps and anxiously rang the bell. The woman in the doorway stared at him in astonishment.[50]

"What...?"

He stopped her with a hasty gesture, "Please, I have to make contact, right now!"

The telephone message was short and vague; he passed on what he knew, which wasn't much. "They're up to something. I think it's the King David Hotel... Expect another message."

That was the only warning he succeeded in sending that fateful day. Popular historian Thurston Clarke describes what happened on the other end of that phone call:

> General Sir Evelyn ("Bubbles") Barker, the GOC all British troops in Palestine, laughed and looked at his wristwatch, "Well, we'd better be quick," he said, "I understand we're due to be blown up this morning."
>
> Colonel Andrew Campbell felt a nerve twinge. He and Barker sat at a long table in the third-floor briefing room at the northern end wing of the King David. "Morning prayers," the daily briefing for staff officers, had just finished....
>
> "Don't worry, Andrew," Barker said. "We've got a few hours of peace." He laughed again.
>
> "What do you mean?"
>
> "We've been tipped off."[51]

This was the morning of Monday, July 22, 1946, the day the King David was bombed.[52]

---

50. One of several Jerusalem ladies with whom Reinhold was romantically linked (Tamir's report on Reinhold, Jabotinsky Archives); testimony of Avinoam in interview with Tavin, 1954, Jabotinsky Archives.

51. Thurston Clarke, *By Blood and Fire* (London: Hutchinson, 1981), pp. 131–32.

52. General Barker later denied that this conversation between himself and Campbell had ever taken place. According to Thurston Clarke: "The description of the meeting between Barker and Campbell is based on an interview with Campbell. Barker now has no recollection of this meeting nor of the intelligence tip-off about Operation Chick and believes Campbell is mistaken. Nevertheless, the author has chosen

The British were indeed waiting for confirmation from their trusted agent, and when it failed to materialize, they assumed nothing serious was likely to happen.

The second call was never made.

This was one of the worst intelligence failures to afflict the Mandatory Government. This was a failure that the parties involved succeeded in covering up not only externally but internally too. To this day the details are under wraps, and the relevant documents are still classified.

Campbell's version. Campbell has a clear, detailed recollection of this meeting and is absolutely certain that it did occur. In every other matter, Campbell's testimony has proven to be completely accurate" (*By Blood and Fire*, notes, pp. 275).

THE DAY

They arrived, one after another, 25 in all, and were ushered into one of the classrooms of the Beit Aharon school on David Yellin Street in Jerusalem. The time was seven in the morning and traffic in the streets was still sparse. They didn't know for sure why they were there – only that action was in the offing and they had been chosen to take part in it.

Shraga Ellis entered the room. All looked at him expectantly, but he confined himself to some general remarks about the importance of cooperation within the United Resistance Movement.

Israel Levi sketched on a blackboard the salient points of the zone of operation, but said nothing about the operation itself. The detailed briefing would come from the chief operations officer.

When Gidi entered there was a hush. All eyes were turned to him, which only accentuated the tension they were all feeling. He looked more serious than usual. After a moment of silence he said in his quiet voice, "Today we're going to blow up the government offices and Army HQ in the King David Hotel."

Silence again. Not a sound was heard. It was as if all had stopped breathing, staring at the face of their commander, scarcely believing what they were hearing. *Is it possible? Can it be?* Most of them were Jerusalemites born and bred. They knew every stone, every alley, every street in the capital – and they knew what an awesome, impregnable fortress they were targeting. Mobile and armored units were constantly patrolling. You couldn't even loiter outside the hotel without risking arrest, and anyone looking suspicious was hauled off for immediate interrogation by the CID. But as the explanations were given, gradually the looks of incredulity faded and the project took on practical, tangible shape. Gidi was less economical with his words than usual, as he described in detail every stage of the operation and the role of each of the participants.[1]

"Entry to the hotel," he explained, "will be effected by way of the northern entrance leading to the basement, as far as possible without attracting attention. The force will number 25, including the commander and his deputy. It will be divided into three sections: (a) interception; (b) infiltration party (including 'porters'); (c) backup."

Pointing to the diagram pinned to the wall, Gidi continued:

A force of seven men will take over the basement floor and its entrances and isolate it from the rest of the hotel. Anyone found in the vicinity will be confined to the kitchen and allowed no contact with the government workers on the upper floors.

Six men dressed as Arab fellahin will act as porters, transporting the milk churns from the van to La Regence. This team will set out first and wait near the northern entrance until the ground has been secured.

Once the ground has been secured, the porters will unload the containers of explosives from the van in the entrance to the basement floor and take them along the basement corridor to La Regence. Israel Levi will set the bombs and activate the delay mechanisms and when the warning signs are in place, the signal for withdrawal will be given.

First to withdraw will be the porters, followed by the backup squad outside the building, followed by the remainder of the infiltration team.

When withdrawal has been completed, warning messages will be telephoned to the central switchboard of the hotel, the offices of the *Palestine Post* and the French Consulate.

In the event of an exchange of fire with British troops – there will be an orderly retreat with mutual covering fire. A vehicle will be waiting about 100 yards from the hotel, ready to evacuate any casualties.

---

1. Testimony of Israel Levi, "The Bombing of the King David Hotel," Jabotinsky Archives.

All participants to report at 4:00 PM to the assembly point in Givat Shaul, to hand in weapons before dispersing. Good luck.

As Gidi was going through the plan, in a corner of the room Elimelech Spiegel was conducting a separate briefing, showing Israel Levi, the commander of the operation, and Yanai, his deputy, how to activate the bombs.

Avinoam stood some distance away from the others, by the door. All were listening intently to Gidi, while Elimelech – assembling the mechanisms – continued his lecture in a low voice, explaining the structure of the "milk-churn bomb" and all its components.

> I showed how everything worked and wanted to be sure they were taking it all in. Though Israel was paying attention, I noticed that Yanai wasn't concentrating at all. He kept looking around in all directions; he was like a coiled spring. Every now and then he'd get up from his seat, go to Avinoam, exchange a few words with him and come back looking angry and irritated. As far as I could tell, he was asking to be allowed to go and call a friend, but this was strictly forbidden and as time went on I noticed he was flushed and sweating – a real bundle of nerves. After his tenth – or maybe eleventh – unsuccessful attempt to leave the room my patience ran out and I shouted at him, "Yanai, you're not listening to me, you're going to foul everything up!" I was very angry and I must have raised my voice more than I intended, because the room went quiet suddenly, and Gidi paused and all eyes turned to us. Yanai looked scared and uncomfortable, but finally he pulled himself together and started paying attention to me. It seems he'd realized there was no way he was getting out. It wasn't until months later, when his treachery was revealed, that I understood why he'd been acting that way.[2]

Gidi impatiently glanced at his watch. The time was nine. Two hours to zero hour, and no word from Lehi.

The two operations – the King David Hotel explosion and the attack on David Brothers – were supposed to occur simultaneously. According to the agreement between the operations officers of the two organizations,

---

2. Author's recorded interview with Elimelech Spiegel, January 21, 1997.

Gidi and Yaakov Banai (Mazal), the IZL would go into action three minutes before. There were rumors in the air that Lehi had pulled out of the business, but no official notification had been received. Meanwhile, the clock went on ticking.

Two hours earlier the Lehi operations officer, Yaakov Banai, had set out in a taxi from Tel Aviv to Jerusalem. "Needless to say, knowing my luck," he explained, "as we were speeding along, we had a tire blowout.... I was stuck there for an hour, fuming. I got to Jerusalem at nine, and there's my first surprise: Dov[3] telling me that on the orders of Reuven, the local commander, our operation has been cancelled and the men sent home. I gave him a good dressing down and told him to get the men back pronto and fix me an urgent appointment with Gidi."[4]

At 9:15 AM Dov arrived at Beit Aharon to find Gidi rapidly running out of patience. The subsequent conversation between Gidi and Banai was conducted in raised voices. The latter was asking for a delay of the operation for one day, "so everything will be ready."

Gidi insisted that further delay was out of the question. Banai stood his ground and refused to budge. Gidi was adamant that he couldn't change anything without clearance from above.

The time – 9:30 AM. The operation was scheduled for 11:30 AM. "We agreed to meet again at 10:15," says Banai.[5]

In Beit Aharon final preparations were under way.

The men began changing their clothes, and in a flash there were Arabs in long cloaks and *kafiyyeh*s strolling about the room, alongside garage mechanics in oil-stained overalls, and a swarthy Sudanese in a white robe and red sash. The youths exchanged glances and burst into laughter.[6]

It was time for the distribution of weapons; such an arsenal had never

3.   Dov (better known as Blond Dov) was one of Lehi's most audacious commanders. In the War of Independence he joined 88 Commando Unit and led the assault force that captured the fortress of Irak Souidan from the Egyptians. He fell in 1948 during Operation Horeb in the fight for Ujja el-Hafir (Nitzana).
4.   Ya'akov Banai, *Hayalim almonim* [Unknown soldiers] (Tel Aviv: privately published, 1958), p. 468.
5.   Ibid.
6.   Israel Levi's interview with Avinoam, November 15, 1968, Jabotinsky Archives; Shai, *Kadei ha-halav she-ra'amu.*

before been seen in operations in Jerusalem – a Bren, 5 submachine guns, 11 pistols, 30 grenades, all this in addition to the explosives already loaded on the green van.

And when all were ready for departure, something happened which was most unusual in the ranks of the IZL; with less than ten minutes to spare, one of the team approached Shraga Ellis, his face contorted, hands clutching his stomach, "I can't do it," he groaned, "I've got a terrible pain in the gut…"

"This was a shock for me," said Shraga.

The guy was supposed to be driving the van, transporting the explosives. He'd been chosen for his oriental appearance: in a *jellaba* and a *kafiyyeh* he really looked an authentic Arab. *How the hell am I going to find a replacement now?* I wondered – almost aloud. And then, out of the corner of my eye I saw Yehoshua Goldschmid (Gal) taking the *kafiyyeh* from the driver's head and covering his own blond hair with it. "I'll take his place," he said simply, and before anyone had the chance to discuss it with him, he'd put on the *jellaba*, too.[7]

SETTING OUT

When Gidi returned to Beit Aharon he'd already decided to go ahead as planned, without waiting any longer for Lehi.[8] Too much precious time had been wasted. Because of the dispute with Lehi the operation had already been postponed from eleven to twelve, and from here on every minute could be critical.

At 10:45 AM they set out for the objective.

The blockade groups were the first to leave Beit Aharon, in two pairs, each pair pushing a handcart laden with vegetables – concealing cans of petrol and six and a half pounds (three kilograms) of TNT. One team set out toward the David Brothers building – across the intersection of Yemin Moshe and St. Julian – led by Aharon Sadovnik. He'd been given the job by Yehoshua Gal at seven that morning. "In the event of exchange of fire,"

---

7.   Author's interview with Shraga Ellis, October 1996.

8.   The argument between the operations officer Banai and the local commander Reuven, who resolutely opposed the operation, continued almost until "zero hour." At 11:25 – according to Banai in *Hayalim almonim* – it was clear that Gidi would not be coming back, and they returned to Tel Aviv.

he was told, "you're to push the cart into the middle of the road and set off the petrol and explosives, blocking the way to motorized reinforcements from the south."

His assistant, Nissim Cohen, was playing the part of the Arab "vegetable peddler" with obvious relish. All the way he behaved in authentic urchin style, shoving the hand cart and swinging on it and sometimes riding on it, while Aharon followed, puffing and panting.

A few yards before the intersection Nissim felt "tired" and sat down on the pavement to rest. He fumbled in his pockets and pulled out a cigarette. When the time came, this would be used to light the fuse. Nearby a British policeman was patrolling, armed with a rifle and fixed bayonet; he glanced at them in a bored fashion.[9]

Near the French Consulate building, outside the souvenir shops – where the "telephone girls" were waiting – the northern blockade pair was in position.

Next to set out was the first-aid vehicle, a commandeered taxi driven by Peri (Efraim Lanchansky), "a poor man's ambulance" the boys called it sarcastically. In the back seat Ariela (aka Hadassa Tabak-Sadovnik) clutched the bag of medical supplies and prayed she wouldn't need to use them. The Bren-gun crew also hitched a lift in the taxi which was parked, as agreed, near the filling station to the west of the hotel, at one end of the alley leading to the French Consulate. Peri didn't forget to point the bonnet of the vehicle toward the east – and the temporary clinic in the Old City.

At 11:30 it was the turn of the "porters," five men in oriental garb, led by David Yaakovi (Saul), slim and sharp featured, succinct of speech. "We were told to be at the hotel within half an hour and we caught a number 1 bus to the commercial center. The driver, an old friend, couldn't take his eyes off me; he tried to start a conversation but I pretended I didn't know him and muttered a few sentences in Arabic. He left me alone after that."

Yitzhak Toviana ("Amnon") had a no less embarrassing experience: wearing a *kafiyyeh* and a gown he boarded the bus with his fellow "porters" and found himself sharing a seat with his next-door neighbor. She stared at him in astonishment, asking with a laugh if Purim had come early this year. He replied in Arabic, hastily turning his face away. As he left the bus

---

9. Author's interview with Aharon Sadovnik, November 21, 1998.

she was still muttering something about his "amazing resemblance" to an old friend…

The nickname given to Yosef Avni – "Abu Jilda" (after a notorious Arab bandit of the 1930s) – didn't fit his fatherly and genial appearance. He was the quartermaster, and when he arrived at Beit Aharon, he was told they were short on manpower. He volunteered without hesitation and was attached to the "porters" squad. The others were already on their way to the hotel, so Abu Jilda was given a personal briefing and a bundle of tattered Arab clothing – whatever was left over. He was told to make his way to the alley and await the arrival of the green van.

"I arrived on schedule," he said, "but there was no time to relax – too many soldiers looking at me suspiciously. I started walking up and down, and advised the other 'porters' to do the same. When the van arrived I must have been looking the wrong way and I missed it. I went on waiting…"[10]

At 11:40, just minutes before zero hour, a commercial van, with a green canvas cover, arrived at Beit Aharon. First they loaded up the milk churns – slowly, cautiously, as if handling fragile glass.

And then it was the turn of the assault-and-control party. All eight of them crawled under the green canvas, silently eyeing the explosives. They had been carefully chosen, in accordance with their individual talents: the commander Israel Levi, his deputy Yanai, the volunteer driver Yehoshua Goldschmid (Gal), Aharon Ashkenazi, Yitzhak Tzadok, Aharon Abramovitch, David Yaakovi, and Hanukka Mizrahi.

For some of them this was the first baptism under fire. At all stages of their journey they encountered army and police patrols. "We were ready at any moment to leap out of the vehicle and open fire on the soldiers," said Levi, "and our only worry was that this would hold up the operation." In St. Julian Street (now King David Street) the van turned right, into the alleyway of Emil Botha, site of the French Consulate; to the north of it stretched a wire mesh fence, with a gate set in it. The van and its passengers passed through the gate unchallenged, stopping about 15 yards from the entrance to the basement and kitchen.[11]

From this point onward, events moved quickly.

---

10. *Yediot Aharonot*, July 22, 1966.
11. Israel Levi's interview with Avinoam, March 3, 1967, Jabotinsky Archives.

Two of the youths relieved the Arab watchman of his weapon, while three others ran down the corridor toward La Regence café, securing all the passages and entrances and ushering anyone they came across into the kitchen. Within less than three minutes, all the hotel workers in the vicinity – some 35 of them – had been rounded up and were confined to the kitchen, Abramovitch watching over them with a drawn revolver and Yaakovi keeping guard at the door. The passage to the stairway was guarded by Aharon Ashkenazi, and Tzadok was stationed at the dining-hall door.

No one tried to resist.

The British army intelligence report on the King David Hotel episode and the testimony of Constantin Joanides, the clerk responsible for the receipt of goods at the basement entrance, confirm the speed with which the attackers took control. In the words of the report:

> On 22nd July 1946 I was on duty in the basement of the hotel near the tradesmen's entrance and at approx. 11:45 A M. I remember that a lorry No. M702 drew up to the tradesmen's entrance and stopped. I at once went to the lorry to see what was in it. I saw that it contained between 6 and 7 milk cans. There were also 4 men on the lorry – which is a small vehicle – like a pick up. I asked them for a delivery note and one of the men said to me in Arabic "Taib" which means in English "alright". All the four men were dressed in Arab dress but one [was] wearing clothing like a waiter. I then came back into the building and suddenly saw two of the men walking behind me. One of the men was the "waiter". He was holding a revolver and the other one was carrying a tommy gun. I looked at them and one said to me in Arabic "Uskut" which means "quiet" otherwise you will be killed. They took me to my office…. Then he again left the office for about two minutes and returned again and asked us about the telephone. We again answered him that there was none. Then he left. I then saw through the window of my office a man holding a tommy gun standing at the door of the basement and two other men were carrying the milk cans inside the building. One of them was dragging a sack – it was a large sack – I did not know what was inside the sack.[12]

_____

12. Conclusive report dated August 15, 1946, of the British army's Special Investigations

Taking control took less time than had been expected, and was less problematical. But there was no sign of the "porters" who were supposed to be unloading the milk churns and carrying them into the basement. Time was passing and Levi couldn't afford to wait.

> I called off the guard who was watching the stairs and told him to cover both entrances, and the other three I told to start unloading the churns from the van. In the end, we all did our share of the portering – assault party, drivers, commander of the operation – everyone available. We loaded the dangerous cargo on our shoulders – seven churns packed with TNT, a total weight of about 880 pounds (400 kilograms). We carried them in pairs into the basement, then dragged them along the corridor to La Regence café – a distance of about 50 yards. We made the journey three times, praying the awful racket wouldn't be heard by the British sentries. When the "porters" finally showed up, the job was already done.[13]

When Levi began putting the mechanism together he discovered to his astonishment that the detonators were missing. They had been in Yanai's pocket, and Yanai was standing there pale and agitated, claiming he must have lost them while helping to unload the churns from the van. Yehoshua Gal, standing nearby, kept a cool head. "You come with me," he said to Yanai and gripped his arm firmly, "We're going to search every inch of the ground until we find them."

The detonators turned up, scattered on the floor in the basement entrance, "I don't know, I don't understand…" Yanai muttered apologetically, but no one was paying any attention to him. Levi got down to the work of assembly without delay:[14] He had to replace the plugs with the chemical apparatus and insert the inverted bottles, fit the mechanical clocks and wind them up fully, check the churns were standing on a level surface, and

---

Branch (hereafter SIB) on the King David Hotel episode (CID docs., HHA 8138 A) and statement of Constantin Joanides to the Mandatory Police the day after the incident (HHA 32/68138).

13. Israel Levi's survey of the operation, Jabotinsky Archives.
14. Author's interview of Aharon Sadovnik, who heard of the detonator episode from Yehoshua Gal.

withdraw the pins from the anti-handling devices. He remembered what Spiegel had told him just an hour before in Beit Aharon. "You're going to need nerves of steel and a lot of patience if you're going to get it done on time, without messing up the sequence." He took a deep breath: he knew this was the most critical stage.

Yanai was on the verge of despair. His hopes of communicating with his employers had been dashed, and now that his attempt to sabotage the operation had failed, he tried another ploy, shouting loudly, "They're on to us, soldiers coming!" and pointed to the tents pitched in the hotel yard where the guard detachments were billeted. Levi stopped work for a moment and joined his deputy in the basement entrance. However much he strained his eyes, he saw no sign of soldiers approaching. "Stay close to me," he told Yanai, "and you'll come to no harm." He asked Hanukka Mizrahi to keep an eye on him. "I didn't suspect him," he said, "not yet. I was just afraid his anxiety might be infectious."

THE MACKINTOSH INCIDENT

Behind a door opening onto the staircase leading down to the basement, six British WRAC girls, commanded by Sergeant Brown, were operating the military telephone exchange. None of the attackers knew of the existence of the exchange – not even Aharon, who had been ordered to guard that entrance.

What happened in those crucial minutes is described by Sergeant Brown:

> A few minutes before 12 o'clock mid-day on 22nd July 1946, Capt. Mackintosh, Royal Signals, brought her an official letter into the exchange. He left the exchange at 12 o'clock, leaving by way of the grill door, which leads into the hotel basement corridor. Two or three minutes after he left Sgt. Brown went to close the grill door and lock it from the inside. However, when she got to the door she saw two men dressed in khaki clothing with Transjordan Arab head dress forcing Capt. Mackintosh at the point of a tommy gun along the corridor towards the South East end of the building. The person armed with the tommy gun saw Sgt. Brown, went towards her and ordered her back. She did as she was ordered and when she got back into the exchange she called the

Maintenance Signalman, then telephoned No. 4 Security Post, the Military Police and then the Duty Signals Officer, informing them of what was happening.[15]

Aharon was the first to see the officer descending the stairs. For a moment he froze.

> Suddenly this big British officer comes out of a door on the staircase and heads straight toward me. A real giant, must have been nearly seven feet tall and weighed more than 200 pounds. As for me – well, even now I'm not exactly huge – but back then I was just a minnow. I'd ditched school that day, skipped an exam. Anyway, I pulled a gun on him and told him to put his hands up. He tried to knock the gun out of my hand and started back up the stairs. I wanted to shoot him but our orders were clear: get the bombs planted without attracting attention. I ran after him and grabbed his belt, and we both fell down and started wrestling. I had no choice – I pulled the trigger and that stopped him.[16]

Muhammad Ahmad Abu Saleb, a porter employed by the hotel and a witness to the Mackintosh incident, said in his statement to the police, that soon after twelve noon he heard something like a fight going on in the hotel basement and went to investigate.[17] He saw a British officer climbing the stairs with a man on his back, wearing a white "kombaz," a red sash, and a tarboosh. Under the kombaj he was wearing khaki shorts. The officer was holding on to a long-barreled pistol and trying to wrest it from the grip of the man on his back. He managed to climb about a dozen stairs and then two other armed men came along and grabbed his legs, pulling him down. The officer fell, and during the struggle he was shot at close range by the man who had been wrestling with him.

The witness said that he contacted Army HQ and told them what was happening. Then he returned to the basement and was pushed into the

---

15. Sergeant Brown's statement to SIB military investigator (CID docs., HHA 8138/41/A).
16. *Yediot Aharonot*, July 22, 1966.
17. CID documents on the King David Hotel episode, also SIB report dated August 15, 1946 (HHA 8138/A).

kitchen where the other members of the maintenance staff were being held. In a sudden fit of panic, he switched off the refrigerator and climbed into it.

While all this was happening, Israel Levi (Gideon) went on dragging milk churns to La Regence café. He didn't hear the sound of gunfire and had no inkling of the Mackintosh incident. He was concentrating on one project only: setting the explosive charges in the right places – and activating them. It was for this he'd been chosen to command the operation, and he was determined to do it without being distracted by problems; there had been no shortage of these, ranging from the non-appearance of the porters to his deputy's failure of nerve. The clock was ticking, and time was short. When he passed Aharon he noticed nothing out of the ordinary. "Come and help with the unloading," he commanded, grabbing another churn.

Later, when questioned by Avinoam about the incident, he shrugged almost apologetically. "I was totally occupied with the churns. I remember there was some whispering going on among our guys, but there was no time to investigate and I didn't want to know about problems. All I wanted was to get the job done quickly, and done properly."[18]

But the Mackintosh incident had far-reaching implications and came close to wrecking the whole operation.

In his book *The Palestine Triangle*, Nicholas Bethell describes the operation as courageous, but also as "a wretched combination of efficiency and negligence." Although it seems that in the circumstances there really was no alternative but to shoot Mackintosh, how could it be that the planners of the operation had no knowledge of the existence of the military telephone exchange? And an even more serious mistake – why was Sergeant Brown allowed to return to the exchange, and not confined to the kitchen with the others, as per instructions?

Whatever the explanation might be, Sergeant Brown's return to the exchange led to dramatic and unexpected developments. Just a few minutes were the difference between a successful mission and abject failure, even the elimination of the participants. Only the technical skills of the commander, Israel Levi, and his uncompromising commitment to the objective, together with the resourcefulness of the other young men, covered

---

18. Avinoam's recorded interview with Israel Levi, November 15, 1968, Jabotinsky Institute.

over the cracks of incompetence and gave them the two or three minutes that would prove decisive.

Sergeant Brown wasted no time. She put on her headphones immediately and contacted Royal Signals HQ and the Military Police, informing them of the attack on Captain Mackintosh and calling for armed reinforcements. "Don't come by way of the corridor," she warned. "The Arabs are still there." When she had made her calls she glanced at her watch: 12:05.[19]

They all arrived at once, skirting the corridor and climbing into the exchange by way of the window overlooking the garden. Lieutenant Chambers appeared a couple of minutes later, accompanied by two corporals armed with tommy guns, at almost the same time as the machine gunner from number 4 security detachment. Through the mesh of the exchange window overlooking the basement, Chambers tried to get a clear view of the corridor leading to La Regence. Two men in Arab Legion headdress turned their tommy guns on him and he stepped back hastily. Then he called the duty signals officer and informed him "that preparatory action could be taken in the event of a breakdown of line communications." By the time he steeled himself to take another look out of the window, the IZL team had already left the building. The corridor was deserted but still he didn't dare venture into the basement, and it wasn't until he heard the all-clear siren that he returned to his office – and then came the great explosion that shook Jerusalem.

Lieutenant Chambers didn't forget his military training. He was sure that the blast would be followed by an all-out assault on the building, and he immediately organized a defensive cordon around the offices – or what was left of them. He was proud of his quick thinking and initiative, and didn't omit to mention them in his statement the following day.[20]

Sergeant Tilley of the Military Police, accompanied by three soldiers, hopped into a jeep and headed for the telephone exchange, approaching from the rear of the hotel. Sergeant Devonald of the Intelligence Corps arrived on the scene soon after. The report that a British officer had been shot in the hotel basement reached Captain Fayne of the general staff of

---

19. Sergeant Brown's statement to the police – CID docs., HHA 8138 A.
20. CID docs., HHA 8138/A (8).

the Palestine Police at 12:05. A summary of his description of subsequent events follows:

> Accompanied by Major Nichols...I was directed by some person to the Ladies' toilet room, where I saw the officer, Capt. Mackintosh, Royal Signals, lying on the floor with a gunshot wound in the stomach. He was being attended to by two of the Hotel waiters, who were applying cold water packs to the wound. The officer was conscious but appeared very dazed. Major Nichols questioned him as to how he had come by his injury, and he replied, "An Arab shot me outside the military [telephone] exchange. At that time a shot was fired and appeared to have come from the direction of the staff entrance in the basement, immediately below the window of the Ladies' Toilet Room. We both looked through the window and I saw a person dressed like an Arab, i.e., striped ghalabia, white hatta and black agal, in the area immediately beneath the window. He fired a shot in our direction and we both took cover behind the windows. Major Nichols drew his pistol and fired a single shot at this man,[21] who was then running towards the gate of the drive leading to the staff entrance. Immediately after this a burst was fired from a TSMG [tommy gun].
>
> I looked into the Ladies' Toilet Room and noticed that Capt. Mackintosh had been taken away. I then made my way to the hotel main lounge.... Whilst conversing with...an officer...and a corporal... [from] Tel Litwinsky...a terrific explosion occurred.... The North West corner of the building, housing the offices of the Secretariat...had been completely demolished.[22]

Sergeant Petty, of security position no. 1, received Brown's message and set out at once for the basement, ignoring the advice to avoid the corridor. When he reached the service entrance he was fired on from outside, apparently by Yehoshua Gal on his way to the van. "I saw a man dressed in a white and blue check *gellabia*, standing in the doorway with a Sten. He shouted: 'Halt! Halt!' I jumped back behind the corner. No more shots were fired. I went back to the entrance and saw a lorry, and the man who had

---

21. Nichols later identified the late Aharon Abramovitch as the man who shot at him.
22. Conclusive report of SIB dated August 15, 1946 – HHA 8138/A.

shot at me crouched down behind it on the far side. He got up and fired at me again with his Sten."

Sergeant Petty was forced to take cover. He made his way to the telephone exchange and from there to the garden, where he met Lieutenant-Colonel Campbell.[23]

A few minutes before this, Barber, the machine gunner, had reported the Mackintosh incident to Campbell, and they both set out to inspect the scene. "When [we were] about level with the Telephone Exchange," Campbell said, "a bomb exploded. I could not see where the explosion actually occurred…. [A] telephone operator…leaning out of the window of the telephone exchange…asked if they – the telephone operators – should get out of the building. Thinking that there might be another explosion I ordered them out of the exchange…. When they were out, I told them to go through the garden to the rear of the annexe." At the basement entrance he came across a huddle of confused and fretful hotel workers, but he couldn't get any hard information out of them. Of the attackers there was no sign.[24]

WRAPPING IT UP

The southern wing of the King David Hotel, where the British administration had taken up residence, was supported by La Regence café. It stood, in fact, on precarious foundations – like the whole of the Mandatory structure in this country. All the supporting pillars of that building had their base in that exclusive café, and Levi took care to position the seven milk churns around the central pillar, on which the entire ceiling was supported. Only when the timing and anti-handling devices had been fitted to his satisfaction did he allow himself a sigh of relief. Whatever happens now, he thought, there's no power on earth that can stop the explosions. He glanced for the last time at the "ticking churns" – and gave the signal to withdraw.[25]

Throughout the operation, Israel Levi had kept calm and stuck doggedly to the task. Even after the essentials of the mission had been completed, he still felt obliged to carry on according to plan and not to overlook the smallest detail. Before leaving the scene, he personally instructed the hotel workers confined in the kitchen to wait five minutes and then run

23. CID docs., HHA 8138/A (23).
24. CID docs., HHA 8137/A (24).
25. Avinoam's interview with Israel Levi, March 3, 1967, Jabotinsky Archives.

for their lives via the northern exit. They were also asked to warn anyone else they met along the way that there were bombs in the basement and the building was about to go up.

As he was walking slowly up the steep ascent to the outside gate accompanied by Yehoshua Gal and Yanai, he suddenly spotted the abandoned van. *Never leave equipment in enemy territory*, he remembered the iron rule that he himself used to instill in his subordinates, and immediately ordered Gal to return to the vehicle and drive it to the base. He didn't like leaving loose ends.

Outside, for the moment there was no disruption of the daily routine. No one was aware of the drama that had been played out just minutes before. Levi waved distractedly at the telephone girls, waiting in St. Julian Street near the alleyway leading to the French Consulate. But before he had time to cross the street, the rattle of submachine guns echoed in the void. "I turned toward the source of the gunfire," he said, "and saw Gal and two of our fellows who'd been left in the building dashing toward the first aid vehicle, while returning fire at the windows of the hotel. It happened quickly and before I realized what was going on, they'd already disappeared in the emergency vehicle. I was consoled by the thought that we'd all be meeting again soon, as planned, in one of the western suburbs of Jerusalem."[26]

While Gal was on his way to the van, gunfire was suddenly heard from the hotel basement. Still there on the ground floor at that time were Aharon Abramovitch (Avidor), Yitzhak Tzadok (Kastina), and David Yaakovi (Saul). They were on their way out when a British officer, one of those alerted by Sergeant Brown, became suspicious of the three "Arabs" walking around openly carrying arms, and ordered them to halt. Tzadok fired first; the officer fired back. Gal abandoned the van and went to help them. The sounds of gunfire alerted the guard detachments and a hail of bullets was aimed at the fugitives.

Gal emptied his magazine firing at the soldiers, and the others made a dash for the exit. Aharon Ashkenazi said:

At that moment we came under fire from windows on the upper floors. Avidor was running beside me and he took a whole volley of bullets.

---

26. Testimony of Israel Levi, "The Bombing of the King David Hotel," Jabotinsky Archives.

He stumbled, shouting, "I can't go on!" I supported him, but he was a big, heavy guy and we hardly made it to the taxi. He had to sit on Yaakovi's lap – there was no room for me. I threw my pistol inside and the car shot away like something out of a James Bond movie. I ran all the way to Yemin Moshe, threw my Arab disguise in a well, and carried on walking to the Bethlehem road. From there I got a bus to Jaffa Gate.[27]

After the exchange of fire in the basement, Tzadok and Abramovitch continued their retreat, hoping to cover the remaining ground safely. Buckell, one of the machine gunners, saw them running and opened fire. "Suddenly," said Tzadok. "they were strafing us with automatic fire; we found shelter in some abandoned building in the garden. Abramovitch went out first and got a bellyful of bullets. I returned fire with the Sten and made a dash for the road. I got a bullet in the leg and fell, but got up and managed to make it to the first aid vehicle."[28]

Yaakovi was about 15 yards from the exit gate in the fence, when he heard an English shout of "Halt!" Out of the corner of his eye he saw Tzadok turn and fire. The two of them began running as bullets whistled around them. Suddenly Tzadok was limping. Yaakovi urged him on, "Faster!" "I can't," he replied. "I've been hit." Amnon turned on his heel and supported him as far as the taxi, which by now was full. There were seven crammed into it, plus Abu Jilda, who was hanging on the running board.

At the road intersection to the south of the hotel, Aharon Sadovnik and the tired "vegetable peddler" Nissim had been waiting patiently for nearly an hour, and nothing had happened.

Suddenly gunfire was heard.

"That's it!" said Sadovnik.

Nissim lit the fuse with a smoldering cigarette and pushed the cart into the middle of the road.

They both turned toward Yemin Moshe. They walked at first, then broke into a run. In Yemin Moshe Nissim stripped off his oriental disguise, and Aharon took off his *kafiyyeh* and wrapped his pistol and bullets in it.

---

27. *Yediot Aharonot*, July 22, 1966; Avinoam's interview with Israel Levi, March 3, 1967, Jabotinsky Archives.
28. Radio program, n. 7 above.

As they were on their way to the central station, they heard the thunderous detonation as the incendiaries and explosives on the vegetable cart went up, but they didn't turn to look and half an hour later they were on a crowded Arab bus, heading for Jaffa.[29]

> Moshe Barazani, a member of Lehi (Fighters for the Freedom of Israel) was captured on Sunday, March 9, 1947, at a road intersection in Jerusalem, with a Mills grenade in his pocket. His target was the commander of the Ninth Division, Brigadier Davis, who used to drive past this point every evening. This took place during the period when martial law was in force, and within less than a week, in a trial lasting just an hour and a half, he was sentenced to death by a military court. When the sentence was announced he sang "Hatikva" and shouted to his judges, "You won't scare us with hangings!" On April 21, 1947, he blew himself up together with his comrade Meir Feinstein – a few minutes before the hangman was due to do his work.

The heroism of these two mesmerized the Yishuv, and the poet Natan Alterman, not a supporter of underground movements, gave expression to this in his *Tur ha-Shevi'i* [Seventh Column] ("Night of the Suicides," *Davar*, April 25, 1947), in part as follows:

> We cannot avert our eyes. Futile to deny
> The glory of that night hour.

At about 12:10 Constantin Joanides, a captive in his own office, pressed the alarm button. "At that time an employee…came in through the door and the armed men took her to the kitchen. I took this chance and pressed on the alarm," he said.

> Five minutes later I saw a young chap wearing a blue shirt and long green trousers. He was bareheaded. I could not see his face. He had curly black hair. He was running in and when he reached the door he spoke in Hebrew to the armed man who went in. When they reached the door I heard them speak in Hebrew to those who were in my office

---

29. Author's interview with Aharon Sadovnik, November 21, 1998.

and left the building. I was told that they said "finish". Later I saw a British Sergeant I think of the Army follow the armed man to the door. The armed Jew with the tommy gun turned back and fired some shots in the Sergeant's direction. The Sergeant returned into the entrance. I then heard some shots being fired from the hotel building directed towards the armed men. About three minutes later I heard the first explosion. Then I heard the siren. We all left the building and went into the road near the tradesmen's entrance.... I do not know when I sounded the alarm but I can say it was about 15–20 minutes before the second explosion.[30]

The alarm signal activated by Constantin came over loud and clear in the police emergency room. A radio car, commanded by Inspector Hadingham,[31] was immediately dispatched to the scene, arriving just as the "handcart bomb" went off near Salameh's office on St. Julian Street, about 50 yards from the King David Hotel. All the office windows were blown out. At 12:20 the emergency room sounded a general alarm siren. Within a few minutes police investigators arrived and concluded the damage caused wasn't serious – and at 12:31 the all-clear was sounded.

The other incendiary device was soon found, in a street to the north of the hotel, outside an Indian tailor's shop. It was defused and caused no damage.[32]

Lieutenant Tilley was the last to arrive in response to Sergeant Brown's appeal. He came rushing up with three more men in an army jeep, skirting the front of the hotel and heading for the telephone exchange.

In the process he noticed six men in Arab clothing, running down the road in a southwesterly direction. He had time to see them clambering into a blue taxi, without license plates, which raced off toward the Old City. Lieutenant Tilley set out in pursuit, but after a few minutes of careering through narrow alleyways he despaired of catching up and the chase was abandoned.[33]

Peri pressed the accelerator hard down to the floor. In the rear-view

30. Conclusive report of SIB dated August 15, 1946 (CID docs., HHA 8138/A).
31. Hadingham served as Commander of Police, Jerusalem Region, in 1946.
32. Nicholas Bethell, *The Palestine Triangle: The Struggle between the British, the Jews and the Arabs, 1935–48* (London: Andre Deutsch, 1979), pp. 209–10.
33. CID docs., HHA 8138/A.

mirror he could clearly see the army jeep trying to catch him, and it took all his maneuvering skill to evade the pursuer. In the commercial center he stopped for a few moments and those who were still in one piece got out of the vehicle. "There were three of us who got out there," Yaakovi recalled.

> Amnon, Abu Jilda, and me. I started ripping off my clothes (we were wearing khaki underneath). People gathered around and stared, seeing Arabs suddenly turning into Jews. There was a bit of commotion, but no one dared come near us. Each of us got away by a different route. I went in the direction of Musrara, heading for Meah Shearim, and I remember as I ran I was pursued by an Arab shouting, "Hajji, your glasses have fallen off…" I ran until I was near the Edison cinema and then I heard the explosion. I dashed across the Musrara neighborhood and ran through Meah Shearim to David Yellin Street. It was only then I realized I was covered in blood – Abramovitch's blood. He'd been sitting in my lap in the taxi. I changed my clothes at a friend's house and went to my hotel. Later I got dressed again and set off for Givat Shaul. On the way there were already roadblocks in place but my forged papers stood up to inspection. I was the first to get to Tel Aviv and give an account of the operation at Ha-Tir Club.[34]

Abu Jilda only became aware that the operation had started when it was over. He was still standing there, waiting for the van, when the first shots were fired. Only then did he realize he'd missed the whole event. He saw Abramovitch slumped over the first aid vehicle and helped to put him inside, then perched on the running board of the taxi. As they drove he stripped off his disguise and in the commercial center he jumped down from the vehicle and caught a bus. At that precise moment the alarm siren was heard and all traffic ground to a halt. He continued on foot, bitterly disappointed. "I was sure the operation had failed," he said later. "In fact, I was so upset I didn't even hear the explosions…"

He reached Givat Shaul in a despondent mood.[35]

As Tzadok and Abramovitch were stumbling – both wounded in the

---

34. Aviezer Golan's interview with David Yaakovi, *Yediot Aharonot*, July 20, 1966.
35. Radio program, n. 7 above; *Yediot Aharonot*, July 22, 1966.

exchanges of fire – towards the first aid vehicle, Yehoshua Gal was still be-hind the van covering their retreat. Suddenly the shooting stopped and si-lence returned. He realized he was alone there – all the others had already left the scene. When he turned towards the exit, he found it blocked by a squad of soldiers. He threw away his Sten, hid his pistol behind his blue overalls and approached the Tommies, calling out in halting English, with an Arab accent, "Jews put bombs…go that way…," pointing in the direc-tion of the basement. They charged off in the direction he had indicated, and Gal continued on his way towards the road.[36]

THE WARNING

One of the toughest roles was that assigned to the "telephone girls" – Sarah Goldschmid-Agassi and Adina Hai Nisan. They had to wait on the pave-ment outside the hotel while the drama was unfolding in the basement. "When the last of our fighters leaves the building, you're to dash to the phone and pass on the warning," they had been told.

Of the two of them, Sarah's was the more awkward predicament – sud-denly seeing her brother (Yehoshua Goldschmid [Gal]) driving the van. He wasn't supposed to be taking part in the operation at all, and she had no knowledge of the last-minute switch that had occurred.

The youths soon began emerging from the basement, and then the shooting started too. Sarah saw a Bren on the hotel roof opening fire, and Abramovitch jerking spasmodically as the bullets hit home, making a last, desperate effort to stagger to the taxi and collapsing in the doorway. A mo-ment later her brother appeared, running. "I think I've been hit," he panted, "my chest is all wet." She put her hand inside his overall and let out a sigh of relief: it was only sweat. "I've got a pistol here and some stun grenades," he whispered in her ear. She took them from him without hesitation. The stun grenades she discarded in an empty lot, but she kept the revolver.

Adina saw Israel Levi give the agreed signal and hurried to carry out her assignment. She turned to the nearby pharmacy, which she had pre-viously checked out herself, and when the proprietor came running out, on hearing the sound of the exploding incendiary bombs, she seized the opportunity to slip inside and dial the number of the King David Hotel switchboard. She read the text of the message in Hebrew and in English,

---

36. Testimony of Israel Levi, "The Bombing of the King David Hotel," Jabotinsky Archives.

following Avinoam's instructions, "I'm speaking on behalf of the Hebrew Underground. We have planted bombs in the King David Hotel. You must evacuate immediately. You have been warned!"

From there she hurried to a telephone booth on King George Street, and called the French Consulate. She repeated the previous message word for word but added, "You are advised to open your windows. We have warned the hotel – please warn them again."

Without waiting for a reply she put the receiver down and ran to the nearby paint store to phone the editorial office of the *Palestine Post*.

All the telephoned warnings were the work of Adina, but Sarah stayed by her side until the job was done. "I had to stick with her, as a backup in case anything prevented her carrying it through."

Then Adina made her way to the Mahaneh Yehuda district and took refuge among relatives. Sarah ran to her father's shop, which was just around the corner.

> I persuaded him to come home with me; we were living then in Givat Shaul, and all traffic was at a standstill (the sirens had started wailing immediately after the exchange of shots outside the hotel). We went on foot. When we reached Mahaneh Yehuda we heard the explosions. I looked at my watch: 12:35. We carried on to Romema. A roadblock had been set up and people were being searched, but out of respect for my father's age they didn't stop us.[37]

Mrs. Deborah Podensky (Lindner) was the telephone operator who received the warning call from the IZL at the editorial office of the *Palestine Post*; Miss Miriam Cohen, the editorial secretary, was also present. Subsequently, they were both subjected to prolonged interrogation on the part of the CID, clearly intended to squeeze false statements out of them regarding the times of the warnings – statements that would serve the purposes of the authorities and of their official reports. But to no avail: all efforts to put words into their mouths proved fruitless.

This didn't prevent the British authorities publishing on August 15, 1946, in an official report from the Special Investigations Branch of Army Intelligence, a distorted version of the statements that the two of them had made

---

37. Author's interview with Sarah Goldschmid-Agassi; *Yediot Aharonot*, July 22, 1966.

to the police. According to the report, "Miss Miriam Cohen confirms the fact that the time the message was received was after the all-clear siren was heard at 12:31. It is therefore evident that the warning was issued between 12:31 and 12:37, the latter being the time of the explosion."

The author of the report went on to suggest that copies of this should be distributed "to all interested parties in Army Staff, Palestine."

In their interrogation by the police July 26 and 29, 1946, both Deborah Lindner and Miriam Cohen insisted they didn't remember the exact time the message was received. "It was definitely after twelve," said Miriam Cohen, while stressing the fact that she hadn't heard the first explosion – nor the alarm and all-clear sirens that had followed it.[38]

Deborah Lindner made the point that at the time the message was received she wasn't wearing a watch and there was no clock in the office, so she couldn't be sure exactly when all this happened. The following is her statement (translated by the CID from Hebrew into English), as recorded by the investigating police officer (Erwin Reindner, no. 1263) on July 29, 1946:

> I started work on Monday the 22nd of July 1946 at 8 A M. I had no watch with me. During the hours of mid day I heard an alarm signal and afterwards the "all clear" siren…. During that time I received a telephone [call] from a girl, who talked not very well English: "Jewish Resistance Movement. We just put bombs under the King David Hotel. They were warned". I did not wish to take the responsibility on myself and told her, "Just hold on". She replied to it, "I have not got time". MIRIAM COHEN who is a Secretary, stood behind me and I let her receive the announcement. She received correctly the same announcement like I received it. The girl closed the telephone at once…. MIRIAM COHEN rang up No. 4321 and informed the Duty Officer of Police HQ about the announcement. That is all…. As I said before, I had no private watch with me and there is also no watch in my working room. I can not know when all the matter happened.[39]

Twenty-six years later – in a Kol Israel radio program – Deborah Podensky

---

38. CID docs., HHA 8138/A (15).
39. Ibid.

(Lindner) repeated her assertion that the warning was indeed received at around midday and immediately passed on to the British: "I remember that at about twelve a girl phoned me and, speaking very quickly, asked me to warn the King David Hotel that there were explosives in the basement. She added that they'd already been warned. My instructions were to pass on any communication from the underground, so I phoned the British headquarters without delay and informed the officer on duty."[40]

THE GETAWAY

Hadassah, the pretty combat nurse, was sitting in the taxi during those frantic moments, watching the kitchen entrance of the hotel, the first-aid kit on her knees. "You're to wait until the last of the boys have come out" had been the unequivocal order. It was a relief when she saw the comrades emerging. And then the shooting started and everything around her was moving with dizzying speed.

Abramovitch reached the door of the taxi and almost fell into her lap. "Quick, get in!" she yelled at him, so scared she barely recognized her own voice. "I'm all shot up," he groaned, and then she saw that Tzadok was limping too; a couple of the boys helped to cram them inside. At that moment Gal came running. "That's the lot!" he panted, "Get going!" Peri stepped on the gas and the car sped away.

At the corner of Mamilla Street all the uninjured got out. Hadassah was left alone with the driver, the two casualties, and the weapons. They turned towards the Old City. Their instructions were to go via Zion Gate, but the driver lost his way, and they found themselves facing Jaffa Gate.

By this time the alarm siren was sounding. "In front of us was a truck loaded with wood," Peri recalled. "Hadassah shouted: 'Go on, overtake it!' but I told her to shut up. 'We mustn't be overheard speaking Hebrew,' I said. I just had to crawl along behind it, as the streets were very narrow and there were a lot of holdups. The police were checking all vehicles. It was too late to think about changing plans, and with the traffic jammed up there was no way I could turn back."

Hadassah glanced nervously at Abramovitch; he was losing a lot of blood and drifting in and out of consciousness. "I bent over him," she said, "using my skirt to cover his wounds as best I could. It seems the police were

---

40. Radio program, n. 7 above.

amused by the spectacle of a Jewish girl smooching with a couple of Arabs and they waved us through. We drove on at a maddeningly slow pace, with Arabs peering at us and laughing."

It wasn't only Arabs who glanced: a Jewish passerby, a friend of the family, recognized Hadassah and couldn't believe what he was seeing: a girl of good family, from an Orthodox household, lounging with a young Arab in the back of a taxi, in a highly suggestive manner. "What's the world coming to?" he muttered to himself. Later that evening, he told her father what he had seen, and when she returned home, pale and exhausted, all her mortified father had to say to her, in a broken voice, was, "As you make your bed, so you must lie upon it..." Having been sworn to secrecy, she couldn't explain what had happened and she fled the room in tears. It wasn't until months later that he discovered the truth and humbly begged his daughter's forgiveness.[41]

In the improvised clinic, a rented room in the Old City, the nurse, Noa (the nickname of Tzipora Ashkenazi), was waiting for the casualties. Abramovitch's condition was deteriorating, and a doctor had to be found for him without delay. Noa had a taxi at her disposal and the two girls set out to call on the services of Dr. Yitzhak Heffner. "We told Peri to drive in front of us," Hadassah recalled. "His vehicle was stained with the blood of the wounded, and we decided if there were any problems, he'd abandon it and join us. And sure enough, on Mamilla Street we came across a police roadblock, and he stopped and joined us."

The time was 12:50 PM, and some of the Arabs who saw the driver abandon the vehicle and run away flew into a panic and began yelling that the Jews had left a car loaded with explosives in the street. A few minutes later the police arrived and on searching the vehicle found a number of pistols, a tommy gun, Arab clothing, and a few grenades. The back seat was covered in blood.[42]

Dr. Heffner was the unofficial physician to the IZL and Lehi underground in Jerusalem. When the two girls reached him, they found him with his medical case, ready to leave.

---

41. Author's interview with Aharon Sadovnik, 1998.
42. SIB report dated August 15, 1946 – HHA 8138/A.

A while before they'd informed me some operation was imminent, and I made sure I was prepared for any contingency," he said. "I didn't know yet what was happening. They told me I had to go with them to the Old City, so I went…. They took me to a room where two young men were lying, still wearing Arab *jellaba*s. One of them, Aharon Abramovitch, I recognized. He'd taken a full clip of bullets in the stomach and I knew at once I couldn't save him. I gave him a pain-killing injection and that was all I could do. The other one couldn't walk. He'd taken one bullet, which had penetrated the knee and severed the tendons…. I was about to start treating him when one of the girls started shouting, "The British are coming!"

"I heard the noise of the soldiers' boots," said Hadassah, "and the barking dogs, too. I climbed out through the window and escaped. In the street there were boys of 14 and 15, keeping watch…and it was they who warned us the soldiers were coming."[43]

Yitzhak Tzadok was known at that time as "Kastina," named after the air-field which had been the target of IZL attack. As a professional carpenter he'd had no trouble finding a job in a British army camp in the south of the country. This was his weekly day off and he'd chosen to spend it in the night club of the King David Hotel – at midday, a fact which would have surprised his British employers if they had only known. They were to find out about it soon enough. Meanwhile, he was lying bleeding in a bare room in the Old City, his unconscious friend dying beside him.

Dr. Heffner gave both men pain-killing injections and the nurses did their best for them. When the warning came through that the army had cordoned off the area and was searching house-to-house, they asked Tzadok if he could walk. He tried – but sank back again with a gasp of pain. The women and the doctor left, and Tzadok was alone with Abramovitch. As he relates:

He was opposite me on the stretcher-bed; I was on a mattress on the floor. He asked me how I felt and I said, "Fine," and I asked him how

---

43. Radio program, n. 7 above.

he felt and he said, "Fine, everything's okay…" And we carried on like that for some time…asking questions and giving reassuring answers…

After about two hours he stopped breathing. He died at two in the morning. His eyes stayed wide open. I admit it was a bit scary. The room was bare, dark, and sealed, and it was as if in all the world there was just the two of us: Abramovitch, who was dead, and me.

Early next morning the British found us (acting, I think, on a tip). They broke down the door and burst in with revolvers drawn. First of all they checked out Abramovitch, pinching his ring and his wristwatch, and then they turned their attention to me. They set about giving me a sound thrashing – but when they found the Army identity card in my pocket, they called their sergeant. He recognized me from the camp and ordered them to take me down to the jeep. They drove me to the Kishleh and from there to the Russian Compound. They kept me there for 31 days, strapped to a bed, before they operated on me and took the bullet out of my leg. They never interrogated me as such, but they put me in a lineup, bringing in two Jewish carpenters from the King David who knew me very well but pretended they'd never seen me before. I was suspected of involvement in the attack, but it couldn't be proved, so I didn't stand trial. One day they transferred me to Latrun, and from there – to Kenya."[44]

In an intelligence report dated August 15, 1946, there is no hint of the circumstances surrounding the discovery of the room, and of Tzadok and Abramovitch. All it says is that "At dawn on Tuesday, July 23, 1946, a combined force of military and police personnel conducted wide-ranging searches in the Old City district of Jerusalem, and at 0930 two Jewish terrorists were discovered in a classroom on the second floor of the Talmud Torah school in the Jewish Quarter. One was dead, and the other had gunshot wounds to the knee. The deceased was later identified by Major Nichols as the man who fired at him. This individual had been under police surveillance for some time."

The commander of the operation was not involved in the exchange of fire. He heard the sound of shooting from the hotel at the very moment he saw

---

44. Ibid.; *Yediot Aharonot*, July 22, 1966.

the two girls hurrying away to complete their task. He turned towards the YMCA building nearby and there, behind a stone wall, he stripped off his Arab gear – Sudanese *jellaba*, broad red sash and tarboosh – and stowed it all under a boulder. In khaki shorts and white shirt he continued on foot to Rehavia. Near the Rejwan building he handed over his weapon – a revolver – to two young IZL members waiting for him there and turned towards his home in Nachalat Achim.

Israel Levi wasted no time. He told his mother he had to go to Tel Aviv for a while, and immediately set out for Givat Shaul.[45] This place had been chosen on the assumption that following the explosion a curfew would be imposed and all routes out of the city sealed. From Givat Shaul there was a way through to Motza, and from there there was a bus service to Tel Aviv. Almost all the participants in the operation arrived there, reported, and were sent out of Jerusalem. On arrival in Tel Aviv they turned to Ha-Tir Club at the seashore, and there they were told to go and "get lost" for a while, preferably in kibbutzim.

Only three failed to make the rendezvous: the two casualties and the deputy commander of the operation – Yanai. Israel was under strict instructions to debrief all those involved in the action and prepare a thorough report for the national operations officer; rumors about the two casualties reached him during the evening, but he was still waiting for Yanai.

Meanwhile the sirens were blaring and a general curfew had been imposed on the capital. Army and police patrols were prowling the streets, arresting suspects, and all routes in and out of the city were sealed. Under these circumstances it was unwise to try to get to Tel Aviv, and the problem was where to find a refuge for the night. What could be safer than an asylum for the mentally ill? Such an institution was not far away, and its staff were known to be IZL sympathizers.

All this time Abu Jilda stayed close by Israel's side. He was in a despondent frame of mind, convinced that the operation had failed and blaming himself. They set off together, heading for the asylum. "I must have said something about failure," Abu Jilda recalled, "and Israel stared at me. 'What failure?' he said. 'The bloody hotel's not there anymore...' I was so overjoyed I started dancing and leaping around, and if the warden of the asylum had seen me at that moment – he'd have admitted me as a patient."

---

45. "The Day the Hotel Fell Down," *Ha-aretz*, May 1979 [Hebrew].

They were warmly welcomed by staff and inmates alike and were given not only accommodation for the night but "appropriate disguises" as well. "I was obliged to put on ragged clothing and battered orthopedic shoes, and my appearance was changed beyond recognition: unshaven face, untidy hair, a crazy look in my eyes – I was an intimidating creature all right. No wonder the detectives who turned up that evening (on information received, it turned out later) couldn't bear to look at me" – Israel recalled,[46] explaining how the British authorities, just a few hours after the explosion, missed the opportunity to arrest the commander of the attack on the King David Hotel!

Next morning the duo succeeded in slipping away to Tel Aviv, and during the four days of curfew imposed on the great Jewish city, Israel Levi was in hiding in Shenkin Street, under the noses of the British, along with a senior IZL commander, Eliyahu Spector, code-named "Eli Dam."[47]

For all their efforts, the British failed to arrest a single one of the King David Hotel conspirators.

---

46. Testimony of Israel Levi, "The Bombing of the King David Hotel," Jabotinsky Archives.
47. Avinoam's recorded interview with Israel Levi.

ECHOES OF THE BLAST AND HISTORICAL POLEMIC

Ninety-one persons died in the King David Hotel explosion: 41 Arabs, 28 Britons, 17 Jews, and 5 of other nationalities.

"It was a terrible tragedy," said Menahem Begin.

> Among those killed were Jews, something that we shall mourn for the rest of our lives and which even today remains a wound in our hearts; and among the Jews who died, there were some who identified strongly with the IZL and some who helped us in our campaign. Nor did we want to harm any civilians, British or Arab – and that was how we planned the operation. We all assumed the hotel would be evacuated and no one would be harmed – that was the morality of our campaign. After all, this wasn't the first time we had bombed a British military installation, and if there were civilians present we used to send a warning and give them time to evacuate. That's what we did on this occasion too. But the outcome was different.[1]

While the operation succeeded in its intended goals, the unintentional loss of life carried devastating consequences on every level.

---

1. Radio program, "The Milk Churns That Roared."

The bombing of the King David Hotel grabbed the headlines of the world's press: the IZL had succeeded in penetrating to the heart of British power and blowing it apart.

At 12:37 PM, July 22, 1946, Jerusalem was shaken by the sound of a huge explosion. "One whole wing of a mighty building – seven stories of stone, concrete and steel – cut off as if with a knife," BBC News reported.

"Yitzhak Sadeh, operations officer of the Haganah, was wrong," says Menahem Begin in *The Revolt*:

> Gidi, operations officer of the IZL, was right: the former claimed that the effects of the explosion would reach only the second or third floor of the King David Hotel. Gidi insisted that they would go all the way to the top; the sealed basement would add to the force of the explosive gases. Those milk-churns reached all the floors, from the basement to the roof. In spite of his youth, Gidi had a lot more experience of this kind of warfare than the operations officer of the Haganah.

"The behavior of the Haganah was strange," Begin complained.

> In spite of the directive not to publicize the identity of the perpetrators – the evening of July 22 I received a note from Galili, asking us to declare publicly that it was the Irgun Zvai Leumi that carried out the attack on the King David Hotel. Galili added that the Haganah for its part would make no announcement. We complied with the Haganah's request and without delay published a factual account of what had happened at the King David Hotel. Only one fact was omitted – that on July 1 the Haganah had told us to go ahead with Operation Chick...[2]

Menahem Begin continued to treat his partners in the leadership of the Hebrew Resistance Movement honorably. They in their usual fashion repaid him with lavish doses of hypocrisy: the task had been entrusted to the IZL because the chiefs of the insurgency movement were well aware of the difficulties of the operations and didn't want to expose themselves to the dangers involved; they worked on the assumption (correct in itself) that the IZL had more experience with operations of this kind. At the same

---

2. Begin, *The Revolt*, p. 223.

time, neither Sneh, nor Galili, nor Yitzhak Sadeh (as will be seen at a later stage) had any intention of letting the IZL claim sole credit for the operation. They wanted it for themselves.

It was only when the scale of the death toll – resulting from the failure of the British to evacuate the hotel – became known that they hurriedly asked Begin to take exclusive responsibility for the action, clinging desperately to Yitzhak Sadeh's dishonest assertion that "the operation was not conducted according to the agreed timetable."

Despite his vacillations and inconsistencies, Israel Galili has admitted:

> When the IZL was given the directive on implementation of the bombing of the King David Hotel building, it was asked not to reveal the identity of the body responsible. We assumed that a statement would be made on behalf of the United Resistance Movement and not on behalf of the individual bodies, thus maximizing the political impact of the operation. When this directive was issued we had no idea how things were going to work out. Then the situation changed…and we appealed to the IZL to reveal the identity of the body responsible.[3]

"The IZL did as we asked," Galili declares complacently. What he fails to mention is the leadership's other, unpublicized agenda – the hounding of the "dissidents." The first shots in a vicious and dishonest propaganda campaign against the IZL were fired by its comrades in arms and partners in struggle – as represented by the underground radio station "Voice of Israel," official mouthpiece of the Hebrew Resistance Movement.

"The Haganah didn't keep to its side of the bargain," is Begin's bitter comment. "The next day the Voice of Israel broadcast a statement as follows: 'The Hebrew Insurgency Movement denounces the carnage resulting from the actions of dissidents in the King David Hotel.' *Denounces…dissidents…* This was the first time in many months that a Haganah spokesman had used the expression 'dissidents.' The implication was not only irresponsible, it was immoral as well…evasion of responsibility and an affront to the morale of warriors."

That day, July 23, Galili sent Begin a personal letter, displaying a degree

---

3.   Testimony of Israel Galili, Yad Tabenkin Archives, Unit 15, Box 172, File 6, Doc. 1.

of defensiveness over what had happened between them as well as grave concern over future developments:

> *To M. Shalom!*
>
> *The serious consequences of your actions in Jerusalem have led to unforeseen developments.*
>
> *The reaction, as publicized in the press, took no account of our guidance and was probably unavoidable in the circumstances.*
>
> *The situation is liable to cause tragic and serious complications regarding continuation of the struggle, and to prevent this it is essential the two of us meet urgently – tonight (July 23, 1946, at 2:00).*
>
> *Please make an effort to attend. I shall wait for you in the place we last met. Our meeting tonight has to precede tomorrow's meeting.*
>
> *– I.G.*[4]

Regarding his motives for sending the letter Galili explains:

> I heard about the explosion on the radio. At first we were astonished that it had taken place at all, and this was immediately followed by another surprise: Yitzhak Sadeh's impassioned claim that he'd been deceived regarding the time of the operation. He saw this as the reason behind the high death toll. He wrote me an agitated note asking to be relieved of his post.[5]
>
> The press was going wild and the world was indignant. Internally, there was confusion and lack of trust. The Agency leadership claimed complete unawareness of endorsements given and withdrawn.... [6]
> Their opinion was that if the Haganah or official representatives of the

---

4. Begin, *The Revolt*, p. 224.
5. Testimony of Israel Galili, Yad Tabenkin Archives, Unit 15.
6. At the time it was agreed with Galili that Sneh would inform the leadership of the Agency of the proposal to bomb the King David Hotel before it was submitted to the x Committee for approval. A few days after the explosion Galili met with Golda Meir and was astonished to hear that she hadn't had the faintest inkling of the scheme to attack the hotel. "She was surprised to hear," according to Galili, "that the IZL had been given two instructions in writing – the first regarding the operation, the second regarding postponement of the operation." Galili adds, "I don't know with whom Sneh spoke before the Committee meeting." (Yad Tabenkin Archives – Unit 25M, Series 6, Box 6, File 13).

community let it be known that at some stage the operation at the King David Hotel had been approved, this would be interpreted as responsibility for the killing and as justification for brutal retaliation against the entire Yishuv.... I made it clear to my contacts in the Agency leadership that they shouldn't be surprised if such an announcement did indeed come from the IZL – their position had to be understood as well.... It couldn't be denied that on July 1 approval had been given on behalf of the United Resistance Movement....[7] The fact that we came through the crisis peacefully, without bloodshed, was to the credit of all concerned.[8]

I don't personally remember a more difficult time. I wasn't happy denouncing an operation we had authorized. There was no one I could consult. There was a danger that denial of responsibility in this case would be seen as a denial of the entire campaign. We had a spokesman, Gedalia Zochowitzky, who had contacts with the press and I instructed him to concentrate on the issue of the deaths resulting from the IZL and Lehi action at the King David Hotel. We focused our denial on the killing, not on the bombing. Incidentally, there were some who accused me of not condemning the IZL strongly enough, but to my mind the IZL had come in for enough condemnation in the press and in Voice of Israel broadcasts.

In his book *The Revolt*, Begin describes our meeting, and the exceptional measures taken to ensure privacy and security. It was a heavy responsibility I was taking on myself, inducing the leader of the IZL to come out of hiding....[9] I was very much afraid that Sadeh's denunciations would drive the IZL out of the fold, and the purpose of this meeting was to prevent the severing of the threads. Begin mentions the letter from Yitzhak Sadeh that I produced at the meeting; it was full of vitriol against the IZL.[10]

Begin relates:

---

7. Yad Tabenkin Archives, Unit 15, Box 172, File 5.
8. Galili, "Address"; "Clarification," n. 20 above.
9. Yad Tabenkin Archives, Box 172, File 5, Doc. 11.
10. Galili, "Address"; "Clarification," n. 20 above.

I went to the meeting with Galili, with a heavy heart. I reproached him over the attitude of the press and he again insisted that the press had "exceeded its brief" and hadn't heeded the guidance of the Haganah on this occasion. But I was especially critical of that vicious Voice of Israel broadcast.

"What does this mean" – I asked Galili – "Don't you know what, and who, is responsible for all those deaths? Why are you denouncing us? The plan was approved, the boys followed their instructions and a warning was given – why don't you people tell the truth?"

At this stage Galili told me that the Haganah intelligence branch had received a transcript of a conversation between a British police officer and Sir John Shaw.[11] At my request, Galili promised that Shaw's remarks would be publicized on the next Voice of Israel broadcast.

He asked me not to make any public statements that might complicate the situation. I agreed.

And then came the big surprise: he took a piece of paper from his pocket and handed it to me to read. It was a note from Yitzhak Sadeh to Israel Galili. I read it, and the world seemed to go dark. Sadeh alleged – no more and no less – that we had deceived him, that Gidi had told him the attack would take place between the hours of two and three in the afternoon, i.e. during the lunch-break when the government offices would be empty. "How is it possible to work with people like these?" – was the plaintive question of the operations officer of the Haganah and chief of the Palmah, Yitzhak Sadeh.

I couldn't believe what I was seeing: did the points raised in the letter correspond in *any* way to reality?

We had indeed discussed the King David Hotel operation many times, but the suggestion of doing it in the afternoon never arose. It was always going to be the hours leading up to midday. On one occasion a time between 4:00 and 5:00 PM was suggested, but it was rejected immediately because it couldn't be coordinated with the LHI [Lehi] operation. "Gidi went to a meeting with Sadeh, after IZL command had already agreed on the time for the operation," I told Galili,

11. Israel Galili told Begin that according to the Haganah intelligence service, when Sir John Shaw was informed that Jews had planted bombs in the King David Hotel and were demanding the evacuation of the hotel, he replied, "I'm not here to take orders from the Jews, I give *them* orders." (Shaw vehemently denied making this remark.)

"and on his return from the meeting he gave me a detailed account and following on from that another command session was convened. Gidi has never lied to me!" I insisted, "and you don't even need to trust him the way I do – what is the point, or the logic, of supposing that he conveyed to Sadeh something different from what had been decided in his presence and at his suggestion? Why hide from his commander and his colleagues a promise that he, allegedly, made to the operations officer of another organization? The fact is that I've never heard, and no member of my staff has ever heard, of 2:00 PM as a time for the operation. If Gidi had received a directive like that, it would no doubt have led to a debate and then there would be two possibilities: either accept it, or reject it and appeal to the Insurgency Movement to have our original decision reinstated. In either case there would be a debate. But we never debated this issue – never."[12]

Galili was stunned. He had never seen Begin so incensed. "It wasn't hard for me to understand the difficult situation he was in following the tragic outcome and the political ramifications," he said. "In the end all I told Menahem Begin was that I hoped there'd be no further complications."

Summing up the meeting and its implications, he recalled:

There was a lot of tension. We were both reserved, and cautious. Menahem Begin seemed to me conscious of the seriousness of the situation…. He insisted, emphatically, that they had acted in accordance with the plan agreed with Yitzhak Sadeh and not deviated from it. He utterly rejected Yitzhak's accusations and suggested a meeting be convened between Yitzhak Sadeh and Amihai Paglin in the presence of us both.

The truth needed to be told, and I tried hard to persuade my friend Yitzhak Sadeh to agree to this unorthodox encounter with Amihai Paglin. He was older than me, sensitive, and easily hurt. I believed in the mutual trust between us, but I decided not to insist on participation as an order. An inquiry could only be held with his free acquiescence.[13]

---

12. Begin, *The Revolt*, p. 225.
13. Testimony of Israel Galili, Yad Tabenkin Archives, Box 172, File 5.

Menahem Begin invited Gidi to meet him and talk things over, and repeated to him Sadeh's accusation. Gidi couldn't believe his ears. First he fixed Begin with an incredulous stare, then burst into astonished laughter. "I was never asked," he said, "about the time of the operation. That subject just wasn't on the agenda in my meetings with Sadeh. We discussed the explosives and the effects they were likely to have, and the time to be allowed for the evacuation of the hotel, and various other fundamental operational issues. Sadeh wasn't interested in details and this detail, when the operation would be carried out, wasn't mentioned even once."[14]

Yaakov Yanai, who served as an aide to the Haganah chief and knew Yitzhak Sadeh well, writes in his account of the King David Hotel episode, "As one who knows how Yitzhak Sadeh operated, I reckon he told the IZL to make sure there weren't any casualties – and left it at that."[15]

THE INQUIRY

Yitzhak Sadeh didn't hide his annoyance at the suggestion of an inquiry. "Nothing like this has ever happened to me before," he stormed, before drawing from his sheath his tried and tested weapon. "This is fascist behavior! I don't see myself as party to that dreadful slaughter. It could have been prevented... It's true that moving the milk churns into the café when it was full of people might have endangered the operatives but they should have taken the risk. It goes with the territory!" the voice of the Haganah chief of staff boomed from behind his desk. "They simply lied, as a way of reducing the danger to the participants." And seeing the look of astonishment on Galili's face he added hastily, "I'm as concerned for the safety of our men as anyone, but consequences have to be taken into account."

When he realized he had no choice but to attend the inquiry, he made it clear to Galili that he would state his case but not get bogged down in arguments. He wasn't a lawyer and had never before been required to participate in such a session. "He looked gloomy and a bit embarrassed," Galili commented, and he added, "I wasn't expecting the truth to come out, but I reckoned that refusal to attend the probe would be interpreted as evasion and possibly even as confirmation of the IZL's contention."[16]

---

14. Begin, *The Revolt*, p. 225.
15. Testimony of Israel Galili, Yad Tabenkin Archives, Box 172, File 6, Doc. 14.
16. Ibid.

The inquiry went ahead as planned – and the results, too, were entirely predictable.

The Haganah was represented by Galili and Sadeh; appearing for the IZL were Begin, Landau, and Gidi. Begin tried to be as objective as possible, asking questions of Sadeh and Gidi on an even-handed basis:

> Maybe, I was thinking, there's just been a misunderstanding here. We put question after question, Galili and I, to Sadeh and Gidi. But the inquiry wasn't decisive. At one point Sadeh irritated Galili with one of his answers when he said he didn't need to take an interest in "these details" when approving operational plans. Galili asked him with undisguised exasperation, "Well then, which parts of an operation *are* you interested in?" Sadeh replied that he was interested in the overall technical aspects, and Galili turned to me with a wink, "At least he's not casting doubt on the principle of the operation…"[17]

One important – and perhaps crucial – detail was discussed at the session; it was Gidi who raised the point and Sadeh confirmed it:

"Do you remember me telling you, that at the time of the attack there'd be no guests in La Regence café and we'd need to overpower 15 or so Arab laborers and cooks?" asked Gidi.

"Yes," Sadeh replied. "You told me that, but I'm quite sure it was agreed between us that the operation was going to take place during the lunch break."

Gidi persisted, "How could we have meant to do it in the lunch break, when the café would be full of guests?"

At this stage Galili called a halt to the discussion, saying to Sadeh, "It's obvious that what's happened here has been a misunderstanding and not an act of malice."[18]

"The two positions couldn't be reconciled," Begin concluded.

> The business of the cooks had been discussed in planning sessions and it was stated explicitly, they would be the only ones in the hotel basement

17. Begin, *The Revolt*, p. 225.
18. *Yediot Aharonot*, July 22, 1966; Yad Tabenkin Archives, Box 172, File 5, Doc. 1.

at the time of the attack and it would be necessary to overpower them, without harming them. It was also understood that we were choosing to attack at this time, when there was no one in La Regence but these operatives, specifically to avoid any premature confrontation and injury to civilians.... How could Gidi have explained that at the time of the attack there would be only Arab workers in the café – and yet be expected to schedule the attack for the lunch break, when the café would be filled to overflowing?[19]

"Gidi stated his case with confidence, putting his points in an orderly, almost erudite fashion," Galili admitted. "Yitzhak Sadeh spoke simply but reluctantly, as if he wished he was somewhere else – anywhere else. Nothing new emerged. Both sides stuck to their guns, and that's how it ended."[20]

Because the inquiry had reached no formal conclusions, Begin suggested to Galili that it be abandoned, and instead a judicial hearing should be held to examine the dispute between the IZL and the Hebrew Resistance Movement. He suggested that the presiding judge should be Yitzhak Gruenbaum, or Dr. Magnes, or Mr. Tabenkin. The proposal was rejected.

Galili felt he had fulfilled his obligations in the first inquiry. If he had doubts about his friend Yitzhak Sadeh's version, he preferred to keep his own counsel. After all, Sadeh's allegations served the purposes of the Hebrew Resistance Movement in its attempts to blur its collusion with the IZL in the King David Hotel operation, and shrug off any responsibility for the outcome.

"In our public pronouncements about the IZL we didn't mention the fact that they didn't inform us of the timing, because that would imply there had been contact and coordination from the start.... In the circumstances," Galili admits, "our aim was to obscure rather than clarify the whole issue of prior collusion."[21]

But despite his efforts to adhere consistently to Sadeh's version in all official communications, he wasn't always able to disguise his doubts in less guarded statements. "The day after the inquiry," he relates, "we met,

---

19. Begin, *The Revolt*, p. 225.
20. Yad Tabenkin Archives, Box 172, File 5, Doc. 1.
21. Testimony of Israel Galili, Yad Tabenkin Archives, Unit 15.

Zev Feinstein (deputy Haganah chief) and I, with Yitzhak Sadeh. We both thought he needed cheering up, and we told him we'd stand by him. The question hanging in the air was: 'Did they deceive – or had there been a terrible misunderstanding?'"[22] Galili knew the answer and however much he tried to suppress and erase it, it kept coming back. Twenty-two years later, it finally emerged from his subconscious and made it into print.

On August 9, 1968, the editor of a history of the Haganah, Yehuda Slutzky, wrote to Israel Galili (then serving as a government minister), asking for his version of the King David Hotel episode, "I'm drafting the chapter on the King David Hotel, and I have, among others, two testimonies at my disposal: that of Mr. Begin (in his book *The Revolt*) and that of Dr. Moshe Sneh, which I received a few weeks ago." Slutzky concluded his appeal to Galili with a question, "Who gave the IZL the order (or permission) to carry out the bombing?" In this context Slutzky raises the hypothesis (a not entirely implausible one) "that the national command decided after July 19, 1946 [the day after the x Committee accepted Weizmann's ultimatum to suspend all activities against the British – *Author's note*] that the dissidents should be allowed to execute their plan, because they didn't accept the political leadership of either Dr. Weizmann or the x Committee."[23]

Galili's reply was the central testimony on which Slutzky relied in the King David Hotel chapter in *The History of the Haganah*.[24]

The text of the original article went through numerous revisions and in the end several sections were omitted, some of them handwritten (apparently by Galili) – sections tending to refute the allegations of Yitzhak Sadeh that Gidi was not acting in accordance with the agreed timetable.

An example is the following sentence which appears in two drafts of the King David Hotel chapter, but not in the finished book: *Confirmation of the operational side of the action was given, in conventional United Resistance Movement fashion, to Yitzhak Sadeh, who was convinced by the operations officer of the IZL, Amihai Paglin, that there was no possibility of penetrating the building during the night.*

Furthermore, the published edition of *The Haganah* contains the statement, "The milk churns had to be taken by the IZL team to the basement

---

22. Ibid.
23. Testimony of Israel Galili, Yad Tabenkin Archives, Box 172, File 6, Doc. 2.
24. Yehuda Slutzky, *Sefer toledot ha-Haganah* [History of the Haganah] (Tel Aviv: Am Oved, 1972), Book 2, p. 898.

under the southern wing of the building, entered by way of La Regence café,"[25] but it omits what follows and appears in all the drafts, explaining why there was no choice for the attackers but to opt for midday: *Because the café would be full of people when the workers in the government offices took their lunch break, the planners scheduled their incursion to occur during office working hours, on the assumption that the warning to be given half an hour before the explosion would allow sufficient time for the clerks and civilian office employees to leave the building in safety.*

This statement, constituting further corroboration of Amihai Paglin's account of the timing of the operation and further refutation of Sadeh's version was simply erased from the Haganah history – and not by chance.

But most serious of all is the omission of the results of the inquiry that pitted Amihai Paglin against Yitzhak Sadeh.

In the published book[26] it is stated simply, "The inquiry ended inconclusively," nothing more. In two drafts of the King David Hotel chapter, based on Israel Galili's testimony, it is stated explicitly, in manuscript (apparently Galili's): *Paglin asserted that the entire scheme depended on getting the explosive materials into the café, something only possible during working hours in the offices.* And then comes the (handwritten) conclusion: *It became clear to all those present that this point, apparently, had not been scrutinized at the time with sufficient rigor, in the discussions between Yitzhak Sadeh and Paglin...*

In another draft a handwritten note is found: *It appeared that the precise timing of the operation had not been adequately clarified in discussions between Yitzhak Sadeh and Paglin.*[27]

It seems that the historians of the Haganah put themselves through a number of contortions in their efforts to defend the credibility of the chief of staff of the United Resistance Movement, Yitzhak Sadeh. In the end they despaired of it – and simply erased the offending sections from the official history.

THE BLAME GAME

Yitzhak Sadeh was in a state of panic. He went out of his way to shrug off all

---

25. Ibid.
26. Ibid., p. 900.
27. Yad Tabenkin Archives, Unit 15, Box 172, File 4, Docs. 14–15.

responsibility for the King David Hotel debacle, running from one public figure to another and endlessly repeating his mantra, "Gidi didn't keep to the timetable we agreed, and that's the only reason so many were killed." His subordinates were not spared this treatment either,[28] and one of those whom he used to call in for heart-to-heart conversations was Yigal Allon. "He was pale and agitated," according to Allon, "and he said they were trying to lay the blame on him because he approved the plan that led to such carnage. 'They didn't act according to the plan I approved,' he kept on saying, choking with emotion.

"Later," Allon continues, "I heard from Sneh and Galili that they were appalled by the slaughter and couldn't understand what had happened, because Yitzhak had assured them there would be no loss of life..."[29]

"It's said that Yitzhak Sadeh displayed *military fortitude* in fighting the Arabs. I cannot argue with that and have no wish to, but I must say, that in the King David Hotel episode, *civic fortitude* was not among the qualities displayed by the chief of the Palmah," concluded Begin sadly.[30]

Begin was not alone in this assessment of Sadeh. Twenty-nine years later the historian Yigal Elam came to the same conclusion. In his Hebrew-language book *The Haganah: The Zionist Path to Power*, he comments on the accusations leveled at the IZL in the King David Hotel episode: "It has to be said that neither Moshe Sneh nor Yitzhak Sadeh showed sufficient moral fiber in this context and their conduct bordered on evasion of responsibility for the bombing."

In an interview recorded in 1999, Yigal Elam gave a more detailed account of his meaning in that marginal comment:

> The decision to blow up the King David Hotel was made in the wake of Black Sabbath. Haganah command decided then to conduct three reprisal operations in the name of the Resistance Movement: one to be entrusted to the Haganah, and the other two to the IZL and Lehi. The IZL was assigned the task of destroying the premises of the Chief

---

28. Testimony of Israel Galili, Yad Tabenkin Archives, Unit 15.
29. Testimony of Yigal Allon, Yad Tabenkin Archives, Unit 15, Box 172, File 6, Doc. 7.
30. Begin, *The Revolt*.

Secretariat of the Mandatory Government in the King David Hotel. It's important to stress that all three operations, including the King David, were approved by the x Committee.

A few days before implementation was due, Chaim Weizmann's ultimatum arrived, demanding the suspension of all military activity against the British. The x Committee caved in and informed Haganah command, "Gentlemen, you're to call it all off!"

Sneh and Sadeh, two of the key figures here, were incensed. Sneh, who was in fact chief of the national staff, didn't pass this decision on to the IZL. As he's quoted as saying in *History of the Haganah*, "I saw this as our internal business." The precise meaning of "our internal business" in this context is worth examining – the most reasonable and logical meaning would be that this directive was aimed at the Haganah alone and not at the other elements constituting the United Resistance Movement. And Sneh goes on to say, "I reckoned that if I told them, they would disregard the order, creating a precedent of defiance of the United Resistance Movement and I didn't want that…" Wonderful! So he didn't pass on the directive to the IZL, and in the meantime he was about to leave the country, heading for Paris.

As for the note he sent Begin, asking for "a few days' delay," such a note was indeed sent on July 19, as confirmed by Begin's testimony and the *History of the Haganah*. And it's important to remember: the decisions to act were made on July 1, 1946, and for a period of two weeks all operations were on hold. The Haganah went no further with its operation, but the IZL continued its preparations in good faith. No one was telling them anything. Lehi, meanwhile, had been badly mauled in a disastrous assault on oil refineries in Haifa. They were sensitive about their losses and in no position to coordinate activities with the IZL.

At this time, Sneh sent two handwritten notes to the IZL: in one of them, he tells Begin to expedite "Malonchick" as soon as possible; in the other, on July 19, three days before the operation and just before his departure for Paris, to delay it "a few days." He didn't tell them it was off! Begin did indeed delay it a few days. He blasted the hotel on July 22 and could claim in all innocence, "Okay, I waited a few days…" especially as – and there's no argument about this – the IZL received no notification that United Resistance Movement operations were canceled. Hence, the request for a delay could have emanated from any number of political considerations, and the IZL was entitled to interpret it that way. If I'd been handling public relations for the IZL I'd have said: "Three days seemed quite long enough for me – especially as there was no contact between us…"

And then the hotel went up, and the angry responses began, responses which it seems even Haganah command was unable to control. The public that the Haganah identified with was appalled by the heavy loss of life, as were the leaders of the Jewish Agency who sincerely believed that Sneh had ordered all operations halted. They didn't know what Haganah command knew, that the IZL had received no instructions regarding suspension of action…

This was the moment when Sneh or Sadeh, or both of them together, should have had the guts to stand up and say, "We didn't pass on to the IZL the instruction to halt operations. There was a breakdown in communications." And since the one who was in the country then was Sadeh, it was his duty as chief of staff of the United Resistance Movement to establish the facts, rather than hiding behind all kinds of flimsy excuses in a desperate attempt to shrug off responsibility and dump the blame on the IZL.

The highest degree of responsibility, without any doubt, is that of Sneh, but it shouldn't be forgotten Sadeh was a player too, and so, incidentally, was Galili. It was they who held the inquiry and all that. This whole story gives off a strong whiff of hypocrisy – what with Sadeh clinging to his version of the timing, which is nonsense anyway; weighed against all the other aspects of the operation, it just looks like a pale and pathetic excuse. And that is precisely what I meant when I made the comment in my book *The Zionist Path to Power* that neither Moshe Sneh nor Yitzhak Sadeh displayed sufficient moral fiber in this episode and their conduct bordered on evasion of responsibility for the explosion. They didn't have the guts to stand up and say, "We didn't tell them to halt all operations; we let them go ahead and they acted in good faith."

Instead of this, they were intent on complicating things and hiding behind Sadeh's allusions, "It all went wrong because the IZL didn't keep to the timetable," and the like. None of that lot cared about the truth. No wonder Begin and the IZL were offended; they knew *they* hadn't broken any agreements.

The Haganah chief and the chief of staff of the United Resistance Movement didn't dare come out publicly and admit the IZL had been in the right all along, and that is precisely what I was referring to. Incidentally, it's very likely that Sadeh's version was a total and deliberate fabrication from the start, and it wouldn't be the first time something like that has been cooked up, all in the "public interest" of course![31]

Two lies fueled the insidious propaganda campaign directed against the IZL in the aftermath of the King David Hotel episode, and naturally enough they focused on the man responsible for the detailed planning of the operation, the late Amihai Paglin.

One of these lies – the invention patented by Yitzhak Sadeh, according to which "Gidi didn't keep to the timetable we agreed on" – has been dismissed by the historian Yigal Elam as "hypocrisy" and as a "pale and pathetic excuse," an attempt to absolve himself of responsibility and lay the blame on the IZL (see the full text of the interview with Yigal Elam, above).

The other lie concerns the warning. The British went out of their way to try to prove there had been no warning. They clung to this lie as if it was an article of faith, and hitched to it all the official propaganda machinery available to them in Jerusalem and abroad. They conducted their campaign of deceit with such skill and professionalism that many were tempted to believe them. They were so proficient that, incredible though it may seem, they even succeeded, momentarily, in convincing none other than the commander of the Irgun Zvai Leumi himself.

According to Gidi:

When I arrived immediately after the explosion at Menahem Begin's house in Tel Aviv, he was under the impression, after hearing the official radio reports, that something had gone wrong and we'd been unable to warn people to leave, and then, before I had the chance to say a word, he told me in that quiet voice of his, "If there was a problem, don't take the responsibility on yourself. We're all equally responsible. Even after I'd explained to him exactly what happened, I knew I was never going to forget that attitude, so characteristic of him."[32]

---

31. Author's interview with Yigal Elam, 1999.
32. "Interview of the Week" with Gidi, *Yediot Aharonot*, September 19, 1977.

In the official report of the interrogation of Emil Carey, the telephone switchboard operator who received the warning call at the King David Hotel, it is stated that the conversation took place one minute before the major explosion.[33]

In Haganah intelligence service documents (communicated on Aug. 4, 1946) there is a report of an interview with Matilda (hotel switchboard supervisor):

> The above-mentioned worked at the hotel switchboard until twelve when she was relieved by Emil Carey. The latter informed her that at 12:10, 12:15 at the latest – a girl rang and said the building was about to explode and must be evacuated.
>
> Emil immediately informed the manager, Mr. Hamburger, who seemed disinclined to take it seriously but began advising people to leave the building.[34]

Deborah Lindner, the telephone operator at the *Palestine Post* who received the warning from the IZL, repeated her assertion that the police made every effort to persuade her to say she had received the warning after the explosion.

The British continued to rely on the fib that they themselves had invented. They carried on with this even after the British Forces newspaper in the Middle East, the *Middle East Mail*, reported in its July 23, issue (the day after the explosion) that "15 minutes before the explosion, the telephonist of the King David Hotel received an anonymous tip-off, warning that the hotel was about to go up and she should run for her life."

The leaders of the United Resistance Movement maintained a dignified silence.

After all, the British lie accorded well with Yitzhak Sadeh's flawed version of events.

The two lies came together, complementing one another perfectly, in the project of laying the blame for the deaths in the hotel blast exclusively

---

33. CID docs. – HHA 8138/A, 13.
34. HHA 1049/112 (47).

at the door of the IZL. "Responsibility for this horrific death toll is due to the IZL and the IZL alone," charged the Haganah journal.[35]

Haganah command knew the whole truth – and kept silent.

Israel Galili, one of the leaders of the United Resistance Movement, said in his account of the King David Hotel episode that he heard about the explosion on the radio and it came as a total surprise. If this is indeed the case (and I'm inclined in this instance to believe him), then his fellow commanders were keeping things from him. Intelligence chiefs, and no doubt the commander as well (Sneh), were definitely in the picture – before and after the bomb.

The day before the operation the Central Intelligence Office received a full report on advance preparations in Jerusalem, including such details as the false license plate numbers of the van to be used for the Lehi attack on David Brothers. The document listed the names of all the participants in the action, and the functions they were to fulfill.[36]

In another document dated July 26, 1946, it is stated (quoting Shimshon) that the operation was carried out at the request of the United Resistance Movement and with its approval, and that he (Shimshon) had actually seen the written approval.[37]

Sarah Agassi (Goldschmid), who with her friend Adina Hai Nisan was responsible for transmitting the telephone warning, said in her statement that as she was waiting between the filling station and the side entrance of the King David Hotel, she saw a young man in khaki shorts and white shirt strolling about in front of the hotel. When she drew her friend's attention to this she replied, "Don't worry, that's a Haganah man who knows about the operation. Later, when Avinoam turned up, he too reassured her, "That's an observer on behalf of the Haganah, they know what's going on."[38]

A Haganah intelligence memorandum, Jerusalem district, July 25, 1946 – under the heading "Role of the Senior Clerk" – states, "After the first explosion outside the hotel, some of the clerks (most of them Arab) tried to leave the building, but Senior Clerk Antipa told them to stay where they were and carry on working."[39]

---

35. *Ha-Homah* [The Wall].
36. HHA 1049/112 (10).
37. HHA 1049/112 (12).
38. Statement of Sarah Goldschmid-Agassi, October 20, 1968, Jabotinsky Archives.
39. HHA 1049/112 (7).

A Haganah intelligence report dated July 26, 1946, to encoder (B) from informant 61104 states, "Giles Eysham, the defense officer responsible for security at the King David Hotel, said that some of the telephone operators received prior warning of the explosion and were thus able to save themselves."

In a report dated July 26, 1946, to encoder (B) from informant 41104, it is stated that the waiters at the King David Hotel say that after the first explosion the manager of the hotel, Mr. Hamburger, was seen running around in all directions, warning everyone he met to leave, because their lives were in danger.

"In this manner," the report concludes, "the lives of many guests and hotel employees were saved."[40]

In response to these reports and others, which inundated the Haganah Intelligence Service center on July 28, 1946, an *urgent* cable was sent to the intelligence representative of the Jerusalem region (code-named Yanai):

> From a number of sources I have received information that in the offices of the Chief Secretariat it was definitely known that something was about to happen – before the explosions. Even prior to the first, smaller blast there was undoubtedly a tense atmosphere. It is said that clerks were absolutely forbidden to leave the building. Please check details immediately: who knew, who received, and who conveyed this instruction? We attach the highest importance to ascertaining: Who is the murderer? Devote all efforts to this point and inform me as soon as possible.[41]

The Jerusalem intelligence representative replied to the above request from the encoder two days later (July 30, 1946):

- Junior clerks in the Secretariat state that Clare Rousseau received a telephone warning of the explosion and ran to tell the chief clerk, *Antipa* [emphasis in the original]. The latter rebuked her, told her not to start a panic and dismissed her from his office. According to Mr. Medzini,

---

40. HHA 1049/112 (13).
41. HHA 1049/112 (25).

immediately after the first explosion Hamburger, the hotel manager, approached Shaw and told him that the building was in danger and its occupants should be evacuated. To this Shaw replied: *I don't take any orders from Jews.*

[The intelligence representative comments: This account is consistent with information received on Tuesday morning from an anonymous source.]

- On July 22, 1946, between 11:45 and 12:00, Novomiesky sent a letter to Shaw by office messenger. The messenger was unable to deliver the letter, because the Chief Secretariat was sealed off by troops with rifles and submachine guns who were allowing no one to enter.
- A Christian Arab clerk by the name of Ruch told a Jewish clerk named Sonnenschein that a number of clerks, himself included, wanted to leave the building before the explosions – but were not allowed to do so.

  [The intelligence representative comments: The information that the chief clerk, Antipa, ordered employees who wanted to leave to go back to work is confirmed by another source.]

- In the editorial office of the *Palestine Post* there is a written message from the IZL, according to which the warning was given 22 minutes before the explosion.

  Continuing to check details.[42]

In a report to encoder T (B), also dated July 28, 1946, informant 0013 relates, "On July 25, 1946, the Hebrew press wanted to print an admission on the part of senior Army officers that they were warned in advance of the King David Hotel explosion, but this item was erased by the censor."[43]

Another document records the testimony of Simha Libbi, a clerk in the Chief Secretariat and a close friend of Clare Rousseau:

There were three people in the telephone exchange. Clare happened to be in the room between 12:10 and 12:20.

When the warning of the explosion came through, Clare went to Simha "in a very agitated state" and told her of the warning.

They both hurried to Antipa's office and passed on the message.

---

42. HHA 1049/112 (32).
43. HHA 1049/112 (31).

Antipa sent them away, telling them they were not to leave the building. Simha saw Rousseau a few minutes before the explosion – for the last time. It seems she returned to the telephone exchange and was killed there. The Armenian telephone operator who was on duty at the time was severely injured.[44]

On August 7, 1946, informant 41104 reported to encoder (B):

Cousins, director of the military accommodation department, had been invited to a meeting in the Chief Secretariat, at 12:30 on July 22, 1946. On hearing the alarm siren, he contacted Bradley to ask whether the meeting was going ahead. The latter replied that the meeting had been canceled and he should avoid the place – since the situation in the building was unstable and trouble was anticipated.[45]

On August 12, 1946 – three weeks after the King David Hotel explosion – informant 00004 submitted to encoder (B) a conclusive report, saying, among other things:

Hamburger, the hotel manager, received a message from the switch-board operator, Emil Carey, saying that he, Carey, had received a telephone warning that the building was about to be blown up and everyone should be evacuated. The warning was given between 12:10 and 12:15 (Matilda). Hamburger immediately advised guests to leave the building, and La Regence café was cleared of customers. According to two sources, Hamburger passed the message on to Shaw, who retorted that he didn't take orders from Jews, or from Jewish terrorists...

The same day, additional information was received from Gavison, assistant to the chief administrator, confirming the account of Clare Rousseau's warning to the chief clerk. According to him, the warning was given 12 to 15 minutes before the second explosion.[46] The following day Gavison's account was corroborated, on the basis of a personal inquiry conducted by Ben David.[47]

---

44. HHA 1049/112 (41).
45. HHA 1049/112 (53).
46. HHA 1049/112 (58).
47. HHA 1049/112 (62).

When the first alarm was heard, following the small explosion, all doors leading to the Chief Secretariat were sealed and no one was allowed in or out.

Many clerks quit their offices, intending to leave the building, but were forbidden to do so by the chief clerk. There can be no doubt that Antipa was acting in accordance with prior instructions from his superiors: Shaw or Gatch.

The report concludes:

The outcome of the operation was clear proof of lack of organization and unpreparedness for emergencies. Clerks in the Secretariat state that Shaw was relying on Gatch, who was responsible for the security of the Secretariat. On the other hand there are reports that Secretariat chiefs, having contacted senior Army officers, were confident that the Army could cope with the situation.

Overlapping authorities, creating confusion in the higher echelons, on the one hand – and on the other, Shaw's obsessional refusal to take orders from Jews – these were the factors preventing those responsible, who knew what was liable to happen, from giving urgent instructions to leave the building.[48]

The documents quoted above are only a small sample of the flood of reports and statements which swamped the Haganah command's intelligence center and were, naturally, passed on to the leadership of the United Resistance Movement – from the day of the explosion and for many days after. And yet in spite of this, the Haganah commander in chief and chief of staff, and members of the national command structure, who were well aware of the truth – as indeed were the British – took refuge behind a wall of silence and buried the truth in the deepest recesses of the archives.

It took 30 years for Israel Galili to pluck up the courage to state publicly what had been tucked away inside him for many years. Commenting on the episode in 1978, he said:

---

48. HHA 1049/112 (46).

I'm not alleging that the IZL ever intended to shed innocent blood. No one denies that a telephone warning was given in advance. It is beyond any doubt that the issue of evacuation was addressed casually, with fatal results, and I cannot understand the behavior of the British. They had every reason to take the warnings seriously.

Since July 22, 1946, to this day, I have never wavered in my belief that the British are not to be absolved of blame, in that they failed to expedite the evacuation of staff from the offices.

At the time we received information from intelligence sources that when the telephone warning was brought to Shaw's attention, he retorted, "We are not here to take orders from the Jews, but to give them orders." In my first meeting with Menahem Begin after the explosion, I brought this to his attention. The disputes between us and the IZL, as acrimonious as they might be, should not be allowed to obscure the responsibility of the British.[49]

It took the British a little longer – 33 years – to admit that a warning had been given by the IZL: Lord Janner, formerly president of the Zionist Federation and not a political ally of Begin, made a speech in the House of Lords on May 22, 1979, absolving the IZL of responsibility for the heavy loss of life caused by the bombing of the King David Hotel in Jerusalem in 1946.[50]

The following is an extract from this speech:

There is one thing I should like to add. I think it should be said. There is an attempt made to defame the present Prime Minister of the State of Israel – who, incidentally, is here to talk to many important people....

As your Lordships know, I am against terrorism of any kind and for any purpose. But I think we must be fair. I was informed that on a radio interview Mr. Begin a few days ago explained the line that his friends took when he said that under no circumstances did they plan attacks on women, children or civilians.

I think the House is entitled to know some facts that I came across in the course of some professional inquiries I have been making in respect of what happened at the time of the King David Hotel

---

49. Yad Tabenkin Archives, Box 172, File 5, Doc. 1.
50. *Ma'ariv*, May 24, 1979.

incident. I came across them not very long ago; I am saying this with the consent both of the people who have been in touch with me and also of the doctor concerned. I want to wipe away the suggestion that no warning was given. I propose to read a letter from a Dr. Crawford in Bournemouth. I quote:

"It was very kind of you to phone me today and I sat down at once to write to you."

I met Dr. Crawford at another venture of Israel which is well known to many people – the Magem [sic!] David, which is the Shield of David Ambulance and Health Services. I happened to meet him at a conference held in Bournemouth. Casually he told me that he knew something about this. He says in his letter:

"Further to our recent conversation in Bournemouth, I am writing to confirm that the officer…who wrote to me in 1946 concerning the King David Hotel 'incident' was Major-General Dudley Sheridan Skelton, CB, DSO, FRCS, formerly DGMS in India, Hon Physician to HM The King and to HE the Viceroy of India. He retired from the forces about 1937…. In 1946, he was head of a hospital in Palestine near Jerusalem and was a frequent visitor to the King David Hotel; apparently he was there on the very day of the explosion and he wrote me that 'a warning' was passed on to the officers in the bar in rather jocular terms, implying it was 'Jewish terrorist bluff'. But despite advice to 'ignore the bluff' he decided to leave and thus was out of the hotel when the explosion took place….

"I hope these facts will be of some help to you. Many of my friends knew this story at the time but few have survived; my sister-in-law will remember it clearly as she was friendly with the Brigadier and lived with us at the time. If you think it worth-while, I could contact her" –

I did ask him to contact her and she wrote a letter confirming what Dr. Crawford said. As your Lordships are well aware, I do not approve of terrorists of any kind. The Prime Minister of Israel explained a few days ago what happened and I hope that the letter I have read out now will, in all fairness, answer the accusation that has been made about this incident. I am very grateful for the attention the House has given me.[51]

---

51. Hansard, HC Deb, 5. s. Vol. 400, cols, 281–83.

WHY DID SHAW NOT ORDER THE EVACUATION OF THE HOTEL?

Twenty-three years after the explosion – when he was interviewed for a Voice of Israel radio program – this was still a mystery to Menahem Begin:

> There are several hypotheses. There are some who allege that it was deliberate malice, not allowing the evacuation of the hotel; it is a fact that British police and soldiers had orders not to let anyone leave, and some of those who did succeed in getting out have testified that shots were fired at them. I'm not sure this hypothesis is correct, and when I wrote the King David Hotel chapter in my book *The Revolt* (I was writing in 1950, when everything was still fresh in my memory) I suggested another possibility: it could be that it didn't occur to them that we really had smuggled explosives into the hotel. As I've said before, it was a fortress, and it was hard for them to imagine us succeeding in penetrating the wire fence, evading the mobile patrols and the machine gun emplacements and all the rest; and then there's the matter of the incendiary bomb outside, the one that preceded the main explosion – maybe they thought that was it, end of story! Perhaps they thought it was all a joke at their expense, meant as a blow to the prestige of the British government and the British Empire; the Jews wanted to see the British ruling class running in panic from the hotel.... They all should have got out, and what would it have mattered if it did turn out to be a false alarm, or just a smoke-bomb or something? If they assumed the warning wasn't serious and the intention was to humiliate them, that could explain why they preferred to stay put.
>
> And there's a third possibility: they were simply afraid to come out. Perhaps they thought we wanted to get them out of the fortress and into the open so we could ambush them. But of course these are only speculations. No one will know for certain, so long as Mr. Shaw declines to explain his reasons for not evacuating the hotel, despite the warning that was received.[52]

Amihai Paglin, operations officer of the Irgun Zvai Leumi and the one who planned the King David Hotel action, points to another consideration that could have influenced Shaw's decision:

---

52. Radio program, n. 7 above.

Reluctant though I am to engage in a pointless wrangle with Mr. Shaw, who was then chief secretary of the Mandatory Government and without doubt the one responsible for the non-evacuation of the hotel, in my opinion, when issues of historical importance are being addressed, what is needed is comprehensive and thorough analysis of the full range of the facts....

When we come to examine the causes behind the heavy toll of casualties resulting from the assault on the hotel, we cannot confine ourselves to determining whether advance warning was given or not, because there were other factors of importance that may have influenced the decision not to evacuate.

One factor: it has to be remembered this was the period of the United Resistance Movement, which grouped together the three underground organizations under the control of the official institutions of the Yishuv.

Whereas the Irgun Zvai Leumi, which carried out the operation, saw the striking of a blow against the center of civilian and military government as another link in the chain of activities designed to undermine that government, members of the official leadership, acting through the intermediary of the Haganah, saw the aforementioned operation as an emergency measure, with the objective of destroying the documents seized by the British from the premises of the Jewish Agency, documents that could prove very damaging to leaders of the Yishuv currently being detained. As a result of this there were serious differences of opinion between the operational arm of the IZL, led by me, and the supervisory apparatus of the Haganah, headed by Yitzhak Sadeh, about the length of time the British should be allowed for the evacuation of the building. The Irgun wanted to set the timing for the usual interval – 70 minutes, whereas the Haganah, represented by Sadeh, insisted the delay should be no more than 30–40 minutes, thus allowing less time for the retrieval and removal of the crucial documents. Clearly this decision, combined with other circumstances yet to be examined, was of critical importance for the outcome of the operation.

The other factor: at that time the British decided to plant an informer in the ranks of the Irgun Zvai Leumi in Jerusalem, preferably in a senior combat command role, a position that would guarantee the British advance notice of all operations planned by the Irgun in the Jerusalem area.

The informer did indeed serve as commander of one of the back-up units in the bombing of the King David Hotel. Beforehand, he tried to get away from the briefing room to make contact with Shaw, but the security rules in Irgun combat units were strict and he wasn't allowed to leave, even though it wasn't yet known he was an enemy agent. So the above-mentioned went into action and was even forced into an exchange of fire with the British police units arriving on the scene.

Lack of information from the noted informer was apparently one of Shaw's major considerations in deciding to ignore the warning given him.

Absence of information on the one hand and serious miscalculation on the other – an assumption that the docile leadership of the Yishuv would not dare sanction such an extreme action – these, in my opinion, led to Mr. Shaw's fateful decision not to evacuate the building.[53]

And there may be yet another reason why the order to evacuate was not given: this has been suggested by Elimelech Spiegel, in whose workshop, in Feierberg Street in Tel Aviv, the bombs were assembled.

When he had finished giving his instructions and putting the mechanisms together in Beit Aharon – Gidi told him to return at once to Tel Aviv. He recalled:

I felt a sudden impulse to take a last look at the King David Hotel, and I asked the driver of the car to pass by it. I wished I had a camera with me, so I'd be reminded of how it looked before the explosion!

When we'd gotten as far as Abu Ghosh, I asked the driver to pull up. I glanced at my watch, to fix the moment of the explosion in my memory. And sure enough, it happened as I expected – but sooner than I'd planned. All the chemical and mechanical clocks were set, by me, *at 45 minutes*. I checked them myself. I knew the time the boys set out, and by my calculation, even if everything was done precisely according to the timetable, down to the nearest minute – the explosives couldn't have gone off before 12:45. *That being so* – I thought almost

53. *Ma'ariv*, February 15, 1972.

aloud – *that being so, somebody moved the churns in an attempt to defuse them.*[54]

Fifty-three years later, Elimelech Spiegel is still convinced the milk churns exploded prematurely.

> I'm the one who fitted the chemical and mechanical clocks to the churns that were smuggled into the basement of the King David Hotel, and the warning period was set at 45 minutes, not 35. I'd stake my life on it. Someone tried to dismantle the bombs and that's why they exploded prematurely. I reckon that's why the Brits were in no hurry to evacuate: they thought they could neutralize the explosives and when that didn't work, they had to do something to clear themselves of the charge of homicide so they made up that story about getting no advance warning.[55]

The suspicion that the British tried to defuse the bombs was not confined to Spiegel alone. It was also a topic of great interest to the intelligence branch of the Haganah. Intelligence documents from this period are crammed with information pointing in that direction. In one of them, sent on July 25, 1946, from Yanai (Jerusalem district) to the Haganah inelligence center, the following report appears:

> Bishop, a foreign correspondent, told our informant that he and his friend Steel (a journalist employed by British intelligence) were sitting in the bar of the King David Hotel shortly before the explosion, drinking cocktails. By his estimate, at 12:10 a burst of machine gun fire was heard, and the two of them went out to the balcony (above the main entrance) to see what was going on. They saw soldiers barging into the hotel basement and checking the identity cards of the Arab workers. They stayed on the balcony for another 20 minutes or so, until the explosion.[56]

---

54. Author's interview with Elimelech Spiegel, October 1996.
55. Ibid.
56. HHA 1049/112 (7).

The intelligence representative (Yanai) adds the comment, "This story proves that the Army knew, 20 minutes before the blast, that there was reason to check which of the Arabs in the basement were genuine employees. This indicates that they suspected a bomb had been placed in the building by men dressed as Arabs."

In a document dated July 30, 1946, there is a reference to attempts on the part of the British to dismantle the explosive charges in the King David Hotel. In a report from 41104 to encoder (B) it is stated that "the baker says there was an attempt by soldiers to defuse the bombs planted by the IZL. The attempt was made a few minutes before 12:00 by a group of soldiers who had been summoned to the basement."[57]

On August 5, 1946, 00004 sent to encoder (B) a report in the name of "the baker": "Among clerks in the Chief Secretariat there is no longer any doubt that a warning was indeed passed on to the Secretariat by the management of the King David Hotel. The man responsible for the security of the Secretariat contacted Army top brass and asked them to send bomb disposal experts and they were sent."[58]

The newspaper *Davar* reported the day after the explosion, "It is rumored that the bomb in La Regence café exploded as police were attempting to defuse it."

In an intelligence document sent on August 6, 1946, to encoder (B), 00004 reports that "after the first explosion outside the building, at the personal request of the chief secretary, Shaw, a team of bomb disposal experts was sent, most of them NCOs and a few officers with them as well."[59]

A more detailed account of the attempt to defuse the bombs is to be found in the intelligence report dated August 7, 1946, from 01104 to encoder (B):

> *Henry Baker* reports that immediately after receipt of the warning (before the first explosion), *Gatch*, responsible for security in the Chief Secretariat, contacted the security officer at Army HQ, and as a result of this, the order was given to send bomb disposal experts.
>
> Henry Baker does not refute the notion that Shaw knew what was

---

57. HHA 1049/112 (42).
58. HHA 1049/112 (43).
59. HHA 1049/112 (52).

going on but he (Baker) thinks Shaw left it up to Gatch to tackle the problem.[60]

THE CORONER'S INQUEST

The quashing of the findings of the first coroner appointed by the British to examine the issue of the King David Hotel bombing adds one more to the long series of question marks regarding the behavior of the British in this episode.

On August 26, 1946, the High Court of Palestine ruled that the findings recorded on August 3, 1946, at the coroner's inquest convened in Jerusalem in the wake of the bombing should be set aside. The official reason given: "Insufficient proof." There was no reference to the identity of the coroner whose findings had been set aside by order of the court; in fact there is no mention of his name anywhere. On the other hand, the High Court ordered the opening of a new inquest into the deaths of 78 of the victims, and it was specified that "This inquest will not be conducted by the same coroner who conducted the inquest on August 3, 1946."

In accordance with the instructions of the court, on September 3, 1946, the High Commissioner, Sir Alan Cunningham, appointed the judge Lionel Alexander William Orr, deputy president of the Jerusalem District Court, to conduct the new inquest. All this vacillation and indecision (unchar-acteristic of the naturally conservative British) gives some indication of the confusion and embarrassment prevalent in the higher echelons of the Mandatory Government and the desperate attempt to obscure facts incon-venient to senior military and civilian authorities. The inquiries previously made, from the day of the explosion onwards – as is clear from various statements (see, for example, the testimony of the switchboard operators of the King David Hotel and the *Palestine Post*) – had been aimed at pre-senting a picture suiting the requirements of the British and covering up their failures.

It should be noted that in Judge Orr's letter of appointment there is an important limitation: "He is to confine himself solely to inquiring into the circumstances of the deaths of the victims of the explosion." In other words, he was not expected to examine such details as the following: was

---

60. HHA 1049/112 (52).

a warning received in time? Who prevented the evacuation of employees from the hotel? Who was responsible for the lapses in security?

Judge Orr refers to this himself in his judgment, with a hint of veiled criticism: "I have confined the scope of my inquest solely to establishing (a) the identity of the bodies, (b) time of death and physical causes thereof, (c) circumstances in which each of the deceased met his or her death. These were the procedural limitations imposed on me, and naturally they have not allowed me the opportunity to investigate the issue of the explosion which occurred at the King David Hotel on July 22, 1946."[61]

In private conversations, Lionel Alexander William Orr was more outspoken. In an intelligence report dated September 15, 1946 (to encoder B-D from 00004), an anonymous source is quoted: "Judge Orr said in a private conversation, 'I have at this moment sufficient evidence to arraign a number of senior officials in connection with the murder of 91 persons. Those chiefly responsible are *Shaw* and *Hadingham* [emphasis in the original]. But my instructions are to confine myself to determining the fact of death and its causes, and not to explore other issues.'"[62]

On the quashing of the findings of the original inquest, on Judge Orr's conclusions and the ignoring of the warning, a *Davar* editorial of September 17, 1946, has the following to say:

> Under pressure from the security forces, the government of Palestine has been obliged to set up a new inquest into the King David Hotel fatalities…and the public demand for an inquiry into the failure to prevent these fatalities has not been addressed…. At all events, His Honor Judge Orr's inquest has refuted the notion, promulgated by the Government Information Office in Jerusalem at the request of the High Commissioner and the Chief Secretary, that no person in an official position was warned of what was about to happen in the hotel.
>
> The commander of police, Jerusalem district, Mr. Hadingham, testified that the manager of the hotel, Mr. Hamburger, told him that explosive materials had been placed under the Chief Secretariat offices.

61. CID docs. (C. 138–1/2/46/1) – HHA 138/8A (58).
62. HHA 1049/112 (56).

Mr. Hadingham immediately ordered a search, but this was not carried out because there was insufficient time....

The police could have called the hotel manager to account, had he not immediately informed the Chief Secretariat of the imminent danger. But it is clear that Mr. Hamburger warned all parties, evacuated guests from the hotel, called the Chief Secretariat offices and the police, and reported to the police commander at the earliest opportunity. He was not negligent.

As to when the matter became known to Mr. Hamburger – that too can be determined precisely, since the *Palestine Post* was alerted and immediately called the police, and the time was logged. The call from the *Post* included the information that the hotel had already been warned. Officer Taylor testified that police headquarters had received an internal alarm signal from the hotel at 12:15, i.e., 22 minutes before the major explosion, but it was not clear whether the hotel alarm referred to the explosives detonated outside or to the danger within – further investigation is required....

If senior officials simply never envisaged that such a thing could happen, and for this reason did not expedite evacuation of the offices – then they should admit it, and let the record show their tragic error.

And if clerks and secretaries wanted to flee and their superiors forbade it, this too needs to be determined.

And *Davar* concludes:

Senior staff of the Chief Secretariat should have been apprehensive. They were aware that attacks on their servicemen and installations were not impossibilities. The judicial inquiry should have confirmed or refuted the allegations on the part of survivors that more lives could have been saved by timely evacuation, and not only did this not happen – there were explicit orders to stay!

It is time to establish the truth about responsibility for the failure to save life and the prevention of escape.

THE LEGACY

"It isn't the men who matter – but the man" was one of Napoleon's favorite sayings.

If it had been necessary to penetrate the King David Hotel according to the conventional notions of modern warfare, the combined forces of the IZL and the Palmah would have been insufficient. Gidi chose eight young men for the task – men lacking real combat experience, average age 19 – armed them with a few revolvers and Stens and pitted them against the Sixth Airborne Division, veterans of the war in Europe, of Normandy and Arnhem – to break down the "wall of Jericho" of Mandatory power in this land.

And they did it: with courage, resourcefulness, and astonishing efficiency. The whole operation lasted less than ten minutes, and was almost flawless. Had it not been for the chance encounter with Captain Mackintosh of the Royal Signals Corps, they would have suffered no casualties and gone leaving no traces behind, nobody knowing when or why they had been there.

Such an operation required more than courage and cool nerves, it required careful and meticulous planning, procedures that were exhaustively calculated – but were also precise and effective. These were the qualities with which Amihai Paglin, the man who devised the operational plan, was amply endowed. He also knew his enemy – and knew the way he thought.[63] His opponents were schooled in the academy of modern warfare, equipped with the most sophisticated weaponry available; his weapons were ingenuity, improvisation, and adaptation to changing circumstances.

With these weapons he planned and executed the Acre prison jailbreak, conquered Jaffa in the War of Independence, and turned into a farce the martial law imposed by the British on the major cities of the land.

The bombing of the King David Hotel was without doubt the crowning achievement of underground activity in Palestine (and with few equals in the world at large). In the words of Colonel Grey,[64] "It was among the factors leading to the decision to abandon Palestine."

It was an operation arousing awe among friends, rivals, and enemies alike.

Richard Crossman, then a leading member of the British Labour Party,

---

63. He fought the British from an ideological viewpoint but did not hate them: "I didn't hate the British in the days of the Mandate. Such bitterness as I felt came about when they started sending our people to the gallows." *Yediot Aharonot*, September 16, 1977.
64. British police commander in the country in 1947. Reuven Gal, *A Portrait of the Israeli Soldier* (Westport, CT: Greenwood Press, 1986), p. 134.

wrote that shortly after the explosion Chaim Weizmann, president of the Zionist Federation, had told him, with tears in his eyes, "You can't deny their courage. If it had been the headquarters of the *Wehrmacht* that they blew up, they would all be in line for Victoria Crosses."[65]

A tribute also came from an unlikely source, none other than Sir John Shaw himself, formerly Chief Secretary of the Mandatory Government, the man widely blamed for the failure to evacuate the hotel, whose own life was saved by a miracle. "It has always been my opinion: from an operational point of view – all credit to your 'terrorists.' They performed their task with exceptional skill and audacity. This was the beginning of a series of Jewish victories, which came to its peak in 1948."[66]

On the fiftieth anniversary of the bombing of the King David Hotel, July 22, 1996, the *Jerusalem Post* wrote in a leading article that "Time has not erased the memory of this historic, desperate event. The perpetuation of this memory is due not only to the mourning of the victims' families, but equally to the success of this terrorist mission and its subsequent political significance – it led directly to the creation of the State of Israel."

And it concludes that despite the importance of the bombing, controversy over the issue has prevented accurate documentation of the chain of events leading to it. Official reports of the attack have only recently been released to the general public by the British Ministry of Defense, having been kept secret for 30 years, and it may be that there are still relevant documents locked away in the archives of Britain's Foreign Office.

According to Neil Cobbett, Britain's state archivist, certain documents pertaining to the bombing are kept closed because they may "cause distress to former members of the government, or personnel, or to public opinion."

In that same issue of the *Jerusalem Post*, Alexander Zvieli, formerly an employee of the *Palestine Post*, wrote that in the air there was a widespread sense of denunciation of a horrific act. But – and no one dared say this – there was also admiration for the courage of the perpetrators and

---

65. *Ma'ariv*, July 18, 1986. (It is hard to believe that this was said by the same Chaim Weizmann who just a few days before had demanded the cessation of all hostile activity against the British – *Author's comment*.)
66. Interview by Moshe Vardi, *Yediot Aharonot*, March 27, 1964. Shaw added: "The Arabs tried to give me a hard time too with terrorist acts, but their operations never showed the same imagination and flair."

their skill and inventiveness. How did they manage to strike at the heart of this bastion of British power?

And he concludes that there is little doubt that in the wake of this explosion, the British cabinet began to consider more seriously the abrogation of the Palestine Mandate. The tragedy of the King David Hotel marks the turning point in the history of Eretz Israel and the Mandate.

The British have a high regard for the Bible. The story of Gideon and his 300 warriors in the Book of Judges fired the imagination of one of their greatest commanders, Major-General Orde Charles Wingate, who saw in the biblical Gideon a symbol and a model to be followed in guerilla warfare – first in this country, taking on the Arab gangs, and later, during the World War II, in Ethiopia and Burma.

The forces at the disposal of the modern-day Gideon (or Gidi, aka Amihai Paglin) numbered no more than 25 young men, of whom only eight went into action – less than an infantry squad – and one of *them* was an agent provocateur planted by the British!

And with this force the IZL set out to storm the most strongly defended British fortress in the land, perhaps in the entire Middle East. And most amazing of all – it succeeded.

On Monday, July 22, 1946, at 12:37 PM, destiny registered the first beat in the countdown towards the departure of the British from Eretz Israel.

THE JERUSALEM RAILWAY STATION BOMBING

The sound of gunfire was not heard by Gidi, who by that time was on his way to Tel Aviv, completely unaware of the bloodbath in progress at the railway station. But Avinoam, then in the first aid station in Ramban Street, most definitely heard the sounds and knew precisely what they meant. At three in the afternoon – 24 hours too late – from his room in the German Settlement he sent a two-word message to the chief of Staff, Haim Landau: Yanai traitor! *Two words, which a day earlier could have changed the fates of men. For Meir Feinstein and his friends they came too late.*

THE OPERATION

On Sunday, October 27, 1946, final preparations were completed in IZL headquarters for an attack on the central railway station in Jerusalem. The plan had finally been approved by Gidi and details passed on to Heinrich Reinhold (Yanai), who had been appointed to command the operation. The final date wasn't specified but he was told to stay in his room and await further contact, within the next 48 hours.

Monday morning, Adina Hai arrived with a message: a meeting with Gidi was scheduled for the following day at 3:00 PM.[1]

Yanai wasted no time. He hastily packed a suitcase, told his landlady, Mrs. Katz, he was going out for a while – and was never seen there again.[2] That afternoon he turned up at Yitzhak Finkelstein's apartment in Haifa, with a strange story about a "present" that he'd been asked to deliver to some address on Carmel. Finkelstein knew Yanai was active in the ranks of the IZL, but even so this seemed a little odd, and he decided to follow him. To his surprise, he saw his friend turn towards the residence of CID inspector

---

1. Tavin's interview with Avinoam, 1954, Jabotinsky Archives.
2. HHA 1229/112 (79).

Schindler; he stayed there a while and on his return said he hadn't found the address and the "present" hadn't been delivered.[3]

As it turned out later, Yanai's long trek to his friend's house had not been wasted: on arrival he immediately handed over a bundle of handwritten papers, and soon after they were on the desk of the British investigations officer, Conquest. Lights in the Haifa CID offices were burning into the small hours of the morning, and telephone contacts with CID Headquarters in Jerusalem continued until dawn.

By the morning of Tuesday, October 29, 1946, the intelligence data handed over by Yanai had already been edited, typed, and divided into three reports (see appendix).

The first (no. 006–130, dated October 28, 1946) contained all the information that Yanai had been able to glean regarding the IZL, with special reference to the plan to bomb the Jerusalem railway station, an operation that he was supposed to be commanding personally.

The second (no. 006–126, dated October 29, 1946) dealt with the organizational structure of the IZL, operational methods, and immediate tactical objectives, as well as the state of relations between the IZL, the Haganah, and the Lehi.

The third (006–123) was a continuation and summary of the first and second, concentrating on the organizational and financial state of the IZL, with details of the senior commanders and targets for attack outside Palestine.

The first report was the most crucial, containing the information that served as a foundation for the wave of arrests on the night of October 29–30, 1946, and the bloody ambush set by the British the following day at the railway station. It included proposed objectives for attack, names and addresses of Irgun commanders, arms caches, and meeting places.

Yanai didn't know the men's real names (the conspiratorial methods of the IZL had their uses!), and except in the case of Dov Cohen (Shimshon), whom he had known since they served together in the British army – he could give only nicknames and physical descriptions. The "brotherhood of warriors" didn't prevent him informing on his former messmate, without a twinge of conscience but with a hint of admiration: "Man in charge

---

3.   HHA 1229/112 (64–65).

is ex-sergeant major Cohen…formerly in Commandoes in Abyssinia and Western Desert – a very brave man" (see appendix B, Report No. 1).

Amihai Paglin's natural caution – his instinct not to become more closely acquainted with Yanai than his job required – served him well. Once Yanai saw him in the doorway of his house – and that was once too often, as it nearly cost him his freedom.[4] The description of Gidi in Yanai's report shows the importance the latter attached to him on the IZL ladder of command, and also his forlorn hope of getting to Begin through him. The following is an extract from the report:

> Another important place is in Yehuda Levy Street [in Tel Aviv], or it may be the Mikveh Street in the Post Office side of the Railway…. The house is called passage "Gardelin" it has two entrances in 2 streets and several escape routes. A very important member lives in this place with his parents, who are very rich. 5′10″ black wavy hair, thin, 26–27 years of age, nice type of man. This man is the most important man I know – all plans made in the country must be vetted by him. I don't know his name. I know him as "Gideon."

At three in the afternoon on October 29 Gidi and Avinoam were waiting, as agreed, for Yanai, to discuss final details of the operation scheduled for the next day at 8:00 AM. They waited in vain. The messenger sent to him had a fruitless journey: "He's not at home."

At 5:00 PM it was Adina Hai who knocked on his door in vain.

By seven, Gideon and Avinoam had run out of patience; with heavy hearts they made their way to his room. Avinoam recalled:

> We asked for Mr. Reinhold and the landlady told us he'd been missing since yesterday. I asked if I could leave a note. On the table there was a vase of flowers but what caught my attention was the piece of paper beside it, with one sentence, in English, written on it: "See you later," signed "Mary." On closer inspection I decided this was a man's handwriting, not a woman's. We began to suspect something wasn't right here: our first thought was he'd been kidnapped by the Haganah – since the King David operation relations between the organizations

---

4. Statement of Amihai Paglin (Gidi), July 8, 1957, Jabotinsky Archives.

had yet again been strained[5] – and the second possibility was that he'd been arrested.

Strange though it may seem, despite all the suspicious circumstances, the idea of treachery simply never arose. As Yaakov Amrami, at that time head of the IZL intelligence network, remarks, "I don't suppose Avinoam had any reservations at all about Yanai when he didn't find him at home – otherwise he'd have canceled the operation immediately, as sometimes happened for less serious reasons."[6]

The operation wasn't canceled. The decision was deferred to the next day; the participants had already been summoned to report at 7:00 A.M. Meanwhile the night curfew had come into force in Jerusalem, and Gidi's intention to return that evening to Tel Aviv was no longer practical. So there was a problem of overnight accommodation. "I had a room in the center of town," Avinoam says, "but it was impossible to get to it because of the curfew."[7]

Another emergency safe house was the "Prophet's Room" in Kiryat Shmuel, and they set off in that direction.

Avinoam was already putting the key in the lock when some obscure sense stopped him. "Maybe it's not such a good idea staying here tonight..." he turned suddenly to Gidi. "After all, Yanai knows this place!" He was surprised to hear himself saying this.

"I was acting as required by the rules of caution," he explained years later to Yaakov Tavin. "We were afraid Yanai had been abducted or arrested, and maybe he wouldn't stand up to the pressure of interrogation. Another possibility," he admitted, "just didn't occur to us."

The two of them carried on towards the Abu Tor neighborhood and found refuge in Mike's apartment.[8] Next day it turned out that British de-

---

5. Yaakov Amrami (Yoel) in his statement on the Yanai issue, July 3, 1958, asserted that in his opinion there was no reason to suppose Reinhold had been kidnapped by the Haganah. "In any case, I don't think we could have suspected then (on the eve of the railway station action) that he had been kidnapped by the Haganah, since contacts between them and us were continuing, and it was a conflict confined to slogans." Jabotinsky Archives.

6. Testimony of Yaakov Amrami (Yoel), July 3, 1958, Jabotinsky Archives.

7. Amrami's interview with Avinoam, 1968, Jabotinsky Archives.

8. Mike – code name of Shmuel Amitai, serving at the time as regional secretary in Jerusalem, later to be regional commander in Netanya.

tectives had indeed visited the "Prophet's Room" – another lucky escape for Gidi.

THE NIGHT OF ARRESTS

Wednesday, October 30, 1946. At 4:00 A M, while Gidi slept in Mike's apartment in Jerusalem, the signal was given. Special police units, backed by troops and armored vehicles, simultaneously raided houses in the three major cities – Tel Aviv, Jerusalem, and Haifa – and made a series of arrests and arms confiscations on the basis of preprepared lists.

A squad of camouflaged snipers took up positions on the roofs of the Jerusalem railway station and the print shop next door as well as on the hill opposite.

At dawn army and police units surrounded the building on Mikveh Israel Street in Tel Aviv, which according to information received was Gidi's residence. "All the men were taken away for a lineup and made to walk one by one past the hatch of a tank, and there's no doubt at all that Yanai was sitting inside it," Gidi testified. Confirmation of this is also to be found in the official report, signed by the head of the Jewish Department, Jerusalem CID Headquarters, John O'Sullivan: "House at Golden Lane, Tel Aviv occupied by very important leader. Raided by Police, suspect not traced, now under observation" (see appendix H – Appendix IV to CID Report).

Before dawn, detectives raided a basement flat at 146 Dizengoff Street, Tel Aviv, temporary residence of Nahum Slonim and Shmuel Krushnevsky, IZL senior commanders. They were both arrested and bundled into a police van; a masked man identified them with a nod of the head.[9]

Concurrently there was a series of arrests among IZL activists in Haifa, including the regional commander, Yitzhak Friedman (Elitzur).

The "Prophet's Room" in Jerusalem was described in the CID dossier as "the residence of a senior commander[10] and an important meeting place." Accordingly, it was treated to a nocturnal visit, which failed to yield the anticipated fruit: "Raided by Police, occupant absconded, documents seized" (see appendix H – Appendix IV to CID Report).

---

9.   Yehuda Lapidot, *Be-lahav ha-mered* [In the flame of the rebellion] (Tel Aviv: Ministry of Defense, 1996), p. 197.

10.   The reference is to the regional secretary, Haim Reznik (Yoram).

In Givat Shaul, on the other hand, the British were luckier, uncovering a small cache of weapons.

All in all, that night the police succeeded in rounding up a dozen IZL activists, most of them rank and file. But the major drama was due to unfold the following day, in the assault on the railway station.

LAST PREPARATIONS

Wednesday night, Meir Feinstein went to bed early, leaving the window by his bed open. He told his brother he was expecting to be called first thing in the morning, as he had to be up early for "an important errand." Six weeks had passed since his discharge from the British army, after two and a half years of exemplary service. "The war is over!" his CO had told him, slapping him warmly on the shoulder and handing him his commendation. *Wrong!* he thought to himself: *The war's only just beginning.* A few days later he joined the ranks of the IZL.

At 5:30 AM he was awakened by his friend's sharp whistle.[11] Down in the street, Aryeh Eshel was waiting for him.

"I'd met him before," he said,[12] "but not as a member of the Irgun. This time we got acquainted through Sima. When we reached the Edison Room it wasn't yet seven o'clock, but most of the team were already there. None of us knew what the mission was going to be."

Sima Huisman (Fleischaker) had joined the IZL at an early age. Now a qualified nurse, she was responsible for first-aid services in her unit. Usually she turned up for operations in her nurse's uniform, apparently feeling more comfortable and less vulnerable that way. She'd been told of this meeting the day before by her commander, Israel Levi: "You're to report at 7:00 AM," he told her.[13] There was nothing unusual about this. She was about to leave, when he said something that stopped her in her tracks: "This time you'll be dressing for a party...not in your nurse's outfit."

"What kind of party...?" she asked, thinking it must be a joke.

"The posh kind..." he smiled. He didn't explain.

11. Yosef Nedava, *Sefer olei ha-gardom* [Martyrs of the gallows] (Tel Aviv: Shelah, 1952 [reprinted 1966, 1974]), p. 251.

12. Yitzhak Avinoam's interview with Aryeh Eshel (Yariv), "Railway Operation," November 3, 1968, Jabotinsky Archives.

13. Avinoam's interview with Sima Fleischaker, December 26, 1967, Jabotinsky Archives.

It was Wednesday, and the future of the operation was still in doubt.

Inwardly, Gidi and Avinoam were still hoping that Yanai would arrive for the operation as planned, and his absence yesterday turn out to have been a mistake. Another messenger was sent to his home – but he too had a wasted journey: Yanai had disappeared as if the earth had swallowed him.

From seven o'clock on six youths and one girl stealthily made their way into the "Edison Room" in the Succat Shalom district of Jerusalem. First to arrive were Moshe Horovitz and Daniel Azulai, closely followed by Aryeh Eshel, Meir Feinstein, Yoav Levi (Kushi) and Masud Betton; the glamor element, without any doubt, was provided by Sima Huisman, resplendent (at this hour of the morning!) in evening gown and all the trimmings, her hair elegantly coiffured. Everyone stared at her curiously, while she smiled awkwardly and blushed. Someone politely offered her a chair.

Time crawled by, slowly. Up the road, Gidi and Avinoam were still conferring – though a decision was slow in coming.

As they conferred, the first reports were filtering through about the arrests and searches among IZL activists. "We heard first from Gal[14] that two training centers in Jerusalem and an arms cache in Givat Shaul had fallen into the hands of the Brits," Avinoam recalled, adding, "After we heard the 'Prophet's Room' had been searched it was agreed the operation should be delayed until the reasons for the loss of the arms caches became clear, and at the same time we wanted another security inspection of the railway station area. It was also decided to appoint a new commander for the operation, and the choice fell on Aviel [Eliyahu Levi], who'd been involved in the advance planning."

At 10:00 AM Aharon Salomon was sent on his motorbike to check the zone of operations.

By this time the ambush squad was already in position and well camouflaged. Camouflage had always been the British army's specialty, and during World War II they'd turned it into a fine art. Sure enough, at first sight there was no change to be seen in the area, certainly not from the perspective of a motorcycle rider.

After a leisurely tour with his girlfriend, Salomon returned 20 minutes later and announced, "No unusual deployments of troops or police."

---

14. Gal – code name of Yehoshua Goldschmid, at that time commander of the Jerusalem combat squad and responsible for weapons stores in the capital.

At eleven o'clock the booby-trapped suitcases arrived at the Edison Room – three of them. They were piled cautiously in the corner and appearing soon after was Gidi – an imposing figure, whom none of those present had seen before. There was a tense silence, which he made no attempt to break. He stood leaning against the wall, silently surveying the team.[15]

Soon afterwards, Aviel was introduced to the combat squad: young, swarthy, in a suit and a colorful tie. Gal told them this was the commander of the operation, and the men exchanged glances: IZL commanders didn't usually go into battle dressed to the nines. Kushi, sitting beside Sima, couldn't resist whispering in her ear, "He looks like he's going to his wedding!" Before she could reply, Aviel had taken over and was going through the stages of the operation.

Nothing was said about the timing.

At 1:00 PM there were no more questions to be asked in the Edison Room. They all knew their roles, and waited tensely for developments.

Gidi left the room, accompanied by Gal. "We can't hold this up any longer," he declared. "I'm going to meet Avinoam. If you don't hear from me by zero hour – Aviel is to proceed as planned."[16]

He turned to go, but stopped at the door, "Send someone to check the area again…"

Salomon jumped on his motorbike, again with his girlfriend riding along. This time he was in no hurry, making sure he got a good look around. The young couple walking arm-in-arm could have been any pair of lovers, snatching a moment of intimacy amid the hubbub of the station concourse.

In spite of all his efforts he discovered nothing suspicious or unusual in his surroundings. This time, too, he missed the soldiers in their ambush positions. The scene was normal and routine. He was satisfied.

"Everything's okay!" he announced on his return, shouting above the

---

15. Avinoam's interview with Aryeh Eshel (Yariv), November 3, 1968, Jabotinsky Archives.
16. Heinrich Reinhold (Yanai), who was supposed to be commanding the operation in question, had been briefed on all the details, and according to his report to the British secret police, the attack was due to take place at 7:00 AM, or at 11:00 AM or at 3:00 PM (See appendix B, Report No. 1). In fact the action took place at 3:00, in accordance with the pre-arranged timetable (it was not yet suspected that Yanai had betrayed the team). All newspapers reported the following day that the assailants arrived at the station at around 2:30, and this would place departure from the Edison Room at 2:00 or a few minutes later.

racket of the motorbike. Aviel heard and looked at Gal, a questioning look in his eyes. Gal nodded, "Proceeding as planned!"

POINT OF NO RETURN

Avinoam paced back and forth in Tachkemoni Street,[17] waiting for Gidi to arrive.

Since early morning he had been trying to dredge up every scrap of information about the searches and arrests across the city. Report followed report. At midday he was told of the discovery of another arms cache in Givat Shaul (in a place that had already been searched that morning, without result); this time considerable booty had fallen into British hands.[18] They had even found and confiscated the IZL staff car. While he was still trying to digest the significance of these events, the first reports of arrests in Tel Aviv and Haifa began to arrive. All the signs pointed in one direction – Yanai.

By the time Gidi arrived his mind was made up. After a brief conference between the two it was decided to order an immediate halt to the operation. But it was too late. A few minutes after 2:00 PM Gal had sent the team on its way, with a parting cry of *"Abi gezunt."*[19]

The lot had fallen. The hands of fate were moving on and there was no stopping them now.

"Neither Aviel nor Salomon is to be blamed in any way for what happened," Gidi was to say years later. "Zero hour was fixed, and if no order countermanding the operation was received before that time, Aviel was authorized to go ahead. If there is any blame to be apportioned," he insisted, "then it's down to us, the organizers, who were maybe too slow to act that day, and should have acted a good deal sooner than we did…"[20]

As Aryeh Eshel was to comment, "One of the things that made Gidi such a great and inspiring commander was the way he always stood by his

---

17. Author's telephone interview of Yitzhak Avinoam, March 17, 1999.
18. The arms confiscated from the cache amounted to twelve revolvers, one submachine gun, and two hundred rounds of ammunition.
19. The Yiddish blessing *Abi gezunt* (As long as you are healthy) became the standard equivalent of "Good luck" as used by IZL members when going into action.
20. Aryeh Eshel's recorded interview with Gidi in 1976. In this interview Gidi pointed out, inter alia, that "there was an agreed zero-hour." (See also n. 17.)

subordinates and was ready to take on personal, direct responsibility for any failure in the field, even if there were others involved."

The two taxis turned one after the other, an interval of a few minutes between them, from Agrippas Street to King George, and from there directly to the railway station. The vehicles had been commandeered a few hours earlier. Daniel Azulai and Yoav Levi (Kushi), disguised as Arab porters, sprawled comfortably in their seats. They were supposed to arrive a little ahead of the others. In the entrance to the station, near the fuel pumps, Arusi stepped on the brakes, but kept the engine running (he was to stay there, ready to evacuate any casualties if necessary). The two of them parted from him with a wave of the hand. The final 200 yards to the waiting room they covered on foot.

In the green taxi the other members of the attack squad were crammed together: the smart "groom" (Aviel), the elegant "bride" (Sima), two armed backup men (Aryeh Eshel and Moshe Horovitz), reserve "porter" (Masud Biton) and the driver (Meir Feinstein).

There were also three black suitcases crammed with explosives. They were piled on the folding seat and all took turns glancing at them apprehensively. They looked even more worried when Aviel took three acid-bottle timers from the "bride's" handbag, fitted them into position and activated them.

For most of the occupants of the taxi this was their first IZL operation, and the knowledge that they were sitting on 150 pounds (70 kilograms) of TNT, the time clocks already ticking, did nothing to ease the tension.

"When we reached the station, the 'porters' were still on their way to the waiting room," said Aryeh Eshel. "Aviel told the driver to do another slow circuit of the station, to give them time to get into position. Meanwhile, the awareness that every passing moment brought the explosion closer, and any disturbance or technical hitch could speed up the process didn't leave me for a moment."

When the second circuit was done the two porters were already waiting in place. Kushi, in *kafiyyeh* and robe, nonchalantly chewing a bagel,[21] glanced at his confederates in the taxi. Aviel responded with a nod of the

---

21. Avinoam's interview with Yoav Levi (Kushi), October 23, 1946, Jabotinsky Archives.

head and Meir stopped the vehicle, as planned, about ten yards from the entrance, pointing towards the center of the city.

So far, everything was proceeding like a well-rehearsed, choreographed theatrical piece: the groom stepping down first from the taxi and chivalrously helping the bride out of her seat; a bevy of porters swooping on them, loudly advertising their services; the groom staring around him, bemused and perplexed by the commotion, and then just "happening" to point to Kushi and Daniel; they take two of the cases and set off towards the waiting room amid the protests of the others. The third case is carried by Masud Biton – and bringing up the rear, the happy couple arm-in-arm, eager to set out for their honeymoon.

Meir Feinstein remained glued to the wheel, Moshe Horovitz beside him with the Schmeisser[22] cocked in his lap. Aryeh Eshel, two Mills grenades in one pocket and a revolver in the other, stepped down onto the concourse.

The hustle and bustle of the traveling public formed the backdrop for the little drama unfolding now before the eyes of the security forces charged with the protection of the railway station.

From the roof of the station building and the balcony of the print shop, the Tommies watched the tableau with a smile. They'd been here since dawn, waiting impatiently for "two men and a woman… armed with pistols," who will try to take control of the station building, "followed by two men carrying three suitcases with explosives."[23]

According to their information, the attack was to take place at 7:00 or 11:00 AM, or at 3:00 PM.

The two earlier times had passed with nothing happening, and there was still about half an hour to go before the third. The frustrated squaddies continued to scour the station and its environs, but nothing suspicious was to be seen. Their attention focused for a moment on the green taxi, which had pulled up at the entrance to the concourse, and from which a muscular, elegantly dressed young Arab had just emerged, accompanied by a young woman all dolled up in a green evening gown. The youth's hand

---

22. Schmeisser – submachine gun of German manufacture.
23. The information supplied to the British by Yanai, October 28, 1946 (see appendix B, Report No. 1).

never left the girl's shoulder and all the signs indicated a vivacious couple off on their honeymoon. They were immediately surrounded by a noisy throng of porters – another sight that the soldiers were well used to. Some of them tried to relieve their boredom with lewd remarks at the expense of the bride, whom they watched until she disappeared into the waiting room.

The familiar routine continued.

DANGER! EXPLOSIVES!

In the waiting room the tumult was the same as it was every day. As the young couple turned towards the ticket seller's window, the "porters" positioned the suitcases against the wall, and in the process pulled out the pins. From now on, any attempt to move them would cause instant detonation. The chemical clocks still provided a half-hour interval for the evacuation of the public.

A few more minutes passed, and the porters began slowly trudging back towards their transport. First to arrive was Masud. He took his place on the back seat, Daniel and Kushi squeezing in beside him.[24]

Aviel and Sima were still in the waiting room; their job wasn't completed yet. Despite the risk of exposure, and in defiance of all the rules of caution and camouflage, Sima had been assigned the task of placing the warnings. Those were her instructions[25] and she followed them meticulously: she took a white cloth from her handbag, unfolded it and, in full view of all, spread it over the three linked cases: clearly visible even from a distance were the *Only Thus* symbol of the Irgun Zvai Leumi and beside it, in three languages and in large red letters the words: **DANGER! EXPLOSIVES!**

A young Arab who had been watching the "bride's" movements with interest was the first to read the message. He pounced on her, clutching at her clothing and demanding an explanation. For a moment she panicked, punching him in the face and tearing herself from his grasp, ripping her dress in the process – not that she noticed this at the time – and fleeing

---

24. Statement of Aryeh Eshel (Yariv) – *Ma'ariv*, October 29, 1976; Avinoam's interview with Aryeh Eshel, November 3, 1968.

25. The bombing of the Jerusalem railway station was the first operation carried out by the IZL after that of the King David Hotel – and the trauma of what had happened then was still fresh. Thus, the insistence on ensuring that not only was a warning given, it was *seen* to be given – at any price. (In actual fact, the price paid was heavy.)

with all the strength she could muster. Aviel, already on his way to the taxi, turned around on hearing the disturbance.

From where he stood on the concourse, Aryeh Eshel couldn't see what had happened in the waiting room. Suddenly he saw Aviel and Sima running for their lives and two young Arabs chasing after them. One of them caught up with the girl and a scuffle began; Aviel rushed to her aid, but in moments they found themselves surrounded and were virtually invisible in the throng.

Of the backup team, Aryeh Eshel was the only one on the scene; he knew he was responsible for the safety of those two and he had only seconds to decide. "I knew physical intervention would be useless," he recalled. "I took the revolver from my pocket and fired a few shots over the heads of the crowd." Moshe Horovitz saw what was happening from the taxi and fired a long burst with the Schmeisser. The Arabs dispersed in panic, scattering in all directions. Sima and Aviel reached the taxi, Aryeh close behind them. All eight of them were now crammed into the vehicle, and Meir Feinstein was pumping the accelerator.

But the sound of gunfire had roused the ambush troops from their torpor – and the whole picture was turned upside down. Suddenly, and without any warning, a flurry of bullets slammed into the fleeing vehicle. The effect was devastating.

No one knew where the firing was coming from. The volleys came down like a hail storm, perforating the tin body of the car and turning it into a sieve, piercing the living flesh of the traumatized passengers. Aryeh Eshel, last into the vehicle, was sitting on the knees of Daniel Azulai, his head slumped on his chest. He didn't so much see as feel his friend's blood pouring over him. Daniel's leg was shattered and blood was streaming from his arm, and there was no way they could stop, not even for a moment. Arusi's first-aid vehicle had disappeared from the scene – no use to them at all!

Seven young men and a girl kept as close as they could to the floor of the taxi – the only one upright was Meir Feinstein, at the wheel. "Hey, look, guys, I'm driving with one hand!" he suddenly announced calmly. *Joking as usual, and at a time like this*, Aryeh Eshel was thinking. He knew Meir's carefree nature and his sense of humor. For years afterwards he couldn't forgive himself for taking this as a witty remark; the boy really was seriously injured, his left arm cut to ribbons. But despite the excruciating pain Meir succeeded in maneuvering the vehicle, one-handed, out of danger, turning down a dusty side street, away from the field of fire.

THE GETAWAY

The taxi pulled up with a squeal of brakes on the edge of a wadi in the outskirts of Yemin Moshe. Two girls waiting there took from Aviel a thick canvas bundle, containing the weapons he'd collected from the passengers during the retreat.

People dispersed in all directions: Aviel headed towards King David Street; Horovitz, a bullet wound in his shoulder, trudged with Biton to the commercial center, where they were intercepted by a squad of Arab Legionaries who didn't miss the opportunity to give them a sound thrashing. Bruised and bleeding, the two men were taken to the Russian Compound. Horovitz was detained for treatment in the government hospital, and Biton was sent to prison.[26]

Meir Feinstein slumped over the wheel, barely able to move; having accomplished his mission and rescued his friends from danger, he was suddenly overtaken by exhaustion; the tension, the mental concentration, and loss of blood were taking their toll. Sima helped him out of the vehicle. His left arm hung limp at his side and his sleeve was drenched with blood. With his right hand he clutched her shoulder and the two of them hobbled towards the buildings nearby. She could feel his strength ebbing away with every step, and as a professional nurse knew he might collapse at any moment. She didn't hesitate to barge her way into the first house she came across, where a shocked elderly couple stared in disbelief at the wounded and bleeding man, and howled with indignation.[27] Ignoring their protests, Sima put Meir down on the nearest bed, and with deft hands tore up a sheet and bound the damaged artery. As she was tending him, a young lad came in, panting, and warned her the police were on their way here, following the bloodstains. "I told him to cover the stains with dust," she related, "and left the apartment as quickly as I could. The police were already closing in, and in my torn and stained dress I would have looked suspicious. So I ducked down as if to fasten my shoe and the police passed me by; like hunting dogs

---

26. Testimony of Moshe Horovitz, quoted by David Niv in *Battles of the Irgun Zvai Leumi*.
27. This was the house of the Stein family (opposite the King David Hotel). Mrs. Aliza Stein gave evidence in court that "Meir came into the house – and collapsed…. As [her] husband was about to call a doctor, the police arrived."

tracking their prey, they followed the trail of bloodstains leading directly to the house where Meir Feinstein was lying wounded."

Daniel Azulai was bleeding quietly, unable to move.

In the taxi, as full of holes as a sieve, only he and Aryeh Eshel were left. The others had all left, fleeing in all directions. Aryeh bent over his wounded friend, whose face was pale and tormented, hoisted him on his back, and with a supreme effort began staggering up the hill towards the neighborhood. Daniel's blood was still streaming, staining the clothes of both men and leaving clear traces on the ground. "When my strength gave out," he recalled,[28] "I went into the first house I came across. There was a woman there of about 50,[29] and she started yelling her head off. I ignored her, left Daniel on the bed and went outside. It was only then I realized I was injured too – my right hand. I was in an awkward situation, covered in blood and with all the local kids swarming around me."

A girl of about 17, Rahel Arieli, saw what was going on through her window and came to his rescue. She took him into her apartment, supplied him with clean clothes belonging to her father, and agreed to testify that he'd spent the entire afternoon in her company. After two days of detention – along with 60 men from the neighborhood rounded up for good measure – he was released and sent home. "I owe her my life," he says simply.[30]

On October 30, 1946, Constable Smith, an arms and explosives expert in the regional police force, was with an army unit searching Givat Shaul in Jerusalem.[31] At 2:30 PM Lieutenant Mayton, the army's explosives specialist, received a call regarding a suspected bomb at the central railway station. He was ordered to go there immediately; Smith asked permission to accompany him and his request was granted.

When they arrived at the station, the officer inspected the suitcases and decided they were definitely dangerous, and the place should be cleared immediately. Lieutenant Mayton himself was told to leave the building without delay, but Constable Smith insisted on trying to defuse the bombs, and

---

28. Author's telephone interview with Aryeh Eshel, March 11, 1999.
29. The lady of the house was a widow named Rahel Tawati, as emerged later in court.
30. "The Blue-Eyed Traitor," *Yediot Aharonot* (weekend supplement), April 9, 1993.
31. Searches in Givat Shaul on October 30 were conducted following receipt of information from Yanai.

when he received permission he moved the first suitcase out of the waiting room to the station concourse. He concluded that the detonating mechanism was attached to the handle of the case.[32] He returned to the waiting room and as he tried to lift the second case there was a thunderous explosion. Smith was killed instantly; the station building was reduced to heaps of rubble. A few moments later the bomb on the concourse exploded too.

THE HUMAN COST

Eight set out on October 30, 1946,[33] to destroy the capital's railway station – a central artery in the transport and communications network of the Mandatory administration.

Three returned to their homes that day unscathed – Eliyahu Levi (Aviel), Yoav Levi (Kushi) and Sima Huisman (Fleischhaker).

One, Aryeh Eshel, returned two days later.

Two, Moshe Horovitz and Masud Biton, returned five months later, after a military trial and acquittal.

One, Daniel Azulai, returned 18 months later, having been sentenced to death and subsequently pardoned.[34]

The only one who never returned was the heroic Meir Feinstein.[35]

---

32. Elimelech Spiegel, who assembled the "suitcase bombs" used at the railway station, is adamant that only two of the cases were fitted with anti-handling devices, and it was Smith's misfortune to choose first the one case of the three which could be moved without causing immediate detonation. When he tried to repeat the procedure, the case exploded and he was killed instantly.
33. HHA 1229/112 (51).
34. It later emerged that Daniel Azulai was an agent planted by the Haganah, who became accidentally involved in the railway station attack, almost losing his life in the process. Following intervention on the part of the Haganah – which since the King David Hotel operation had resumed cooperation with the authorities – his death sentence was commuted to life imprisonment. He was released after a year and a half.
35. On March 25, 1947, five months after the bombing of the Jerusalem railway station and the capture of Meir Feinstein, severely wounded, in Mrs. Stein's apartment – Feinstein was arraigned before a military court along with Biton, Horovitz, and Azulai. Meir arrived in court having had his left arm amputated, and without counsel. He refused to defend himself and denied the court's authority to try him. Biton and Horowitz were acquitted for lack of evidence, and Feinstein and Azulai were sentenced to death. On April 17, 1947 the GOC confirmed Feinstein's death sentence, although that of Azulai was commuted to life imprisonment. Four days after confirmation of the sentence,

On April 21, 1947 – 175 days after the railway station episode, Meir and his comrade in destiny, Moshe Barazani,[36] cheated the hangman; they put two grenades between them, and – with a last embrace and a cry of "Hear O Israel, the Lord our God is one Lord" – blew themselves up and died the deaths of martyrs.

---

on April 21, 1947, at midnight, Feinstein blew himself up together with his comrade in destiny, Moshe Barazani, with two hand grenades smuggled into their cell.

36. Moshe Barazani, a member of Lehi (Fighters for the Freedom of Israel) was captured on Sunday, March 9, 1947, at a road intersection in Jerusalem, with a Mills grenade in his pocket. His target was the commander of the Ninth Division, Brigadier Davis, who used to drive past this point every evening. This took place during the period when martial law was in force, and within less than a week, in a trial lasting just an hour and a half, he was sentenced to death by a military court. When the sentence was announced he sang "Hatikva" and shouted to his judges, "You won't scare us with hangings!" On April 21, 1947, he blew himself up together with his comrade Meir Feinstein – a few minutes before the hangman was due to do his work.

The heroism of these two mesmerized the Yishuv, and the poet Natan Alterman, not a supporter of underground movements, gave expression to this in his *Tur ha-Shevi'i* [Seventh Column] ("Night of the Suicides," *Davar*, April 25, 1947), in part as follows:

We cannot avert our eyes. Futile to deny
The glory of that night hour.
Do not be silent, when the flame speaks,
Whereby those two burned themselves to death…

THE YANAI EPISODE: INFILTRATION OF A BRITISH AGENT

His IZL code name was Yanai. In Germany, where he was born in 1916 to his mother Leah and his father Abraham Reinhold, he was given the name Heinrich, or Heini for short. The British preferred to call him Henry, the Jews Yehiel. Women whom he befriended during wartime service in Europe knew him as Harry.[1]

In his childhood he studied in a *yeshiva* and in 1933, after a spell in a *hakhshara* (training farms toward agricultural settlement in Eretz Israel), emigrated to Palestine. He embarked on his new way of life in Petah Tikva and in 1939, on the eve of World War II and in the wake of bloody domestic riots, joined the guards (*ghaffirs*) of the Jewish Settlement Police and served in Safed.

Even at this early stage his behavior was regarded as eccentric: in spite of his role as a Jewish guard, he preferred to socialize with British police personnel; the link between them was a Jewish officer attached to the CID,[2] Max Schindler, formerly an attorney and criminal investigator in Berlin. It wasn't hard for the two of them to find a common language; it was a case

---

1. The multiplicity of names and nicknames helped him to confuse even his lovers...
2. CID – Criminal Investigation Department – detective branch of the British police force.

of "birds of a feather." A secret and shadowy bond soon developed between them, its basis being service to the interests of the British administration in Palestine.

They met often, and kept in close touch even after Schindler was transferred to Haifa.[3]

In 1943, acting on the advice of his friends in the British secret police (as was to emerge later), Reinhold enlisted in His Majesty's Armed Forces and became an undercover intelligence agent.[4] He was posted, and not by chance, to the Third Battalion of the "Buffs,"[5] specifically to 28 Platoon, a unit composed largely of Haganah activists, many of them engaged in stockpiling weapons and organizing illegal immigration – an issue of great concern to the British authorities at that time.

Throughout this period, regular correspondence continued between Reinhold and Schindler. Beyond the innocent exchange of opinions and impressions, between the lines, there were subtle hints, incomprehensible to anyone but the correspondents themselves, such as this sentence, concluding a letter from Schindler dated November 19, 1945: "I don't know whether you should not have taken the commission. I am anyhow glad that it was offered to you."[6]

Cultivating Schindler's friendship was not untypical in the complex network of contacts that Reinhold was weaving around himself. Back in the days when he was serving as a guard in Safed he had made a point of befriending an officer in the British CID, Norman Talbot, and this connection wasn't severed even when the latter was transferred to Jerusalem CID HQ. (In defiance of all logic, Reinhold was careful to keep all his correspondence – with detectives or with lovers.) From exchanges of letters that have survived, it may be inferred that in the summer of 1940 he approached his friend Talbot, asking for his help in obtaining a certain post (unspecified) in the secret police. In his reply, dated July 19, 1940 (on CID-headed notepaper), Talbot remarks, "I've spoken about you – and I will do my best…,"

---

3. Most of Reinhold's activity in Haifa consisted of locating Jewish underground activists in the north of the country (interview with Shmuel Perl who in the early 1940s served as IZL commander in Safed).
4. Employed by the British espionage service.
5. The Buffs – a British regiment that incorporated a number of Jewish infantry companies during World War II.
6. Photocopy of this letter in author's possession, courtesy of Jabotinsky Archives.

and on August 2, 1940, he writes at greater length, "I saw Lieutenant Danin this afternoon and he wants you to come up and see him. I told him your qualifications, that I thought you were the right man for the job. Let me know when you can come to Jerusalem. I will tell him…. Of course I cannot promise anything."

In another letter from Talbot, dated September 2, 1940, it is stated, "I myself saw the recommendation. I am sure that you will get a favorable reply in the near future."

The nature of the assignment suiting Reinhold's talents isn't defined explicitly in the correspondence,[7] but there's no need here to resort to guesswork. By dint of meticulous study of his biography (in the Jabotinsky House archives and Haganah Historical Archives) it emerges that in the years 1941–42 Reinhold was employed by the coastguard service. The conjunction of his service in that capacity with his negotiations conducted through the CID officer Talbot leaves little room for speculation. From a secret intelligence document it may be inferred that in those years Reinhold carried out a number of important assignments for British intelligence, including several secret missions to Syria and Lebanon. From the same document, we learn that while returning from one of these missions he was detained in Ein Gev but released following intelligence intervention.[8]

Later, during the period of his service in the British army, having aroused the suspicions of the Haganah activists in the platoon, he was summoned by them to an inquiry. In his testimony on this occasion he freely admitted that before enlisting he had served in the German section of the secret police in the north of the country.[9] All the signs are that what he was really doing there was helping the British track down illegal Jewish immigrants, trying to enter the country via Syria and Lebanon.

From various records and documents preserved in the archives it emerges that Private Reinhold was suspected by the Haganah even then of collusion with the British. He himself used to boast to fellow soldiers of his "friends in the CID." In a report submitted by an intelligence operative known as "Gad" to Haganah HQ, dated November 23, 1943, it is stated that "Private Reinhold Yehiel, who served in 28 Platoon, has been transferred

---

7. Photocopies of this correspondence in the author's possession; most originals deposited in Jabotinsky Archives.
8. HHA 1229/112 (68).
9. HHA 1229/112 (3).

to unit 4. In Platoon 28 he offered our comarades help should they need it, since he has friends in the CID and in this unit, too, he has already managed to propose this." And Gad concludes, "Reinhold is a resident of Haifa and has served in the police force in Atlit."

Following Gad's warning, intelligence personnel began investigating the issue, and to the dossier quoted above, on November 27, 1943, the handwritten note was added, "Ben Israel has been asked to inform us of all that is known of the subject's activities in Haifa."[10]

Ben Israel's reply was received a month later, January 4, 1944: "The subject served in the auxiliary police force in Atlit for two or more years. He was then transferred with the rank of corporal to the coastguard service and served there for one year." [For some reason the informant omits any mention of his service as a *ghaffir* in Safed – *Author's note*.] Ben Israel continues, "He was once questioned by one of our senior operatives in connection with various matters. In this conversation he said he had worked in the German section of the secret police in the north of the country, and that he had been the victim of negative publicity within Yishuv circles. He had even received threatening letters, which he claimed were sent by Jewish institutions, although he didn't know the reasons behind them." And Ben Israel concludes, "It's difficult to say anything definite about his character: his admission of police connections can be interpreted in a number of ways."[11]

Ben Israel probably did not realize just how accurate this assessment was. The deeper Reinhold's character and the reasons for his actions are probed, the clearer the impression becomes of a split personality: a man of no scruples, incapable of choosing between his Jewish roots on the one hand, and on the other his admiration for all things British: British power, British culture, and the British way of life – a way of life he did everything he could to emulate.

Once he had proved himself in the role "appropriate to his talents" – as a "hunter of illegals" in the north – his intelligence handlers gave him weightier assignments in the same line of work: foiling the immigration of Holocaust survivors from Europe and identifying organizers of illicit

---

10. HHA 1229/112 (2).
11. HHA 1229/112 (3).

immigration among the ranks of the Jewish auxiliary forces. Enlistment was the logical step.

So it was that on January 4, 1943, intelligence agent Yehiel Reinhold (the name registered in the recruitment office) exchanged his civilian garb for military uniform and took up his posting to 28 Platoon, Third Battalion, the "Buffs."

His comrades-in-arms testified that he was a courageous and disciplined soldier – who sometimes took discipline to absurd lengths. He spared no effort or expense in the attempt to buy the affection and trust of his messmates. This was the period of the White Paper and he was often to be heard railing against the Mandate administration in the most acerbic terms and calling for resistance. In spite of this – and without knowing precisely why – the others treated him with caution and were careful not to share with him information regarding immigration and arms acquisition.

An intelligence report dated March 30, 1947, states, inter alia:

> During the subject's period of army service in the Brigade, based in Holland and Belgium, he used to engage in all kinds of black market activities on behalf of his officers.
>
> He once told one of his comrades of his connection (familial, apparently) with Inspector Schindler of the Haifa CID. He even claimed to have shared a house with him (Sea Road on the Carmel).
>
> The subject used to give (unauthorized) instruction in sabotage techniques, specializing in the use of primitive devices. He used to call these "home economics" classes.[12]

The atmosphere of reservations and suspicions surrounding Reinhold continued throughout his army career. An intelligence document dated September 17, 1947, relates how, immediately after enlistment, Reinhold made the acquaintance of a Jewish soldier who had deserted from the French army and who had in his possession maps of the El Alamein front. Two days after they first met, he asked to see these maps – and they vanished

---

12. HHA 1229/112 (45).

into thin air. "It must be assumed they were passed on to Yehiel Reinhold's superiors," the author of the report concludes.[13]

From letters to his friends it emerges that on July 27, 1945, he went AWOL, and set out on a mysterious journey through Belgium, France, Germany, and Austria. He never explained what he was up to.

In his book *Life in the Ranks*, Haganah activist Zvi Brenner stresses that in Haganah circles, Reinhold was regarded as an agent planted by the British. He backs this up with the following anecdote: in the course of a divisional training exercise near Kiryat Haim, he was sent an assistant instructor from another platoon, named Reinhold. "At the same time I received a note from his platoon sergeant, Eliyahu Hershkovitz: 'He's a good instructor, but keep a close eye on him, he's suspected of having links with the CID.' I decided to get rid of Reinhold as quickly as possible," Brenner goes on. "I let him take one class and then went to the commanding officer and said, 'Ben-Artzi[14] is making fun of us; he's sent us an instructor who's totally useless!' Reinhold was soon back in his own unit."

Yehiel Reinhold, Army number 38454, was officially discharged from His Majesty's Armed Forces on May 25, 1946. Rank on discharge – sergeant-major. In his service record, in the "conduct" section, the two letters v.G. appear – very good. An extravagant tribute indeed – bearing in mind his unauthorized absences from bases in Europe…

Two months previously, on April 1, 1946, he had been placed on the demob list, and a few days later, without waiting for his discharge certificate, began working as an accounts clerk in the NAAFI[15] offices in Haifa. It was time for the sergeant major and part-time secret police agent to cultivate a new civilian identity.

This was the short-lived Golden Age of the United Resistance Movement. Hostile actions against the Mandate administration were being extended in scope and taking on a more nationalistic aspect. Worrying rumors were filtering through to British intelligence agencies, according to which the IZL and Lehi were planning assassination attempts on figures of authority in Palestine and in Britain – including the High Commissioner,

---

13. HHA 1229/112 (68).
14. Efraim Ben-Artzi was the platoon commander who sent Reinhold to act as instructor.
15. NAAFI – Navy, Army and Air Force Institute – British military canteen service.

GOC Armed Forces, and even the foreign secretary, Bevin. Reliable information regarding the intentions of the underground organizations – the IZL in particular – became an urgent priority, and Reinhold's controllers couldn't afford to waste any time. Reinhold didn't disappoint them. While still in his period of transition to civilian life, with typical German efficiency, he turned immediately to two of his friends, from opposite poles of the political spectrum.

First he approached Yehuda Koppel, a senior Haganah commander in Haifa and a former comrade-in-arms. As he expected, Reinhold had no difficulty getting a warm recommendation from Koppel for admission into the ranks of the Haganah. Not only that: he was also invited to attend a command course in Kibbutz Alonim. Rumors of his friend's involvement with intelligence Koppel dismissed airily as cheap gossip.

Later, when Reinhold's treachery became known, Koppel's precipitate recommendation brought suspicion of collusion with the authorities to bear on him as well. "For two or three years he was Reinhold's closest and most trusted friend, and I suspect he was involved himself," declared a senior Haganah activist, who had served in the British army with Koppel, in October 1947.[16]

Yehuda Koppel, whose recommendation had smoothed Reinhold's path into the ranks of the Haganah, never forgave him. "I'm going to find that man…" he was still saying bitterly, years later. "I'm going to find that man and kill him!" He was not alone in this aspiration – which remained unfulfilled.

At the same time, Reinhold turned to Yitzhak Finkelstein from Haifa, a veteran IZL activist and close family friend; the two of them had grown up together in Germany. Finkelstein's apartment, at 92 Herzl Street, had often served him as an emergency hostel and postal address. Knowing his friend's ideological background, Reinhold had no difficulty picking the right theme: the destruction of European Jewry and the immigration embargo. "We can't sit around anymore with arms folded!" he fulminated, repeating words he had heard Finkelstein himself use on several occasions. "We have to work for the expulsion of the British and the establishment of a Jewish state." The other couldn't believe what he was hearing, but Reinhold hadn't finished

---

16. HHA 1229/112 (74).

yet, "I don't care who does it" – with a wistful, provocative stare into the middle distance – "I'll join any outfit that has the guts to act. If the religious parties declare war – I'll be right behind them!"[17] The hint was clear.

Finkelstein was overjoyed: countless debates had finally born fruit. He could barely refrain from embracing his friend; boys like Yehiel didn't turn up every day on the IZL's doorstep in the communist stronghold of Haifa. He was well aware of his skills with explosives and his valor on the battlefield – but not his theatrical talents. It never even occurred to him that the whole performance was a sham. The next day he warmly recommended him to Eliezer Sudit – whose IZL code name was "Kabtzan" (Beggar) and who was in Haifa at the time on a special assignment for Amihai Paglin – planning the destruction of a British warship. The image of Reinhold, as described to him, aroused his interest and his curiosity: it only remained to see whether the man matched the image. The two of them met that evening.

It wasn't enough that Reinhold's data came up to expectations – he seemed too good to be true: a former soldier, 30 years old, with a wealth of combat experience, an explosives expert, fluent English-speaker, solid build, fair hair, blue eyes – in his rosiest dreams Kabtzan couldn't have imagined someone better suited to the job for which he'd made the trip to Haifa. In his mind's eye he already saw Reinhold, in the uniform of an officer of the Royal Navy, smuggling into the port the two barrel bombs that would wreck the British destroyer. Most of all he was impressed by his sincerity, the way he talked openly of his contacts with intelligence during his military service. At 21 years of age, Sudit had acquired some experience of combat in the field; his notions of intelligence were drawn from spy fiction and movies. Secret agents, he remembered, don't advertise themselves in the marketplace. Reinhold also made no secret of his approach to the Haganah, and the command course he had been invited to attend. Kabtzan knew all about this, but he was pleased to be getting further evidence of the man's openness. In fact he had already decided he should be inducted immediately into Ha-Ma'amad (an alternate internal name for Etzel) even if this meant bypassing the normal formalities and procedures.

"He's just the man for the job," he told Gidi. "He's prepared to join us as a simple soldier and give up the Haganah command course."

"Why should he give it up?" Gidi interrupted him with a smile. "No,

---

17. HHA 1229/112 (68).

he should do the course, make some contacts..." He was already toying with the mischievous idea of implicating the Haganah in the attack on the British destroyer, and the notion suddenly seemed feasible – and gloriously neat as well! He could barely restrain his mirth.

So Reinhold completed the course in Kibbutz Alonim and passed with flying colors. He impressed his instructors with his aptitude in handling explosives, and his talent for constructing improvised bombs and primitive devices from everyday, commonplace materials. "He knows more than the instructors!" was the whisper among his fellow trainees. "You have to gain the trust of your comrades and your commanders," Sudit told him, and characteristically Reinhold followed his instructions to the letter. "Nothing surprising in that," Kabtzan commented drily, years afterwards. "He always did a thoroughly professional job – for the IZL, the Haganah, or the Brits... He was a conscientious worker, whichever master he was serving."[18]

While Reinhold was displaying his talents on the combat-command course, Gidi was finalizing the plans for the sabotaging of the British destroyer: two iron barrels linked together with steel wire, two-thirds filled with explosives (the remainder left empty, for flotation purposes), were ready for transportation to the docks. According to the plan, Kabtzan, in diving gear and with the assistance of a Haganah diver (who thought he was working for the United Resistance Movement) was supposed to tow the barrels to the bows of the ship, fitting one on each side. But as zero hour approached – with Reinhold, disguised as a British naval officer, already driving a Royal Navy jeep into the harbor complex, the barrels of explosives stowed in the back – information leaked to Haganah command in Haifa and a furious row ensued on the dockside, stopping only just short of a violent brawl. In the end the IZL operatives were forced to abandon the scene, leaving behind them the two barrel bombs.

There's no knowing how things would have worked out if the Haganah hadn't gotten in first and foiled the operation – and no ruling out the possibility that British intelligence was in the picture and preparing a warm reception for the divers. It is a fact that when IZL members tried their luck again, they discovered to their surprise that the warships had put to sea and had anchored at a safe distance offshore. "At first we put this down to bad

18. Author's interview with Eliezer Sudit-Sharon (Kabtzan).

luck," said Gidi in 1957, "but in light of what we know today, it's virtually certain that our plans were leaked to the British by Reinhold."[19]

The failed attempt to sabotage the British destroyer had the effect of blowing the cover of both Kabtzan and Reinhold, and they left for Tel Aviv that very evening. The following day a Haganah team searched Reinhold's room and possessions – but found nothing. They were told by his room-mate (Yitzhak Finkelstein) that he'd gone to Jerusalem.[20]

While Gidi was deliberating on where to reassign him, Reinhold was energetically gathering information on IZL commanders in the region, their addresses and meeting places. (He himself was temporarily staying with Nahum Slonim.) It took all his considerable powers of persuasion to induce Sudit to take him to Gidi's house on Mikveh Israel Street. "I was very angry when I came out of the workshop and saw Yanai there," said Gidi,[21] "but the Kabtzan assured me it was okay, as it was impossible to tell which apartment I came out of."

In the end Reinhold's transfer to Jerusalem was approved. The decision was influenced, among other factors, by the imminent return of Shraga Ellis to Tel Aviv and the urgent need to find a replacement for him as com-mander of the combat squad in the capital; all felt that Reinhold had the potential to make a success of the appointment (after a brief period of in-duction under Shraga's tutelage). For this, consent at the highest level was required and Bezalel Amitzur, head of the national command staff, met Reinhold for a long exploratory chat.

Fifty years later, details of that meeting were still clearly etched in Amit-zur's memory. "The boy made a good impression," he said.

> You could say, it was too good... Perhaps that's what made me uneasy. His admission of former links with British intelligence sounded genu-ine and convincing, but there was something there that set faint alarm bells ringing. I reckoned someone should keep an eye on him, at least in the early stages, and who was better qualified to do that than Yit-zhak Avinoam, with his years of experience in IZL intelligence? That's

---

19. Statement by Amihai Paglin, July 8, 1957, Jabotinsky Archives.
20. HHA 1229/112 (6).
21. Statement by Amihai Paglin, July 8, 1957, Jabotinsky Archives.

why I sent Yitzhak that note, short and to the point: *Respect him – and suspect him!*[22]

Yitzhak Avinoam strongly denies receiving that note. "Bezalel Amitzur sent me no note that said 'Respect him and suspect him.' And what's more, he never held any conversation with me about Yanai. Not before he was transferred to Jerusalem, and never during his whole time in Jerusalem. There's no basis either to the claim that for two years I was commander of Delek. My total time at that assignment was four months."

Bezalel Amitzur for his part does not take back his words. He stands firmly by his version.

INFORMATION GATHERING IN JERUSALEM

Towards the end of June 1946, Reinhold moved his field of activity to Jerusalem; from this point onward he would be known by his code name – Yanai. He soon got himself involved in the training program in the capital, instructing platoon commanders in the use of explosives and in techniques of sabotage, sometimes in field-craft too. He always demonstrated a high level of knowledge and expertise and gained a reputation as a fine instructor. At the same time he was careful not to exceed his professional brief, making no attempt to fraternize with junior commanders or with privates. When the training session was over, he would return to his private life and private concerns,[23] about which very little was known to the responsible authorities in the capital.[24]

Shraga Ellis was still serving at that time as commander of the Jerusalem combat squad, but he was awaiting transfer to the national planning committee and he already had "one foot" in Tel Aviv. His replacement, Yanai, was introduced to him by Avinoam. "Try to find out a bit about him," the latter suggested. "Take him on a tour of the city."

"His appearance was certainly impressive," recalled Shraga Ellis. "Tall, muscular, radiating confidence – the very image of a fearless warrior."[25]

---

22. Author's interview with Bezalel Amitzur, December 22, 1998.
23. Tavin's interview with Avinoam, 1954, Jabotinsky Archives.
24. The fact is that Reinhold's movements and habits were not tracked, as he was a mere newcomer to the IZL. That nonfeasance raised the risk of shedding precious blood and of losing the lives or freedom of some of the IZL's best fighters.
25. Author's interview with Shraga Ellis, October 1996.

For a long while the two men strolled in a leisurely fashion, like a pair of bored tourists, under no pressure of time. Yanai listened attentively to Shraga's explanations, saying little; his few comments were considered and practical. But whenever they stopped to look at a potential objective, his reticence would suddenly disappear, to be replaced by a barrage of irksome questions: had the attack plan been finalized? What stage had the planning reached? And dates – he was particular eager to know the dates of future operations. Shraga would reply patiently and with a laconic air, "I don't know the timetable, that's not my department. I haven't the faintest idea about dates." When this exchange had been repeated a number of times, the atmosphere between them became rather strained, coming to a head when they stopped in front of the King David Hotel. This time Yanai wasn't content with pestering Shraga for dates. He wanted to know why top priority wasn't being given to attacking this objective, and striking a blow at the very nerve center of the Mandate administration.

Shraga was stunned. "If this boy really is as genuine as he looks and sounds," he told Avinoam, "Jerusalem has got itself a first-rate commander – and one with a head on his shoulders, too."

Four months later, October 28, 1946, CID headquarters received from Yanai a full list of all attacks planned and projected in Jerusalem, including the attack on the central railway station that he himself had been appointed to command.

As time passed, and trust in him remained unshaken, his self-confidence grew, and his contempt for his commanders and their poor judgment peaked in the aftermath of the King David Hotel operation – when he arrived a day late for the debriefing in Tel Aviv. On being asked by Avinoam to account for the delay, he replied that after the operation he had been detained as a suspect and released only after he had phoned his pal Inspector Schindler at Haifa CID headquarters....[26] Incredible as it seems, his story was taken at face value by Avinoam, and no red lights started flashing in his mind when he heard of the involvement of a British detective.

"The consideration that convinced Avinoam that Yanai was 'okay' after all was apparently the meeting that he convened in Tel Aviv for the

---

26. Tavin's interview with Avinoam, 1954, Jabotinsky Archives.

debriefing of participants in the operation," Yaakov Amrami (Yoel)[27] writes in his book (in Hebrew) *Things Are Bigger Than We Are.* "Avinoam met Yanai and the others by the Ha-Tir Club as planned, and it's a fact that he didn't betray them.

"Yanai apparently had the sense not to inform on that occasion, to avoid suspicion," is Yoel's cynical comment. And that was not all: when Yanai saw how easy it was to hoodwink his boss, he had the nerve to ask for permission to go to Haifa "to thank Schindler for his help."[28] This request too was granted, and as a result he had *carte blanche* to travel to and from CID offices in Haifa without arousing suspicion and without anyone bothering to report his movements to higher authority. The true nature of his contacts with Schindler first became known to the IZL leadership only four months later – following his desertion and treachery at the time of the railway station operation (see page 190). The intelligence chief of that time, Yaakov Amrami (Yoel), assigned the task by his colleague Haim Landau, compiled a retrospective report. This report was one of the contributing factors leading to the death sentence passed on Yanai[29] (a sentence never put into effect – see below).

The events of October 30, 1946, in the Jerusalem railway station – and all that followed – were the direct result of that blunder.

Within a day of arriving in Jerusalem – a few weeks before the King David Hotel bombing – Reinhold began systematically gathering information on the command structure of the IZL. He missed no opportunity to make contacts in the higher echelons of command, using all kinds of excuses in the pursuit of his goals. Shmuel Tamir, deputy regional commander in the capital at that time, met him for the first time, by chance, at the "Prophet's Room."[30] "I'd arranged a meeting with Avinoam," he related,

---

27. Yaakov Amrami (code name Yoel), served at this time as commander of the IZL intelligence branch.
28. Lapidot, *Be-lahav ha-mered*, p. 205.
29. Testimony of Amrami (Yoel), July 3, 1958, Jabotinsky Archives.
30. The "Prophet's Room" in Kiryat Shmuel in Jerusalem served as a meeting place and temporary hostel for commanders from the capital and the surrounding districts, and for the first five weeks of his time in Jerusalem Reinhold was in residence there. The address is included in a list of meeting places given to British detectives by him.

and I arrived there early. A stranger came out to meet me, someone I'd never seen before, and he asked what I wanted. I murmured something about looking for Mr. X, and was told there was no such person. I apologized and left. Later I was told by Avinoam this was the new commander of the combat squad, a rising star, staying there temporarily.

A few days later I had another meeting scheduled to take place in the "Prophet's Room," and I met Yanai again. Avinoam was late and as I now knew who he was, I got into conversation with him. He didn't know me personally, but he assumed I was a senior commander and he started talking about a new idea he had for constructing railway mines…. I suggested he should wait for Avinoam and take it up with him, but he said there was no time for this, it was urgent and it had to go right to the top…. He wanted a meeting with someone at the highest level, or the person in charge of production. I promised to look into it for him – but I didn't fix him up with a meeting.[31]

Having failed in his approach to Tamir, Yanai tried his luck with the Jerusalem regional commander. Avinoam recalls:

One sunny day in August 1946 Reinhold came to me with a strange request; he asked to be introduced to a senior staff officer, because he had ideas about developing a new type of bomb and he wanted to unveil his plan to someone highly placed in the command structure. I got him an appointment with Shraga Ellis but he wasn't content with that; he wanted someone higher up the ladder. I arranged for him to meet Gidi. The two of them talked for some time, and at the end of the conversation he asked for an introduction to the commander of the Irgun, to show him the broad outlines of the plan. Gidi heard him out patiently but told him he didn't see anything special here, anything that would justify a meeting with the boss.[32]

In the words of Amihai Paglin himself:

31. Testimony of Shmuel Tamir, May 23, 1958, Jabotinsky Archives.
32. Tavin's interview with Avinoam, 1954, Jabotinsky Archives.

He was tireless in his pursuit of the objective. He was driving me nuts with all kinds of suggestions, trying to get me to fix him up with a meeting with the commander of the Irgun; this started when he was in Haifa and it got worse when he arrived in Jerusalem. He was particularly interested in the identity of our technical expert.... He bombarded me with complicated sketches and diagrams, in the hope of confusing me so I'd refer him to the specialist. When he got really tiresome I used to tell him I wasn't authorized to meet the man whenever I felt like it, and in the meantime he should leave the plans with me; if I happened to meet the "tech specialist" – I promised – I'd pass on the idea.[33]

A natural instinct for caution, sharpened over the years of underground activity, stood Gidi in good stead in this instance, warning him not to identify himself as the one responsible for research and development in the field of sabotage. "I wasn't suspicious of him at this stage," he explained. "It just seemed to me that a new recruit didn't need to know that the operations officer was also the technical specialist."

It may be safely assumed that Yanai's trip to Haifa, after his meeting with Avinoam at the Ha-Tir Club in Tel Aviv, wasn't planned with the sole purpose of saying "thank you" to his old friend Schindler. There can be little doubt (especially in view of what was to follow) that this less than exuberant occasion (following his failure to prevent the destruction of the nerve center of British administration) saw the inception of "Operation Shark" – four days of curfew and house-to-house searches in Tel Aviv, on the basis of detailed information received by British military intelligence that the King David Hotel bombers had gone to ground in the big coastal city (British War Office document 275/29).[34] And who was better placed than Yanai – coming directly from the debriefing at the Ha-Tir Club – to supply such solid information?

The fact that after his meeting with Schindler he returned to normal duties in the ranks of the underground and even took part in sabotage activities (such as the mining of the railway line near Nahariya), without betraying

---

33. S. Lev-Ami's interview with Amihai Paglin, Hebrew University, Dept. of National Documentation, reel 1593.
34. PRO WO 275/29.

anyone, suggests that the British were in no hurry to dispense with his services and wanted him to stay in place; they were still hoping that one day he would deliver to them the most senior staff of the IZL, including the commander himself. So he returned again and again to the lions' den. The time for burning bridges and disappearing was not yet ripe.

When the days of curfew and wide-ranging searches in Tel Aviv and environs came to an end, and tensions eased a little, the young men began gradually moving back to their homes. Among those returning to the capital was Yanai. "For security reasons" he moved out of the "Prophet's Room" and went to live in Rehavia, at 45 Alfasi Street; his landlady was a Mrs. Katz. Here he could hatch his intrigues undisturbed.

"At that time we had temporarily suspended active operations," Avinoam recalled, "and we were concentrating on training. I remember telling Yanai to go for three days of training at Beit Iksa. To my surprise, he turned to me with a very strange request: he wanted a letter of introduction on behalf of the Betarists – 'in case of problems with the police.' Of course, I refused this absolutely."[35] This was evidently an attempt on Yanai's part to gather incriminating evidence in writing against the Betar movement, not, at that stage, an illegal organization.

Reinhold missed no opportunity to add to the stock of information that would be handed over to his British masters when the time came. Shmuel Tamir recalls:

> One summer night in 1946 we were planning a series of explosions all over the capital. I was asked by Avinoam to tell Yanai to stay off the streets that night. As I was on my way to his house, a stray dog attached itself to me.... After I'd given Yanai the warning, he stood at his door and watched me as I walked away. He didn't know my name, but he thought he knew where I lived, and the only other information he could give was a description – of me and of the dog that he took to be mine. Incidentally, there was a boy from Egypt staying with my parents at that time – and he looked very similar to me.[36]

---

35. Tavin's interview with Avinoam, 1954, Jabotinsky Archives.
36. Testimony of Shmuel Tamir, May 23, 1958, Jabotinsky Archives.

Wednesday, October 30, 1946, the day of the action at the Jerusalem railway station, was also Shmuel Tamir's wedding day. He spent his honeymoon in Haifa and thus missed the wave of arrests that came in the wake of Yanai's treachery. The British CID made a point of visiting his parents' house. "They didn't ask for me by name but described my appearance," Tamir goes on to say, "and they seemed particularly interested in knowing whether we had a dog…"

Ironically, suspicion fell on the youth from Egypt, Edwin Shomer, who was housed with Tamir's parents. On the instructions of John o'Sullivan, head of the Jewish Department of MI5 (the counterintelligence branch of British security),[37] his name was added to the "most wanted" list and his description circulated to all police stations in the region, including Egypt, where the British assumed he had taken refuge.[38]

NEVER ONE OF US

The image of Reinhold in the British army (as described by other members of his unit) was totally different from his image in the ranks of the IZL. On one point the two camps were in agreement: there were strong reservations about the man. "However hard he tried, Reinhold was never one of us," Zvi Brenner writes in *Life in the Ranks* (in Hebrew), "maybe because of his police connections in the past. Sometimes the fellows would tease him and say 'Tell us, Yekke, are you really working for the CID?' and he'd say, 'Sure, and one of these days I'll have you all locked up…' People were wary of him, but he could be so charming when he chose to be…no one suspected he was really up to anything."

In a similar vein, Yitzhak Avinoam commented in an interview with Yaakov Tavin in 1954, "He was a reclusive type and only mixed with people when he had a training job to do…. I had reservations about him and it's hard to explain why. Maybe I'm naturally suspicious of 'original' people – and that's the way he came across…. I didn't encourage him to socialize with senior commanders…. Maybe it was subconscious caution…"

---

37. MI5, the arm of the security services charged with the suppression of political terrorism. The Jewish Department was headed by John O'Sullivan, a talented officer of Irish extraction, who played a crucial role in the Yanai affair. MI5 acted in this Eretz Israel under military cover, in the guise of the DSO (Defence Security Office). The DSO provided logistical services to all branches of the British intelligence community.
38. CID docs., HHA.

Avinoam adds, and explains:

The question has been asked, "if there were suspicions, why weren't they acted on?" My considerations were based on internal factors.... Yanai knew about meeting places, knew the men and some of the commanders, even knew the number of the car used for transporting weapons – and yet none of these was targeted at the time. Still, I decided to put him through a decisive test and put him in command of the Jerusalem railway station operation, a situation where he'd maybe get caught in an exchange of fire with British troops, risking injury and even death. This was his breaking point. Maybe he was a coward all along, or his British handlers decided this was the time to squeeze all the information out of him and spirit him away.... It seems his training in subterfuge wasn't that effective.... If he'd been more methodical and more patient, the damage he could have done to us, as a professional agent provocateur, would have been incalculable.[39]

Shmuel Tamir, serving at that time as head of IZL intelligence in Jerusalem, was asked by Yaakov Amrami to examine all the available material concerning Yanai's treachery and to put his conclusions into writing. In the detailed report that he submitted on November 11, 1946, to IZL command (full text in the Jabotinsky Archives), he sums up his character: "unemotional, practical, cool-headed, with a talent for administration, intelligent, cynical attitude towards women...prone to mood-changes...enjoys taking chances..." The next item in the report is the most striking: "He has a strange interest in the Christian Church, and I have a theory that he is not of Jewish parentage on both sides."

A further indication of the reservations surrounding Yanai is the account given by Yaakov Amrami, in his book *Things Are Bigger Than We Are*, of his behavior the night before an operation:

He was one of 15 combat squad members who assembled in a room at 256 Dizengoff.... Because the men knew they had to leave early in the morning, they went to sleep early, bedding down on the floor. But

---

39. Yaakov Amrami's interview with Avinoam, 1968; Tavin's interview with Avinoam, 1954, Jabotinsky Archives, Yanai/Reinhold file.

two or three of them didn't sleep, and one of them was Yanai. He was of German ancestry and I remember looking at him and seeing a fair-haired youth, of Christian rather than Jewish appearance.

Though I didn't speak to him, he came over as a cocky, stubborn young man, with a strong personality, determined to get his goal – if he had one. I was doing paperwork in the next room, and he behaved as if I wasn't there, staring at some point in space and not saying a word, not a word. I didn't encourage him to talk, because I wasn't interested in talking to him, but I reckoned he didn't look like a typical IZL type: he was more neatly dressed than most, and had a more military air about him: he could have been a regular soldier on parade, awaiting inspection...[40]

When Heinrich Reinhold's *modus operandi*, during the short period of time (five months in all) that he spent in the IZL, is analyzed, the almost self-evident conclusion is that his handlers wanted to use him to get to the leadership and in particular to the commander, Begin himself, thus striking the underground movements a mortal blow and paralyzing their activity for a considerable length of time. This also explains the lack of interest that Yanai showed in the rank and file and in junior field commanders and the fact that they weren't immediately betrayed when the opportunity arose, as in Avinoam's debriefing in Tel Aviv for participants in the King David Hotel action, or the evening before the mining of the railway lines on October 8, 1946, when the pick of the combat squad commanders met in Slonim's apartment in Tel Aviv. "We demonstrated the new homemade devices," said Gidi, "and Yanai, who was responsible for mining in the Nahariya sector, also took part in the demonstration and did his job effectively. The British had the opportunity to arrest everybody there, but it seems they wanted Yanai to deliver bigger fish," he concluded.[41] Furthermore, the sequence of events lends support to his hypothesis that Yanai was working at that time not for the British secret police, but for the Intelligence Service, specifically for MI5. The methods of this institution do not necessarily conform to the conventions accepted by civilian intelligence agencies and almost any

---

40. The reference is to an unsuccessful attempt to sabotage a British warship in the port of Haifa.
41. Statement by Amihai Paglin, July 8, 1958, Jabotinsky Archives.

means are justified by the end, including permitting the agent in place to participate in limited hostile actions against the government, to gain the trust of his co-conspirators.

However, it's not to be supposed that operations of military and political significance and wide-ranging implications, such as the bombing of the King David Hotel, could be categorized as such. In Jerusalem – it has to be remembered – was concentrated the whole of the power infrastructure of the Mandate government, which made the city a prime target for the underground movements. And here Reinhold came into the picture. "Planting" him in the ranks of the underground in Jerusalem was no small coup for the authorities. "It gave them a certain sense of security in Jerusalem," was Gidi's comment at the time. "They believed that from now on Yanai, as a high-ranking IZL commander in the capital, would be capable of giving advance warning of any serious operation. As I understand it, a hint along the lines of 'the terrorists won't take us by surprise again' was delivered at the time in the British Parliament," Gidi noted.[42] "And of course, all along the British never lost sight of their main objective: to use Reinhold to expose the IZL leadership and get their hands on Begin."

The period of Yanai's activity in Jerusalem – up to the time of the King David Hotel operation – was characterized by a relative lull in hostile actions against the British. During this period the IZL had been planning an assault on Jerusalem's central prison, and Yanai was to command one of the units. In the end the operation was deferred to a later date – "And that was lucky for us," said Gidi, "because Yanai would have been in on all the details of the operation and there's no doubt at all there would have been a leak – and the British would have held a warm reception for us, as they did at the central railway station."

Amihai Paglin didn't know just how accurate his assessment was: CID documents released in the 1990s show that among the items of information supplied by Yanai to the British on October 29, 1946, the central prison in Jerusalem was noted as an objective for attack: *"Arrangements to attack the Central Prison, Jerusalem, were planned a long time ago but lack of money prevented the attack being carried out. The release of certain prisoners there is vital to the I.Z.L."* (see appendix C, Report No. 2).

The only serious operation that Reinhold took part in (involuntarily)

---

42. Ibid.

was the King David Hotel bombing, and this was his greatest failure as a British-run agent: not only was he unable to foil it, he had no option but to participate in it, risking his life in the process. The outcome from his personal point of view was painful and humiliating. That morning he had known something was afoot and suspected the King David was the target, but his efforts to convey the information to his employer came to nothing. All he managed was a brief telephone message and the promise of further details (see above, page 120).

The British went on waiting for conclusive information from their trusted agent and when none came, they decided nothing serious was imminent and returned to their routine.

Heinrich Reinhold was never a professional agent in the classic British mode. He would be more accurately described as an amateur adventurer. He was attracted to danger and enjoyed defying it – to a certain level. Because he made no secret of his former links with the British CID he had no need to apologize for his contacts with police agencies, and he could neutralize any suspicions arising against him from that quarter. Secretly he must have been proud of the way he was mocking and teasing everyone: his comrades in the underground movement with his boasts of friends in high places; his controllers with his brazen accounts of his role in operations against them.

It is strange that, even after his treachery was exposed and it was revealed how he had fooled his line commanders in Jerusalem throughout his time in the capital, there are still some who maintain that he defected to the British only after the King David Hotel operation; this would be convenient for those seeking an excuse for one of the worst blunders in the history of the IZL, its failure to track down the spy despite all the glaring clues that he left behind him.

Those who take this view rely on a CID report dated December 1, 1946, according to which some five weeks before, on October 25, 1946, Heinrich Reinhold was arrested by detectives in Haifa, "cracked" under interrogation, and revealed all he knew about IZL operations and command structure (see appendix A, cover page to the CID report).

Aryeh Eshel, one of the IZL commanders in the capital, who investigated the Yanai case, took the trouble to try getting confirmation on this from John O'Sullivan himself, at that time head of the Jewish Department at CID headquarters.[43] "Although he was fully cooperative, O'Sullivan couldn't answer all my questions," Eshel states. "This, he explained, was because his superior, Deputy Chief of the CID Richard Kittling, kept his cards very close to his chest in sensitive areas such as these, so that he, as chief of the Jewish Department, knew only what was absolutely necessary for the performance of his job."

The CID document on which so much reliance has been placed was composed more than a month after the episode to which it refers, and all the signs are it was a deliberate fabrication designed to cloud the issue, because the British hadn't yet dispensed with Yanai's services, and also for reasons of their own (secret rivalry between police and intelligence services). It is a fact that on November 6, 1946, Jaffa police issued a "wanted" notice[44] naming Yehiel Heinrich Reinhold, *a former soldier, associate of Finkelstein, a known terrorist in Haifa* – and this almost two weeks after the above-named had supposedly been interrogated by detectives in Haifa.

All the facts and the chain of events in the Yanai episode (as recorded above) demonstrate beyond any doubt that Heinrich Reinhold was an agent planted by the British even before he joined the British army and that he continued in this role throughout his career in the underground organizations.

Reinhold was an accomplished saboteur – there is no denying that. His expertise in explosives he acquired during his service in the British army, and he made astute use of it in consolidating his position in the ranks of the underground.

Towards the end of his time in the IZL he began showing signs of anxiety, but the British had not yet obtained their primary objective – Begin's head. Reinhold began examining other escape routes – from the IZL and from British intelligence. One of his lady friends admitted that they had been forging passports and entry visas for the USA. At the same time he began inundating the British with bogus information that only a fertile imagination like his could have devised, such as a bizarre list of terrorist

---

43. Aryeh Eshel, "The Search for Written Evidence of Heinrich Reinhold's Treachery," *The Nation* 124 (1996).
44. HHA 1229/112 (14).

objectives, including the Jerusalem Municipality. He also allowed himself a touch of humor, apparently, when he said with reference to the projected assault on the Jerusalem railway station, "It will be commanded by a Jew of German extraction named Yanai, of whom nothing else is known…" (see appendix B, Report No. 1).

But the most startling report that he sent to his superiors alleged that "It is doubtful if Beigin [sic!] ever existed. Old timers have never seen him" (see appendix D, Report No. 3). The purpose behind this is clear. If Begin did not exist, there was no point in carrying on the search for him. Reinhold's job would be completed and he could be let off the hook.

Explosives are dangerous toys and Reinhold loved playing with fire. By nature he was a compulsive, almost an obsessive gambler. The higher the stakes, the better he liked it. Only one thing he wasn't prepared to gamble – his life.

He was bold – but lacking in fortitude; and he certainly had no intention of sacrificing his life for his employers or for any ideal. The only value that mattered to him was himself. And when this "higher value" was endangered, he abandoned everything and fled for his life.

His hobbies were wine, women, and cards, and success with women made up for his losses as a card player. High society women whom he cultivated were only too happy to "lend" him money, while romantic partners from the underground movements were rewarded in a novel fashion: before burning his bridges and disappearing over the horizon[45] Reinhold passed on their names and addresses to British detectives, and those who didn't escape in time were arrested and imprisoned.

The last word on the Yanai episode should go to Amihai Paglin:

---

45. As a result of his treachery, a sentence of death was passed on Yanai by the IZL Command. He was located in Belgium but attempts to abduct him failed and he escaped again, seeking temporary asylum in England, which was granted. In 1948 his trail was picked up once again, in continental Europe, and a question was sent to the IZL commander, who had recently emerged from hiding: "What is to be done with the traitor?" The reply was: "Today we have a Hebrew state and a Hebrew government. It is no longer the function of the IZL to carry out death sentences." So Yanai was spared for the second time – and vanished into obscurity.

Besides Hilewitz, who wasn't an IZL member, I know of only one instance of treachery in the ranks of the Irgun: a scoundrel by the name of Heinrich Reinhold, whose IZL code name was Yanai. At first he operated in Haifa, and then transferred to Jerusalem. He used to come to me with all kinds of ideas, trying to engineer a meeting with the commander. He wanted to know who the Irgun's technical expert was (at that time there were rumors circulating among the British that Soviet agents were working with us as advisers…). The British were well pleased that "their man in Jerusalem" could warn them in advance of any sensitive operation, but on the other hand they didn't for a moment give up on the idea that one day he would bring them Begin's head on a platter.

Neither he nor his handlers imagined he would be caught in the embarrassing situation of having to participate in a high-profile operation as one of the commanders, without any chance of passing on a warning, as happened in the King David Hotel action. And as if that wasn't enough, he had to get into an exchange of fire with his British employers – and almost got himself killed. It came as a severe shock to him, and he couldn't face the prospect that such a traumatic experience might be repeated. He asked his handlers to release him, but they hadn't finished with him yet, and were still hoping he'd "get Begin" for them. Indications are that they reached a compromise: if he was ever to be trapped in a similar situation, the British would utilize to the utmost all the information he had amassed, and smuggle him out of the country. They kept their word.

Thanks to the security procedures followed by the Irgun, Yanai knew about the railway station operation, but not the date of implementation. When he heard I was going to the capital the next day, he assumed that was when it was going to happen and he went running to his handlers in Haifa, who decided it was time to act on all the information he had. That was the night there were raids all over the country, using pre-prepared lists of names, with that bastard identifying some of the suspects from a car with blacked out windows. After that he was spirited away to Europe.

At the end of the day, the worst damage he did to us – apart from the betrayal of some good men – was foiling our attempt to sink the flagship of the British fleet in Haifa, a scheme he played an active part in himself.... It all fell apart when the warships suddenly, without any warning, put to sea and anchored offshore. At the time we thought it was bad luck. Today I'm convinced it was Yanai's doing.

It's important to stress the fact that despite all the harm he did to the IZL, Yanai didn't succeed in preventing a single significant operation.... It is my firm belief that Reinhold was in the pay of British intelligence long before he joined the Irgun, and he did not defect in the wake of the King David Hotel operation, as some seem to think.

After his disappearance we tried to eliminate his controller, Schindler, but we only succeeded in wounding him (he lost a leg) and he was immediately transferred to Germany.

This was the only case in which an enemy agent ever succeeded in infiltrating our organization. It's important to remember: Yanai was with us for less than four months, before we caught on to him.[46]

---

46. S. Lev-Ami's interview with Amihai Paglin, Hebrew University, Dept. of Contemporary Judaism, 1970; author's interview with Amihai Paglin, 1969.

MARTIAL LAW

Towards the end of 1946, the British government decided to adopt an "iron fist" policy towards the Yishuv in Eretz Israel. It was hoped that emergency regulations and disruption of economic life would punish the Jews "by striking at their pockets," to quote General Barker, and this in turn would lead to greater willingness on the part of moderate elements among the Yishuv leadership to cooperate in suppressing the terrorism of the underground movements. The British also believed that the USA would ultimately agree to a scheme whereby only a minute proportion of the remnants of European Jewry would be allowed to enter the country, all the others returning to their countries of origin and staying there. They were convinced that in order to prevent Soviet expansion into the Middle East, the United States would agree to a continuing British presence in Palestine, as Mandatory power or in some other capacity.

The year 1946 was not a good one for the British army in its war against the IZL and Lehi. Although Operation Agatha had been intended to give the army the means required to crush the terrorists, by the autumn of 1946 it was clear that there had been little or no effect on the frequency nor scale of terrorist operations. Montgomery and Dempsey could not understand how this was possible; they looked around for a reason, and their attention was focused on the High Commissioner. They alleged that the civil administration was persistently curbing the activities of the military arm and was therefore responsible for the disappointing results of operations conducted by the army. This pretext was refuted by General Barker, acting GOC (Palestine), who wrote to Dempsey on November 21, 1946, declaring that the accusations were unfounded. "Cunningham," he asserted, "did not interfere with or inhibit military action."[1] He tended rather to blame the strategic bankruptcy that had characterized the campaign in Palestine, claiming that current operations had more to do with raising morale than with fighting terrorism. But Montgomery insisted on his interpretation of events, declaring that if only the Army were to be allowed to act at its own discretion – without first having to seek the approval of the civilian arm – there was no doubt the situation in Palestine would be improved. The cabinet sided with Montgomery.[2]

On February 18, 1947, the British foreign secretary, Ernest Bevin, announced the government's intention to refer the Palestine question to the United Nations. The announcement did not specify precisely what the government would be asking the United Nations for; a more explicit statement was that of Colonial Secretary Creech-Jones: "We are not going to the UN to surrender the Mandate. We are going to the UN…asking for their advice as to how the Mandate can be administered."[3]

THE MARCH 1 ATTACKS

The leadership of the IZL, tensely watching every move of the British and their leaders in Parliament, decided for their part on intensification of the struggle.

On March 1, 1947, the IZL unleashed a series of surprise attacks, hitting military targets all over the country:

- Near Rishon Letzion a military vehicle hit a mine – two soldiers injured.
- A military munitions truck hit a mine near Rehovot – one soldier injured.

---

1. MEC Cunningham Papers 1/3, Telegram, MILPAL to MIDEAST, November 21, 1946, Doc. No. xxi.
2. Bruce Hoffman, *The Failure of British Military Strategy in Palestine 1939–1947* [Hebrew] (Ramat Gan: Bar-Ilan University, 1983), p. 28.
3. David Niv, *Battles of the Irgun Zvai Leumi*, pp. 101–3.

- A military vehicle fired on near Petah Tikva – a number of soldiers injured.
- A transport hit a mine near Kfar Sirkin – six soldiers injured and one killed.
- A mine exploded near Tulkarm – an officer and two soldiers seriously injured.
- Near Bet Lid, a British sergeant and a private killed and two others injured.
- Mortar and machine-gun fire directed at army camps near Pardes Hanna, Hadera, Kfar Yonah and Bet Lid – scores of injuries, some of them fatal.
- A number of objectives hit in Haifa and environs – in the lower city, ten military vehicles destroyed in a parking lot.
- Near Kiryat Haim, a military vehicle hit a mine – three soldiers killed and two injured.

The climax of the March 1 attacks was the assault on the British Officers Club in Goldschmidt House in Jerusalem, in the very heart of a military security zone.

"It was a calculated decision," Gidi recalled, explaining the circumstances that led to implementation of the attack on the Sabbath:

> At that time there were rumors that Field Marshal Montgomery, the chief of the Imperial General Staff, was in the country incognito, advising army authorities on how to fortify their installations. The Officers Club, Goldschmidt House, was supposed to be a model for that style of fortification – although it was hard to tell whether its location, beside the Jewish Agency and the Yeshurun Synagogue, was for strategic reasons or out of the (misplaced) hope that it would constitute insurance against attacks from the underground movements.... One way or the other, the British made sure it was protected all around. Besides an army camp, there were four defensive emplacements around it and another three on the roof. On the main access road there was a military roadblock, and an armored car patrolled the perimeter of the compound every few minutes. The main worry was the municipal buses that used to pass by the site at regular intervals. If one of these was in

the vicinity at the time of the attack, there were liable to be casualties among the civilian population, something we wanted to avoid at all costs – even at the cost of canceling the operation. And after further reconnaissance of the site along with Shraga Ellis we both came to the unavoidable decision that the idea of an attack on Goldschmidt House just wasn't on; the risks were too great.[4]

Pensive and disappointed, they turned to a nearby barbershop, and while Gidi was having his hair trimmed, Shraga Ellis glanced at the headline of an evening paper – and exclaimed angrily: *British troops attack refugees on the* Haim Arlosorov – *Many casualties.*

"There and then," said Gidi, "we decided to go ahead with the operation regardless, and hit that very building. We worked out our tactics, based on a small team of attackers, for maximum effectiveness and minimum casualties. The problem of the buses was still there, and then it occurred to us to schedule the operation for the Sabbath, when there'd be no civilian traffic."

The same day Gidi presented the plan to Begin and obtained his approval to operate on the Sabbath – a rare occurrence in the history of the IZL.

All participants in the operation were from Jerusalem, and it was commanded by Dov Salomon (Yishai), also a native of the capital.

Avshalom Haviv was second-in-command and leader of the Bren team, which took up position behind the concrete wall adjoining the Yeshurun Synagogue, opposite Goldschmidt House. Another unit, commanded by Aryeh Eshel (Yariv), was assigned the job of blocking the road by flooding it with gasoline and setting it alight, to keep reinforcements at bay. An extra backup unit was stationed by the Agency building, with instructions to open fire on the army camp nearby.

As Dov Salomon has described the course of the operation:

We set out from [Menahem] Madmuni's apartment in the Mishkenot district. In the alleyway behind the house a military tender was waiting. We all crawled under the canvas cover, the whole squad except for Elimelech. He was the most British-looking of the lot and could easily be mistaken for a Tommy, especially in uniform, so it was his

---

4. S. Nakdimon's interview with Amihai Paglin, *Yediot Aharonot*, September 29, 1972.

job to drive. We drove slowly towards the Officers Club, but at the entrance there was a line of vehicles so we decided to do a few circuits until the way was clear. On the third circuit, I gave the order to head for the building.

Once we'd overpowered the sentries at the gate, I gave the order to break into the compound. At the same time the backup and interception squads went into action: Avshalom Haviv opened up with the Bren, targeting the windows of the building opposite, where the British had set up defensive positions. The interception squad stationed by the Agency opened fire on the tented camp, blocking any reinforcements from the southwest.

The first volley of fire sent the rest of the guard detachment scurrying into the building – and we were hard on their heels, Yoav Levi (Kushi) with one consignment of explosives and Naim Yosef[5] with the other. As we ran, we tossed a few grenades towards the army camp and the windows of the club. By the time the grenades exploded we were already inside the building and setting the charges (88 pounds; 40 kilos apiece) by the two central pillars of the staircase. Once we'd lit the fuse (12 inches; 30 cm. in length) – I gave the order to withdraw.[6]

The whole operation had lasted no longer than a minute and a half. During this time an armored car had appeared on the scene, and while the sabotage squad was busy inside, the Bren team opened fire, hitting the commander of the vehicle, who was exposed in the turret, and three other soldiers who ran from their bunkers to assist the crew of the armored car.

After the operation, Gidi was curious to find out who the machine-gun marksman had been, scoring a "bull's eye" with every shot – and to his surprise it turned out to be a former Palmah member, Avshalom Haviv,[7] who had only recently joined the IZL, after a two-week machine gunners' course in the orchards of Petah Tikva, and was experiencing combat for the first time.

In the thunderous explosion that followed a few minutes later 17 officers

---

5. Naim Yosef is the brother of Rabbi Ovadiah Yosef, leader of Shas.
6. Testimony of Dov Salomon (Yishai), Beit Jabotinsky Archives.
7. Avshalom Haviv was captured on May 4, 1947, following the Acre prison raid, and was subsequently hanged.

and men – including some high-ranking intelligence personnel – were killed and 27 wounded. The three-story building was in ruins.

As they withdrew, the IZL fighters still had time to pour gasoline on the road and set it alight, blocking access to the site. Not a single IZL member had been hurt in the operation.

MILITARY REGULATIONS IMPOSED

The attack on the Officers Club, at Goldschmidt House in Jerusalem, in the heart of a military security zone, shook the foundations of the Mandate administration and caused outrage in Britain.

The London *Sunday Express* published a leading article on Palestine under the heading: "Rule or Quit." The article went on to say that the problem of Palestine must be solved – and solved at once. British prestige was being trampled underfoot, and British lives sacrificed for no reason.

In an official communiqué published in Jerusalem it was reported that the High Commissioner had decided to impose martial law in the districts of Tel Aviv, Ramat Gan, Bnei Brak, Petah Tikva, and the Meah Shearim quarter of Jerusalem, on the basis of the emergency regulations drawn up in 1937 and for reasons of public safety:

- In each district, all authority is to be transferred to the Army and to the Army commander appointed by the High Commissioner to act as Military Governor.
- All civilian government offices and courts are to be closed. A military court will be established as well as courts authorized to reach rapid verdicts.
- The Military Governor is empowered to order the closure of banks and post offices.
- Telephone services are to be suspended.
- The Military Governor has the authority to confiscate land and buildings.
- Civilian police personnel will be subject to military authority, and every member of the Armed Forces will have full powers of arrest.
- The Military Governor may bar individuals from entering the district as he sees fit.
- Cafes, restaurants, and hotels are to close at 10:00 PM precisely. All cinemas in Tel Aviv are to be closed indefinitely.

- All these regulations also apply to Arab villages in the districts specified.
- All roads in the Haifa municipality are to be closed to civilian traffic.

According to official estimates published in Jerusalem, some 240,000 people would be affected by the military regulations: this figure included 180,000 Jews in Tel Aviv, 17,250 residents of Petah Tikva, 10,200 in Ramat Gan, 5,760 in Bnei Brak, and 25,000 in Jerusalem.

The advantages which martial law was supposed to give the armed forces were set out in a report compiled by the "Joint Planning Team," which concluded, "These measures, which will impair both the freedom and the prosperity of the private citizen, will perhaps encourage him to co-operate [with the army] in giving information about terrorists and denying them shelter."[8]

According to the historian Bruce Hoffman,[9] this report is the clearest summary available of the reasons for which martial law was adopted, and what it was expected to achieve.

Cunningham reported to London, February 13, that the Yishuv was "paranoic" with fear lest these regulations be enforced. He wrote that "In martial law the Jewish community see economic disaster, as well as widespread hardship."[10] In the army's view, money was the "Achilles' Heel" of the Yishuv.[11] According to one intelligence report, "The making of money is almost a second religion with the Jewish race," and it goes on to describe the discontent that the regulations would impose on the Jews, inducing them to offer the kind of cooperation that other measures had failed to achieve, while another analysis of the situation envisaged that these conditions would spur the Jews to "go on a manhunt to save themselves and their pockets."[12]

8. PRO CO 537/2299 Report, from Director of Plans to Director of Joint Planning, March 21, 1947.
9. Hoffman, *The Failure of British Military Strategy in Palestine*, n. 2 above.
10. Ibid.; Weekly Intelligence Summary Telegram, Cunningham to S. of S. Colonies, February 13, 1947.
11. PRO WO 216/194 Telegram, C.-IN-C., MELF, to War Office; Order issued by General Sir Evelyn Barker, July 23, 1946.
12. PRO WO 275/58 Sixth Airborne Division Intelligence Summary No 33, "Jewish Affairs," March 1947, and No 34, March 14, 1947.

MAKING A MOCKERY

The British were mistaken – and grievously so. If they imagined that martial law would paralyze the underground organizations, they found out soon enough that their optimism had been excessive.

"Combat units commanded by Gidi and Shimshon swept like a flame across the country," Begin boasted.[13] As a matter of historical fact, a handful of fighters, led by Gidi and Shimshon, made a mockery of martial law in spite of the hundred thousand British servicemen standing behind it.

Amihai Paglin recalls:

When martial law was declared in the districts of Tel Aviv, Petah Tikva, and the Meah Shearim quarter of Jerusalem, we succeeded, a number of commanders, including Shimshon, in slipping away to Netanya and from there we organized a series of raids against the British. Shimshon excelled himself, standing out as one of the central figures of the underground war; trained in field-craft during his service in the British army, he showed the full range of his skills in that state of emergency. He was in his element. Every evening he'd gather a group of young men, hand out machine guns and mortars, and go out to attack army camps in the vicinity. In this respect [Gidi smiled] he reminded me of the Biblical Shimshon [Samson], and his raids on the fields of the Philistines....

On his return, he'd describe each and every detail of the experience and laugh at his exploits. There was something in his uninhibited, almost childish laughter that we all found infectious. When he was in action, on the other hand, he was serious and calculating, saying little and weighing every step meticulously. Afterwards, when it was over, you'd hardly know he was the same guy – laughing and joking and keeping our spirits up. We used to sit down together and compile bulletins. We couldn't contact Irgun HQ in Tel Aviv and there were no newspapers in circulation, so there was a gap to be filled. We produced a daily bulletin, using stencils, and signing ourselves "Field Command."[14] ...Shimshon made sure that his robust sense of humor was reflected in the stenciled bulletins....

---

13. Menahem Begin, *The Revolt*, p. 93.
14. The only surviving bulletin issued by "Field Command" is reprinted in *Collected Sources and Documents*, vol. 4 (p. 20), Jabotinsky Institute Publications.

The day martial law was declared, we carried out some 25 sabotage operations across the country, and this continued throughout the time the restrictions were in force.[15] But the crowning achievement was without doubt the major assault of March 12 on the "Schneller Camp" – at the heart of Jerusalem's security zone – the site of barrack blocks and some of the most important installations of the British military apparatus in the Middle East.[16]

To quote Begin,[17] "This was one of the toughest and most audacious operations carried out by the IZL since the beginning of its war, and it was a

---

15. The following is a partial list of operations conducted in March 1947:
    - March 2 – In Hadera a military vehicle damaged by a mine planted by the IZL.
    - March 3 – An army camp in Haifa under rifle and grenade attack mounted by Lehi.
    - March 4 – An army camp in Hadera under fire from the IZL, two soldiers injured; RAF jeep damaged by a mine near Rehovot.
    - March 5 – Lehi activists blow up government offices in Haifa. In Jerusalem IZL units strike a number of objectives, including the strongly defended "British Fortress."
    - March 6 – Camp 71 near Hadera under automatic fire and grenade attack from an IZL unit, five soldiers injured.
    - March 7 – A series of attacks launched on British army bases, lines of communication, and vehicles. Two officers killed and two injured in Lehi attack on army jeep in Jerusalem. An IZL unit attacks the police station at Sarafand-al-Harb near Nes Ziona.
    - March 8 – Operations throughout the country: British military personnel and installations under automatic fire and grenade attack, and road mines detonated, in Jerusalem, Tel Aviv, Haifa (assault on Allenby Camp), Sharona, Hadera, Even-Yehuda.
    - March 9 – Lehi attack on Camp 72 near Pardes Hanna, 11 British soldiers killed, 18 injured.
    - March 10 – IZL attack on Camp 87 near Hadera, one soldier killed and six injured; communications sabotaged and vehicles damaged by road mines. Near Bet Lid, British army patrol under fire from IZL units, numerous casualties.
    - March 13 – British army patrols fired on by IZL units in Tel Aviv and near Kfar Salameh.
    - March 14 – "British-Iraqi" oil pipeline blown up and three large storage-tanks destroyed. Installations in the Haifa refinery area set on fire.
    - March 15 – Army camp near Hadera attacked, officers' quarters and food and equipment stores destroyed. Damage estimated at many thousands of pounds.
    - March 16 – Haifa-Kirkuk oil pipeline sabotaged near Haifa and near Kfar Hasidim.
16. Author's recorded interview with Amihai Paglin, 1969.
17. Menahem Begin, *The Revolt*, p. 94.

real test of Gidi's tactical skills, based as they were on the exploitation of surprise and the use of small forces to inflict heavy blows."

It was all done with clockwork precision: under the cover of sniper fire, forestalling any resistance on the part of the security forces, a five-man commando squad penetrated the external defenses, made a frontal assault on the offices and housing blocks, activated the explosives, and retreated safely. Armored columns hurrying to the scene of the attack were forced to stop, pinned down by ferocious fire from the backup units.

In the explosion, a few minutes later, extensive damage was caused to the barrack blocks and the administrative offices.

A more detailed account of the attack is given by Yitzhak Avinoam:

> My orders were to carry out an all-out attack and we chose Schneller Camp, located on the border between the western suburbs, which were under restrictions, and the area outside the restriction zone. I entrusted command of the operation to Yehoshua Gal.
>
> We didn't have all the weapons we needed for the operation. Gidi supplied us with the Bren, as well as a quantity of explosives. We also had a few Stens – not much for such an ambitious operation. And then it turned out that the Bren had been stowed in a place we couldn't get to when H-hour arrived…but Yehoshua volunteered to cover the others using a conventional Sten – and that's exactly what he did. We knew the British could call up tanks and armored cars to the operational zone – and the question facing us was how to stop this. Under normal circumstances we'd have blocked the access roads with mines, but traffic restrictions under the emergency regulations meant that we were short of explosives. Then Gal suggested, "Let's put empty barrels at all the access points to the camp and put signs on them: "Danger – Explosives." That should hold them up for a while, and give us time to finish the job."
>
> We took up this suggestion – and a very effective ploy it turned out to be…
>
> Throughout the operation Gal kept a cool head, giving covering fire with his Sten and even scoring a long-range hit on a sentry at the gate. He waited until he heard the explosion before giving the order to withdraw. In spite of the curfew and the tanks rolling in from every

direction, the boys succeeded in getting away, through backyards and across fences, and made it to their homes safely.

The British suffered considerable casualties, but the figures weren't publicized. Not one of the attackers was hurt.[18]

The reverberations of this action were felt throughout the country and the world; they were felt in the British Parliament, and in Britain there was mounting pressure to quit Palestine for good. The attack on Schneller Camp finally shattered the delusion that terrorism could be defeated by strong-arm tactics.

Army intelligence reports confirmed that martial law had had no appreciable effect on the level of terrorist activity. While soldiers were conducting searches in the towns, terrorist attacks were talking place elsewhere.[19] The intelligence officer of the Sixth Airborne Division drew attention to the fact that "In spite of all the restrictions, acts of sabotage and murder continue on an increasing scale; the Illegal Forces are going all out to 'thumb their noses' at the authorities and their fellow countrymen."[20] After 13 days of martial law, only 24 terrorists had been detained, and of those not one had been arrested in an area subject to the restrictions.[21] Continuation of martial law is liable to lead to riots and other forms of disorder."

Cunningham was at his wits' end.

GIDI'S VICTORY

On March 19, four days after the attack on the Schneller Camp in Jerusalem, 15 days after the imposition of martial law, the Palestine government published a communiqué announcing its official abrogation.

The Government Press Office admitted that during this period no fewer than 68 terrorist acts had been recorded, but in London there was stern criticism of Cunningham following his decision to abrogate martial law.[22] The mood of the cabinet meeting convened on March 20 was grim;

---

18. Tavin's interview with Avinoam, 1954, Jabotinsky Archives.
19. R. Dare Wilson, *Cordon and Search: With 6th Airborne Division in Palestine* (Aldershot: Gale and Polden, 1949), p. 262.
20. PRO WO 275/58 Sixth Airborne Division Intelligence Summary no. 34, March 14, 1947.
21. MEC Cunningham iv/1 Security Conference, March 14, 1947.
22. PRO FO 371/61770 E 2382/46/31 March 19, 1947; Telegram, Cunningham to S. of S. Colonies, 16 March 1947.

among its other conclusions it was stated that "The withdrawal of martial law after so short a period had given an impression of weakness and must have encouraged the Jewish community and the terrorists to think that they had successfully resisted it."[23]

There was pressure to reimpose it, and this time nationwide.

Cunningham defended his position indignantly, pointing out that the recommendation to abrogate martial law had come from the army, not from his office. Indeed, as Montgomery has confirmed, "The problem then became how to preserve law and order for the next six months,"[24] and in this connection, he adds:

> It was suggested that it might be necessary to impose martial law over the whole country. I was opposed to this. Such action would have led to paralysis of economic life and to cause unemployment; it would bear hardly on Jew and Arab alike, and overall, would be damaging to the country The High Commissioner already possessed very great powers under the Defence Regulations, and these were adequate – if he had the courage to use them.[25]

Cunningham declared, "There are various methods in which present anti-terrorist methods can and will be improved, but renewed imposition of Martial Law on the present model is the only practical proposition."[26]

When the issue was debated in the cabinet, the majority view was that the results achieved by martial law had been disappointing. A few arrests had been made but terrorism had not been defeated; terrorist activity was not only continuing, it was increasing in scale. It was decided there would be no renewal of martial law in Palestine.

In conclusion, martial law did indeed paralyze the economic life of the Jewish community but in the longer term did equal damage to Britain: the Mandatory Government lost many thousands of pounds in tax revenue, while the cost of the security operation rapidly devoured the limited budget allocated to it.

---

23. PRO CAB 128/9 C.M. (47) 30th Conclus. March 20, 1947.
24. The period remaining until the expiry of the Mandate.
25. Sir Bernard Law Montgomery, *The Memoirs of Field Marshal the Viscount Montgomery of Alamein* (New York: New American Library, 1959), p. 423.
26. MEC Cunningham Papers iv/1 Security Conference, March 14, 1947.

Despite all the army's efforts, a total of only 60 terrorists were arrested.[27] "This was Gidi's victory," said Menahem Begin:

Paglin was the operations officer, the planner and the instigator, a strategic genius and an artist in the devious acquisition of weapons, one who acted with lightning speed and regularly caught his enemies napping. He organized sabotage squads and sometimes led them himself, though he was under no obligation to do so. During those six weeks I saw him only once or twice; reporting to me in person would have been too risky, and I received his reports through others. Those were hard times for all our boys… But when we achieved our great victory over the British with the lifting of martial law, Paglin came to see me in a neighbor's apartment and I still remember how he looked then: dirty, unshaven, exhausted…and even at a time like this he kept to the protocol, coming into the room and standing to attention! I embraced him warmly with a cry of, "Hey, Gidi, this is your victory!"[28]

27. Tavin's interview with Avinoam, 1954, Jabotinsky Archives.
28. Menahem Begin, *The Revolt*, p. 323.

THE STORMING OF ACRE PRISON

From Jerusalem, Reuters reported the embarrassment of the British authorities, faced by the escape of so many arch-terrorists and the waste of months of searches, arrests, trials, and interrogations. The blow was apparently unbearable. In the House of Commons one minister declared, "Such a thing has never happened before in the history of the British Empire." The chorus of angry voices demanding an end to the British occupation of Palestine rose to a crescendo.

THE BLAST HEARD AROUND THE WORLD

The time was 22 minutes past four, the afternoon of Sunday, May 4, 1947. A violent explosion shook the walls of the ancient prison of Acre, a mighty tongue of flame soared for an instant above the courtyard, and a pall of dust hung in the air.

The echoes of the blast from outside were accompanied by two smaller explosions on the inside – a bundle of thunderflash grenades, detonated in the open, added to the chaos and confusion. Through the fire and smoke, amid the heaps of rubble in the courtyard, panic-stricken figures were seen running in all directions. There was shooting from all sides and Arab prisoners at the gates of their cells bellowed like cattle led to the slaughter-house, convinced their end had come. They were extricated by their allies in the yard and all rushed out in a frenzy, adding further to the confusion. There were already casualties as the sentries opened fire, infected by the overall bedlam, but the shock of the explosions and the grenades thrown from outside by the attackers soon put the security forces, all 150 of them, out of action and within moments the prison was undefended. The cries of the patients in the mental-hospital wing mingled with the roars of vehicle engines outside – and chaos reigned.[1]

---

1. Jan Gitlin, *The Conquest of Acre Fortress* (Tel Aviv: Hadar, 1962).

247

The only ones who stayed calm were the attacking forces and their allies on the inside. In an audacious and well-planned operation, a combat unit of the Irgun Zvai Leumi succeeded in blowing open the southern wing of the fortress and releasing 41 prisoners (30 members of the IZL and 11 Lehi activists). It was a superbly coordinated combined attack by outside forces and prisoners on the inside; the planning was so thorough and discipline so tight that there was no sign of confusion or panic among the escapees.

"It was probably the most carefully planned operation of any they undertook, and its reconstruction later showed that those taking part had an accurate knowledge of the prison, buildings, and the routine observed in them," Major Wilson, an officer of the Sixth Airborne Division, was to say years later.[2]

The effect worldwide was stunning:

"The military achievement of such an attack surprised everybody," the *Jewish Herald* wrote on May 9, 1947, going on to quote General Bolt, commander of the Sixth Airborne Division, as saying, "These Jews are some of the bravest and the best soldiers in the world."

"The prison break was the most daring and sensational one yet made by the underground," the *New York Times* wrote the following day. "This may have been the underground's pay-off for the hanging of four convicted terrorists in the same prison on April 16. The assault that broke down the walls that Napoleon had not been able to reduce," the paper added, "was planned and executed with the usual dash and precision of the terrorists, many of whom had served in the armies and partisan forces of the Allies."

All others were outdone by Ben Hecht, in an open letter to the underground fighters of Palestine published on May 14, 1947, on the front page of a number of New York papers, beginning:

My Brave Friends,

You may not believe what I write you, for there is a lot of fertilizer in the air at the moment. But, on my word as an old reporter, what I write is true. The Jews of America are for you.

You are their champions.

You are the grin they wear.

You are the feather in their hats.

---

2. Wilson, *Cordon and Search.*

> In the past fifteen hundred years every nation of Europe has taken a crack at the Jews.
>
> This time the British are at bat.

The statement included a section which is still remembered and often quoted in Britain, "Every time you blow up a British arsenal, or wreck a British jail, or send a British railroad sky high, or rob a British bank, or let go with your guns and bombs at the British betrayers and invaders of your homeland, the Jews of America make a little holiday in their hearts."[3]

Reactions from all over the world laid particular stress on the blow to the prestige of the British government. "The attack on Acre Prison," the London correspondent of *Haaretz* reported on May 5, "is seen here as a serious blow to British prestige, after the executions on the eve of the UN session which were intended to show that Britain was firmly in control.... Military circles have described the attack as an act of strategic genius."

London newspapers devoted half their columns to the events in Acre, which overshadowed all other news.

"The Jewish underground tonight engineered the escape of 251 Jewish and Arab prisoners from the powerful Acre fortress in the biggest and most spectacular mass jail delivery of modern times," wrote the *Daily Mirror* on May 5, 1947.

The Acre jailbreak took place during the deliberations of a special session of the United Nations General Assembly, convened to discuss the problem of Palestine at the request of the British government. From Bevin's point of view, the very fact of appealing to the UN was a kind of retreat, but it was a calculated one to a position prepared in advance, from which international approval of his policy in Palestine was bound to emerge eventually.

For seven days the debates proceeded placidly, with the Americans showing clear understanding of Britain's problems and willingness to help her out of an awkward predicament. And then came the explosion at Acre prison, landing on the heads of the British like thunder from a clear sky; the morning of May 5, 1947, representatives of 52 nations, along with newspaper readers all over the world, read of the heaviest blow ever inflicted by the IZL, or by any underground resistance movement.

---

3.   Bethell, *The Palestine Triangle*, p. 247.

On May 6 the UN correspondent of *Haaretz* reported from the Assembly, "Events in Acre have caused a tremendous sensation here; it is seen as the most significant jailbreak in history."

Radio Moscow, in a departure from its normal policy, devoted a comprehensive and detailed report to the jailbreak, but the real sensation was witnessed in the forum of the United Nations: Andrei Gromyko, the Soviet representative, astonished delegates with the announcement that his country now favored the establishment of a Jewish state. "It is well known," he said, "that bloody events are taking place in Palestine.... The fact that the government which holds the Mandate has itself brought the problem to the Assembly for discussion, can only be interpreted as admission that continuation of the present situation in Palestine cannot be countenanced."[4]

The special sitting of the United Nations organization concluded its deliberations with the decision to appoint a commission of inquiry to examine the Palestine question. "And when the UN delegation arrived in the country," Begin relates, "some of the delegates met me and said: 'In New York, at the special session, when we heard of your assault on Acre, we knew straightaway that Britain's days in Palestine were numbered.' Those same delegates," Begin added, "later voted for the establishment of a Jewish state."

ORIGINS OF THE PLAN

The plan to break into Acre prison began to take shape towards the end of 1946. On April 2 of that year, an IZL unit had been captured near Bat Yam while returning from sabotage activities against the railway network in the south of the country, on behalf of the United Resistance Movement. Thirty-one men were taken prisoner, including the chief operations commander of the IZL, Eitan Livni. They were held at first in Jerusalem, and later transferred to Acre.

Gidi takes up the story:

From the first day of their imprisonment we felt we were obliged to free them, and this feeling weighed on us all the more heavily as the conditions of their detention worsened; it intensified when they were transferred from the prison in Jerusalem to Acre, and became unbearable when our other comrades were led to the gallows, just yards from

---

4.   Samuel (Shmuel) Katz, *Days of Fire* (Garden City, NY: Doubleday, 1968).

the cells of the 31. We felt as if we were leaving wounded comrades on the battlefield, and we were absolutely determined to do something, to free them and bring them back into the bosom of the fighting family.

As this was the way we thought, you can understand how in this case we were prepared to take risks that we'd have avoided in a conventional operation. I'm talking here of both the planners and the perpetrators. This feeling was shared by Shimshon (Dov Cohen), who commanded the operation and met his death in it.

It should be remembered that the Acre operation was carried out in a period of relative quiet, since the Palestine issue was then being debated by the United Nations, and as I understand it, there was even an unofficial pledge on our part to the South American delegates, not to exacerbate the situation while the debates were continuing.

All this was before the hangings. We were convinced that the British were intent on carrying out the sentences, and we were planning to rescue our comrades from the death chambers (first in the central prison in Jerusalem and later in Acre), but the British caught us short by bringing forward the implementation of the sentences. They did this like thieves in the night, behind a smokescreen of lies and broken promises.[5]

Twenty-two years after these tragic events, Gidi could still barely control his disappointment and resentment, as he continued, "The British hangman beat us by less than 48 hours. The first date set for the Acre operation was April 18, 1947,[6] but the British took them to the gallows on April 16, having broken their promises. We felt we could stand it no longer and couldn't leave our other comrades to the mercy of the government."

While Gidi and Shimshon were looking for ways to spring their comrades from the prison, Eitan Livni lost patience and started devising a plan of his own. "The prison at Acre was under a heavy pall of gloom," he writes in his memoirs. "No wonder, that after our first taste of the place we began questioning veteran prisoners about prospects for escape…. What we heard

---

5. Taped interview with the author, 1969.
6. See also Matti Shmulewitz, *Be-Yamim Adumim* [On red days] (Tel Aviv: Ministry of Defense, 1978), p. 261.

wasn't encouraging: not one single prisoner had ever succeeded in escaping from Acre..."

He soon came to the conclusion that the only way of breaking out of the prison was by means of a large-scale operation, and within a few days he had a detailed plan in hand and this was sent, in code, to IZL Command for approval. As he describes it:

> According to the plan, we were going to climb on the roof of the lavatory building, which was one story high, overpower the sentry on guard there and cross to the roofs of the low Arab buildings adjoining the wall, and a force would be waiting for us outside, ready to get us away through the alleyways of the old city.... The reply from Headquarters was short and to the point: "Plan unacceptable. Suggest alternatives."[7]

Gidi relates:

> Command told me to examine the feasibility of Livni's plan. I went to Acre, and after a short tour of the sector, it was clear to me the plan was sheer fantasy, fruit of the imagination of people who've been cooped up so long between prison walls they've lost all sense of reality. It might just work in a movie, but it was completely impractical. In general terms it depended on getting control from inside, climbing on the roof of the prison, eliminating the guard post there, slipping out into the street, and sneaking through backyards of houses to the alleys of the old town. All this, of course, with assistance from outside, which would ensure orderly withdrawal to a place of safety. It was a plan for guaranteed suicide: even if, as the first stage, they succeeded in getting control of the roof – and that was doubtful – no one would get off that roof alive. Obviously, the plan was rejected.
>
> The success of the Acre prison break – as with other Irgun operations – depended on the first blow falling with the impact of an earthquake, a blast that would stun everyone in the target area and paralyze for a few moments the response capability of the security forces. This short period of shock and loss of focus was something our men were adept at exploiting, working quickly and efficiently and getting the

---

7. Livni, *Ha-Ma'amad*, p. 224.

job done. Obviously, this effect couldn't be achieved with a few pistol shots, as the young men in the prison envisaged. By the end of that first reconnaissance, I was in no doubt about this.

As for the reconnaissance itself – I came to Acre with Aharon Mizrahi, who spoke fluent Arabic, and we were both dressed as Arabs. While inspecting the area, we found to our surprise that part of the wall around the prison, about 20 yards high, bordered on the main street, which was open to civilian traffic.

Moreover, the arch of the old Turkish bathhouse adjoined the wall and as a result of this the effective height of the wall bordering on the street was reduced to some four yards above ground level. It seemed too good to be true, and I decided to compare what we'd seen on the ground with the Public Works Department's maps of the prison site. When our examination was complete, I still couldn't believe what I was seeing: the map matched the picture on the ground.

I assembled a few members of the combat squad and showed them the maps. All agreed that we'd found the weak point in the fortress. If indeed one of the walls of the prison bordered on the main street – all that remained for us to do was to blast through that barrier standing between our friends and freedom. We couldn't imagine why the British hadn't considered this possibility.[8]

One aspect of the plan – the security forces on the roof of the building – was not too much of a worry to the combat team. "Almost certainly they'll be in shock after the explosion – at least for the first ten seconds," Gidi declared. "In any case, they can be silenced by firepower from the ground.

"No one underestimated the importance of the mission we'd taken on," Gidi stressed, continuing:

To get an idea of the scale of the Acre jailbreak in modern terms, we'd need to compare it with raiding the central prison in Damascus, extricating a number of prisoners and flying them to this country in safety. That's what it was like, attacking Acre prison in 1947: in the heart of a hostile Arab city, surrounded by army camps and under the noses of prison guards.

8. Author's recorded interview with Amihai Paglin, 1969.

At first sight, you'd think it impossible.

We thought otherwise.

The next step was to make direct and unmediated contact with Eitan Livni. Families of prisoners were allowed to visit their relatives and even bring them packages of food. I joined one of these groups. Eitan Livni was given advance warning and was asked to signal to me, somehow, the location of their cells. It was decided to exploit the visit to smuggle into the prison a quantity of explosives and detonators, for making thunderflash grenades.

I poured gelignite into jam jars, filling them two-thirds full and adding orange jam of the same color. In the entrance to the prison there was a long table, and the packages had to be laid out for examination. One of the guards stuck a skewer into the jam jar and when he pulled it out there was a globule of gelignite, mixed with jam, sticking to the end. He tasted the concoction, grimaced, and spat in disgust. For a moment he seemed to hesitate and my heart missed a beat: would he send the jar for analysis? But no. He closed the jar, his face blank, no doubt thinking the prisoners were welcome to the filthy stuff, and didn't bother to check the other jars. When the inspections were done I approached the gate. I saw the commandant of the jail, Deputy Commander Charlton, standing there casually, leaning against the gate to the right of the entrance.

When Livni saw me he started walking towards me with a cry of "Hey, you're from Tel Aviv, aren't you? Can you give my regards to my parents?" He didn't see the Englishman standing there, and I was afraid he'd say too much and give the game away. I gave him a cautionary wink, and he took the hint. "Where do your parents live?' I shouted back at him. He approached me and uttered a single word, "*smitri*" – "look" in Russian – and turned his head to the southern side of the wall, the place where the break-in was going to be made...and so, in the course of a shouted conversation, interspersed with Russian words, he showed me where their cells were. It fitted the information we already had.

I glanced outside the wall and noticed the turrets of two mosques on the skyline. I estimated their position relative to the prison and decided to use them as landmarks on the operational map. In the process

I also checked again that the external wall of the prison bordered on the road as the map indicated, and I felt mightily relieved.[9]

Gidi was indeed relieved, but characteristically, he wasn't content with first impressions. He set out for another reconnaissance, this time accompanied by Shimshon. The cover was "marketing bakery ovens" – a business in which Gidi was well versed.[10]

The purpose of the survey was to check out the crossroads near the fortress and devise a plan for controlling the access and exit routes of Acre city. As they walked, the fortress on one side and the sea on the other, they reached the Safed-Acre-Nahariya intersection.

At such a busy intersection, they had to keep in mind that a British military convoy could turn up at any moment and wreck the entire operation. To deal with such an eventuality, it was decided to set up a well-defended observation post, with a select squad of six, headed by Shimshon, equipped with arms and ammunition including a machine gun, bombs, mines, and Molotov cocktails.

As their tour of inspection continued, the two turned towards the southern wall of the fortress, the area of the planned break-in. Since the police station was located in the new, northern sector of the city, it was decided it should be isolated from the southern sector by means of two blocking squads, one to the west of the fortress and one to the east.

In Gidi's own words:

> Once we'd made up our minds to storm the fortress, we conveyed the general lines of the scheme to our friends inside, allowing them some latitude about their part of it but insisting on one point: they were to use thunderflash grenades to block any reinforcements arriving in the prison yard from the administration block. This task was to be entrusted to the ones not taking part in the break-out. They replied they could do better than this: they'd set fire to kerosene[11] in the entrances

9.   Ibid.
10. The Paglin family business was the manufacture of bakery ovens.
11. British reports use the term "paraffin," the equivalent of which in American usage is kerosene.

to the offices, and cover their comrades that way. Which indeed they did – and very effectively too.

As the plan took shape, it became increasingly clear that the crux of the operation was the withdrawal – not the assault. Shimshon went out in the jeep to tour side roads leading from Acre to the nearest base, at Shuni.

At the end of a two-day tour accompanied by an Arabic-speaking youth (from the start we preferred to route our retreat through Arab rather than Jewish areas), he returned with a detailed itinerary, starting at the Acre-Safed intersection and continuing via the valley road to Binyamina and Shuni. He surveyed the region two or three times, and when he was satisfied I joined him for another "spin." The proposed itinerary was flawless and met all our requirements. This, we decided, was it!

From this point onward, the center of gravity shifted to the organizational area. In the planning section it was accepted practice that any complicated or unusual operation would be commanded by a member of the combat squad who had been in on the original scheme. The lot fell on Shimshon and this was, to my mind, the best choice in those circumstances. I myself wasn't a candidate (as chief operations officer, I was barred from going into action) but anyway – of the two of us, Shimshon was the better suited – I can't think of anyone more capable of commanding this operation. Besides, it was a right he demanded for himself. As virtually the only one to slip through the net when the 31 activists were arrested at Bat Yam, he felt a special responsibility to lead the operation to rescue his friends from their incarceration at the hands of the British.[12]

"And that is what he did – although it cost him his life," Gidi concludes with a regretful nod of the head.

THE BRIEFING

It all began on the Sabbath, May 3, 1947.

At 4:00 PM a group of young men assembled in a diamond factory in Netanya. It was a one-story building and the administration office, usually

---

12. Author's recorded interview with Amihai Paglin, 1969.

deserted on non-working days, was now filled with clouds of cigarette smoke, both its windows closed and covered with white curtains. The youths sat at ease on the concrete floor, exchanging jokes and impressions. They knew they had been summoned for some operation, but had no idea what it was to be.

Into the room came a blond, blue-eyed man, short and sturdy, who looked for a moment at the faces of the assembled company and left without saying a word. Some knew him by his codename, Shimshon, and only a few knew his full name, Dov Cohen. But his heroism was a byword and his reputation preceded him as one of the most able commanders in the ranks of the Irgun.

While the boys were still pondering the meaning of this unconventional meeting, on a Sabbath too, a local hairdresser arrived and without much ceremony began treating them all to a British-style "short-back-and-sides" – with results that naturally became the occasion for laughter and witticisms.

After they had waited for an hour and a half, Gidi arrived. All now moved to the next room, where there were big maps and sketches pinned to the wall. Gidi stood at a blackboard propped up on one of the benches, his gleaming eyes scouring all those present. They sat still, waiting tensely for him to speak.

"The target this time," he said slowly, as if weighing every word, "is Acre prison." And after a short pause, as if giving them time to digest what they had heard, he added firmly, "The objective: to free our people imprisoned there."

The men in the room were transfixed as if by an electric current. A soft murmur and whispers of surprise. Some couldn't believe their ears: *to storm Acre prison, the British Bastille? Is such a thing possible?*

Gidi raised his eyebrows and then continued quietly, as if unaware of the storm his words had just aroused: "This operation is set to be one of the most daring in the history of the Irgun and is likely to have far-reaching political consequences – more important still, it will lead to the release of our best comrades, whom we need so much at this time. There is no doubt," he added, pausing for extra emphasis, "that this operation will make an impression in the world and will have many repercussions. But – and this is what you have to remember – the scope of our achievement depends on the extent of our success. The operation itself is not as tough and complicated as it may seem to you now. Every detail has been thoroughly planned, and if everyone does the job assigned to him and follows instructions to the letter, success is assured."

There was a pause. Gidi took a sip from his glass of juice and began detailing the plan and the role of each group:

Unit number one, consisting of four men,[13] will be led by Shimshon, the commander of the operation, and will travel in the command jeep, with Bren gun mounted. When the explosion is heard it will block the Nahariya to Haifa road, and set fire to the gas station by the main road, to add to the general confusion.

Unit number two, of four men,[14] led by Dov Salomon, the deputy operation commander, will breach the wall of the prison and escort the escapees to the transports. Two members of the unit will hang the explosives on the windows of the southern wall of the fortress. Through the gap created by the explosion, our imprisoned friends will escape to freedom. The explosives will be passed to them wrapped securely in bundles, with hooks for hanging.

Unit number three, of three men,[15] commanded by Avshalom Haviv, on hearing the explosion, is to mine the road leading from Acre police station to the alleyways of the old town, and set up a Bren position to cover the withdrawal route.

Unit number four, of two men,[16] led by Menahem Ostrowicz, is to mine the road leading from Acre police station to the *souk* and to the prison, and after the explosion will open fire and pin down the sentries on the southeastern section of the wall.

As he spoke, Gidi marked on the blackboard every position, every alleyway, and every road in the operational zone. His instructions were given in a simple and easily comprehensible form:

---

13. Besides Shimshon, Unit 1 included Benyamin Shomryahu, Zalman Lifschitz, and Yosef Hazan.
14. Besides Salomon, Unit 2 included Yehuda Apirion, Moshe Hamermann, and Meir Amiaz.
15. Besides Avshalom Haviv, Unit 3 included Meir Nakar and Yaakov Weiss.
16. The other member of Unit 4 was Amnon Michaeli.

The blocking squad, commanded by Moshe Levi, will number four men,[17] and will approach from the direction of the municipal offices. Its job is to mine the section of road to the south of Acre, near Naaman Bridge, and cut off the town from any outside contact for as long as possible.

And last of all, *the diversionary squad*, of three men,[18] commanded by Akiva Cohen [Yoav], will launch a mortar attack on the local headquarters of the Sixth Airborne Division. After the operation it will withdraw northward.

"It is essential that we avoid fatalities among the Arab population of the town," Gidi stressed. "If the need arises, firing in the air should be enough to scare them off. And remember," he added with a smile, "you are to conduct yourselves in a manner becoming members of His Majesty's Forces, and if you encounter any British soldiers, try not to arouse their suspicion. But" – no longer smiling – "if they're on to you, then give them a taste of lead, don't think twice. Any questions?"

Silence.

There were no questions.

THE BREAKOUT

The next day all made their way to the jump-off point at Shuni. At 2:30 PM the signal was given and a convoy of 34 fighters (most of them in British army uniforms) set out in three vehicles – a three-ton military truck and two vans – with the command jeep up ahead, flying a green flag to mark the head of the convoy. Beside the driver, "Captain Shimshon" sat back comfortably, festooned with medal ribbons and in his pocket a movement order signed by "Major Skeller": *To transport 20 soldiers, on leave, from Sarafand to Beirut, via Acre.*

The jeep had barely left the gate of Shuni when a British military convoy appeared on the road from Zikhron Yaakov. The gate was closed again and the drivers switched off their engines. To avoid arousing suspicion, Shimshon kept moving forward until suddenly the engine went dead. The commander of the British convoy pulled up alongside Shimshon and offered to

---

17. The other members of the interception squad: Moshe Amiel, Margalit Abutbul, and Shulamit Mehulal.

18. Other members of the diversionary squad: Yosef Shitrit and David Dahari.

help. Shimshon rejected the offer politely, assuring him it was a trivial problem and he had already figured out how to fix it. The two "officers" parted company on cordial terms, and when the British had gone, a mechanic was sent out from Shuni to repair the fault, and the convoy was on the road again, to all appearances a regular unit of Royal Engineers. Naturally, no one suspected the two civilian cars that tagged along: in one of them, members of the diversionary squad, disguised as Arabs, and in the other, two young couples in civilian dress, who had chosen a novel way of whiling away their precious time together: mining roads and blocking bridges.

About an hour later, another squeal of brakes. Someone lifted the canvas at the back of the truck and a military policeman peered inside. There were impatient murmurs, "Hey, mate, don't hold us up, we're on leave…" The Briton mumbled something unclear and walked away. In the command jeep, the inspection proceeded smoothly enough: Shimson produced his fake movement order, accompanied by some juicy curses. The MPs smiled sympathetically and saluted – and the convoy moved on.

At 4:10 PM the assault force started deploying in its positions. Shimshon's command jeep was the first to take up position at the major Acre-Safed-Nahariya intersection. The three camouflaged vehicles – the truck and two vans – moved south towards the fortress. The truck was too big to pass through the gate of the old town and had to be left outside the walls. The mortar crew in the civilian van headed northward, to the Sixth Airborne Division camp at "Sydney Barracks"; the blocking squad had moved up from the municipality sector and was drawn up close to Naaman Bridge, opposite the Kurdani base, ready to block the road south of Acre.

Tension among the 41 prisoners destined for escape reached a climax. "The hour of 16:00 passed," writes Eitan Livni,[19] "and after that the minutes passed with maddening slowness. I looked at my watch, it was 16:15…and we were already wondering how to get the explosives, detonators and fuses back into the hidden caches…and then, at 16:22, an almighty explosion shook the walls of the prison…"

When the infiltration party reached its destination, it was already 4:15 PM. The commander, Dov Salomon, who had already reconnoitred the

19. Livni, *Ha-Maʾamad*, p. 237.

area, had no difficulty identifying his surroundings. One glance at Gidi's sketch was enough to confirm the location of the mosque, and not far from it, the outer wall.

Members of the blocking squads, led by Avshalom Haviv and Nahman Zitterbaum, took up the positions allotted to them and began planting mines in the roads leading to the fortress.

The military van stopped by the bridge. Two ladders were pulled out, along with "equipment for repair of telephone cables." The demolition squad set off towards the Turkish bathhouse, with its vaulted roof adjoining the wall of the fortress. In Dov Salomon's own words:

> I ordered two of my men to secure the site and block access to it from east and west, and the first hitch happened when we came to set up the ladders: they were each made up of two sections that could be combined into one. The day before they'd been painted and slotted together, and now that the paint was dry it was impossible to separate them. One wouldn't open at all, while the other, which could be extended slightly, reached to about a yard short of the edge of the roof. I was determined to get the job done no matter what. I told my second-in-command, Yehuda Apirion, to climb onto the roof of the bathhouse, which he did by dint of supreme physical effort – and I followed with a bundle of explosives on my head; when I got to the top of the ladder, he leaned over and took it off me and then we repeated the exercise. Once the explosives had been brought to the roof, we pulled the ladders up after us, positioned them against the two windows in the fortress wall and, as carefully as we could, climbed up and hung the bundles of explosives on the bars, using the hooks prepared in advance.
>
> We activated the charges at once, removed the ladders, and didn't hesitate to jump down from the dome to the street. We'd given ourselves 30 seconds and sure enough, just as our feet touched the ground, there was a sound like a thunderclap and the earth shook. For a moment we were stunned ourselves.[20]

When the sound of the explosion was heard, the three groups of prisoners moved all at once:

---

20. Testimony of Dov Salomon (Yishai), Jabotinsky Archives.

Menahem Maletzky, commander of the group of 13, sprang from his cell and set off at a run with his men along the corridor behind the cells. At the corner separating the two wings of the building, the group stopped. Maletzky and Ashbel approached the first inner gate, fixed explosives to the bolts, activated the charges, and retreated to a safe distance. There was a deafening report and the bolts disintegrated. After a moment's pause, the group moved on to the second gate; another loud explosion and they were all running through the haze of smoke and dust towards the fuel store, its two windows open wide.

Simultaneously, Dov Efrat's team set to work. One section, armed with clubs and iron bars – ripped from beds – blocked the corridor, barring entrance to security staff and Arab prisoners; the other section cut off the administration block from the prison yard and isolated the escape route, using a barrier of fire and smoke produced by an inflammable mixture of oil and kerosene.

All this time Menahem Schiff's group were lobbing thunderflash grenades at the sentries and keeping them at bay.

An account of events between the prison walls as seen from a British perspective may be gleaned from the report by the prison authorities kept in the CID files.[21] Extracts from the report are given here:

On 4th May, 1947 the prisoners at Acre Prison were on exercise in the exercise yard in the afternoon, when at 4:10 PM, three grenades were thrown from outside the prison into the lunatics section which is at the extreme South Eastern corner of the prison abutting onto a 'bus garage. There was no panic among the lunatics although seven inmates sustained minor injuries from bomb fragments.

Immediately after these explosions rifle and machine gun fire was brought to bear on the Arab guards on the prison walls from all directions and a party of Jews scaled, by the use of light ladders, the roof of the archway over the Suk running adjacent to the Turkish bath. By using further scaling ladders they reached the barred windows in the

---

21. *"Daf me-ha-slik"* [Page from the hiding place], *Haganah Archives Quarterly*, no. 6 (1997).

corridor running along the South side of the prison proper opposite cells numbers 14 and 15 respectively.

The bars of those windows were blown out by the use of explosives and the corridor was entered, the attackers turning right towards the prison school where they blew the gate leading into the school and then, presumably blew the gate leading into the exercise yard.

Jewish prisoners in the exercise yard immediately the explosion was heard took up previously prepared sticks, on the ends of which had been wrapped paraffin-soaked rags, and lighted them and commenced to brandish them. Arab prisoners, panic-stricken, scaled the wire apron of the North wall of the exercise yard and filled the corridor between the exercise yard and the prison offices. At that time two condemned prisoners, one Arab and one Jew, were on exercise in the corridor...under the charge of...Thompson.

The Arab prisoners broke into this corridor and released the condemned Arab. Thompson was the only British office[r] at that time present. He endeavoured to quieten the prisoners and frantically demanded their release and managed to reach the gate leading into the reception lobby, which was locked, and he remained there, having sustained minor injuries, until ASP Mr Glahomo, second-in-command of the Central Prison, Acre, opened the gate in an attempt to rescue him, upon which the Arabs streamed into the reception lobby and pinned both ASP Mr Galhomo and Thompson against the outer blank iron door.

Meanwhile, Mr. Charlton, Superintendent of the Prison, who, at the outset was in the prison hospital and who could not, by virtue of the press of prisoners, leave the hospital had, through an outer window, called for gas. Tear gas was then fired through the vision aperture in the outer blank iron door and the Arab prisoners then panicked in the opposite direction....

The report further tells us that exchanges of fire between prison guards and assailants continued for some time and police and army reinforcements arrived at the prison at 5:10 PM and that telephone lines between the prison and Police HQ had been cut.

A report submitted by the High Commissioner, Sir Alan Cunningham, to the British colonial secretary, stated that at the time of the assault on the prison, diversionary attacks were simultaneously launched by armed Jews in the vicinity of local army camps. Shots were fired at military vehicles, and six mortar-bombs fired into one camp. Mines were laid at seven points on the local roads. At the time of the attack, exchanges of fire between prison staff and assailants continued for a considerable period of time.

ESCAPING — AND PAYING THE PRICE

Outside the wall of the prison, the attackers began losing patience. In the words of Dov Salomon:

> The echoes of the blast had faded long ago. Yehuda and I climbed up on the roof again, but there was no sign of the prisoners.
>
> "Yishai, what's going on?" the lads down below were shouting. "Aren't they coming?" "It'll be okay," I assured them, "they're working from inside." I tried to sound calm.
>
> After a few minutes – which seemed like hours – the first escapees arrived. Part of the roof had collapsed after the explosion, and the boys had to jump over the cracked dome, where there was just a narrow foothold left. As they ran they shouted "It's us!" and although we replied "We're here!" as agreed – they stopped suddenly, panicking: the figures in British uniforms and tin hats looked all too authentic. It took a few moments of confusion before they were convinced these were their comrades in disguise. They were so relieved and overjoyed they pounced on us with hugs and kisses. "No time for that," I warned them, "there's still a long way to go before you're safe."[22]

The party of escapees sped toward the vehicles, covering the 200 yards through the alleys of the old town at a run. The little van was soon full. The thirteenth man aboard shouted "All in!" – the canvas cover was pulled down and the vehicle lurched forward. They passed through the wall of the old town without mishap.

According to the exit route agreed beforehand, they were supposed to cross the Haifa-Acre road near the Muslim cemetery and from there take the unpaved roads skirting Napoleon's Hill to the main Shefaram highway. For some unknown reason, instead of crossing the road, the driver turned

---

22. Testimony of Dov Salomon, Jabotinsky Archives.

right and began heading towards Naaman Bridge, and it was then that a unit of paratroopers appeared, driving up from the seashore; the vehicle aroused their suspicions and they signaled to it to stop. When this was ignored, they opened fire. In the desperate attempt to escape, the car skidded off the road and crashed into a fence of cactuses, turning on its side. The paratroopers kept on firing.[23]

Gidi narrates:

And then, like something out of a movie, Shimshon suddenly appears, in his Airborne Division uniform and his captain's epaulettes, shouting at the top of his voice: "Stop firing, you fools!" The firing stopped immediately, and he calmly flagged down one of the army vehicles, loaded the young men onto it and ordered the driver to get going. All this under the gaze of the astonished soldiers.

Shimshon's position, some distance from the point of the assault, at the Acre-Safed-Nahariya intersection, wasn't by chance. From the start, the withdrawal had been our top priority, and that's why Shimshon was posted on the most sensitive section of the route. So, at the critical moment, he was the right man in the right place.[24]

When the British realized they had been tricked, they opened fire again, with the "captain" responding with bursts from the Bren and forcing them to take cover in a ditch beside the road. Suddenly a bullet pierced the engine of the truck, and the escape vehicle wasn't going any further.

Shimshon uttered a few juicy curses but didn't lose his head: he stopped a truck carrying Arab workers and forced them to abandon the vehicle. Yet the driver refused to budge. Shimshon ran out of patience and fired a short burst in his direction; unfortunately, one of the bullets hit the fugitives' own driver.

The soldiers increased their rate of fire.

A no-way-out situation.

"And here Shimshon showed his true colors, all his courage and resourcefulness," Gidi relates in a tone of admiration. "While he was pinning the British down with steady fire, he urged his men to disperse and head

23. Brigadier (Res.) Mordecai Ziori, *Ma'arakhot* 201, August 1969.
24. Author's recorded interview with Amihai Paglin, 1969.

for the fields. He held his position, giving covering fire until a volley of bullets hit him in the face and silenced him permanently. He died at his post."

Shimshon's last, heroic moments are described by Matityahu Shmulewitz, one of the escapees in the ill-fated tender:

The car was traveling at high speed, and it was like being carried on eagles' wings. Suddenly we hear shooting close by. Volleys from the driver's seat.

"Are they attacking us?"

Yes, we're under fire. From the front seat, someone's firing back. Increasing speed. "Down!" Bullets pierce the canvas and whistle over our heads. Ashbel wounded.

"We're caught in a trap!"

Staying in the car means certain death. We started jumping out through the back door, under fire. Several wounded. Run! Look for shelter! Running along the ditch by the side of the road. The bullets catch up with us. Someone falls beside me: Haim Brenner. Someone else. Must get away from the road. Bullets whistling around our heads, but the enemy out of sight. We made it to the path by the cemetery. Behind that hill there's cover. Maybe we'll get away after all.

I took the lead. We were almost on the hill when a red beret and the muzzle of a Sten suddenly popped up in front of me. I signaled to the other runners to stop, felt a sharp pain in my hand. Wounded. Go back!

We ran down the hill, back to the road.

Suddenly the firing stopped.

When we got to the road, we saw a British officer running towards us with a submachine gun. The paratroopers stopped firing for fear of hitting him.

"Boys, follow me!" shouted the "British officer." We ran after him. It was Shimshon, commander of the operation. Most of us were wounded, and some couldn't run anymore and needed help. The bullets still whistled around our ears. Up ahead there was a military vehicle parked on the road. If only we could get to it…there was still hope.

We made it to the car. Sitting inside it were two British soldiers. Shimshon threatened them and we overpowered them. This was the car the paratroopers had been traveling in before they attacked us.

The two soldiers and the driver stayed put, as they were unarmed. We do our best to restrain them. They're scared and pleading for mercy. Meanwhile, Shimshon's "persuaded" the driver to step on it.

It seems the soldiers who attacked us are armed only with submachine guns, and within a few seconds we're out of their range. The two Brits in the car have realized we're not armed, as well as close to exhaustion, and try to break loose. We get Shimshon, sitting beside the driver, to hand us a revolver and force the two men to jump out of the command car. The paratroopers are still chasing us, on foot. But we're well beyond their range.

Shimshon asks if there's another driver among us. Yes, we still have Shimshon Vilner – the last reserve driver....

Beside the road, by the fuel pump, stands Shimshon's jeep. The driver was told to flood the road with petrol and set it alight, to give the impression we've headed towards Haifa and this is our way of impeding pursuit.... The irony is, through force of circumstances, we *are* on the Haifa road.... It's decided to abandon the idea of torching the gas and instead to arm ourselves with the Bren and all the other weapons that have been left in the jeep.

The British driver is ejected from his seat and runs for his life. All the uninjured help to transfer the arms and ammunition from the jeep to the other vehicle. Shimshon Vilner takes the driver's seat and tries to start the engine – once, twice – nothing doing.... There's a big bloodstain spreading on the floor of the vehicle, and the groans of the wounded are pitiful. The British soldiers are closing in on us, and we'll soon be in range again. Bullets already humming. Someone notices a dark patch on the road under the engine; seems the petrol-tank's been punctured. Less than 100 yards between us and the Brits. Suddenly, a flash of hope: a red truck loaded with Arab workers appears before us.

"Quick, stop that truck!" Shimshon commands, running forward with the Bren. We all trail after him, the lightly wounded helping the more severely injured. The truck stops. One volley of shots in the air and the Arabs scatter in all directions. Only the driver stays put and refuses to budge... The British are getting closer... Shimshon is running out of patience, yelling at the driver to get out, but he's still refusing. A burst from the Bren puts an end to the argument, but also to our last remaining hope. The Arab driver collapses in a pool of blood while Shimshon Vilner, in a hurry to take his place and entering by the other door, is killed by that unfortunate volley.

We'd lost a good friend and our fate was sealed – no driver.

Amnon, the only one among us who had the faintest idea of how to drive, tried to get the truck going under a hail of fire. Wounded in the chest and his arms almost paralyzed, he struggled with the wheel and finally succeeded in slewing the truck across the road.

"Scatter!" shouted Shimshon, from behind the command jeep, opening fire with the Bren and forcing the British to take cover. Their advance was halted, but for how long? We hurried towards the fields. The logical direction to take was to the right; the left led back towards Acre and that was the way the Arabs from the truck had gone. In the distance we saw a field of standing wheat. "If I can just get there," I thought, "hide in the wheat till nightfall – then carry on." Shimshon Vilner and the Arab driver were left lying in the road while Shimshon, the commander, was still standing behind the jeep, shooting at the British.

Panting and wheezing we collapsed in the wheat field. Very slowly I turned my head to look back: the commander of the operation, in captain's uniform, lay in the road, showing no sign of life... In a final effort to save our lives – Dov Cohen, our Shimshon, sacrificed his own life.[25]

The fate of the fugitives who hid in the wheat field was related by Matti Shmulewitz some ten days later, in a personal letter delivered secretly to Eitan Livni from Acre prison.

The following are extracts from that shocking document, describing the inhuman behavior of His Majesty's finest, shooting wounded prisoners in cold blood as they lay helpless on the ground – the ground for which they sacrificed their young lives:

A quarter of an hour later the soldiers arrived in the wheat field and found us. They opened fire although we had surrendered and it was only by a miracle we came out alive. Yosef was injured again. We were saved by the intervention of a police officer, who ordered the soldiers to take us alive. Shimon, Mike, and Baruch weren't so lucky. They were

---

25. Shmulewitz, *Be-yamim adumim*, pp. 267–70.

shot at while lying helpless on the ground, and miraculously, Baruch wasn't hit. They took us to the car, dragging the wounded along the ground and throwing them in like sacks of coal. We lay in one heap, the dead and the wounded together. Only Moshe Salomon, who was uninjured and I, wounded in the hand – could do anything to help. I won't even attempt to describe my feelings.

After we'd pulled the dead off the wounded, I spent the journey talking with Shimon. He knew he was going to die and I tried to deny this and raise his spirits. Mike[26] also knew he didn't have long to live, and in spite of this he lay there cracking jokes. It was hard to believe a guy like that could be on his way out: every now and then he'd utter a groan, immediately adding, "It'll be okay...don't worry..."

An Egged bus full of Jews was standing in the roadway as we stopped to pick up another casualty: Amnon. Mike, seeing the faces of the Jews looking on at the macabre spectacle, shouted at them, "Jews, look, we're dying for you."

Instead of the hospital they took us to Acre police station, where they dumped the wounded on the pavement. To all my pleas, protests, and appeals for medical assistance there was the same answer: Shut up! Shimon was the first to die. He was conscious to the end. It's hard to describe how I felt, watching my friend dying. His main worry was the grief that his parents and friends would suffer as a result of his death. "Give my best wishes to all the boys," he said. "Tell them not to grieve – but carry on. Write to my parents and sisters and try to console them." His last words were, "Matti, avenge me, a-v-e-n-g-e..."

Levi died in terrible pain. He was wounded in the lungs and he choked to death. It was a ghastly experience for me, being there beside them and unable to help...

Mike went on cracking jokes to the last moment. The same old Mike. I held his hand and felt him going cold and yet it was still hard to believe he was dying. Right up to the end he was comforting *me*, "Don't worry, it's going to be okay, we'll pay them back."

Nicho was lying there quietly, the blood oozing from a bullet hole

26. Mike is Michael Ashbel, who was sentenced to death in 1946 and reprieved following the kidnapping of British officers from the Hayarkon Hotel in Tel Aviv. While still in the condemned cell, he composed the popular song "On the Barricades," which became the virtual anthem of IZL fighters in the pre-State years.

in his back. I moved him onto his side and told him not to move. He was also wounded in the leg and it was hard for him to lie on his side. After a few minutes he asked me in a submissive tone, "Matti, can I turn over? It's hard to lie like this." When the doctor finally arrived, he sent him to join the others, because he said he felt better.

There's no doubt that most of those who died of their wounds could have been saved, if they had received medical attention. They were left to bleed for six hours...

The commander of the diversionary squad, Akiva Cohen (Yoav), took up position with his two assistants, Yosef Shitrit and David Dahari, in the little pine grove. They parked their vehicle in the shade of the tree, set up the mortar, and calibrated it for the center of the camp, HQ Depot of the Sixth Airborne Division.

From time to time they glanced towards old Acre, waiting impatiently for the agreed signal. When the sound of the explosion was heard from the direction of the prison, the first bomb slid into the muzzle of the mortar and flew off towards its target. Yoav fired off the missiles at a brisk rate and they exploded with thunderous crashes in the center of the camp. The surprised soldiers, caught in the middle of a game of football, ran about in all directions, stunned and panic-stricken.

When the bombs were used up, the mortar was taken back to the vehicle and it sped off toward the north. According to the plan they were supposed to withdraw in the direction of Tiberias, but at the intersection near Pekiin they realized the brakes weren't working. They were speeding down a steep slope and at the last moment the driver, Yosef Shitrit, decided on a desperate solution: he steered the vehicle straight at the rock face. There was a deafening impact, the car flew up in the air, turned over several times – and there was silence. The cab section was embedded in rubble, the rear section some 50 yards down the road.

They were lucky, and came out of it with barely a scratch.

The Arabs of the nearby villages rushed to the scene, clearly amazed to find the three occupants of the wrecked car still alive. But they made no attempt to help them get to Tiberias. In the end Musa Mahmud, a Christian Arab from the village of Rama, was persuaded to drive them to Tiberias in his truck, in exchange for a generous fee.

Fifty years later, Yosef Shitrit visited their savior in Rama and invited him to the celebration of the anniversary of the Acre prison raid, held in Tel Aviv's Hall of Culture. "Were it not for him," said Shitrit with feeling, "there would have been 16, rather than 13, Jewish victims of the noose…"

After the first group had left via the gate of the old town, the rest of the fugitives were ushered towards the remaining vehicles. Some got into the second van, others continued on foot towards the big truck parked outside the wall. Suddenly the engine of the van died, and the occupants started pushing it in an attempt to start it.

By this time the Arab residents of Acre had realized what was happening and had set out in pursuit of the fugitives. They closed the gate in the wall and started pelting the young men with stones, sticks, whatever came to hand. The commander of the attacking force, Dov Salomon (Yishai) was forced to fire in the air to disperse the unruly mob. Meanwhile, they had succeeded in getting the tender moving, and forcing open the locked gate. On the other side the big truck was waiting. "We clung to it with the last remnants of our strength," said Eitan Livni, "we climbed aboard…and off it went…heading east towards Napoleon's Hill, in the direction of Safed. The van went ahead of the truck and one of its occupants was a wounded Lehi activist, Haim Appelbaum, who'd been wounded in the stomach during the withdrawal."[27]

On the main road to Safed the fugitives came across three youths from Shimshon's unit – Binyamin Shemer, Yosef Ronen, and Meir Amiaz. They reported that they'd been given the job of mining the Safed-Nahariya intersection, and having set fire, as planned, to a small filling station, were waiting in vain for the command jeep to pick them up.

"From what they told me," Livni recalled, "I gathered that Shimshon's command squad had been held up by unforeseen circumstances." The bitter truth of what had happened became known to them only late that night.

The two vehicles – the van and the truck – drove up the hill in the direction of Shefaram-Nazareth. The gradient became steeper and steeper. Up ahead appeared a military convoy led by a command jeep.

Zvi Wolf (Hillel), in command of the van, immaculate in his British uniform, poked his head through the cabin window and saluted his

---

27. Haim Apfelbaum died of his wounds on the way; the day after, members of Kibbutz Dalia took his body to Haifa for burial.

"comrades-in-arms." They returned his salute. The cool nerve he displayed undoubtedly saved the little convoy from a fate similar to that of the first van.

The convoy continued southward, on dusty winding tracks, towards the Jezreel Valley. After a while the lurching stopped, and the vehicles were on a smooth asphalt road, leading to the hills of Efraim. They were approaching Kibbutz Dalia, and at six in the evening the residential quarters could already be seen in the distance. They left the vehicles and set out on foot towards Binyamina, reaching the rendezvous point at around midnight. They spent the night in Nahalat Jabotinsky and the following day they dispersed around the country.

All efforts on the part of the British to find them came to nothing.

The blocking unit by the Acre police station, commanded by Avshalom Haviv, waited in vain for the bugle call. The signal for withdrawal never came. A glitch, which to this day has not been explained, cost the lives of three of the IZL's best fighters, Yaakov Weiss, Meir Nakar, and Avshalom Haviv. They had been ordered not to leave their post until they heard the bugle. But when Dov Salomon, at the end of the operation, wanted to sound the retreat, the bugler was nowhere to be found. He had simply vanished without trace.

When the third (and last) fugitive vehicle passed by Avshalom, the young men called to him to join them, as it was all over, but he still waited, like the disciplined soldier he was, for the signal to retreat. "It's all right," he waved them on, "I have to stay put. See you later!"

The escapees sped on their way. Avshalom and his two subordinates had a long wait ahead of them. They defended themselves to the last bullet, and only then did they surrender, to be taken to the fortress – and sentenced to death.

Members of the other blocking squad – Amnon Michaeli and Menahem Ostrowicz – also waited in vain for the bugle call. They too were arrested when their ammunition ran out.

When the operation was over it emerged that the number of prisoners who had succeeded in gaining their freedom amounted to 27 (20 IZL men and 7 Lehi). Nine fighters had been killed in confrontation with British forces (six escapees and three liberators) and eight of the escapees, some of them wounded, were arrested and taken back to the prison. Also in custody were five members of the attacking force, who were unable to return to their base.

SHIMSHON

Gidi admitted 22 years later:

> When I heard the news of Shimshon's death I was stunned. In all my years of active service in the Irgun this was the only time I couldn't take in the notion that someone had stopped a bullet and was dead. Someone, maybe, but Shimshon? I just couldn't get my head around it. I was sure the bullet that would put an end to Shimshon's life hadn't been made yet. For months and years afterwards. I still had a hard time believing Shimshon wasn't around anymore."[28]

After a thoughtful pause, Gidi continued:

> What impressed me most of all was the cool head he showed in emergencies. It wasn't just that he could get out of any jam, it seemed he actually enjoyed the danger. His mastery of the Bren was total – and awe-inspiring. That boy could run with the Bren, shooting from the hip, spraying left and right and scoring a "bull's-eye" with every burst. And we're not talking about field exercises but the real thing, the heat of battle. The way he used to play with that gun – it was like watching a maestro with a violin.
>
> He was of less than average height, but his build was muscular and athletic, and he had the face of an older man, deeply etched with wrinkles – the legacy, perhaps of his experiences both in the British army and the Irgun. There was a strange sort of inconsistency between his mature face and young body, but the overall impression he made on you was that of a determined, fearless youth, who could be relied on 100 per cent. Any assignment he took on himself, you could be sure he'd do it whatever the circumstances – and do it well.
>
> Indeed, in all the years of my active service I never knew a fighter so keen, so much at home on the battlefield. And if I needed further proof, I got it in the raid on the airfield at Lod, the operation that he

---

28. Author's recorded interview with Amihai Paglin, 1969.

commanded, the famous "night of the airplanes." ...There were setbacks on that occasion; the airfield at Lod was already on alert, after we'd blown up the main transformer...and suddenly there were searchlights blazing and rockets flying in all directions. The British were expecting an attack; we could hear the announcement coming over their loudspeakers. Not only was Shimshon undeterred by this, it spurred him on to even greater effort. It was at times like this, when something happened that wasn't in the game plan, he showed his real strengths. Like a warhorse scenting gunpowder, he came to life and stormed at the target. The considerable combat experience he'd gained during his time in the British army in World War II, his natural abilities and professional talents, gave him excessive self-confidence, which may well have been justified. "If there's a war," he used to say, "I'll be a part of it." He told me a lot about the battles he fought in, in East Africa: daring commando raids like the taking of the horn of Africa. He came to regard himself as invincible, invulnerable...

To him, war was the spice of life and it seems to me that without the tension and the danger, he'd simply have withered away. Put him in civilian life, he'd be bored stiff in five minutes. And we were given further proof of his exceptional abilities on April 2, 1946, in an operation near Ashdod. In the course of a series of attacks on the rail network in the north and south of the country, one of our units, which had just sabotaged the railway station in Ashdod, ran into a British army ambush in the neighborhood of Bat Yam. As a result of this encounter, 31 of our men were taken prisoner, including the chief operations officer of the IZL at that time, Eitan Livni. Only two succeeded in slipping through the net and making it safely to Bat Yam: one of them was Haim Golovsky-Gilad, and the other Dov Cohen, alias Shimshon. They simply disappeared in the sands, under the noses of the British, as if they had never existed.

I don't remember how I got the news, but that evening I set out for Petah Tikva, curious to hear firsthand what had happened. But the fellow wasn't at home; his landlady told me he'd gone to the movies. I wasn't surprised: after two days of grueling reconnaissance on foot, after a night battle and demolition of a railway station, followed by a dramatic escape among the sand dunes of Bat Yam, the young man deserved a little recreation, didn't he? One of the local movie theaters was showing a Western, and sure enough, that was where I found him, totally engrossed in the action on the screen.

"How's it going, Shimshon?" I slapped his shoulder lightly. He glanced at me, with an air of mild irritation. "Oh, it's you…," he said hurriedly, "wait a moment, there's something important happening here," and he turned back to the screen. I smiled to myself; that was Shimshon all over – concerned only with the matter at hand and apparently oblivious to recent events.

He impressed me with his simplistic approach to the most complex issues. Once he was assigned the job of attacking a train between Rosh Ha-Ayin and Lod. Getting to his objective meant leaving the main road (behind Petah Tikva) for a side road and carrying on from there to the railway tracks. He took a couple of fellows with him, put a Bren, plus a few rifles and grenades, into a sack, hired a taxi and loaded it up with all the goodies. He told the driver to take a side road through the plantations, and after about ten minutes of bumping along on dusty paths the taxi driver, thoroughly perplexed, asked, "Hey, have you guys got the faintest idea where you're going?"

"Sure," Shimshon replied, "so step on it and don't waste any more time!" Near the railway lines he told the driver to stop, took the rifles and the Bren from the sack, set up the machine gun, and opened fire on the speeding train; from the windows, fire was returned, and the young men threw grenades and the engine went up in flames. Shimshon calmly put the firearms and other equipment back into the taxi and said to the driver, "Take us home!" But the unfortunate fellow, who had no idea what was going on, had been caught in the crossfire and taken a gunshot wound in the leg, which made driving very difficult. In the end, when his leg had healed, he joined the Irgun…

In short, Shimshon showed his talents to the full in the thick of the action, and it's no wonder that during World War II his British mates used to call him "the little Devil"![29]

A British officer who witnessed the raid on Acre prison told his friends that if the commander of the operation had fallen into his hands alive, he would

29. Ibid.

have saluted him in recognition of his heroism – and then shot him, on account of the danger posed by men like him to British people everywhere.[30]

After a long silence, during which he seemed for a moment to have switched off and drifted into the recesses of the past, Gidi resumed:

> There is something else I'd like to say about him, something that's been in my heart for ages. It has to do with the moments I spent with Shimshon, before parting from him for the last time.
>
> Two or three minutes before departure, with the drivers already revving their engines, I received worrying news about unusual movements of troops in the region, suspicious departures from the routine. In the past, such information had been sufficient grounds to postpone ordinary operations, but this was no ordinary operation: what we were about to do was the kind of thing that's fated to happen only once in a generation – an opportunity which, if missed, might never arise again. Time was pressing, and I needed to make a quick decision. I called in the only two combat squad leaders who were on the scene at the time – Shimshon and Shraga Ellis. I put before them the information that had just arrived and asked for their opinion. I didn't opt for any position myself, wanting to hear their input before deciding. They were unanimous in insisting the operation should go ahead, without delay. (It had been agreed from the start with our friends imprisoned in Acre that in the event of the operation not taking place as originally scheduled, it would go ahead the following day, in the morning or at 4:00 PM.)
>
> The arguments against delay were persuasive: until yesterday, the date of the operation had been kept secret; from today onward, dozens of men in Acre prison would be aware of it. They had been preparing homemade thunderflash grenades and civilian clothing, and were in a heightened state of tension and expectation. In these circumstances, a leak to the prison authorities could not be ruled out; we might arrive tomorrow and find ourselves in a trap.
>
> Any other operation would have been postponed indefinitely, but

---

30. Haim Gilad, *Be-tsel ha-gardom: Sipurei shel mefaked be-Etzel* [In the shadow of the gallows: The story of an Etzel commander] (Tel Aviv: Israel Defense Ministry, 1983), p. 100.

the Acre prison raid wasn't just any operation; it had been designed from the start as a scheme for the rescue of our comrades-in-arms, living in the shadow of the gallows, and for this reason we were prepared to take on ourselves greater risks than ever before. Every stage of the plan had been thoroughly assessed – and the consensus had been: it could be done, and done successfully. And then, as I was still wavering, Shimshon turned to me and said, "What are you worried about? I'm going to be there, keeping an eye on things, and if anything goes wrong, I'll sort it out straightaway. Don't worry, it's going to be okay, I promise you." These were the last words Shimshon ever said to me. They still reverberate in my ears – and they tipped the balance.

Even today, 22 years later, I still think it was the right decision. If we hadn't carried out the operation on that occasion, it would never have been done at all. It was a single, unique chance, never to be repeated.

In spite of Shimshon's reassurances, the parting was poignant. I remember Shraga Ellis and Shimshon didn't only shake hands, they were locked for some time in a fond embrace – the kind of emotional display not characteristic of the Irgun. For myself, I made an effort to suppress my feelings and merely laid a hand on his shoulder, wondering, heavy-hearted, if we would ever meet again…[31]

GIDI'S ANALYSIS

"And yet," Gidi said, "it could have ended differently, and without any loss to our side."

The plan of the operation was flawless and based on a number of fundamental principles which were largely vindicated:

The first, camouflage in the guise of British servicemen – which passed the test of authenticity.

The second, setting up positions at key points in the city of Acre – no police force succeeded in even getting close to the scene of the action.

The third, planting mines in a 2-mile (3-kilometer) radius around the city of Acre – preventing the dispatch of reinforcements.

---

31. Author's recorded interview with Amihai Paglin, 1969.

The fourth, the mortar attack on the Airborne Division camp – pinning the troops down and preventing any approach to the site of the attack.

If the operation had been conducted according to the original plan, it would have been concluded without losses.

The basic problem arose when one of the essential components of the plan – camouflage – came unstuck. This happened when the first truckload of fugitives from Acre prison came across a British military vehicle and was ordered to stop. The driver panicked and tried to get away; the British fired warning shots and the boys, hidden inside in civilian clothes, jumped out and were identified as escaping prisoners… from this point on it all fell apart, ending with their recapture and the death of Shimshon as he tried to defend them.

As for the losses, the greater proportion of these came from the British shooting at prisoners after they had surrendered (some of them already wounded). But the important thing to remember is that the operation achieved its goal: the storming of the citadel of Acre (a project reckoned to be impossible), the release of dozens of prisoners and getting them to a place of safety. From a military point of view, an action on such a scale would be considered a stunning success even if our losses had been greater – to say nothing of the political implications of the operation.

And finally, when we analyzed the operation, as we did more than once, we came to the conclusion that had the action been carried out on another day or under different conditions, there is no guarantee that the results would have been better in terms of casualties – if it would have been carried out at all.[32]

Only 50 years later – after the release of British police documents concerning the Acre jailbreak, and with certain key personnel in the British security services proving willing to reveal a little of what they know about the subject – has it become clear just how accurate Gidi's assessment was, and how justified his natural instinct not to delay the operation for even one day.

Edward Horne, a senior officer in the Mandatory police, revealed in 1982 in his book *A Job Well Done*, that on May 3, 1947 – the eve of the

---

32. Ibid.

raid – the decision was made to increase the height of the prison wall in the sector where the breach was due to be blasted, and apparently this work was scheduled to begin the following day, i.e., the day of the operation.

According to Horne:

> Then the CID had information that a big escape was going to be made but was not certain when and how. On 29th April the prison commander was warned to keep special attention for possible escape bids, aided from outside…. Checks were made upon censoring letters to and from Jewish prisoners as well as visitors who called to see them. Then on 3rd May a decision was made to raise the height of the wall to the prison garden, so that the prison authorities now felt they had done all they could be expected to do.[33]

Indeed, from various CID documents, from memoirs of British police officers and from interviews with them, it emerges that the intention to attack Acre prison and release Jewish prisoners was known to the authorities, and they were taking measures to forestall or prevent such an attack. It has also become clear that the soldiers on the Acre seashore were not there by chance.

In one of the CID documents preserved in the Haganah archives,[34] the Acre prison commandant writes on December 9, 1946, to the commissioner of prisons (Palestine):

> *Top Secret. Attached herewith a diagram, showing general topography of Acre Prison, with a number of guard positions marked. The diagram was found December 8, 1946, and was apparently dropped by a prisoner of the Jewish Shuni group. The interesting point about the diagram is the inclusion of the manhole cover in the outer yard (I have marked this with an arrow) and it is clear that the diagram has been prepared with a purpose, evidently with a view to escape or attack. I am unable to draw definite conclusions or suggest appropriate counter-measures, but ascertaining the lay-out of the drainage system is my immediate priority….*

33. Edward Horne, *A Job Well Done* (Eastwood: Anchor Press, 1982), p. 309.
34. *Haganah Archives Quarterly*, issue 6.

> *Please expedite dispatch of the regular troops allocated for exterior defence.*

The letter is handwritten, evidently for security reasons; having it typed would risk its exposure to prying eyes, some of them Jewish. It seems it was passed immediately to CID, and arrived on the desk of the deputy chief of the political department, Mr. John Bryant, with a handwritten, unsigned memo attached:

> *The Hebrew notation on the diagram requires accurate translation and if possible, fingerprints on the reverse of the diagram should be compared with those of members of the Shuni group.*

The CID invested considerable effort in attempting to solve the mystery of the diagram, but came up with nothing. In any case, it was a warning of sorts of the planned breakout, five months before the event itself.

John O'Sullivan, the British MI5 officer serving as assistant to the inspector-general of police and head of the political branch of the CID, revealed in an interview given in October 1980 to Aryeh Eshel[35] that the British not only knew of the intention to attack Acre prison, they even knew the day of the week: it would take place on a Sunday. Furthermore, he added, "we knew, or believed it was scheduled to be at 15:00."[36] He even stated that they had been informed beforehand.

According to him, on three successive Sundays army, police, and detective units were stationed at various points in Acre, and only on the Sunday of the fourth week (the day of the operation) were these arrangements canceled. The police and CID units were withdrawn, leaving just the army. The soldiers were supposed to be on guard, but as tension seemed to have eased, they went down to the bathing beach – in swim trunks but keeping their weapons with them.

O'Sullivan stressed that the soldiers were in Acre on duty and not by chance. "If the attack had taken place on one of the previous Sundays," he

---

35. One of the IZL commanders in Jerusalem.
36. John O'Sullivan, interviewed by Aryeh Eshel in London, October 1980.

said, "they would have wiped out the attacking force…. The alarm was raised, and the soldiers on the beach alerted, but the response wasn't as effective as it would have been the week before, or the week before that… the outcome then would have been completely different."

O'Sullivan's testimony finally solved a puzzle that had perplexed the planners of the Acre operation, Gidi included, for years: the apparent paradox of the presence on the scene of British soldiers, obviously dressed (or undressed) for the beach and therefore presumably off duty – but fully armed and ready to leap into action.

So, it wasn't a case of blind chance after all. The British were expecting an attack and the paratroopers were part of the deployment of troops prepared to meet it. And yet, they were unable to thwart it. In the battle of wits between the British generals, graduates of Sandhurst and Camberley, and the 25-year-old Amihai Paglin of Tel Aviv – it was Gidi who came out on top.

As in previous instances – the King David Hotel, the Jerusalem railway station – the planning of the Acre prison raid was so thorough and ingenious that the British were unable to foil it despite the advance warning they received and all the countermeasures they adopted.

Thirty-four men – the sum total of the force assembled by Gidi for the Acre operation. They consisted of three electricians, four diamond polishers, one student, one high school senior, five merchants, seven drivers, seven engineers, six clerks – a total of 34, the youngest 17 years old and the oldest, 34. And with this force he struck a blow not only against the impregnable walls of fortress Acre but also against the prestige of Great Britain.

"To move thirty-four men and four vehicles into a heavily patrolled British area, blow the side out of a prison in the midst of an Arab city, and anticipate driving out before the British could react was not actually as improbable as it sounded," writes J. Bowyer Bell.[37] Indeed, "improbable" was a concept that did not exist in Paglin's lexicon.

---

37. Bell, *Terror Out of Zion*, p. 209.

BRITISH FRUSTRATION

Some impression of the frustration and despair felt by the British in the wake of this and other audacious IZL operations orchestrated by Gidi may be gleaned from the report of the High Commissioner, Sir Alan Cunningham, to Colonial Secretary Creech-Jones, consisting mainly of apologies for failing to prevent the attack. Cunningham stated that "no amount of soldiers or policemen would be able to defend the country from attacks on buildings, railways or pipelines, which [could] be executed at any time, day or night – a situation that [had] existed for many years." In that report the High Commissioner also noted that "the dissidents in Palestine are trained with the same underground stratagem which was used by the European Underground in the Second World War."

In reference to the Acre prison raid, he admits the British did not believe such an operation could succeed: "This prison is an ancient fortress, built of sturdy masonry, in an Arab town. It was deliberately chosen as the site for detention of some leading Jewish terrorists, because it was reckoned that in an exclusively Arab town the likelihood of an attack was reduced, and if such an attack were to take place, it could be resisted pending the arrival of reinforcements."

The frustration felt by the British Mandatory authorities over their failure to thwart the jailbreak was exacerbated when it became apparent that, while most of the Arab criminal convicts had been recaptured, not a single Jewish fugitive had been netted. To quote Sir Alan Cunningham again:

> Of those who succeeded in escaping, not one has been caught, despite determined efforts on the part of the army and the police. Security forces throughout the country were placed on alert shortly after the raid. Mobile units have patrolled all roads, especially those in the vicinity of Acre, and mounted police units have patrolled the hills in the region of Safed, following reports that fugitives had been seen in the area…. On the outskirts of the major cities all cars entering and leaving have been searched and from the North to the South of the country buses and taxis have been stopped and all passengers required to give proof of identity. But all these efforts, I repeat, have been unavailing.

The last commandant of the Mandatory police force, Colonel Grey, admitted in 1960 that the Acre prison raid was one of the three operations[38] that shook the foundations of the British administration and hastened the decision to leave Palestine. He said that the conquest of Acre prison, which symbolized more than anything else British power in the country, had been compared in the public consciousness to the fall of the Bastille, which symbolized the victory of the French revolutionaries.

In 1958, when Menahem Begin was asked the question, "Which was the most decisive operation carried out during the revolt?" he replied without hesitation, "The conquest of Acre prison."[39]

If the bombing of the King David Hotel marked the beginning of the end of British rule in this land, the Acre jailbreak symbolized the end itself. Six months later, on November 29, 1947, despite British opposition, the UN decided in favor of the establishment of a Jewish state – a decision prompted not least by the blow struck by the IZL in the assault on Acre prison.

---

38. The other two operations cited by Colonel Grey in this connection were the flogging of officers and the hanging of the sergeants.
39. Menahem Begin on the IZL, *Ha-Olam ha-Zeh*, April 8, 1958.

DEFEATING THE GALLOWS

Of all the 200 operations planned and implemented during the time that he served as chief operations officer of the Irgun, one episode troubled Gidi's mind and weighed on him more than any other – the hanging of the sergeants. "When you think of two helpless men, their faces hooded, dangling before your eyes, you know you have crossed a barrier. It's not war anymore, it leaves a stain, it weighs on the conscience…" Gidi confessed years later in a newspaper interview.[1]

"That being said," he added without hesitation, "I'd do it again tomorrow if the need arose." And he continued:

> Throughout our war against Mandatory rule, I felt no blind animosity towards the British as such. I had strong feelings, and a great deal of anger and resentment, over all aspects of British policy towards the Jewish community, and for this reason I fought without compromise, without mercy, using all the means then at my disposal. But British soldiers I didn't see as enemies, rather as tools, implementing a policy not of their devising. Furthermore, I respected them as fighters – although

---

1. Yosef Lapid, "The Scar Left by the Hanging of the Sergeants," *Ma'ariv*, July 22, 1967 [in Hebrew].

I despised their masters in London, sitting comfortably in their padded seats and imposing on their servicemen the contemptible task of harassing Holocaust survivors on the high seas and slamming the gates of the country shut in their faces. In the course of our operations, scores if not hundreds of vulnerable British servicemen crossed our paths – and we did them no harm.

Until the hangings came – and left a heavy legacy. And after that – the shooting of our soldiers taken prisoner in the Acre prison raid.

All these things were not to be forgiven.

The killing of our men in cold blood, with cynical cruelty, under the guise of emergency regulations, was not to be passed over in silence on our part. General Barker had promised to hang Jews from the lampposts – and it was necessary to prove to him and to the Jewish people that hangings would not be the lot of Jewish underground fighters alone; they would be directed against His Majesty's Forces too.

And we acted accordingly – although with gritted teeth. But the lesson was learned, and the hanging of the sergeants put an end once and for all to the ignominy of the gallows in this country. Thereafter – and until the end of the British Mandate – no more Jews were hanged in Eretz Israel.

WE SHALL RESPOND TO GALLOWS WITH GALLOWS

Sergeants Mervyn Paice and Clifford Martin were serving with the British Intelligence Corps in the Netanya region. They were kidnapped while leaving a café and held as hostages by the IZL, in an attempt to prevent the execution of three of their comrades – Avshalom Haviv, Yaakov Weiss, and Meir Nakar – captured in the aftermath of the Acre prison raid.

The objective was not achieved. The British decided on a display of firmness: on Tuesday, July 29, 1947, the three men went to the gallows.

The day after, the IZL hanged the two sergeants.

Paice and Martin were not the first British hostages kidnapped in tragic circumstances for the purpose of saving the lives of underground fighters. They were preceded (at different times) by seven army officers, three sergeants, a judge, two policemen, and two civilians. Most of them were released unharmed; three succeeded in escaping by their own efforts. Until that time, no Jew sentenced to death had gone to the gallows. This convention, of not using the gallows against Jews, was broken for the first time following the kidnapping and flogging of British servicemen, in retaliation for the judicial flogging of a young IZL activist. That night three of the floggers were arrested, when whips, ropes, and weapons were found in their car. The three – Mordecai Alkahi, Eliezer Kashani and Yehiel Dresner – were sentenced to death, on a charge of "carrying weapons and possession of materials for the manufacture of explosives."

The three of them were held in the death cell of the prison in Jerusalem, together with Dov Gruner. The IZL did not sit idly by. The planning committee devised a scheme to break into the prison and release the young men. For this an armored car was needed. "Day after day Shimshon went to the main road with a party of men and waited for an armored car.... By April 14 we hadn't got our hands on an armored car," Begin writes in *The Revolt*, "and that day Gruner, Dresner, Alkahi, and Kashani were transferred to Acre Prison."

Two days later they were executed.

While these dramatic events were unfolding, in a separate development unconnected with the transfer of the condemned men to Acre, the IZL was engaged in feverish preparations for one of the most audacious actions in its history, the storming of Acre prison. This operation was to take on additional significance as a suitable response to the execution of Gruner and his friends.

No one imagined that this operation, which from a professional viewpoint was crowned with success, would present the IZL command with a new and painful challenge: three of the participants in the operation were arrested and condemned to death. The Irgun's warning this time was unequivocal: *We shall respond to gallows with gallows.* The British reacted with stringent security measures: all their personnel were confined behind walls and wire fences and forbidden to walk the streets except when on armed patrol. All attempts to seize hostages came to nothing. In Netanya, IZL members were ordered to prepare a suitable hiding place for holding "British prisoners" who had not yet materialized. Eliyahu Tomarkin, one of the local Irgun commanders, was appointed to lead a team in preparing a sealed bunker under an abandoned diamond factory in the Tobruk district. The bunker was constructed of non-metallic materials, to avoid exposure by mine detectors.

Two days after confirmation of the death sentences on the three men, a squad commanded by Binyamin Kaplan finally succeeded in snatching Sergeants Paice and Martin as they left the Rose Garden café. The duo, serving in 252 Field Security Unit, were in civilian clothes and relaxing in the café with a Jewish civilian employee of their base camp, Aharon Weinberg.[2] The Jew was released and the two sergeants were chloroformed and taken to the hiding place in the sealed basement, under the watchful eye of David Dahari.

Amihai Paglin heard the news of the kidnap of the two Britons at an early hour of Saturday morning. He knew now that the lives of the trio in Acre depended on the fate of the hostages. His main concern was over the security of the place where the two Britons had been taken.

Gidi gathered together a number of young men and set diversionary measures in motion to deceive the army and police. Rolls of bandages, a chloroform bottle, and stretchers were loaded on a truck which was sent to Netanya and from there along the coast road to Herzliya; near the village of Jaljulia they abandoned the vehicle and continued on foot towards Tel Aviv leaving clear traces behind them, thus creating the impression that the two Britons had been taken to Tel Aviv.

At around 11:00 AM Gidi set out in his car for Netanya, carrying oxygen canisters. He went first to the house of the local IZL chief, Avraham Assaf, and the men made their way to the bunker. From a distance the factory looked empty and derelict. In the room above the bunker, apparently just a disused office, Dahari and his friend were sitting calmly on the sofa covering the trapdoor. A specially designed hydraulic mechanism raised four of the floor tiles, and the two commanders cautiously descended the ladder.

"Good morning!" Gidi said affably. The two hostages rose to their feet and mumbled something in reply.

"We're convinced there's been a mistake here," said Paice. "We're soldiers, and we're not involved in politics. Why have you kidnapped us?"

"I've come here to sort out some things you need," was Gidi's reply. They were shown the oxygen canisters and Gidi explained how they were to be operated, in case the ventilation slits needed to be closed. Martin asked if he and his friend could be allowed out now and again for a breath of fresh air. Gidi promised to consider this positively, conditions permitting – and

---

2. Haviv Kanaan, "The Lesson of the Gallows in Netanya," *New Look* (July 26, 1967).

the hostages were indeed occasionally taken up to the shop floor of the factory for this purpose.

Before leaving Gidi said, "Your fate is not in our hands; it's British army command in Palestine that's responsible for your lives."

"We understand."

Gidi returned to Tel Aviv. In the meantime the army was threatening to impose curfews and martial law, and Gidi ordered extra supplies of oxygen, food, and water for the bunker; he also instructed Dahari to leave the place if the army came anywhere near the factory.[3]

Dahari attended to the needs of the hostages, supplying them with food and drink and emptying the bucket that served as a latrine. "As intelligence men they understood Hebrew, and one of them spoke Arabic too," he recalled. "As time passed a bond developed between us."[4]

The British response to the kidnapping was furious: thousands of soldiers and police personnel scoured the region. Most of the searches were concentrated in Netanya, where the entire population was placed under house arrest, but no trace of the hostages was found. According to Dahari, in the course of their searches British troops were close to locating the bunker: "They came into the upper building, saw it was derelict and left."[5]

For more than two weeks the two sergeants were kept in hiding, in the Tobruk district, while the country was in ferment. Members of the Haganah were asked by the official institutions to make every effort to find the sergeants, but they were no more successful than the British had been.

At the end of July 1947, British foreign secretary Ernest Bevin ordered the implementation of the death sentences. The Jerusalem attorney Asher Levitzky was called to police headquarters in Jerusalem and notified that the High Commissioner had rejected appeals for clemency and the families of the condemned men should prepare themselves. Levitzky hurried to the house of Chief Rabbi Herzog and from there tried to contact the High Commissioner's residence, in a last attempt to obtain clemency. The High Commissioner's aide, Major Chichester, replied drily, "Sir Alan wishes to inform you that he has taken his decision after long deliberation."

---

3. Haviv Kanaan, *Gardomim be-Netanya* [Gallows in Netanya] (Tel Aviv: Hadar, 1976), pp. 51–53.

4. Radio program on the hanging of the sergeants, broadcast on "IDF Airwaves," presented by David Dayan

5. Ibid.

It was the rabbi's turn to try: "Please inform His Excellency that if he defers implementation of the sentences, I shall continue my efforts to save the lives of the kidnapped soldiers."

"You've already had plenty of opportunities to work on their behalf," the aide replied. "In current circumstances, His Excellency sees no purpose in granting a stay of execution."

An appeal from the president of the Va'ad ha-Le'umi (National Council), Yitzhak Ben-Tzvi, was equally unsuccessful. "His Excellency is aware of public opinion, but his decision is irrevocable."[6]

On July 29, 1947, before dawn, the three condemned men were put to death.

The same day it was decided in IZL headquarters that gallows in Acre would be matched by gallows in Netanya. The assignment was entrusted to the chief operations officer, Amihai Paglin.

That doleful morning the focus of attention moved to the ancient cemetery of Safed. At 11:00 AM the three executed men were laid to rest there. The two thousand Jewish residents of Safed accompanied them on their last journey, in defiance of the curfew imposed by the authorities. Avshalom Haviv, Yaakov Weiss, and Meir Nakar were interred alongside the other four martyrs – Dov Gruner, Mordecai Alkahi, Yehiel Dresner, and Eliezer Kashani.

As the congregation of residents of Safed stood in silence next to the freshly dug graves, Gidi was speeding in his car from Tel Aviv to Netanya along with a member of the planning staff. Most of the way he kept silent, his thoughts focused on the tragic events in the Acre death cell, and anger surging in him. He knew there was now no choice but to hang the two sergeants. Otherwise, there would be no end to the "march of the gallows" in this land. His mood grew gloomier: despite the pain and the rage that he felt when recalling the fate of his friends, whose young lives had been cut off so cruelly, he was not overwhelmed by any lust for vengeance against the two hostages, who also had families and were just as eager to live as Nakar, Haviv, and Weiss had been. *For what ideal must Paice and Martin forfeit their lives?* he reflected bitterly. And yet, irrespective of logic, he knew that things were now beyond his control. Responsibility for what was happening lay in London – in Downing Street.

---

6. Kanaan, "The Lesson of the Gallows" (see n. 2 above).

A cycle of violence without end, without prospect of solution – unless some way of breaking it could be found…

THE HANGING OF THE BRITISH SOLDIERS

The policemen in place at the Bet Lid police station showed no particular interest in the ancient car and waved them through. Soon afterwards the car stopped outside the home of Assaf, IZL chief in Netanya. "The people are living in terror," he told them. "The Haganah has spread the rumor that the town will be razed if the hostages are hanged." He suggested that the job should be done in the outskirts of Tulkarm. Gidi was inclined to accept this but suspected that the Arab town, with all the army camps around it, might be inaccessible. "How about one of the orchards near Hadera?" was his own suggestion, and the two of them went out to look for a suitable place.

When they returned to Netanya, the town was already in darkness. After much deliberation, Gidi came to the decision that there was no option but to hang the hostages in the basement of the diamond factory, and then take the bodies to one of the plantations on the outskirts of the town. Zero hour was set for 10:00 AM, the following day. Gidi returned to Tel Aviv, having finalized all the details with Assaf. Among other things, he told him to prepare explosives to mine the site where the bodies would be left.

Next morning, Assaf gathered a dozen young men and told them to stand by; their role was to help transfer the bodies from the bunker to the eucalyptus grove. At 9:00 AM, Gidi arrived with some of his men. At 10:00 a number of youths were seen walking towards the derelict factory. Dahari was waiting for them, with four of his assistants. All were armed and agitated. When Gidi appeared, the tension rose to a climax. He was no less stressed than his subordinates, but outwardly he maintained an air of composure, and set to work quickly and decisively, determined to let no sentiment or outside interference impede the performance of this painful task. He knew that as a commander it was his duty to stand by his subordinates at this difficult time, one of the most grueling he had ever known in all his years of service in the Irgun. He stayed with them until the bitter end of that drama, knowing that what he had just witnessed would never be erased from his memory: a barrier had been crossed, a point of no return. At the same time, he felt there had been no choice; the decision was out of his hands.

Yoel Kimhi, one of the senior IZL commanders, was responsible for transporting the bodies to the grove. He had been present at the hanging, and 29 years later he described his feelings at the time as "deep dejection, a mixture of pity and revulsion; it was almost unbearable," he confessed, "and I could tell the other fellows were in torment as well."

Gidi ordered that the bodies be taken to the grove and hung on two trees, side by side. The mines were to be laid on the path between the trees. That evening he returned to Tel Aviv. It had been, he said, "the hardest day of my life."

Yeroham Bartmann, intelligence officer of the IZL in Netanya, and Assaf, the local commander, went out to check the routes between Netanya and Kfar Vitkin, the site where they planned to leave the bodies. On the way to Avihail they encountered an army road block and had to retrace their steps.

They had no choice but to look for a plantation in the region of Even Yehuda, since all other routes were under tight army and police surveillance. The bodies of Paice and Martin were put into sacks and loaded in the back of a van. After a backbreaking journey on unpaved roads, they stopped by a grove near Even Yehuda. "We chose two tall eucalyptus trees, close together," said Yoel Kimhi, "and hung the bodies on them. We mined the area around the trees, in a 2–3 yard radius. There's no truth in the allegation," he added, "that we booby-trapped the bodies as well. We covered up our traces and left."

"After the mining of the site, the IZL was at pains to warn the local Haganah of the danger," recalled Yaakov Amrami.[7]

> I was instructed by Headquarters to approach Mr. Israel Rokach, the mayor of Tel Aviv, and ask him to pass a message to Mr. Oved Ben-Ami, mayor of Netanya, and through him to the local branch of the Haganah, warning them that to avoid injury to their men they should call off their search for the victims. I told Mr. Rokach the precise location

---

7. Yaakov Amrami (Yoel) was serving at this time as the commander of the IZL's intelligence service.

of the grove near Even Yehuda, but he didn't believe me, insisting he had "reliable information" from the Haganah that the IZL intended to hang the two sergeants in Magen David Square in Tel Aviv. It took me a long time to convince him the job had been done and the bodies were not in Tel Aviv but Even Yehuda. Eventually he was persuaded, let out a sigh of relief, and called Mr. Ben-Ami to tell him the news. According to reports from our intelligence service, Ben-Ami informed the British first, and the Haganah only some hours later.[8]

The bodies were found the morning of Thursday, July 31, 1947, in the municipal eucalyptus groves two and a half miles (four kilometers) southeast of Netanya. British security forces sealed off the area and began searching from tree to tree, with mine detectors. Soon afterwards an army ambulance arrived. The soldiers allowed Ben-Ami and the many journalists who had assembled to enter the plantation.

Before long the searchers were confronted by a horrific sight: the bodies of the two hanged men – in undershirts and trousers – suspended from two trees about a yard apart. Both faces were concealed by khaki shirts, and pinned to their chests were indictments issued by the IZL. Detectives scanned the statements cautiously, and the area was again thoroughly checked. Around 10:00 AM an army officer approached the bodies with a saw and began cutting the rope on which Martin's body was hanging. Suddenly the body fell to the ground and a thunderous explosion was heard; it had triggered one of the mines planted between the trees.[9]

To the chorus of orchestrated condemnation from official community institutions and from various public figures, the IZL responded vigorously:

> *When nine of our fighters were led to the gallows by the British, you did not denounce the hangings, or express any sympathy for the bereaved families; it is only when two British spies are executed that you protest and rush to offer your condolences.... We warned the enemy again and again and again that if he dared ignore the rules of war and hang our*

---

8. Yaakov Amrami, *Things Are Bigger Than We Are.*
9. Kanaan, *Gardomim*, pp. 83–93.

prisoners, his prisoners would suffer the same fate. Not as an act of repri-
sal, but as a duty to the people of Israel….

We reject the "morality" of slaves standing meekly before the slaugh-
terer. Never again will Hebrew prisoners be hanged in their homeland,
or else the hangers and their lackeys will die by the same noose.[10]

LONDON'S RESPONSE

It seems that the hanging of the sergeants tipped the balance. Reactions
in the House of Commons verged on the hysterical.[11] In a debate held on
August 12, 1947, Brigadier Mackeson asked:

> What is the position at the moment? So far as I can make out, we now
> have, in round figures, between 80,000 and 100,000 troops in Pales-
> tine…. Since the present Government took office, 79 military person-
> nel have been killed and 180 wounded, 40 policemen have been killed
> and 69 wounded, while the civilian casualties have numbered 16 killed
> and 10 wounded. That comes to about 400 British casualties. Now, we
> have reached the final climax…[12]

A particularly impassioned contribution to that debate was that of a member of the Labour Party, Mr. Lever:

> I urge upon the Colonial Secretary to go to United Nations now,
> before we get dragged any deeper into the morass of vengeance and
> counter-vengeance, and deeper into the rivers of blood as a result of
> the planless hopeless approach to the situation…. Is he going to wait
> until more people are hanged or murdered in some other way?… Are
> the gibbet, the flogging block and the demolition squad to be our sole
> contribution to civilisation in the Middle East?… Britain should take
> the only honest course left and should ask United Nations to relieve
> her of responsibility so as to allow her to call out her troops as early
> as possible.

---

10. Aryeh Eshel, "Breaking the Gallows."
11. Yosef Nedava, *Mi geresh et ha-Britim me-Eretz Yisrael* [Who drove the British out of
    Palestine] (Tel Aviv: Association for the Dissemination of National Awareness, 1988),
    pp. 42–43.
12. Hansard, HC Deb, vol. 441, col. 2307.

There is no moral basis for our presence and no wish on the part of anyone in Palestine that we should remain.... What right have we to demand of the people of Britain that we should make the sacrifice of their lads who go out there to maintain this senseless rule? What right have we to ask the people of Britain to sacrifice 100,000 men from their economy to perpetuate a police State in Palestine.... This is probably the last chance this Government will have of leaving Palestine with some decency and with some semblance of dignity before she is irretrievably committed to a hopeless policy.[13]

A similar note was struck by the historian J. Bowyer Bell, an internationally acknowledged expert on the subject of political terror who has studied underground insurgency movements in Ireland, Yemen, Cyprus, and elsewhere. In his book *Terror Out of Zion* he notes:

It might have appeared that the deaths of the two sergeants vitalized British resistance to the Irgun rebellion, smeared all the Jews with the terrorist label, and set back the dream for a state. This was not so; in fact, it was rather the reverse: the two seargants were the straw that broke the Mandate's back.

In Britain there were full-page pictures of the two sergeants; their bodies hanging like strange fruit in an orchard. The papers, with heavy black headlines and outraged editorials, reported the anguished speeches in Parliament, the mobs daubing swastikas on synagogues, and the looting attacks on Jewish shops. Few in Britain took time to notice the reaction of the *Manchester Guardian* – "Time to Go." The *Guardian*'s writers felt the only hope was the United Nations, which might find a way to release Britain from responsibility, giving Jews and Arabs an opportunity to start afresh. The *Guardian* was perceptive; for the wave of revulsion in Britain was directed as much against British presence and tactics as against Jewish terror: the exhausted *Exodus* refugees dragged screaming back from the Promised Land, the death of two young men trapped in a humiliating and pointless struggle against a persecuted people, the weekly lists of dead and maimed that brought no thanks from either Jew or Arab. So, instead of adamant

---

13.   Ibid., col. 2346–47.

demands for vengeance and reprisals, as some expected, the concensus gradually formed, as the *Guardian* predicted, that the time for evacuation had arrived.[14]

All others were outdone (again) by Colonel Richard Meinertzhagen, who not only did not denounce the hangings but placed the blame for the deaths of the two sergeants on the British government and on Downing Street:

> Two days ago the Palestine Government executed three Jew terrorists caught while attacking Acre Gaol. A just conviction and sentence. The terrorists kidnapped two British sergeants about a fortnight ago and announced their intention to hang them if the sentence on the Acre Jews was carried out. The bodies of the two sergeants were found hanged, yesterday. It is a ghastly retaliation and a brutal act. I am terribly sorry for those two men who only did their duty and I am terribly sorry for our soldiers in Palestine, who have to carry out this revolting policy of the Government. The real men responsible for the killing of those two sergeants are the politicians who sit in Downing Street, the Government of this country and ultimately – the British public. All my sympathy is with the Jews who have been driven by apathy, anti-semitism and broken promises into a state of exasperation. If I were a Jew I should be a terrorist, a violent one, and I would aim at Whitehall.
>
> …Also the Jews have suffered much more persecution than Indonesia has ever dreamed of and have been led to believe by successive British governments that they will be given a home in Palestine. We have turned their home into a shambles and perpetuation of Hitler's policy of extermination.[15]

---

14. Bell, *Terror Out of Zion*, pp. 238–39.
15. Colonel Richard Meinertzhagen, *Middle East Diary, 1917–1956* (London: Cresset Press, 1959). Meinertzhagen was a member of the British delegation to the Peace Conference of 1919, and served as Chief Political Officer in Palestine and Syria in 1919–1920 and Military Adviser to the Middle East Department of the Colonial Office, 1921–1924.

THE BATTLE FOR JAFFA

I see him before me, at Passover 1948, as though it were the day before yesterday, and he is covered in dust and mud, unshaved, his pistol at his side, and he is all radiant with joy as he tells me, "We have conquered Jaffa – we have won!"

And I paid no attention to the dust or the mud – I hugged him and kissed him, I loved him like a son. That was Gidi in the underground days. It could be said of him, he was one of the founders of the State of Israel. Were it not for Gidi, there is no knowing if we could have conducted our war as we conducted it, and if we had not conducted it as we conducted it – there might never have been a State of Israel.

– Menahem Begin, in his funeral oration for Gidi

MUNITIONS — SELF-SUFFICIENCY AND DEVELOPMENT

"Throughout the period that the Irgun Zvai Leumi was active," Amihai Paglin recalled:

> except for the years 1944–45, the IZL suffered from a shortage of explosives. In fact, the scale of our operations was in direct proportion to the quantities of explosives at our disposal. We were chronically undersupplied. Incredibly, operations like Schneller camp were carried out with explosives that reached our arsenals virtually at the last moment, a day or two before the action. Even in the case of the King David Hotel, we acquired them just a week or two in advance. We lived from hand to mouth in this respect, and the shortage was not eased until the beginning of continuous production at the end of 1947, or more accurately, at the beginning of 1948. Acquisitions barely met our minimum requirements. If we'd had bigger stocks of munitions, the operations of the Irgun would have been altogether different – and on a much greater scale.[1]

---

1. Shlomo Lev-Ami's interview with Amihai Paglin, Hebrew University, Institute of Contemporary Judaism, Dept. of National Documentation.

According to Menahem Begin in *The Revolt*:

> He had a rare talent, our Gidi – he combined an inventive mind with dexterous hands; he was both a planner and an executor. His technical and tactical inventions were innumerable. Gidi developed the remote-controlled heavy mortar, which the British, for reasons of their own, dubbed the "v3," from which the famous "Davidka" was later to evolve. Gidi invented the contact-mine for trains, against which all precautionary measures adopted by the British proved unavailing; they could not be dismantled and anyone trying – and British experts did try – paid with his life for disregarding our warnings. Gidi's mind was forever devising new inventions: special road-mines, flame-throwers, milk-jug bombs...the "barrel bomb"...[2]

With the renewal of the armed struggle against the British in Palestine in 1944, production started of the stun grenades that were used in the first attacks on government offices and CID premises in the three major cities.

It was at this stage that Gidi came into the picture.

According to M. Hameiri, "We used to pack TNT, first into cardboard boxes and later into Bakelite containers... We got our instructions from Amihai Paglin, who used to turn up every now and then on a bike."

In the summer of 1944 a room was rented in Jaffa in the Shapira district and there road mines were assembled, using wooden boxes. Triggering mechanisms, batteries, and detonators were manufactured "in-house" while the explosive materials themselves were added at the jump-off point, shortly before the operation. It was also at this time that sabotage devices were developed, including special types of charges for the destruction of railway tracks (the explosive was extracted from shells and road mines "borrowed" from the British).

A more progressive step in the manufacturing process was the move to a house in Feierberg Street in the center of the city, and the delivery of new equipment: a lathe, a drill, and electric saw, and it was there, among other products, that the first stages in the manufacture of grenades was car-

---

2. Menahem Begin, *The Revolt*, pp. 71–72.

ried out. Moreover, it was here that the milk-jug bombs used in the King David Hotel operation, with their anti-handling devices, were assembled.

At the end of 1947, the IZL experienced a critical shortage of munitions, threatening to paralyze a considerable proportion of its planned activities. On Gidi's instructions, priority was given to this area of production, and one of the first measures adopted was the establishment of two divisions: one to focus on mercury fulminate and the other on TNT and nitro-cellulose. Gundar Elitzur was appointed to supervise the explosives division, with Aharon Shani as his deputy. The mercury fulminate division was billeted in a lab for making glass items in the attic of Yosef Mizrahi's house, in Zadok Hacohen Street in Tel Aviv. Working there were Yosef Mizrahi himself, Yosef Greenwald (the "Professor") who was a professional chemical technician, and a third individual named Moshe.

David Grozbard recalled:

After many studies and experiments we succeeded in November 1947 in reaching a decent level, producing mercury fulminate for detonators and grenade percussion caps. Besides the gaps in technical know-how that we had to overcome, we also had the problem of getting the raw material (the appropriate commercial companies were nervous about supplying the gear we needed for fear of the authorities), but eventually we made contact with a commodities agent who was willing to supply us at reasonable prices. According to the testimony of Yosef Mizrahi, they reached a productivity level of 800 grams of mercury fulminate per day over a period of two months – a total yield of 40 kilograms. At a later stage, during the battle for Jaffa, a need arose for anti-vehicle weapons, and it was decided to try manufacturing Molotov cocktails, which were used successfully in the front line.

Experiments in the manufacture of nitro-cellulose began even before the manufacturing division was established. A chemist by the name of Dr. Magrikvich had devised a scheme for extracting explosive material from old reels of cinema film. He tried to develop the idea in collaboration with Lehi – without success. Then he contacted Amihai Paglin, operations officer of the IZL, but even so they were unable to extract explosive material from nitro-cellulose.

With the establishment of the explosives production division, Dr. Magrikvich joined forces with Elitzur, and they tried again to exploit his method.[3]

According to Aharon Shani:

The films, which came to us from various film companies, were bathed in chemicals, cut, heated, and turned into explosive "noodles" with the help of Dr. Magrikvich. The films were either given to us, or simply confiscated. According to Gidi's instructions, we were supposed to pack the explosives we'd made into gasoline cans holding 4, 12, and 22 pounds (two, five, and ten kilos). On Passover night, when all of Israel was sitting down to the *Seder*, we were still putting the charges together, and the moment we reached a total of a thousand kilos – I remember as if it was yesterday – I dashed over to 4 Mikveh Israel Street, to Gidi's parents' house.[4]

Shani goes on to say:

There was another type of explosive, in the form of cotton batting. This was another Amihai Paglin initiative. The material was a mixture of sulfuric and nitric acid. After a process of heating and blending at a certain temperature, we would dip the cotton batting into it several times until all the liquid was absorbed and after drying, the batting was compressed into stiff wads. When it proved effective, we began continuous production in the workshop in the Hatikva neighborhood. We called the product "Antika."

The main purpose was to use it for springing our people from jails, an issue which was of the greatest concern to Gidi. Developing cotton batting explosives was entirely his idea. According to regulations, special category prisoners were entitled to have civilian clothes sent in from outside; it never occurred to the prison authorities to wonder what was in the shoulder pads of those suits....

There was no limit to Gidi's range. He had a fertile brain and

---

3. Yosef Evron, *Magen ve-romah* [Shield and spear] (Tel Aviv: Ministry of Defense, 1992), pp. 68–72.
4. Recorded interview with Aharon Shani, Jabotinsky Archives.

innumerable ideas. When we began working on the tunnel in Latrun, we suddenly came across a huge boulder and couldn't get any further. For a moment it seemed all the work we'd put into it – three or four months of hard labor – was going to waste. The only option left to us was to appeal to Gidi. We got his reply by secret mail: *I'm sending you a dismantled electric compressor, which should solve your problem.*

It was agreed the compressor would be delivered in three or four batches, then assembled and used according to his instruction. But the compressor was only part of the problem: we needed ventilation pipes too. The tunnel was going to be about 100 yards long, and as we were digging lying flat, our air for breathing had to be supplied through a pipe hitched up to a pump in the entrance to the tunnel. This was another of Gidi's solutions. The pipe was delivered to us in three-yard sections, once a week, in crates of oranges. When the British finally discovered the tunnel, they just couldn't understand how we had succeeded in smuggling in a compressor and 100 yards of piping – without any inkling on their part.

Another example of Gidi's inventive powers was his method of sabotaging oil pipelines. In the section between the Jordan and Haifa, the pipe was buried about a yard and a half underground. And then Amihai came up with an ingenious idea: he developed a kind of skewer, made from piping, the lower section packed with explosives and a chemical timing device which was also his own design; all this based on a hollow charge. He would dig the "skewer" into the ground until it made contact with the oil pipe and set the delay mechanism according to the schedule determined from the start; an hour, two hours, or more.

Amihai was always a step ahead, never striking twice in the same place. If the British were concentrating their forces in Tel Aviv, he directed his operations towards another town; if there was a state of alert in Haifa – he struck in the South. And this was the principle he applied to the telegraph pole issue; he devised a way of demolishing scores if not hundreds of telegraph and telephone poles, without endangering our people. We were, after all, very short on manpower; all the disruption nationwide was the work of a few dozen young men, moving from area to area.[5]

---

5. Ibid.

"He did everything in his little workshop in Mikveh Israel Street in Tel Aviv," said Shraga Ellis, going on to relate:

An innocent foundry for making baking ovens was converted during the underground period into a center for the development of sophisticated bombs and elaborate train mines, triggered by the weight of the cars, or the engine – according to the prearranged plan and the timetable agreed. British explosives experts tried to find a remedy for the repeated onslaught on the railways, but without success. Gidi set them a challenge, and they had no answer to it.

He applied similar methods to the disruption of British communications. The basic weapon was a stick of gelignite, containing a sophisticated triggering device, another of his inventions. We used to go out at night with a carpenter's drill, drill a hole in a telephone or telegraph pole, insert the stick of gelignite and seal the hole with a wooden plug, so that nothing showed on the outside. Times of explosions had been set in advance and then – over a period of weeks and months – a blast would be heard and a pole collapse, for no apparent reason. The campaign caused chaos in the administration's communications system – but all they could do was grit their teeth and repair the damage.... It's even said that the Russians (this was during World War II) began taking an interest in Gidi's inventions, to equip their partisans in the fight against Germany....

Gidi was always looking forward in the search for new challenges. One day – this was in 1944 – he came to me and said, "Shraga, the time has come to set up a munitions factory."

I'd given up being surprised by anything Amihai came up with – or so I thought – but this time I couldn't hide my astonishment. "A munitions factory?" I queried, "Do you know what that involves?"

"Yes," he said calmly, "I've thought it all out and I've got a concrete plan; I want you to close your workshop and move over to manage the new plant: Shlomo Dola will help you on the production side and I'll give you any technical advice you need."

"And who's going to finance it?" I persisted.

"The Irgun, of course," he replied. "I've already done the calculation and the total outlay will be about one thousand pounds sterling."

But a thousand pounds sterling was a huge sum of money in those days, and IZL command couldn't afford that kind of expenditure. In the end the figure was whittled down to 750 pounds. (Shlomo Dola and I invested 500 between us, and the Irgun paid the balance.)

We decided the company should be legally registered, and we set up a firm called "Eldest" – combining the initials of Ellis, Dola and Stopnitzky. (This last was an alias of Bezalel Amitzur, representing IZL command, who was supposed to supervise us but in fact hardly ever got involved.)

So the factory was set up at 83 Herzl Street, with an area of approximately 100 square yards. We acquired tools and equipment – everything that we needed for production purposes. All under Amihai's watchful eye. Vigilant as ever, it was he who recognized the potential of the two doors of the premises we had rented: a front entrance and a side exit. "You should split the shop into two halves," he said, and then and there he took out a piece of paper and a pencil and sketched a diagram: an office served by the front entrance, and the main production area behind it, served by the other door…

This was the IZL's first serious industrial enterprise. Admittedly, here and there a few small-scale efforts had been made in the manufacture of products such as bombs and grenades, but these had been specific commissions, to meet urgent needs. The factory in Herzl Street was the first munitions works worthy of the name. We had machinery there, and even a lathe.

The primary production items were mortars and bombs. Even before we'd gotten ourselves properly organized, Amihai came up with a scheme for producing sophisticated mortars, and he had a list of detailed specifications, in terms of dimensions (2-meter barrel with 20 mm. muzzle capacity) and materials. When the job was done, we went out to conduct tests in the sands at Holon. The first attempt was unsuccessful, but Amihai wasn't the type to give up. He took all the components, shut himself away in the workshop and checked and rechecked every feature, assembling and dismantling and assembling again, and a few days later he announced that he'd located the problem. There was no more need for tests; it was time to start producing mortars in earnest – a run of 25, for use in operations nationwide.

The bombs were more problematical; it was a far from simple issue. Gidi worked hard on the development of the bombs and when it seemed we had succeeded, we held tests – the cigar-shaped bomb spun in the air, performed a variety of aerobatics and finally fell some way short of the target. Gidi's response to this was, "We'll give it wings." We started with three wings, moved on to six, giving the bombs a range of 500 to 600 yards, and then Gidi said, "No more trials – we're going into production." We made a lot of bombs.

We used to dig a hole in the ground and insert the mortar, incorporating the automatic triggering mechanism designed by Gidi. It worked very well…

Of the four mortars targeted on Sharona, only one worked (on account of the torrential rain that fell that night), but the one that worked created havoc as well as panic and confusion among the British. [6]

The severity of the impression made by these mortars on the British has been described by Nicholas Bethell:

On 14 May 1945 the IZL issued declarations in Jerusalem. In the words of Major Whitfield, "The declarations were well printed, and in the three official languages. They called upon the 'oppressor government' to evacuate all people – employees and public alike – from all buildings occupied by the British in Palestine: *The civilian population – Hebrew, Arab and other – is requested, for its own good, to refrain, from henceforward until the cancellation of this warning, from visiting any government offices, or even approaching them. You have been warned!*'" [7]

This was no idle threat. That very day, three loaded mortars were found in their emplacements, targeted on the police camp at Sharona, at a range of a few hundred yards, to be detonated by means of a delay mechanism. On May 16, four 40-pound mortar bombs exploded near the same camp, and two other bombs exploded outside the police station in Jaffa. Damage was caused but there was no loss of life. Thirty-five telegraph poles were destroyed, and some 200 others primed to explode. Whitfield noted that

---

6.   Author's interview with Shraga Ellis, October 1996.
7.   Bethell, *The Palestine Triangle*, pp. 167–68.

the damage caused was indeed slight, but not through any lack of effort on the part of the IZL. It was impossible for civilians to evacuate all buildings controlled by the government, as they had nowhere else to go. Mortar bombs fell near the residential quarters of the Sharona police camp.[8]

On May 22, Shertok was warned by the acting Secretary General, Robert Scott, that "the most drastic steps" would be taken to suppress any new upsurge in terrorism. Shertok retorted that the British had done very little – if anything at all – to help the surviving remnant of European Jewry.[9] The IZL continued to deploy its homemade 3-inch mortars and almost every night there were explosions. As mentioned, the British called these mortar bombs V3, after the V1 and V2 German rockets that had fallen on London the previous year. Arthur Koestler mentioned this during his secret meeting with Begin, and the commander of the IZL took it as a great compliment.

Edward Horne recalls that these mortars were very effective. The IZL

> took to telephoning half a dozen [police] stations to warn them that a mortar was aimed at the place and would go off in the night. Usually one station got the bomb and the other five had sleepless nights watching for the attacks that never happened. It was a matter of honor that no station was evacuated… Half a dozen small garrisons played cards or dozed fitfully in a kind of Russian roulette situation… When Field Marshal The Lord Gort took the salute of the Kings Birthday Parade in Jerusalem in June 1945…two mortars [were trained] upon the saluting dias…. A routine search revealed their presence and they were rendered safe.[10]

Though Israeli literature has never had much to say about these mortars, in Horne's opinion they were the biggest single negative influence on British morale.

The munitions factory was in operation for some six to eight months before falling into the hands of the British as the result of a tip-off (after the "Night of the Mortars").

---

8.   WO 169 19744.
9.   S25/33.
10. Horne, *A Job Well Done*, pp. 291–92.

With the seizure of the Tel Aviv factory, manufacture of arms by the IZL came to an end until 1948.

GIDI'S BARREL BOMB

One of Gidi's most fearsome inventions was the "barrel bomb." Begin says of this in *The Revolt*:

> Miraculously we acquired a sum of money, miraculously we acquired half a ton of explosives. Gidi completed the miracles, with the creation of the famous "barrel bomb," the barrel on wheels which one morning was catapulted from an armored car (the first of its kind in Eretz Israel) and shook the whole of the British "security zone" in Haifa and with it British self-confidence in the country at large. It was a technical innovation worked out in great detail, down to the special teeth under the wheels, which prevented the barrel rolling back once it made contact with the wall of the British fortress. The colonialists were very jumpy. They surrounded their security zone with dense barbed-wire fences four to five yards high – and along came this "catapult" and vaulted over the fence. An impertinent barrel indeed… Immediately British authorities ordered that the height of the fences be raised to eight yards! This was done, but Gidi set to work as well. There's no doubt that if the British had stayed longer in the country their wire fences would have risen scores of yards high, and they would still be no protection. Gidi would have found some way of breaching them. Definitely.[11]

Gidi not only designed the barrel in all particulars, he supervised all stages of the operation, which was code-named "Hamb-Af" – a reference to two instances of the expulsion of refugee ships that had shocked the Jewish community at this time: the *Exodus*, whose passengers had been sent back to Hamburg, hence the "Hamb," and the *Af-al-pi-khen* (Nevertheless), hence the "Af."

This was a gigantic barrel packed with half a ton of TNT, fitted at both ends with tractor wheels. It was catapulted from the back of a flatbed truck, and a special mechanism stopped it from rolling back after making contact with the wall of the building.

---

11. Begin, *The Revolt*, p. 209.

It was manufactured in the Oman workshop in Jaffa, with components acquired from various sources, and final assembly was carried out in an orchard near Bnei-Brak.

When the work was complete, the barrel was stored in Abu Kebir, disguised as a seed drill. (When it was necessary to move it out in readiness for the operation – in September 1947 – the IZL operatives were offered the escort of a British armored car that happened to be passing, in case of harassment by the Arabs of Abu Kebir…)

On September 29, 1947, the "barrel" duly landed on British headquarters in Haifa, and the building was severely damaged.[12] The operation was carried out by Moshe Levi (Yariv), Benni Bachar, Avraham Mica, Shula Slonim Polak (Nitza) and Yoel Kimhi (Azriel).

"What characterized Gidi most throughout the development process was the notion: what man can do, I can do," said David Danon.

> I used to say to him, "Leave it, Amihai, there are experts for that," and he'd say, "Forget the experts, I don't have time to look for them." He would sit and plan and construct and operate, without materials, without equipment, without money – just getting on with the job. From delay mechanisms he moved on to devices for blowing up trains, and we got to the point where we could decide from the start which train we were going to attack, what date and which carriage, and all this with improvised methods. Most, if not all, of these developments were the fruit of Amihai's fertile imagination – and his determination. Once he'd decided on the objective, he started working on the means. Once he'd decided on the means, he set them in motion. Nothing could deflect him."[13]

"One of Amihai's talents was the application of things from a technical point of view," said Eitan Livni.

> Sometimes you'd think to yourself, *Hey, that's really simple.* But somebody had to come up with it, someone had to make the right tool for

---

12. Evron, *Magen ve-romah*, pp. 68–69.
13. David Danon's tribute to Gidi, at the memorial ceremony 30 days after his death, 1978.

the job, as well as inspiring confidence that the gear or the gadget would work. That was part of his genius. When we attacked the police station near Ramallah, we used mortars that fired primitive missiles – jam jars filled with explosives. But someone had to prepare them. It was Gidi who did that.[14]

---

14. Recorded interview with Eitan Livni, 1978 (property of the author).

THE RAID ON CAMP 80

On April 6, 1948, at 6:45 AM, Gidi led a combat unit of the IZL, commanded by Yehoshua (Eliyahu Temler) to British army camp no. 80, near Pardes Hanna, where a Royal Artillery battery was based.

In a daring frontal assault the young men took control of the camp, looted the armory and – before the British had recovered from the shock – withdrew with their spoils, amid a ferocious exchange of fire, leaving behind them panic and confusion such as this crack regiment had never experienced before, even in the battles of World War II. For a long time after the assault British troops continued firing indiscriminately – at one another.

In one of the rooms of an ancient Turkish building on a farm in Shuni, 50 young men, assembled some time earlier, were now listening with rapt attention to their operations officer:

"Our objective this time," said Gidi, pointing to a large-scale map, "is to empty the armory of Camp 80, between Binyamina and Pardes Hanna." "We need weapons as we need air to breathe," he stressed, "and what we didn't manage to grab three weeks ago in Beer-Yaakov[1] – we'll get here." Typically, he didn't go in for long introductions:

---

1.   An unsuccessful raid, March 15, 1948, on an army camp in Beer-Yaakov.

Unit Number One, headed by Jackson, will be the first to penetrate the camp, heading straight for the arms store, which is about 50 yards from the gate. [Gidi pointed to a short, solidly built, muscular individual; in his sergeant-major's uniform, decorated with medals, Jackson looked every inch the veteran Tommy. Clearly he was very pleased with the role he had been given – a role he had performed in the past with no little success. As a genuine veteran of the British army, he was fluent in barrack-room slang – including the conventional curses.]

Unit Number Two will set out in the army truck following Jackson and take control of the barrack huts in the left-hand section of the camp. It will be commanded by the Kabtzan [Beggar].

Unit Number Three will take control of the right-hand section.

Unit Number Four will take control of the guardroom to the left of the gate and replace the sentry on duty next to the barrier with one of our men.

All the groups I have just mentioned will be dressed in British army uniforms and equipped with walkie-talkies, keeping in touch with Hillel (Zvi Wolf), who will be with me near the gate, passing on my instructions to you.

Other groups will be dressed in civvies. Their job is to load the arms on the truck once we have control of the camp. Two men [Gidi pointed to them] will blow up the wire fence to the left of the camp, creating an escape route for the trucks loaded with arms.

The assault force set out early in the morning from the IZL base in Shuni in a convoy of five vehicles – two trucks, two armored cars, and a jeep.

Bringing up the rear was a Hillman private car, driven by the deputy commander of the Netanya region, Shmuel Amitai (Mike), who had only recently passed his driving test. Near the objective, the road took a sharp turn to the right; Mike took the corner too fast – and the car flipped over. The two trucks stopped for a moment – but Gidi, traveling in a separate vehicle, waved to the driver to carry on.

Some distance from the gate of the camp, the armored cars halted, having developed "mechanical problems," and while attempts were being made to "repair" them, Sergeant-Major Jackson arrived at the gate, waving an envelope addressed to the camp commandant. In his neatly pressed uniform and with his Scottish accent he aroused no suspicion, and he was sent with his letter to the guardroom, where he explained that he had come to collect supplies, and his CO wasn't taking any chances and had given the trucks an armed escort.

After a few moments the barrier was raised and Jackson's jeep drove through into the camp. The two army vehicles approached the gate. The sentry approached the first and asked for the paperwork. Yitzhak Shulman takes up the story:

> I directed him to the driver on the other side of the cab and as he turned away I drew my weapon. "If you don't do as I say," I warned him in his language, "your blood will be on your head." He didn't seem particularly impressed by the threat, replying with a grin, "Leave it out, mate!" The grin disappeared from his face soon enough when he saw the Sten. "This isn't a joke," I hissed between my teeth. "This is an operation of the IZL, the National Military Organization." His face turned pale and he was shaking like a leaf. I assured him he'd come to no harm if he did as he was told. At my demand, the gate was opened wide and the other vehicles entered. While this was happening our men overpowered the guard detachment, relieving them of their weapons and taking charge of all the positions in the entrance area.[2]

The place of the two sentries, ordered to strip off their uniforms and give them to their captors, was taken by two of the assailants. The barrier was raised again and the two armored cars trundled in and took up strategic positions as planned. One (commanded by Pooni) towards the south, and the other (commanded by Bundi) towards the north, close to the armory. All this happened very quickly and nobody in the camp realized anything untoward was in progress.

"There were about ten of us young men and we easily took over the armory," said the Kabtzan.[3] "There was no resistance. One of the guards was in the middle of shaving and he still had soap covering half his face."

Bundi turned his armored car towards the right side of the camp, where the Shermans were parked. From the direction of the gate there was the

---

2. Recorded testimony of Yitzhak Shulman (Shaika), "The Attack on Camp 80," Jabotinsky Archives.
3. Testimony of Eliezer Sudit-Sharon, codename Kabtzan (Beggar), "The Raid on Camp 80," Jabotinsky Archives.

sound of gunfire; a group of soldiers, headed by a colonel, had arrived on the scene to investigate. Bundi called on the colonel to surrender. He refused stubbornly and the conversation was cut short by a burst of machine-gun fire. He fell dead on the spot.

The course of that short battle has been described by Zvi Wolf (Hillel), who watched what was happening through the fence of the camp:

> Suddenly a man came rushing out of one of the huts in the officers' section. At first sight, he looked like a civilian, and he was in such a hurry it seemed he'd forgotten to put on his trousers. He came out in his underwear…. He immediately began giving orders to the frightened soldiers, oblivious to the fact that he was Improperly Dressed, in clear contravention of King's Regulations. It was clear from his manner that he was a fairly senior officer, whose sense of responsibility kept him immune from the panic that had seized all the other residents of the camp, now resembling something between a circus and a madhouse. He was barking out orders, but all his military energy was incapable of preventing the completion of the operation, which was proceeding precisely according to plan, with the cool nerve and determination that were the hallmark of underground fighters in those days.
>
> One of our boys recognized the warlike potential of the man in underwear and put an end to the "show" with a volley of lead. The man fell in a pool of blood, dying. When the other soldiers realized their officer wasn't coming back to them from the other world, they threw in the towel. Later, it turned out the dead man had been a very senior officer indeed: a colonel, and none other than the commandant of the camp in person.[4]

Attempts by the British to get to the tanks and bring them into action were foiled by ferocious fire from the armored car. "Eventually, they succeeded in getting one Sherman started, and it began moving ominously towards the armory," the Kabtzan recalls.[5] "Our men threw grenades at it; they were so excited they forgot to take the pins out, but the crew of the tank were

---

4. From the diary of Tzvi Wolf – property of the author.
5. Testimony of Kabtzan (see n. 3).

convinced these were Molotov cocktails. Their nerve failed them and they jumped down and ran for their lives, leaving the Sherman to its fate."

At the first sound of shooting, Baruch Weiner (Konous) made a dash, as planned, for the communications room. A thunderous explosion shook the camp and the radio station was in ruins.

All this time the young men were working without a moment's pause. Feverishly the weapons were loaded on the trucks – dozens of rifles, thousands of rounds, Brens, heavy machine guns, submachine guns, some of them chained together. "We didn't have time to cut them loose – even though we'd come equipped with special cutters; we just lifted up the whole caboodle and loaded it," the Kabtzan continues.

While this was going on, Jackson noticed an armored personnel carrier advancing slowly towards the armory. Bundi opened fire from the armored car and the driver, standing up for a moment, took a bullet in the backside and slumped down again. Jackson darted forward, grabbed the wounded man and dragged him under cover, no doubt saving his life in the process, and then without a moment's hesitation took over the controls of the APC, its engine still running, and drove it towards the armory. By this time the trucks were fully loaded. "We virtually swept the armory clean," said the Kabtzan. It should have come as no surprise that one of the trucks was so weighed down, a tire blew out. Again it was Jackson who took the initiative: the load was transferred to the APC.

"I'd been ordered to watch the prisoners in the armory, staying at my post till the last moment," Malkiel recalled.

It was only when all had climbed aboard the APC that Yehoshua ordered me to join them. Like the rest, I was sitting on an ammo box. The whole procession moved towards the gate, with the last armored car at the back covering the retreat. We heard the whistle of bullets over our heads but luckily, we were moving fast and they didn't manage to hit us.

At first the fellows at the gate didn't recognize us (in our army uniforms we looked just like British Tommies), and they almost opened fire on us. Somebody shouted the password – and everyone breathed again. We turned right towards Pardes Hanna. Looking back we could see a lot of movement of armored cars and tanks in the camp. There was shooting from various weapons, including artillery. One tank was seen emerging from the gate but it stopped suddenly, hit by gunfire from inside the camp, someone obviously believing it had been commandeered by the raiders.[6]

Later it emerged that in the aftermath of the attack there had been a ferocious struggle between the British army and itself – between the force blocking the exit and the force setting out in pursuit. Clearly the British uniforms worn by the assailants had confused everyone, and no one knew who was who.

"We carried on towards Pardes Hanna. At a certain point we diverted, as planned, from the main roads and took a side track, winding through the plantations, till we reached Shuni," Malkiel continues his account.

When the weapons had been unloaded, the haul was assessed:

One armored personnel carrier (APC), 3-inch mortars, a light artillery piece, 35 Brens, 2 Fiat anti-tank guns, 2 Browning heavy machine guns, 70 rifles, 65 submachine guns, and thousands of rounds of ammunition.

The weapons and equipment were stored in various arsenals in Zichron Yaakov and the surrounding area.

But there had been a price to pay: in the exchange of fire an IZL fighter, Yitzhak Kaveh, had been killed.

British losses amounted to eight men killed, including a colonel, the camp commandant.

Regarding the fate of the APC, which was to play an important role in the conquest of Jaffa, the Kabtzan relates:

> This was the only APC we ever had at our disposal, and we were sorry to lose it. After consultation with Jackson it was agreed to transfer it to the Petah Tikva region, an area no longer under British control; here the pullout had already begun. Before doing this we changed the number of the APC and gave it the insignia of a different unit. On our way we passed an army convoy moving towards Haifa, including APCs, and their crews waved at us affably. We waved back and congratulated ourselves on our forethought in changing the number.

---

6. Testimony of Yitzhak Mintz (Malkiel), May 9, 1957, Jabotinsky Archives.

At the approaches to Petah Tikva we came across a Haganah road-block. We were politely informed that from this point on, it had been agreed this was a zone "Out of Bounds" to British troops. The commander, struggling to express himself in English, was almost pleading with us to "stop messing about." I answered him in Hebrew and he gaped at me. We offered him some English cigarettes and that calmed him down. In Petah Tikva we took off our British headgear and broke into Hebrew songs. We were still in uniform, and the public greeted us with mixed feelings: they weren't sure if we were Tommies disguised as Jews or vice versa.[7]

7. Testimony of Kabtzan (see n. 3).

JAFFA ON THE BRINK

The night of August 10, 1947 – three and a half months before the UN's proclamation of a Jewish state – a gang of armed Arabs burst into the Hawaii Garden café across the Yarkon, murdered four Jews and injured seven others. The gang numbered about a dozen men, disguised as soldiers and armed with Stens, hunting rifles, and grenades; for a long time they rampaged through the area, unchecked and unchallenged.

The next day Gidi asked for an urgent meeting with Menahem Begin, "What happened yesterday in the Hawaii Garden," he warned, "marks a dramatic turning point. We have reached a historic crossroads; we're on the verge of war against the Arabs. We have to forget the British and concentrate from now on on full-scale war with the Arabs."

Begin gave his trusted lieutenant a long look and answered slowly and emphatically, like a teacher repeating a scriptural text to his pupils, "You can forget the idea that any Arab will dare raise his hand against a Jew in the Middle East. The barrel bomb that you detonated in Haifa, the other momentous achievements that we have scored – they are the guarantee that no hand will ever again be raised against Jews. Don't worry – it won't come to that."

Gidi was stunned. *What does he know about Arabs?* he mused. *He*

wasn't here during the riots of 1921 and 1929; he has no idea how easily orien-
tal mobs can be incited to violence and turned into wild beasts hungry for prey.

"The bloody events of yesterday," he insisted, "show that we're talking here about a trained and organized gang that isn't out for loot and plunder but for the murder of Jews because they are Jews. And if one such gang already exists, it won't be the only one on the scene. You can be sure there are more like this, and their number will grow." Even as he spoke, he knew deep down that he was wasting his words. Begin listened politely, but his blank expression showed that his conviction was firm: no Arab would dare raise his hand against a Jew, in this land or in the entire Middle East.[1]

"I left this meeting disappointed," Gidi was to say later. "It was obvious to me that the murders in the café symbolized a historic turning point, de-manding a radical change in our political perceptions and a fundamental reshuffle in our organization." The events of the following weeks only con-firmed his concerns.

The idea of a "fundamental reshuffle" had been in Gidi's mind for some time before the café incident. Towards the end of 1946, he had discussed this with a number of combat squad commanders, those responsible for most of the planning and the executive action. "With the kind of instinct that is second nature to fighting men," he recalled,

> we felt that a historic and crucial showdown between ourselves and the Arabs was close at hand – and time for preparation was running out. We were unanimous in concluding that a regular military force, ready for battle, had to be organized within six to eight months; we needed trained and fully equipped field units, so we could play our part in the impending war for the destiny of this land.
>
> But while we, a limited caucus of commanders, were pushing for a radical change in the objectives of the Irgun, shifting the emphasis towards the Arabs (for which we were even prepared to suspend all operations against the British), most of those in the higher echelons of command still saw the British as the principle enemy. Every blow

---

1. Amihai Paglin interviewed by Shlomo Lev Ami, January 27, 1970, Institute of Con-temporary Judaism, Hebrew University of Jerusalem.

that we struck brought in its wake a feeling of self-satisfaction and complacency: *Hey, we've shown them again!* I felt we were losing sight of the overall picture, drifting into a war of tit-for-tat where all that mattered was keeping the balance in our favor. Of course, our High Command was right to see the departure of the British from this land as a decisive victory in the continuing struggle of the Irgun – but the Arab element in all this had been almost entirely forgotten. For this, regrettably, we were destined to pay a high price.[2]

HAGANAH PARALYSIS

On November 30, 1947, the day after the UN Assembly's decision, the Arabs of Jaffa went to war against the city of Tel Aviv. They started with sniping, and progressed to bombardment. The defensive barriers erected in the central streets afforded little protection – as lethal firepower unleashed from the Hassan Bek mosque and from the high-rise tenements of Manshiya penetrated to the very heart of the great metropolis, reaching Moghrabi Square, the Carmel Market and the windows of the municipality building. One hundred fifty-six civilians were to be killed and over a thousand wounded – men, women and children – in the five months that elapsed before the conquest of Jaffa by the IZL. The Arabs of Jaffa became more daring and started using mortars, their shells devastating whole neighborhoods in the shared border zone. Thousands of families were made homeless. Newspaper headlines worldwide reported "Battles in Rothschild Boulevard…"

For close to 150 successive days Jaffa continued to challenge Tel Aviv, while the heads of the official institutions and the policy makers of the "organized Yishuv" displayed astounding impotence.

As for the Haganah, three weeks before the invasion of the Arab armies, with Abdullah's legionaries already deployed in the Ramleh-Sarafand-Wilhelma sector – a 20-minute drive from Tel Aviv – the Haganah leadership was still waiting passively for the departure of the last Briton from Jaffa…

"The characteristic feature of all Haganah operations at this time," writes a former senior Haganah commander, Yosef Olitzky, in his book *Mi-Me'ora'ot le-Milhamah* (From Riots to War), "was that our forces were content to destroy enemy strongholds or devastate a particular site, without

---

2.   Ibid.

any attempt to hold on to them. In the public at large there were those who asked – *what's the point of all this fighting, if you can't keep control of the places you've captured?*"

He admits this and goes on to offer the excuse that

> if we had only needed to contend with the Arabs and their "volunteer" hangers-on, the situation would have been simpler. But they weren't alone on the battlefield. The truth is that the third, supposedly "neutral side" was not only providing them with an endless supply of weapons and ammunition but also giving active support and protection.... We were forced to back down not only because of the superior numbers of the Arab enemy, but also out of awareness of the conspiratorial ploys of the third side, making every effort to prevent us straying beyond our border...

In less convoluted terms: the presence of the British in Jaffa paralyzed the Haganah.

These were gloomy days for Gidi. The war of attrition between Jaffa and Tel Aviv was taking on the form of a static stand-off: border incidents, sniping, and acts of mutual reprisal were becoming routine occurrences. By natural instinct he knew what others had not yet grasped: time was on the side of the Arabs; as May 15 drew closer and with no preventive measures taken, Jaffa was ever more liable to become the central base of the invading Arab armies. Only quick and drastic action could change the situation, and the only appropriate action was the conquest of Jaffa. But an operation such as this required trained field forces and heavy weapons, which were not at the Irgun's disposal. *If only they'd listened to me a year ago...*, he reflected grimly. But it was not in his nature to cry over spilled milk. He knew something had to be done – and quickly. In the meantime he set about establishing training camps in the plantations of Petah Tikva and Ramat Gan.

By January of 1948 it was clear to all that war with the Arabs was inevitable. IZL Command convened an emergency joint session with the Planning Section and four strategic objectives were identified as required by the political and military situation on the eve of British withdrawal: the conquest of Jerusalem, of Jaffa, of the Lod-Ramleh sector, and of the Tulkarm-Nablus-Jenin triangle.[3]

At the time these decisions were made, the Irgun had only a fraction of the matériel needed to implement them. The transition from underground operations to war of conquest found the IZL unprepared and ill equipped. The schemes adopted were in fact statements of intent and aspiration rather than realistic propositions. Trained manpower and logistical resources had barely met the requirements of underground activities.

By February 1948 it was too late to start training field combat units on a war footing. For this reason it was decided to focus on just one of the four schemes: the conquest of Manshiya-Jaffa. And even this was only due to Gidi's unflagging obstinacy.

The Haganah, with infinitely greater resources at its disposal, continued to hide its head in the sand and indulge in the pleasant delusion that Jaffa would fall "like a ripe fruit." Yosef Olitzky, in the book noted, *From Riots to War*, reveals that there were indeed schemes discussed for taking Jaffa: one involved conquest of the outer suburbs and another, conquest of the entire city. Eventually, the conclusion was reached that "the city was likely to fall even without assault, like a ripe fruit, and moreover, an assault could end in failure; in the context of street fighting in a large city, victory cannot be guaranteed."

And there was also a strategic consideration, he adds: "Jaffa was disintegrating, and one way or the other, no longer posed a serious threat to Tel Aviv. Storming it would be like plucking a fruit ready to fall by itself, and the duty of commanders is to conserve the manpower at their disposal and avoid unnecessary waste…"

It was convenient for the Haganah to rely on the assumption that if Jaffa was detached from "the Arab centers," it would have no option but to surrender. This also enabled Haganah spokesmen to excuse its inactivity in the face of continuing provocation from the Arabs of Jaffa. This was a perception vehemently opposed by Gidi.

He warned, when the unequivocal decision was finally taken to go on the offensive against Jaffa, "The theory prevalent in Haganah circles, according to which a prolonged siege of Jaffa would lead to automatic capitulation without fighting, is a serious strategic fallacy. It is Tel Aviv that

---

3.   Zvi Shimshi's interview with Amihai Paglin, September 13, 1957, Jabotinsky Archives.

risks finding itself under siege as a result of unchecked aggression on the part of its neighbor."

He continued, declaring:

> The city is open to the sea and can provide a supply artery and a logistical base for enemy forces; it is well fortified and supported by a large population of 70,000 inhabitants; from an economic point of view it could sustain itself for many months, even if forced to rely on maritime traffic alone. Its geographical characteristics transform it into a dangerous hub, a launching pad for large-scale Arab attacks on the center of the country.
>
> What is more, bombardments from Jaffa have so far been confined to primitive, homemade mortars, and even these have caused panic in the southern suburbs of Tel Aviv and driven thousands of families from their homes. It's not hard to imagine what we can expect if the Arabs of Jaffa get their hands on higher caliber mortars or artillery – it's a nightmare that could come true the day after May 15.[4]

It never occurred to the clever strategists of the Haganah that while they were waiting for Jaffa to fall like the proverbial ripe fruit, the Egyptians could take over the port and send their armored vehicles and tanks directly into the heart of Tel Aviv, with the Jordanian Arab Legion joining in the attack from the east.

I'M GOING TO HIT JAFFA

From the moment the command decision on the conquest of Jaffa was made, Gidi began feverish preparations for implementation. The first priority was to gather intelligence. According to Abba Shertzer (Gundar Michael), national intelligence officer of the IZL:

> Towards the end of February 1948 Gidi called me and told me quite simply: "I'm going to hit Jaffa." He showed me a big map of the city, explaining the plan in general outline, and asked me to check out the situation there, from the perspective of defensive dispositions, strength

---

4.   Ibid.

of enemy forces, and if possible, the kind of weapons and ammunition at their disposal. At that time Jaffa was closed and sealed off.

The intelligence report that I received and passed on to Gidi (who was dealing with it personally) stated, among other items: "Some activity is perceptible in the port of Jaffa, and there is talk of the unloading of equipment for the Iraqi army." The mood in Jaffa was exuberant, but economic activity was sluggish. Heavy guns were not visible, but on the other hand, mortars of various calibers had been installed at a number of points. The principal weapons were rifles and mortars. Every Arab urchin was armed at least with a dagger or other light weapon. The British were turning a blind eye to the public carrying and trading of arms.

All sources confirmed that in Jaffa there was no anticipation of attack, and all were calm and confident in themselves and in their British protectors.[5]

In tandem with the gathering of intelligence, Gidi began taking urgent steps towards remedying the shortage of weapons, ammunitions, and other instruments of war. The most serious problem was in the context of explosive materials. The IZL's arsenals were almost empty of this item, and the issue was at the top of the list of priorities. Besides acquisition (by purchase or confiscation), Gidi transferred the emphasis to "in-house" production. And sure enough, in April 1948, the "industrial department" of the IZL succeeded in producing large quantities of explosives.

Something of the process has been described by Aharon Shani [see also previous chapter]:

> I was one of Amihai's assistants, working on the production of explosives, which was another of his inventions; to this day I don't know where he got the idea from. We were extracting the raw material from old movie film. The moment we reached a total close to two thousand pounds I went to Amihai's house, where all the senior commanders, including Menahem Begin, were waiting for news about the explosives situation. I reported that we'd produced almost two thousand pounds, and it was decided the attack on Jaffa would go ahead.

---

5. Testimony of Abba Shertzer (Gundar Michael), March 19, 1957, Jabotinsky Archives.

A number of successful raids on British military camps in February–March 1948 improved the picture immeasurably in this respect, too:

- On February 15, 1948, an IZL unit raided a military armory in Hadera and "confiscated" 40 tons of weapons and food supplies; a month later 12 rifles and machine guns were "confiscated" from the guard detachment of a British army camp in Beer-Yaakov.
- The biggest haul of weapons and ammunition was undoubtedly netted in the daring raid on Camp 80, on February 6, 1948. The total seized was awesome: 35 Brens, 70 rifles, 65 submachine guns, a light artillery piece, 3-inch mortars, and thousands of rounds of ammunition. Also "confiscated" was an armored personnel carrier – the first vehicle of this type to fall into Jewish hands [see the chapter "The Raid on Camp 80"].
- But the most audacious operation, which brought forward the date of the attack on Jaffa (occurring about a week later) and contributed most of all to its conquest, was the attack on the munitions train near Pardes Hanna on April 18, 1948 [see the chapter "The Fateful Train"]. Among the items seized on this occasion were 20,000 3-inch mortar shells – Gidi's "secret weapon," which broke the spirit of the Arab residents of Jaffa and led directly to the capitulation of the town.

Three possible approaches to the conquest of Jaffa were put by Gidi to the command staff of the IZL.

a. Direct frontal assault;
b. Prolonged siege;
c. Eccentric penetration.

From a purely tactical point of view, he explained, option (a) would be preferable, if only they had the equipment required. Option (b) was not feasible, on account of Jaffa's access to the sea, and pressure of time. So the third option remained – eccentric penetration (from the perimeter inwards) through weak points in the defensive ring; progress from house to house and from street to street, avoiding road intersections but blasting holes in the walls of buildings – a slow advance on a broad front.

On the basis of the facts presented, it was decided to adopt the third option, with flexibility for a rapid transition to assault on the center.

The plan had two stages:

Stage one – cutting off Manshiya with a raid on the beach, to be coordinated with a heavy mortar bombardment of central Jaffa;

Stage two – rapid transition to concentric conquest (breaking through to the center of Jaffa and assault from the rear on perimeter positions).

Objectives of the bombardment in both stages were

- Preventing the movement of regular troops in the town
- Breaking the spirit of enemy soldiers
- Creating confusion and panic in the civilian population and prompting mass flight[6]

On Thursday, April 22, 1948, the decision was made. Four members of the Planning Group – Amihai Paglin, Eliyahu Temler, Shraga Ellis, and Menahem Maletzky – met with Menahem Begin at the Paglin family home in Tel Aviv. Gidi presented the plan for the conquest of Jaffa and added that the latest arms acquisitions – the raids on Camp 80 and the munitions train – had supplied all the arms and equipment needed for the attack; the military and political situation, the atmosphere of panic among Arabs in the aftermath of Deir Yassin, "all these factors," he stressed, "make this a uniquely propitious time for implementation of the scheme." At the conclusion of the discussion, Menahem Begin instructed that preparations for the "assault on Jaffa" should be completed within 48 hours.[7]

6.   Amihai Paglin, "Tactics in the Conquest of Jaffa," *Herut*, April 19, 1949.
7.   "Fighting from Wall to Wall" (50th anniversary of the conquest of Jaffa), *Makor Rishon*, 1998 [Hebrew].

ON THE MOVE

On Sunday, April 25, 1948, the signal was given.

At 9:00 AM shells began falling on the center of Jaffa. They landed on the Clock Square, the Post Office building on King George Avenue, on the harbor sector, on the Ajami Quarter, ravaged Bostros Street and sowed ruin and destruction. The two 3-inch mortars[1] installed on the grounds of the Alliance school in Tel Aviv spewed out a relentless hail of fire and brimstone. The mortarmen – David Brisk (Chunky) and A. Kaufmann (the Australian) – had their hands full. Shell after shell was fed into the maw of the mortar, rose in the air with a loud shriek, and fell to the ground with a thunderous crash.

Six hundred soldiers of the Irgun Zvai Leumi were drawn up on

---

1. The two 3-inch mortars had been looted from an RAF camp near Rosh Ha-Ayin on November 22, 1945, in the course of an audacious raid mounted by members of the IZL. Also confiscated on the same occasion were some 70 Sten submachine guns, five Brownings, and a quantity of Mills grenades. Since that time, it had been impossible to operate the mortars for lack of ammunition. Exactly one week before the attack on Jaffa, the raid on the munitions train near Pardes-Hanna (see the chapter "The Fateful Train") netted a vast quantity of 3-inch mortar bombs, thus closing the last gap in the preparations for the assault.

the border of Jaffa – five platoons of infantry, two service platoons, four armored cars, and one APC.

As the frightened residents of Jaffa were anxiously watching the flight of the shells, two combat platoons quietly infiltrated the no-man's-land between Manshiya and Naveh Shalom. One turned towards the railway station, the other towards the seashore.

They moved cautiously, keeping close to the walls of buildings and fences. Suddenly, a deluge of fire and lead: from in front, from behind, from the left, from the right – the sleepy alleyway seemed to come to life all at once, spitting fire in all directions.

"They were well deployed, the sons-of-bitches," one of the fighters recalled. "They had Spandau machine guns, pairs of fortified positions giving mutual covering fire, backed up by regular troops from the Arab states."

The men cursed softly, but kept on the move, slipping through courtyards, breaking through walls. One platoon ran into a defensive wall of fortified enemy positions, the other found its way blocked by a British armored car, approaching from the railway station. Evidently, the Arabs had good professional advisers, setting up "hedgehog" positions in depth: *take one of them and it isn't enough – the others will catch you in crossfire*. It was becoming increasingly obvious that the defensive line in the hinterland of Manshiya was not as thin as had been supposed, while the relentless hailstorm of bullets proved they were not short of ammunition.

"We didn't have an operational map of Jaffa," Gidi admitted. "Night reconnaissance patrols came under heavy fire, and we couldn't get a proper picture of the situation from close quarters. We planned to take a few key positions on the front line, and use them as a base for checking out the defenses in depth, getting a more precise picture and planning the assault accordingly."

Plans are one thing – the situation on the ground something else: from the CID building in Jaffa Street, two heavy machine guns are rattling away; an armored car is spewing bursts of fire. They throw a grenade at it; it responds with a two-pounder shell and keeps on advancing. They throw another grenade; the vehicle stops, hesitates…regains confidence and advances a little further, cautiously, to within throwing range of Molotov cocktails (which don't exist…). They call up the "Frog" armored car. A hail of bullets greets it. As the machine gunner (Konous) keeps his finger on the trigger of the Bren, eyes fixed on the target, the driver (Jackson) is heading straight towards the enemy position. The field of vision is very limited (with the hatches closed), and suddenly there are cries of alarm echoing all around; some of the fellows have taken shelter behind a pile of stones and can't be seen by the driver; one of them has his leg crushed under the wheels of the vehicle.

When the wounded man had been extricated, the armored car advanced more cautiously, looking for the enemy's armored car. The two met face to face, unleashing volleys of fire: one with a light Bren and the other with a heavy machine gun – a bantam-weight versus a heavyweight. Progress was slow and wearisome, the way strewn with wreckage and the rubble of masonry. To the right, the unit that was supposed to be attacking the enemy position had dug itself in, pinned down by ferocious fire. From the window of a tall building someone opened fire on the armored car but this was ignored and the vehicle carried on to within 20 yards of the fortified position. Suddenly, the black barrel of a Fiat emerged from the enemy armored car. A deafening explosion, but the shell missed. A cloud of thick smoke shrouded everything and the crew of the "Frog" could no longer tell what was happening ahead of them; they could hardly breathe and their eyes were watering. Ammunition was running low and there was no choice but to retreat. Even this was far from easy, as the way was narrow and cluttered with rubble. The armored car reversed slowly, still under heavy fire.

The point section finds itself exposed in open ground, without cover, and also begins to withdraw, the whole platoon trailing along behind. Two are missing and there's no way of knowing what has become of them: killed, or wounded, or just separated from their unit. They pause to look for them, find one – and lose another. The platoons can't be delayed any longer. The retreat continues.

In one of the classrooms of the Alliance school, a conference of operations staff is convened. The commanders sit on children's benches and assess the balance sheet of the first day's fighting: the enemy has proved well prepared, his positions fortified and effectively defended. Even the one that was taken had to be evacuated, coming under heavy fire from the others. The first round has ended in failure, with all units pulled back to the starting point after taking casualties.

Gidi hears the report once, twice, three times: he shakes his head, saying nothing. The atmosphere in the room is grim: silence has fallen and all are waiting for him to speak. He turns to the map room and all follow him, dejectedly. It seems the three missing men – Lieutenant Michael Laska (Giladi), Avraham Mizrahi, and Shmuel Wachtfogel – have been taken prisoner by the Arabs, and one of the commanders, Zev Zweig, has been wounded by a sniper's bullet. To emphasize the gravity of the situation, a number of shells explode outside the HQ building.

The consultation between commanders continues. All are aware that the advantage of surprise has been lost. The Arabs' defensive positions have not been weakened, and from now on they'll be more alert. Returning to the former line of advance will involve bitter frontal combat, but abandoning the bottleneck of Manshiya is something no one is contemplating. All are agreed that this is the enemy's weak point.

Summing up, Gidi says:

The conquest of Manshiya will seal the fate of Jaffa. There's no reason for despair. The battle's only just begun. We didn't succeed the first day, but we shall succeed in the future. The boys deserve a rest – after a sleepless night and a day of fighting – and tomorrow we will renew the attack, but adopting new tactics: we will fortify our forward positions with sandbags and advance steadily, sandbagging all the new positions that we take. The sandbags will give the boys minimal protection from enemy fire and enable them to get close to that infernal position that held up our advance today – and take it out.

The conference comes to an end. Gidi's calm and measured words have dispelled the fog of doubt and inspired new confidence in the hearts of the commanders. The decision is unanimous.

By this time Jaffa has absorbed around a thousand shells – 11,000 pounds (5 thousand kilos) of high explosive. There is great confusion and an air of panic in the streets. At nightfall dozens of trucks loaded with passengers leave the city, among the fugitives the first deserters from the ranks of the army.

Monday, April 26, 1948. Reconnaissance patrols begin at dawn. During the morning, the troops assemble at the Alliance school. Gidi chooses the most experienced, battle-hardened veterans among them and divides them into three groups: demolitions, backup sections, attackers.

At twelve noon the attack is resumed – this time, with armored support. The demolition section forms the advance party, destroying one Arab position along with its occupants. They take control of the railway station sector and consolidate their position. The enemy, with British support, calls up armor and mortars and uses anti-tank weapons for the first time.

A squad of attackers is pinned down in a ruined building, unable to move. The "Frog" armored car is sent to assist them and, amid heavy exchanges of fire, is ordered to join the APC which is dumping sandbags along the young men's line of advance – protection of a kind from enemy fire. The "Frog" machine gunner is hit in the eye by a splinter, impairing his vision. The armored car performs some acrobatic maneuvers and beats a hasty retreat.

A fortified enemy position continues to hold up the advance, and at HQ the decision is made to use anti-tank weapons. An armored car is sent to the scene, armed with a Fiat. The gunner manages to fire one shell, before a bullet hits him full in the forehead. The armored car withdraws hurriedly, taking the wounded man to the first aid station, but all attempts to save him come to nothing.

Meanwhile, the situation of the besieged party is becoming more serious. The fear of encirclement by the enemy, which is becoming a more realistic prospect moment by moment, spurs the men on to prodigious efforts: under cover of heavy smoke and using any weapon that comes to hand, they succeed in slipping through the ring of fire and returning safely to the assembly point.

At the same time a fierce battle is in progress in another sector. Demolitions men armed with explosives have advanced towards the "Red Shop House" supported by two armored cars and the APC. At the head of the column is the machine gunner of the "Frog," one eye bandaged and his finger never budging from the trigger. The roar of explosions and collapsing walls is deafening. Suddenly British armored cars equipped with anti-tank weapons and heavy machine guns approach from the flanks. "The first exchanges of fire immediately proved the inequality of forces and the pointlessness of this kind of engagement," said the "Frog" machine gunner. He recalled:

The sound of the Bren was completely drowned out by the racket of the Spandau and the Browning. And that was before the Fiats opened up. We decided we had to retreat but the way was blocked by the APC: a whole wall had fallen on it and put it out of action. The road was so narrow there was no chance of going around it. We were trapped, and running out of ammunition. Luckily the crew of the APC, working under heavy fire, somehow managed to get the vehicle moving and out of the way.[2]

Pitched battles in the bottleneck continued into the hours of darkness – without result. By evening it was clear that a second day of attacks had failed to break through the enemy's defenses. The assault troops were up against a brick wall.

THE AGONY OF DEFEAT

However absurd it may sound, while the fighters of the IZL were pitting themselves against the fire and the steel of the defenses of Manshiya, leaders of the official Yishuv institutions were less concerned over the fate of Jaffa than over the strong groundswell of support for the action from all levels of society. They obviously saw this as a veiled threat to their hegemony.

According to Kenneth Bilby in *New Star in the Near East*, "Ben-Gurion raged to his advisers about the 'scoundrels' and the Haganah high command disowned the attack in bitter language. Yet when Irgun armored cars paraded down Allenby Street after the capture of Manshieh, sidewalk cafés and street corners echoed with applause. At that stage the erstwhile terrorist soldiers were the Robin Hoods of the war of liberation."

And if this was not enough: hovering in the air was the public demand for unification of the fighting forces. An agreement on this issue had been brokered and approved some time before under the auspices of the Jewish Agency and the Zionist Action Committee, although the Haganah, for its part, was in no hurry to implement it, on account of the objections of leftist elements. And the IZL's attack on Jaffa amplified the demands for unity, a project enthusiastically supported by most of the daily press. The leadership of the Haganah could no longer resist public pressure, and so it was that at the height of the second day's fighting, the leaders of the IZL were sent an urgent invitation to attend a meeting with its representatives, "to discuss immediate implementation of the operative agreement."

---

2. Baruch Weiner (Konous), *Jaffa Album* (Hebrew), Jabotinsky Archives.

"I went with Haim Landau, at the invitation of the Agency and the Haganah, to meet Galili and Yigal Yadin," Menahem Begin relates in *The Revolt*. He went on, stating emphatically:

> This was my first encounter with Yigal Yadin and a few days later, after the fall of Jaffa, I introduced him to our Gidi. The two young operations officers hit it off immediately, they were real kindred spirits. Gidi was impressed with Yigal, describing him to me as "a young man who knows what he wants and is full of energy, like one of ours." Yadin was just as complimentary towards Gidi. "If Gidi puts forward a plan of action," said the operations officer of the Haganah and future army chief of staff, "it will be in no way inferior to anything I would come up with. I trust Gidi 100 per cent."

At the end of the meeting between the Haganah and IZL leadership, it was agreed that the operative agreement would come into force immediately. An announcement to this effect was carried that evening by the Haganah's "Voice of Defense" and the IZL's "Voice of Fighting Zion."

It was clear that the attack on Jaffa had accelerated ratification of the agreement, the signing of which had been delayed for weeks. At the same time, the Haganah continued to demand a halt to the operation, out of (almost pathological) dread of entanglement with the British. After exhaustive negotiations, Yadin agreed to allow another 24 hours for the conquest of Manshiya. In a grim mood of uncertainty and consumed by doubts, Begin returned to the operational HQ, to hear a gloomy assessment of the first two days' fighting: no progress.

The tense atmosphere in the operational HQ has been described by Menahem Begin in *The Revolt*:

> I summoned all commanders to a conference. I gave a report of my meeting with heads of the Haganah and their agreement to continuation of the attack, if the enemy lines could be broken within 24 hours. "But," I said, "I don't see why we should carry on beating our heads against those defenses, behind which stand British tanks. For two days we have exerted ourselves to the utmost...and the bombardment of Jaffa may yet yield results. The enemy who has been attacking Tel Aviv

for months, has been forced onto the defensive. We have sacrificed precious young blood. I have no doubt that were it not for the support of the British tanks, we would have carried all before us. But it is a fact that the tanks are there. In these circumstances it is no disgrace – even for the IZL – to suspend the direct assault. We shall hold the line we have taken, and leave a strong vanguard force there for the time being.... Pay no attention to any suggestion that we have failed. The IZL needs no recognition of its fighting prowess.... It is simply that the combined forces of the enemy greatly outnumber ours. The boys have all fought well, but I see no point in beating our heads against the wall."

There was a tense atmosphere in the map room – the tension before the taking of a momentous decision. Gidi was silent for a long while. Other commanders gave their opinions for and against my proposal. Finally, Gidi asked permission to speak. He spoke quietly, with repressed emotion. His opinion was that a final decision should not be made on the basis of two days of fighting. In those two days we had learned a lot. The enemy would not be capable of resisting our attacks for much longer. The present method of attack could still succeed. But if the decision were to be taken to withdraw most of the troops, he wanted to leave a sufficiently large force at the front to renew the attack when the time was right.

After lengthy discussions, it was decided to pull most of the units out of the front line and leave a limited force at the "Alliance." The decision was taken. In practical terms it meant suspension of the direct assault. [3]

The decision was passed on, as an order, to the squad commanders and their men.

When the battles of the second day were at their fiercest – as the heads of the Haganah and the IZL were concluding the draft agreement on unification of forces – the press, at the Haganah's instigation, was crowing over "the failure of the IZL."

Al-Hamishmar: "This was a day of great provocation and great shame....

---

3. Begin, *The Revolt*, p. 365.

Soldiers of the IZL have not stormed central Jaffa, all they have done is to impose themselves on large swathes of the Hebrew city."

Haaretz: "An operation like this requires the deployment of *proper* troops; to embark on it with inadequate forces, just to compete with the Haganah for public support…is nothing but the height of irresponsibility and malicious jealousy."

Most devastating of all was Dr. Azriel Carlebach in *Ma'ariv*: "Those incapable of defending Tel Aviv should beware of endangering it."

And all of this less than 48 hours after the launching of the attack.

The IZL radio station was not slow to respond:

There is celebration in their camp. The IZL attack has failed! And when you listen to their broadcasts and read their articles, you are under the impression that this is good news for Israel. Have you heard? The IZL has failed. What better, more reassuring news could there possibly be?

In the past we have not said a word about Nebi Yehoshua and Nebi Samuel or the scores of other instances in which they have blundered. We have not written in the style in which these scoundrels have written, those who pray for the failure of Jewish arms, just because we are the ones wielding them. We never scratched their eyes out when they failed. That is the difference between us: we pray for their success on the battle-field – for the success of Hebrew fighting forces, while they, in their blind hatred, pray that our soldiers will fall and fail to advance…

We shall pay no heed to them. Our warriors are locked in mortal combat against combined Arab and British forces, a fight in which they are greatly outnumbered. They are shedding their blood, to ward off danger from the Hebrew city.

Such was the exchange of views in Tel Aviv towards the end of April 1948, as the soldiers of the IZL were launching head-on assaults on the biggest and best-defended Arab city in Eretz Israel.

THE STRANGEST MUTINY

Gidi left the meeting with a sense of deep frustration. With every fiber of his being he rebelled against the order he was about to give his subordinates: to "pack up" and abandon the territory. Abandon it to whom – he mused bitterly – to the Arab Legion of Jordan, to the Egyptian army, so their tanks can knock on the doors of Tel Aviv? Something inside told him it would be a grave mistake on his part to order withdrawal when all his instincts were crying out against it. But he'd been outvoted in the staff conference – and a halt to the operation had been ordered. He had never infringed military discipline.

"But that night something strange happened," Menahem Begin writes in *The Revolt*. "For the first time ever, soldiers of the Irgun Zvai Leumi defied me. They simply refused to obey the order to retreat."

The first to mutiny was the Kabtzan (Eliezer Sudit). He recalled:

> Someone came from HQ and told me that we'd be leaving just a small detachment at the front and pulling the main force back to the base in Shekhunat Hatikva. I had the feeling – after two days of fighting – that it would be possible to break through, advancing from house to house. I spoke with the other commanders and they agreed with me. I dashed to HQ, found Gidi and told him: "We're not leaving!" I pleaded for another chance to try the house to house approach. Gidi said it was an order from the top. "We're not quitting until we've had another crack at it," I insisted.[4]

The shadow of a smile flickered across Gidi's tired face: "Tell that to the boss!" He slapped the Kabtzan's shoulder. "I could have hugged him for joy," he said later. It soon emerged the Kabtzan wasn't the only one defying the order to retreat.

Begin wrote, describing this unique situation:

> In the map room delegations began arriving. They spoke in different styles but the message was unanimous: we're not giving up the battle. Let us make one more effort. We're sure we can lick them this time. We can do it!
>
> Something like this had never happened before in the Irgun Zvai Leumi. In every unit reached by the order to retreat, protesting voices were heard: No, we're not pulling back. Let's have one more crack at the enemy. We're ready, we'll lick them! For several hours a bizarre dialogue was conducted in the map room: between a commander ordering retreat and 'mutinous' soldiers insisting on fighting!

---

4.   Testimony of Eliezer Sudit-Sharon (Kabtzan), Jabotinsky Archives.

And Begin continued:

> Gidi returned from a long reconnaissance inspection of the front line. My Gidi, he looked very tired and drawn. He stood before me all covered in dust and mud – having had to crawl through the alleys of Jaffa – but his dark eyes were ablaze with renewed confidence. He said, "I've found new weak points in the line. I'm sure, sure we can break through. We won't go in a straight line again. We'll advance on a zig-zag course, blasting our way through the houses. We won't be hemmed in on two sides again. On the contrary, we'll be the ones putting the enemy in a vice. We'll advance from house to house, reinforcing the line with sandbags. We'll be careful. I shall take the lead myself, as I know the terrain. I guarantee that this time we'll make it. This will be our last attempt, so let's go for it!"

"The discussion came to an end," Begin concludes. "The soldiers' mutiny had succeeded. There was a consensus among commanders and soldiers alike that the previous order should be rescinded. We weren't breaking off the assault: we were resuming it with renewed vigor, under Gidi's leadership, according to his plan…"

Another command meeting was held, and all listened attentively to Gidi's words, as he stressed:

> The main thing we have learned from the first two days of fighting is that seizing isolated pockets in the enemy's defensive line after advancing over open ground under fire does not provide a solid base for further advance. Every time such a position has been occupied, it has been taken back by the enemy, using his control of the approach routes and his ability to bar the way to reinforcements. We, therefore, need to find a route of advance that isn't exposed to enemy fire, so it will be possible to move up reinforcements in the wake of the attacking force, avoiding the streets that are exposed to fire.

All the while, a bold tactical plan was already taking shape in his mind: breaching the interior walls and advancing through houses to the enemy positions.

As for the crossing of open ground, he suggested sandbags should be thrown from the houses onto the pavement: "One soldier will jump out and take cover behind the first bags, and the others will keep on handing him sandbags to build a defensive barrier across the street; as the barrier grows, other soldiers will join in and hundreds of bags will be passed from hand to hand, building an impenetrable shelter behind which the assault units can advance to the next block of houses."

He continued:

> The second problem we have to overcome is the British armored cars. And this problem too has a solution: the streets leading from central Jaffa to the battlefield in Manshiya can be blocked by blowing up big buildings on the left-hand side of the advance-route, filling the streets with rubble and making them inaccessible to armor. Demolitions men will blast holes in the walls of houses along the way, and whole houses will be blown up, collapsing on ground positions and putting them out of action. Sappers will prepare hundreds of sandbags and these will be passed along a human chain to the point-unit, which will hang on by its fingertips to every place it reaches.

The plan is accepted. It calls for rigorous preparation and redeployment of forces.

A brief respite for reorganization is announced.

In Jaffa there is chaos and dejection, a populace living in fear. The Iraqi commandant is making secret plans for escape – taking eight thousand pounds with him for "travel expenses." There are mass desertions from the ranks and pools of blood in the devastated streets; the stench of broken sewers is mingled with the reek of corpses, fractured water mains are flooding the streets. Jaffa is reeling like a drunkard, on the point of collapse in a welter of blood.

GIDI'S PLAN IN ACTION

Tuesday, April 27, 1948. Feverish preparations continue into the early hours. The decisive onslaught is scheduled to begin the next day, Tuesday morning. But Gidi isn't taking any chances this time; under cover of darkness he goes out for a night reconnaissance with a few other commanders, to establish the route of advance and to identify all of the enemy's weak points. All preparations have to be completed as planned, he stresses, even if it means delaying the operation. His face is grim, as he explains everything down to the last detail. "This is the final attempt at breaking through," he declares, "and nothing is to be left to blind chance."

The majority of fighters have been told they won't be taking part in the assault; those left are the experienced, battle-hardened ones – and they are divided into three platoons.

The most important assignment this time has been entrusted to the demolitions men. Dozens of gasoline cans are hastily crammed with explosives – 44 pounds (20 kilos) to a can. These will be deposited close to enemy emplacements, at a distance of five paces. Each can is fitted with a 4-inch (10 cm) fuse. "Light it – and take cover!"

These units are equipped with mines, axes, spades, and hoes, with which they will clear a path for the attack units. A courtyard behind a defended building becomes an improvised sand quarry. Thousands of empty sacks are piled up there; two squads are busy filling them, and two squads of "porters" will carry them down the line, constructing defensive dispositions while the battle is in progress.

New anti-tank and anti-armor teams are organized; their equipment – Molotov cocktails, Mills grenades, and light weapons. They are to approach the armored vehicles by any available means and set them alight. Gidi decides on four waves of assault, one after the other. There will be no respite. He has thrown away the rule book, adopting every ploy that could facilitate the objective: crossing the some 300 yards that separate his forces from the seashore – a sector of densely built housing, some already in ruins; wells; and a network of fortified positions.

At 3:00 PM a diversionary attack is launched in another direction, to the right of the line of advance. The feint is successful: all the enemy's attention is drawn to it. The real assault begins under cover of darkness, as a column of "ants" invades Manshiya – its objective, the sea. Commanders of all ranks stand alongside the fighters, ready for any duty – portering, demolitions – whatever is required, authorized or unauthorized.

One after the other all units and squads take up their positions. This time there is no headlong dash across open space. Lessons have been well learned. The chain of porters sets up positions along the line of advance, as sandbags pass from hand to hand. From now on, every inch that is gained will be held at any price.

At the first street corner the familiar picture is repeated: the same armored car and the same lethal fire from all directions; from right and left, from below and above. The "point unit" from the first day flexes its muscles again, throwing Molotov cocktails at the armored car. They miss, but the vehicle stops firing and withdraws. A solitary demolitions man crosses the street at a run. He gets to within a few paces of the position, lights the fuse and takes cover behind a nearby house which shakes to the roar of the explosion. The boys fire at the wrecked position. No response. They move on to the next.

The street is barricaded by the sandbags which continue to arrive in the chain. The demolitions men charge forward and two more buildings collapse, blocking the intersection and keeping the armored cars at bay. As an extra precaution, an anti-tank team is put in place, armed with Molotov cocktails. Meanwhile the "drilling" through the houses continues. They crawl through the gaps. Just two more streets to cross – but it is no simple task. Near the second street the point unit finds itself cut off and under heavy fire, pinned down in an isolated house – the last before the second street. Someone sets foot outside, and catches a volley of lead between knee and ankle. He collapses and is dragged back inside, his leg paralyzed. This is a death trap. Another attempt to break out ends with another injury. Impossible to advance or retreat. The air vibrates to the roar of explosions. The demolitions men are continuing their assignment.

A long hour passes. The party under siege in the ruined house dares not make another escape attempt. The intensity of fire wanes gradually and the backup unit with the Bren finally reaches the besieged house. The gunner takes up position in the entrance to the house, shooting from the shoulder. They decide to try slipping out under the cover of machine-gun fire.

They dash out and cross the street at a run. The chain joins up again. The waves of attackers mingle together: men who have lost contact with their units join others. Porters volunteer for demolitions duty. The whole line is bursting with life, like a colony of ants on the move. The demolition of houses continues, as does the building of sandbag walls. The wedge is threaded through the breaches in the blocks of buildings, across courtyards and alleyways, flanked by ruined or abandoned Arab positions. In one of them the remains of a meal have been left: pita, onions, olives – a pan still steaming.

Manshiya has one more artery left: Hassan Bek Street. If this is cut off, the scorpion will have no head.

The time of the third watch is approaching. The fighters haven't closed their eyes in three nights. Legs are heavy as lead and heads spinning, and there is just one thought that keeps them going: "To the sea…to the sea!"

At the operations HQ they are aware of the weight and significance of the moment. Gidi is dashing about from one position to another. The order is: "Consolidate at all costs and keep the advance going."

Consolidation means not only building sandbag barricades but also blocking all alleyways and access routes with the masonry of demolished buildings. The demolition teams don't rest for a moment: their men crawl through courtyards, climb fences, dump their charges, light the fuses. Building after building collapses and gradually a winding tunnel is bored between precarious walls and fences reinforced with concrete. The frantic work continues late into the night.

HAGANAH INVOLVEMENT

That same night the Haganah carried out a number of surprise attacks on Arab positions to the south of Jaffa – Tel Arish and Haria and Sakiya. Both villages were captured, but the attack on Tel Arish ended in costly and painful failure; the next day, at dawn, the Arabs mounted a counterattack and forced the young men to withdraw from the heights that they had occupied, suffering heavy losses: 18 killed and more than 40 wounded.

The day before this, the cooperation agreement had been signed by chiefs of staff of the Haganah and the IZL. The topic of the Haganah's planned attacks never arose. "They didn't say a word to us of their intention to launch attacks in the Jaffa region," Begin comments in *The Revolt*. "All that was agreed was that we would carry on with the battle to neutralize the Manshiya salient. News of their attacks reached us that evening."

At noon the following day Haim Landau again met with Yigal Yadin. The latter demanded repeatedly that operations on the Jaffa front be halted immediately, since "the 24-hour deadline agreed upon has elapsed and Manshiya has not been cut off." Landau replied that IZL forces were deployed to attack according to a new plan, and there was no point suspending operations at this stage of the battle.

The two sides parted without any decision being made, and the impression was that Yadin had given retrospective consent to continuation of the assault. Still there was no mention of the Haganah attacks, due to take place in a few hours time.

Most surprised by the Haganah's involvement in the attack on Jaffa were the representatives of the press. From the first day of the IZL's assault the Haganah had been conducting a vicious propaganda campaign, denouncing the operation as "an act of political-military lunacy." "To attack Jaffa, a fortified city included in the Arab sector [according to the UN's partition plan], three weeks before the British withdrawal, is adventurism. It's a crime!"

All of this was said to the press in various forms and with particular vehemence on April 25 and 26, 1948. The evening of April 27 the tone changed: the Haganah had joined the IZL's campaign.

"What's going on here?" was the question on the lips of the foreign correspondents who for three days had heard nothing but denunciation of the IZL's operation. "How is it that the assault on the suburbs of Jaffa was 'an act of lunacy' on April 25, and by the 27th has become a 'judicious act'? What has changed? The British are still in Jaffa, Jaffa's status under the UN scheme is unchanged – so what has happened to explain such a volte-face on the part of the Haganah?"

An official spokesman for the Jewish Agency offered the pretext that "these were solely acts of reprisal – not conquest." The press was not convinced: if it was good to attack Jaffa on April 27, why was it bad to do it on the 25th, seeing that in the interim the political circumstances had changed not one iota? The inevitable conclusion was that the three days of fighting had made a significant difference to the *military* circumstances. This was the line taken by columnists in most of the major newspapers of the USA and Europe.

TO THE SEA!

Wednesday, April 28, 1948. Dawn of a new day. Hassan Bek Street exposed to the rays of the rising sun, and in the distance the gleam of the sea. Only one big concrete emplacement stands between it and the warriors. The men gaze at the scene, entranced.

And suddenly it happened. Even as Gidi was weighing up the possibility of taking the position by storm, there suddenly came a mighty roar, bursting from the lips of dozens of fighters, dashing forward in a wild rush and yelling: "The sea! The sea! The sea!" No one knew where the idea came from. They didn't know themselves. One man shouted, "The sea!" and charged forward as if possessed, and was surprised to find to his left and right scores of others, all shouting the same thing. No one cared about the fortified bunker, which was apparently stunned into inactivity. Before its occupants had recovered their wits, the first of the assailants were already alongside it, firing from the hip and tossing grenades into its open embrasures – then continuing the headlong dash towards the sea. Those who had manned the bunker disappeared into the alleyways at the first opportunity, leaving loaded weapons behind, traumatized by the awesome spectacle of the charge.

It all happened with dizzying speed. When the boys arrived at the seashore it still seemed this was only a mirage. After three days of fatigue and frustration, the relief was intoxicating. Men dabbled their feet in the salty water, embraced one another, larking about and giggling like mischievous children. The news rapidly passed down the line from the seashore to the Alliance school; the wounded tried to climb off their stretchers, the fit were overjoyed, and commanders had their work cut out restoring order.

"Only Gidi wasn't carried away," according to Begin. "Of course, he too knew we had made it, we had conquered and won... But he was a battle-field commander, and the battle wasn't over yet... Gidi knew that the enemy's counterattack could come at any moment, and this was the critical time, between conquest and counterattack. He called his men to order..."

At first the fellows paid no attention to him. In fact, they didn't hear him at all; the triumph of victory had robbed them of all their senses. Gradually the high spirits were cooled and the ranks formed up again.

What happened shortly before the breakthrough to the sea is described by Aharon Shani:

> It was a critical moment. In Hassan Bek Street Arabs were in positions across the roadway, with five or six Brens, firing towards Tel Aviv. Our people were in positions facing them, with the same sort of firepower. It was an absurd situation, the two sides exchanging volleys of shots,

and a British armored car standing on the sidelines, just looking on. Men were falling on our side, every second there was one more dead or wounded – and then Amihai appeared, taking in the situation at a glance and realizing this was a slogging match with no prospect of movement on either side. He also figured out something we hadn't been aware of: the Arabs had been consolidating their positions with concrete emplacements from the inside, effectively creating defenses within defenses.

Amihai said, "Come with me," and we made our way to an empty building overlooking these positions and he said: "This house has got to come down." He brought up the cans of explosives himself – 20 and 30 and 45 pounds (10 and 15 and 20 kilos), dumped the stuff on the second and third floors, told me to go down and get all the others clear, and brought the whole house crashing down into the street, sending the Arabs scurrying away in panic, having no idea where the blow had fallen from. Another example of Amihai's quick thinking. It was then that people started running in the direction of the seashore, and the breakthrough into Jaffa began.[5]

While these dramatic events were unfolding on the seashore, the Haganah approached the IZL with an urgent request for the support of a 3-inch mortar team in an action to extricate casualties from Tel Arish. Gidi immediately gave his consent, although the mopping-up operation in Manshiya was at its height. Chunky and the Australian once again displayed their professional prowess: over three hours they showered the battlefield with accurate fire and did not budge from their post until the last of the young men had been evacuated.

Later that day the IZL again lent the Haganah a mortar crew, to assist in the conquest of Kfar Salameh, and again Chunky was in action, this time teamed up with Konous. "At 2:00 AM," the latter recalled, "we were ordered to launch a heavy bombardment of the center of the village, its approaches and defensive positions. We fired around 500 shells, and the roar of the explosions shook the neighborhood. When Haganah troops attacked at dawn, they met no resistance. The village was deserted; all had fled from the bombardment."

---

5. Recorded interview with Aharon Shani, Jabotinsky Archives.

The change in the situation on the ground was not immediately communicated to the snipers at the Hassan Bek mosque, and they continued to hurl their poison in the direction of Allenby Street in Tel Aviv; that Wednesday another Jewish casualty was rushed to the Hadassah Hospital.

These pockets of resistance had to be eliminated before they gained their second wind, Gidi decided, and he sent instructions to the armored vehicles to break through into Manshiya via Hayarkon and Meah Shearim streets, to help with the mopping-up operation. Haganah soldiers manning the road blocks were sure they had lost their way: "Halt – this is the border!" they shouted. "Not anymore!" the crews replied, "We're going for a bath on Jaffa beach – you're invited!"

At 10:00 AM Gidi ordered some of his units to advance, with armored support, towards the Hassan Bek mosque and storm it. He also gave them a flag and told them to fly it from the minaret of the mosque, to proclaim far and wide Tel Aviv's liberation from the threat of sniper fire. As they approached the mosque the lads came under heavy fire from a two-story house on a nearby hill.

After a brief skirmish the position was overrun and its occupants taken prisoner. The way to the mosque was now clear. Ferocious fire was returned from the sacred site, but those inside, former attackers now forced to defend themselves, soon realized their time was up and a white flag fluttered above the minaret, soon to be replaced by the squad commander, Boaz, with the blue and white flag given him by Gidi – the flag which proclaimed to the people of Tel Aviv that the era of sniping from the Hassan Bek mosque was over.

Five hours later this was officially announced by Eli Katz (Gundar Ali) in the first press conference as such ever given by the IZL.

In a cramped room in an ancient building in a run-down area, field headquarters, "the atmosphere was electric," according to Yitzhak Ziv Av, describing his encounter "with men who only yesterday were underground, in deep cover:"[6]

He continues:

---

6.   Published in *Ha-Boker* (newspaper), May 25, 1948.

Outside, beyond the windows still rattling to the blast of shells, it is five hours since Manshiya fell. Above the Arab police station flies a blue and white flag, above the Hassan Bek mosque flies a white flag of surrender.... The salient of Arab territory projecting into Tel Aviv has been cut off....

Commander Ali – sallow, disheveled, unshaven, unwashed, his combat fatigues grubby and his eyes sore from strain and fatigue, begins with a general report: the fighting has lasted three days and three nights...and was concluded at 07:00 with the conquest of Manshiya, after an 18-hour battle reaching a climax on the fourth night.... The commander of the front, the planner, the guide and executor of the scheme – is still visiting forward positions, supervising their fortification....

The room was already half emptied when the front line commander entered. He stood to attention. The press officer said emphatically: "I have the honor to introduce to you the commander of the operation, Commander Gideon." Clearly a pseudonym. The commander is very thin, his face just skin and bone, with piercing eyes. He is of average height, but his slim build makes him look taller. His voice is lower and his speech more pragmatic than is the case with most of his colleagues. Only the map of the front folded in the pocket of his army shirt sets him apart from the civilians accompanying him....

An operation cannot be judged [Ziv Av continues] after one day, nor can it be judged on the basis of one of its stages. No city is ever conquered in a single day. And in Jaffa, whether it acted for the better or the worse, the strength of the IZL was way below half of the combined numbers of the British and Arab forces pitted against them... This being the case, the "Voice of the Haganah" did a serious disservice to confidence, when a few hours after the start of the operation, it rushed out a report crowing over its failure...although a day later the same radio station was reporting the conquest of Manshiya... As it turns out, the attack on Jaffa shook the spirit of Arabs over a very wide area, and in the ranks of the Haganah there were many thousands who regretted the tone of our earlier broadcast...[7]

---

7. Ibid.

And sure enough, that very day – as if by magic – the tone of all the nation's newspapers changed: the same journalists who only yesterday were vehemently denouncing the IZL attack on Jaffa now veered from one extreme to the other. Thus *Haaretz* opined:

> Yesterday the Manshiya district of Jaffa was conquered. Anyone looking at a map of Tel Aviv-Jaffa will understand at once the military significance of this development: a long spur of Arab territory penetrating close to the center of Tel Aviv has been removed from the control of Arab gangsters.
>
> This zone has not accommodated civilian populations for many months. On the other hand, the Manshiya quarter has provided a mustering point for Arab fighting forces, especially foreign invaders – posing a serious threat to the security of the residents of Tel Aviv and tying down a large number of Jewish defenders along an extensive front line – while the Hassan Bek mosque and other high points in Manshiya have provided a base for snipers harassing and endangering the civilian population of the metropolis. Now the enemy forces have been displaced and their troops forced to withdraw, releasing significant areas of Tel Aviv from their sphere of activity.
>
> The Jewish community cannot allow Jaffa, so close to the heart of the community, to serve in the future as the springboard for Arab attacks on us, at the disposal of the Arab states which speak openly of their eagerness to attack us with their regular armies, backed up by warships and by troop-carrying ships landing reinforcements in Jaffa. The community cannot tolerate the existence of a potential military base on its doorstep.

Such perceptions, never previously heard, assumed great importance in the hindsight school of journalism. To quote again from our old friend Dr. Azriel Carlebach in *Yediot-Ma'ariv*: "Now, thank God, you can sleep soundly at night in Tel Aviv, for the first time in many months. The nights are pleasant now, whether noisy or quiet. And anyone who has nothing better to do, can enjoy them."

THE BRITISH ARE COMING

Meanwhile, IZL fighters were still engaged in the "cleansing" of Manshiya. The next objective was the police station; it was taken by assault and its defenders scattered. It was then that the first Spitfires appeared on the horizon, flying low with a menacing roar, and ostentatiously photographing the battlefield.

Gidi got the message, and his top priority now was to secure the territory occupied. He called his squad commanders together and gave them their instructions: "The next bout will be with the British army," he explained, and all set about feverishly consolidating their positions.

According to Yosef Olitzky:

During the first three days of the battle, when the Arabs were repelling the IZL's attacks, the British army was still supposedly "neutral" and continued to stand aside, observing. Its help was given furtively and indirectly, avoiding overt involvement in the battle...But when the Jews gained the upper hand, the British army could no longer stand aside, and its heavy guns, armor, and infantry went into action against Tel Aviv.... While the fighting was in progress, the British deployed significant numbers of troops in Jaffa and special units, five battalions – a total of some 4500 men – were shipped into the port, to prevent its capture and force the Jews to abandon their gains in Manshiya.... Jewish neighborhoods bordering on Manshiya-Hassan Bek were subjected to an unprecedented level of artillery and mortar bombardment.[8]

One does not have to be a professional military commentator to understand why the British were determined to hold on to Jaffa of all places until May 15, 1948. According to the partition map, the city was included in the Arab sector; keeping it as a sea base in the hands of the Arabs was vital to the success of the invasion by Arab armies – an invasion which the British Establishment, and Ernest Bevin in particular, intended to use as a means of restoring the status quo and scuttling the UN's decision in favor of a Jewish state.

And then came the IZL's assault on Jaffa, threatening to turn everything upside down – no wonder the British were incensed.

But what motive, rational or irrational, induced the Haganah to support the British demand that the IZL operation in Jaffa be halted – and in

---

8.   Yosef Olitzky, *Mi-me'ora'ot le-milhamah* [From riots to war] (Tel Aviv: Mifkedet Haga Tel Aviv, 1951).

the same terms? Was it blind hatred that deranged them, or astounding political and military myopia? It seems that the dominant emotions here were jealousy and anger: the IZL had found the courage to implement a scheme that had been on their agenda, too, but deferred for fear of British disfavor, and in the complacent belief that "Jaffa is bound to fall sooner or later, anyway…"[9]

As things turned out, the Haganah "won," in that its job was done for it by the IZL. This was a slight that it could not forgive.

Thursday, April 29, 1948. For the past seven hours British artillery and mortars have been pounding the ruins of Manshiya indiscriminately.

Until last night all had been working frantically, the heavy sandbags passed from hand to hand, blocking streets and alleyways. Fingers were bent by the effort; blood streamed from ripped fingernails. Some worked at filling big barrels with gravel and rolling them out to bolster the barricades; others blew up buildings, sending ruins crashing down on the desolate streets. The Tel Aviv regional commander, Yosef Levi (Gundar Uzi), volunteered to serve as in demolitions; he succeeded in blasting one building before being mortally wounded by a burst of fire from an armored car. Not far away an IZL armored vehicle was hit by a Fiat shell, and two of its crew wounded. More forces are brought into the battle. Two British armored cars go up in flames. The construction of defenses continues steadily under a hail of bullets. The British bombardment steadily intensifies, shells landing from all directions: from the right, the left, from the front. Buildings collapse like houses of cards; mangled human limbs protrude from the rubble.

---

9. Details of plans by the Haganah (which were never implemented) to detach Manshiya from Jaffa are revealed by Yosef Olitzky in *Mi-me'ora'ot le-milhamah*, pp. 282–83. Much emphasis is laid on the simplicity and ingenuity of the plan – as opposed to the mordant criticism directed towards the IZL, which actually carried it out. "The plan to cut off Manshiya was remarkably simple," he boasts. "All that was required was to break through on a line from Baal Shem Tov Street to the sea…. But the British were still in Jaffa, and they weren't going to allow the Haganah to dismember Jaffa or conduct any kind of military operation there. Our people were even warned that so long as the British retained a foothold in Jaffa, Jewish forces would not be allowed to take it over…. In spite of this," Olitzky continues, "since bombardment from Manshiya continued to threaten Tel Aviv, at the end of March a plan to detach Manshiya was debated in Haganah Tel Aviv Command, and approved with a number of amendments…. In the end, implementation of the Manshiya plan was deferred, as no longer being of vital importance – Jaffa was bound to fall sooner or later, anyway…"

Moans of pain echo in the void and medical orderlies run back and forth. They and the demolition crew are the only ones still active in the field.

The others keep their heads down and wait. For what? There's a saying that two shells never land in the same place – don't you believe it! Three direct hits in the same crater…. The thunder of the guns doesn't let up for a moment. One barrier is convulsed like a living body, its central section flying up in the air. Heavy sandbags are born aloft with surprising ease, shedding their contents all around and adding to the choking haze. The bombardment leaves big gaping holes in the barricades. Four men, including Gundar Yehoshua, run to take up positions by one damaged barricade, armed with a Fiat and Molotov cocktails. As they crawl through the wreckage, a shell explodes close at hand. They are still moving. Tension mounts: will they reach the barricade? They reach it, and all sigh with relief.

No respite in the deluge of shells. Hearts miss a beat with every whine – and then the deafening explosion. The building in which the four took refuge collapses, and again the medics are on the move. You count them: one stretcher, two, three, four – all of them. You can't see anything clearly, just mangled body parts. Don't look.

Explosions resound all along the line; dozens of stretchers are carried out from the inferno; scores of wounded – and there's no knowing how many are dead. No one budges from his post.

IZL command staff meets in emergency session. After consultations Haim Landau sends an ultimatum, via the mayor of Tel Aviv, Israel Rokach, to the representatives of authority: "If by twelve noon the British bombardment has not stopped, the IZL will target 3-inch mortars on British family quarters in the German Settlement in Jaffa."

Around noon the intensity of the bombardment gradually eases. (Has the ultimatum done the trick? – too early to tell.) At intervals a British armored car appears at a street corner, fires a few volleys of shots and withdraws. They don't seem particularly keen to attack. The young men lie still, hugging the ground, unflinching. "They shall not pass!" they whisper.

At 3:00 PM all is suddenly quiet on the front line. They have not passed – but a heavy price has been paid: another 13 fatalities to be added to the list of the fallen.

The combat skills displayed by IZL fighters in Jaffa impressed friends, rivals, and enemies alike. Even Yosef Olitzky, whose hostile attitude towards the

IZL is reflected on almost every page of *From Riots to War*, was forced to admit, grudgingly,[10] "Members of the IZL risked their lives and operated with incomparable aptitude."

Kenneth Bilby, correspondent of the *New York Herald Tribune* and a serving combat officer during World War II, told Begin: "I was in Jaffa, and I spoke with the commander of the British forces. He told me that the young men's street fighting techniques could serve as a model to any army. My soldiers – the British commander added – were so unnerved by the fire power of the IZL they hardly dared poke their heads out of tanks or fortified positions."[11]

According to Bilby's later account in *New Star in the Near East*:

On the first day of the truce I crossed the two hundred yards of no man's land under a white flag and ducked into the heavily guarded advance command post of the British Forces. Major G.J. Hamilton, commanding the 1st Battalion Royal Irish Fusiliers, who directed the assault on the Irgun, met me at the outpost and gave the best explanation I have yet heard on why the Jews were winning:

"Those Jews are bloody good street fighters," he said. "They have it all over the Arabs in a town. They even gave us a stiff fight. They know how to use demolitions and how to clean out a street. They scare the daylights out of the Arabs."

Inadvertently, he also explained why the Jews had not overrun all of Palestine before the Mandate ended and the regular Arab armies invaded.

"After they captured Manshieh, I got orders to save the city for the Arabs at all costs, particularly since the Jews took Haifa. We were reinforced with Cromwell tanks and 75-mm. guns. We hit them hard for two days with tanks and armored cars at the edge of the Manshieh zone. We drove them back several hundred yards to a fixed line which we still hold.

"I think Jaffa is a doomed city when we leave, but you can be sure there will be no further encroachments by the Jews until the Mandate ends. General Murray (Major-General Henry Murray, commanding

---

10. Ibid.
11. Begin, *The Revolt*.

the Lydda Military district) has made it plain to me that we will use everything we have if necessary."

Friday, April 30, 1948. The front line is quiet.

Many boatloads of civilian evacuees; foreign correspondents report 60,000 leaving the city. The British army takes the places vacated by the fleeing gangs and announces its intention of staying in the city until May 15.

The British acknowledge the de facto conquest of Manshiya but put forward, via the Haganah, a two-point ultimatum:

a. To hand over the Manshiya police station
b. To allow free movement of armored vehicles in Hassan Bek Street

The ultimatum is accompanied by threats. The Commander-in-Chief British Forces Middle East has announced that the IZL attack on Jaffa, which is outside Jewish territory according to the terms of the UN's decision, has changed the situation radically and necessitates a redeployment of British forces in the area. The BBC reports that British reinforcements shipped in from Malta and Cyprus have landed on Jaffa beach, to prevent the city falling into Jewish hands.

The Haganah is in touch with the British and recognizes their right to intervene.

Jewish and Arab representatives are invited to a meeting at the CID building. They are introduced to the commanders of land, sea, and air forces. The British governor, Holler, again presents the (expanded) ultimatum, which will expire, he says, at noon on the Sabbath. The terms are the following:

a. The Manshiya police station to be transferred to British control
b. 400 yards on either side of the line of conquest to be held by British troops. Any armed person seen in this zone is liable to be shot.
c. Hassan Bek Street to be open to British military traffic
d. A cease-fire to be observed throughout Jaffa as far as Beit Dagon

The Arab mayor of Jaffa, Dr. Haykel, emboldened by the British position, demands the return of the whole of Manshiya. This enrages the deputy governor, who expostulates, "Have you no shame? In the whole of Jaffa there are no more than 15,000 Arabs remaining – and *they* are only here because British soldiers are protecting them!"

The Jewish representatives – Israel Rokach, mayor of Tel Aviv, and Amos Ben-Gurion (responsible for liaison with the British) – try to negotiate, accepting one clause, rejecting another...

IZL command rejects the ultimatum out of hand, since it means "abandoning territory won with our blood, and renewed danger to Tel Aviv." As for threats to bombard Tel Aviv, the reply was, "If the British are interested in a trouble-free withdrawal of their forces, they should do the math: in the hands of the IZL there are still thousands of 3-inch mortar bombs, and in Palestine there is no shortage of army camps vulnerable to attack."

The Haganah, for its part, pressed for the acceptance of the British demands. "We did a lot of tough talking, in person and by telephone, with leaders of the Haganah, which ended with them appealing to us to accept the British territorial demands, in accordance with the operative agreement between us," Begin recalls in *The Revolt*. "We reminded them that we had carried out the attack on Jaffa on our own responsibility and before the agreement came into force. We suggested they explain this to the British authorities.... Alternatively, they could say that the order to retreat was passed on to the IZL, but the latter refused to comply.

"All of this was to no avail: The Jewish institutions were not inclined to accept my advice," Begin concludes.

Gidi put an end to the debate in his own unique fashion: a few hours before the expiry of the ultimatum, IZL demolitions men blew up the police station in Manshiya, turning it into a pile of ruins, and in the process blocking Hassan Bek Street, the artery connecting Jaffa to Tel Aviv. The British had nothing left to negotiate over and in their typical fashion, accepted the fait accompli and acknowledged that a "a new frontier" had been set by the IZL – a temporary cease-fire line between Jaffa and Tel Aviv – on condition that the other side of the line would be manned by the Haganah, not the IZL.

Sabbath, May 1, 1948. At 2:00 PM the Haganah took over the IZL positions. Gidi shook hands with the commander coming to pick up the baton. "I hope you'll keep what we captured," he said emphatically. "We'll keep every inch of territory we captured," the Haganah representative replied. Journalists were quick to note that both used the expression "*we* captured"...

The British spread out opposite the Haganah line in Manshiya. Now the picture became absolutely clear: there was no longer a military front in Jaffa – only a "political front," with British forces on one side, and Haganah personnel on the other. Residents of Jaffa themselves were by this time on their way to refugee camps in the Arab states, while those remaining opened up an "internal front." The mayor of Jaffa had fled, the Iraqi army commander had fled, newspaper editors had fled. All the public institutions disintegrated.

The remnants of the gangs gathered in small groups, and began looting whatever was left there to take. In the process disputes broke out among them, or between them and British troops who turned up with the same object in mind.

Such was the "internal front" of Jaffa!

The British government, however, was still not reconciled to the defeat of the Arabs of Jaffa and would not allow them to surrender. "Strange though it may seem," Field Marshal Montgomery writes in his memoirs:

> the fighting in Palestine between Jew and Arab brought relief to the British troops, since they were no longer the target for attack by the Jews – as they had been for so long. We ceased to suffer casualties. Instead, the troops were chiefly engaged in holding the ring and trying to ensure a fair deal for both sides. A good instance of this occurred in Jaffa towards the end of April 1948. Heavy fighting was taking place in the town, and reports indicated that the Arabs were getting the worst of it. Jaffa was the only Arab port in Palestine and I was asked by the Government to take all necessary steps to ensure that it did not change hands before the 15th May. I gave orders accordingly, and said that if the Jews captured Jaffa, our troops must retake and hand it back to the Arabs. The C.-in-C. troops on the 28th April and these, supported by Spitfire aircraft, pushed the Jews out and brought about a truce in the town. We had one British soldier killed.[12]

Sure enough, in the first days of May the stream of British reinforcements intensified – by sea and by land – from Malta, Cyprus, and army camps

---

12. Montgomery, *Memoirs of Field Marshal Montgomery*, p. 423.

around the country. In the port of Jaffa patrol boats were seen, and squads of commandos disembarked on the beach.

But all this effort was in vain. Battered half to death, Jaffa was only waiting for the British to leave so it could surrender, unconditionally.

The consul-general of France went to Jaffa to protect the 75 French nationals concentrated in the French Hospital and the "Convent." He ordered the flying of French flags, for purposes of security, and the Arabs, seeing this, also began flying flags – French, American, Dutch, Belgian.

The last remaining member of Jaffa's municipal council, Abu Laban, took matters into his own hands and formed an emergency committee. On May 12, 1948, the emergency committee contacted the Haganah in Tel Aviv, declaring that the town and its residents could no longer be defended, and asking for terms of surrender.

On May 13, 1948, at 10:00 AM, a surrender deputation from Jaffa arrived in Tel Aviv. Discussing the details lasted some five hours, and articles of surrender were finally drawn up at 3:15 PM. One after another members of the emergency committee signed the document. A deathly silence reigned in the hall, and only the rustling of papers and the scratching of pens testified to the momentous event. First to sign was Abdul Rahim Muhammad, a wealthy fruit grower of Jaffa, and he was followed by Amin Andreas and Salah Najar (aide to Hassan Salameh, leader of the gangs in the south). The last to sign, with shaking hand, was Ahmed Abu Laban, of Jaffa's municipal council.

Over and done with.

Jewish forces were drawn up for the victory parade in the streets of conquered Jaffa. Heading the procession was an armored car of British manufacture, long since the property of the IZL, painted with a white *Rak Kakh* (Only Thus) symbol. Following close behind, in a civilian car belonging to Tel Aviv regional command, were the Haganah district commander (General Kiryati) and his IZL opposite number, Petachia Shamir (Steiner). Behind them Haganah and IZL units marched with their weapons. The IZL's armored car leading the parade symbolized more than anything else the Haganah's recognition of the conquerors of Jaffa.[13] This was a brief and one-time gesture of goodwill, inspired by a fleeting historical moment.

---

13. "The IZL in Jaffa after the Conquest," *Jaffa Album*, Jabotinsky Archives.

The Haganah never had the courage to admit that the surrender of Jaffa before May 15, two days before the end of the Mandate, came about as a direct result of the conquest of Manshiya by the IZL, which was a vital turning point in our strategic situation. On the contrary, wherever its hand reached, it tried to disparage the operation and play down its significance.

Thirty-eight years were to elapse before a president of Israel, Chaim Herzog – former IDF general, operations officer, and head of the intelligence branch in the War of Independence and after – finally rectified the historical injustice done to the real conquerors of Jaffa, the fighters of the IZL, "who with the liberation of Jaffa established a decisive landmark in the War of Independence," as he wrote in a letter on the occasion of the thirty-eighth anniversary of the liberation of Jaffa.

The following is the full text of the letter:

From the President
April 28, 1986

To all involved in the ceremony commemorating the 38th anniversary of the liberation of Jaffa, my warmest greetings:

Thirty-eight years have elapsed since soldiers of the Irgun Zvai Leumi broke through into northern Jaffa in a valiant and courageous operation that led to the liberation of the city and its capitulation to the Hebrew defense forces.

The battle for Jaffa was momentous and costly in terms of casualties. On the Arab side British forces were operating in an attempt to frustrate the action and prevent Jaffa falling into the hands of the Jews. There can be no doubt that the liberation of Jaffa was a decisive landmark in the War of Independence. It is easy to imagine the likely outcome, had Arab Jaffa held out for three more weeks, until the invasion of the Arab armies. If the port of Jaffa had been at the disposal of the invading forces, if they could have established a bridgehead in Jaffa, in the very heart of the Jewish State which was just then coming into being – this would have radically changed the nature of the battle. The liberation of Jaffa was of far-reaching strategic importance, providing Israel with a secure hinterland at a time when her soldiers were stationed on the various front lines, engaged in desperate defensive warfare.

In the name of the nation, honor and gratitude are due to the combatants in the battle for Jaffa, who risked their lives for the sake of the foundation of Israel. Let us bow our heads in respect to the memory of the fallen, and may their names be inscribed forever in the annals of Israel, a part of the legacy of Jewish heroism from generation to generation.

– Chaim Herzog

"At first sight, the conquest of Jaffa was not a part of the Hebrew uprising against British domination," Menahem Begin writes in *The Revolt*:

> but from a political and historical perspective the conquest does indeed constitute an episode in the liberation struggle against the oppressor. There was nothing fortuitous about British determination to preserve Jaffa at all costs.... Jaffa was needed, to threaten Tel Aviv after May 15, 1948.... It was supposed to paralyze the city and tie down Jewish forces. Jaffa was a tool in the hands of the British – perhaps the most important tool – in the attempt to subdue the Hebrew community and force it to appeal for British "mediation" and "stewardship." This plan too was foiled...

"The conquest of Jaffa," Begin concludes, "was one of the fateful operations of the Hebrew War of Independence, but the conquest cost us very dear: 38 [the actual number was 41 – Y.E.] commanders and soldiers, some of our finest men – gave their lives for the survival of Tel Aviv and the survival of the nation."

END OF THE JOURNEY

On every bullet there's an address, who knows which one bears his name?

If Amihai has no address – how will the bullet find him?

So, if you want to be alive when the battle is over, my advice,

My advice is to stand two paces behind him…

My friends, shed no tears for Amihai, it will always be too soon,

Live forever, Amihai, Amihai…

– Yaron London

PORTRAIT OF A FREEDOM FIGHTER

We were all recruited for life,
Only death will release us from the ranks...

From Avraham Stern's poem "Unknown Soldiers"

GIDI IN HIS OWN EYES

Twenty-two years after the War of Liberation, Gidi stated in an interview with Shlomo Lev-Ami:

> If I had to start all over again, I would repeat most of the operations carried out by the Irgun in the years 1945–1948. I don't think that the war between ourselves and the British (and it really was a war) went beyond the limits of decency (to the extent that any war can conform to notions of decency.) I felt no blind hatred towards the British. I had very strong feelings, possibly amounting to hatred – anger certainly – in regard to British policy, and that is what I opposed. But I had nothing against the British as such, or the Tommy as such. On the contrary, I respected the soldiers I fought against, although I despised their political masters, hiding behind their backs. British soldiers I saw as victims themselves of the policies that we opposed. The only instance, besides the hangings, in which there was fury directed against the British – and

I mention the issue of the hangings because that really made a deep impression – occurred after the raid on Acre prison, when a soldier opened fire on men from our side who had surrendered, this accounting for the majority of our losses in that operation. To this day I haven't decided whether to accept the British version, that this was the act of a lone soldier in a state of nervous collapse – "running amok" as they called it – "despite efforts to restrain him on the part of officers and fellow soldiers."

…Unlike Lehi, which prided itself on killing British soldiers and policemen, the Irgun confined itself to military operations, never seeing the killing of British personnel as an objective in itself. Ironically perhaps, conventional warfare ("vegetarian" warfare as the Lehi used to call it, dismissively) accounted for more British lives than any of their cloak-and-dagger activities. The only cases in which we carried out operations designed to kill were acts of reprisal for the executions in Acre – whether this took the form of the hanging of the sergeants or the bombing of a troop train outside Rehovot. In all other operations, if the British suffered casualties, these were inflicted in the course of our raids on strategic objectives. I'm not saying we'd have risked our own lives to spare British lives – far from it – though we were in the habit of giving advance warning before the bombing of installations. Speaking for myself, on several occasions I had the opportunity to kill dozens if not hundreds of defenseless Tommies – but I never did. It would have served no purpose. We only ever set out to kill in response to the hangings.

Two things I have never been reconciled to – then or now: the policy of restraint, which we adopted at the time of the "Saison," a policy for which we paid in blood, hardship, and the loss of freedom of some of our best fighters and commanders. And when speaking of blood, I mean the price that we all paid as a result of the failure to establish the State of Israel in its historical boundaries. And this, to my mind, because we were denied any say in those fateful times when decisions were taken. I thought then, and I'm convinced today, that this was one of the Irgun's greatest failures – that it didn't compete to gain power. Any other group of freedom fighters, anywhere in the world, would have exploited its military achievements in the pursuit of political influence and a place at the head table…

The Irgun seemed to take pride in doing the opposite, and the result – besides the injustice done to all our fighters, excluded from any key national role – was the unnecessary shedding of blood in order to attain the borders of the State as they are today; we could have achieved this at the end of the War of Independence and not 20 years later.

IN THE EYES OF OTHERS

Reserved, stubborn, universally loved. Modest, a lover of action who shunned publicity – that was our Gidi. Seeing him, you would never imagine that with his own hands he had written whole pages in the military history of our people. Where did Gidi come from? He was once a member of the Haganah. Idealism brought him to us…

He was young in years, still in his early twenties, when he took over command of the operational planning section of the Irgun. The deeds of this remarkable young man, whose military talents undoubtedly bordered on genius, the British will remember all their days on this earth. The most vital and most daring arms acquisitions were the fruit of his imagination, or the deed of his own hands: the breaching of Acre Prison, the King David Hotel, the destruction of aircraft and military airfields – most notably at Kastina where 20 heavy bombers were destroyed – all of this was planned by Gidi. He was the inspiration behind all these operations. Together with Shimshon (commander of the Acre raid) he harassed the British mercilessly during the period of martial law.

After Simon the Hasmonean, Gidi deserves to bear the title "Conqueror of Jaffa."

Menahem Begin, *The Revolt*, pp. 67, 72

Gidi's reputation was widespread and reached as far as our place of exile in Africa. Whenever his name was mentioned, there was talk of his astonishing technical aptitude, his inventiveness and his courageous leadership in battle. We were sure that Gidi would find his place in the army and rise to the most senior of ranks, and we were all disappointed and indignant when this did not happen. Begin spoke of him as a military genius of whom the nation of Israel had failed to take full advantage.

I remain convinced that it was action on the part of the underground, the national underground – which drove the British to their decision to leave this land. There is no doubt in my mind that the factors which influenced them in this direction – exerting the greatest influence on British public opinion and senior members of the British Parliament – were the blows inflicted on them, including the King David Hotel, attacks on airfields, on police headquarters, liberation of the Acre prisoners and finally, the ultimate act of the hanging of the sergeants. For all their ruthlessness and vigor, these were the things that forced Bevin and his cronies – against their will – to quit Eretz Israel.

Yitzhak Shamir (former prime minister),
interview with the author, 1997

Amihai Paglin was a veritable genius in all aspects of military operations. He had a talent for thinking in unorthodox terms, finding solutions that would not have occurred to anyone else. The IDF, in my opinion, wasted the potential of a man who could have been, who should have been, chief of staff, but who on account of his IZL background was not given the opportunity to enlist and progress to senior rank.

His ideas and insights were often unconventional, and always worth listening to, even regarding topics outside his normal purview. He wasn't a professional engineer, but he tackled engineering and technical issues with no small success despite his lack of formal training.

In the period of his service as the prime minister's adviser on counterterrorism, I was chairman of the Foreign Affairs and Defense Committee, and I know that in that organization there was surprise and even some derision when Begin appointed Gidi to the post. They were used to jobs like that going to former spooks from the Mossad, IDF generals, or internal appointees. They didn't know him and what he was capable of. But very soon they realized who they were dealing with and in the short time he served there, he contributed significantly to the security of the State.

Moshe Arens, interview with the author, 1996

He wasn't interested in political parties or cliques, or anything of that kind. There was a State of Israel, and a People of Israel, and he was committed to serving both of them.

There was no limit to his imagination, but there was nothing frivolous about it either. It was always accompanied by creative energy and manual dexterity, converting the idea into a minutely crafted creation, one of those inventions that made history.

In Eretz Israel, in the great revolt, the backbone of the British Empire was fractured.

When I meet them, the British, even today – journalists, cultural representatives – they're still incapable of taking in the magnitude of what happened then, how the backbone of a great empire was suddenly broken. Gidi played a central role in the breaking of this spinal cord, and in this capacity he will enter Jewish history, and the history of the region, and the history of Britain.

Shmuel Tamir, funeral oration, 1978

Amihai. Dark hair, deep eyes, the face of a monk. He didn't have a lot to say, but he made a strong impression on me. That impression remains...

He was somebody very special. First of all – he was absolutely fearless. I've known very few men in my lifetime who could match his courage. He simply didn't know the meaning of fear. As far as he was concerned he was invulnerable, and getting caught wasn't part of the equation either. It just couldn't happen, to him or to any of us.

I reckoned he had a monkish, ascetic look about him...tall and dark, wrinkled face, taciturn, moody almost. But when he smiled, or told a joke – that was something else! In a flash, the man changed...

In some ways he differed from us. I reckon it was because he came from "the other side," the institutional one, with the values of the established community, with a socialist perspective, although he came from a patrician, not a proletarian household; he had a sort of Israeliness about him, a kind of simplicity, not what we were used to in our camp, with our adherence to Jabotinsky's "glory" principle – an approach bearing the stamp of Jewish tradition and Jewish religion – as opposed to the revolutionary approach (inspired by the Russian Revolution) adopted by "the other side." We were perhaps more Jewish than him, but he was more Israeli than us. For this reason we sometimes felt a little uneasy in his presence – or perhaps that was because he was head and shoulders above the rest of us and his courage was a byword. And if you set out to analyze his most significant operations, from the perspective of that time when resources were meager, everything was primitive and Wingate was the only strategic icon we had – you can't help but be impressed by the genius of that brave and resourceful commander. Without in any way disparaging the roles played by the other Irgun commanders and their contribution to the success of the revolt, it has to be admitted that the man who personified this revolt – in theory and in practice – was Gidi.

This may also go to explain his rejection of political life and his return to civilian life, at a time when all the others were opting for political careers.

It was as if he left the camp, as if he didn't belong there. He played his part – and left the stage...

Gidi was and remains a figure of extraordinary heroism, head and shoulders above the rest, whose destiny it was to take the lead at one of the critical stages in the war against the British. And when the war was over, his job was done.

The IDF of today couldn't accommodate a man like Amihai and cast him in a central role. The IDF is a big, well-oiled machine, operating according to rigid conventions, no place for a revolutionary with revolutionary ideas, no place for a born individualist who demands the right to think for himself. Men like Gidi have no place in the IDF of today.

The IDF of 1948 – that's a different story. In the IDF of 1948 Gidi could have been one of the top brass, as a field commander or strategic planner, although no doubt his wings would have been clipped. In this respect he resembled Wingate, a misfit in the rigid framework of the British army and yet an exceptional commander and leader of special operations. Gidi would have stood out like a sore thumb in the IDF. That at least is my opinion.

From a psychological point of view he was an individualist, refusing to compromise and intolerant of any opinion or line of thought contrary to his own. For this reason too, the IDF would not have been his natural habitat.

Colonel (Res.) Yehuda Naot (Globman),
interview with the author, 1997

He was a solid young man, muscular, lean, tense, as tense as a coiled spring. His energy was unflagging, his diligence and commitment to the objective immeasurable. He was capable sometimes of going without sleep for two or three nights and working 48 or 72 hours straight, if required. And from the moment he embarked on some enterprise, you could tell he was fired up inside, and would stay that way until the job was done.

He was a composite sort of character, combining all the roles and doing everything with his own hands. The IZL was chronically short of weapons (even worse off than the Haganah) so arms procurement was his first priority, and having obtained the hardware he trained his men, made all the preparations, drew up detailed plans on paper, and went out in person to reconnoiter the ground in advance, to guarantee the success of the mission and secure the retreat routes; he took personal charge and did not leave the field until the last casualty had been evacuated to a place of safety. It should not be forgotten that by the standards of those times, these were actions of outstanding audacity.

Amihai wasn't a man given to speeches, but he knew how to inspire people with his astonishing operational talents, his unflagging commitment to the job in hand, his ability to find a solution to any problem. After his death I received a letter from a friend, living at that time in Switzerland [the reference is to former Palmah activist Zev Levin, at one time Israel's ambassador to Kenya – Y.E.]. When Amihai was heading the IZL's operational branch, the other was serving in the ranks of the Palmah. He writes, "You may not know this, as it's something we've never discussed, but to me and to my generation Gidi was a kind of living legend, the embodiment of the qualities that were so important in our lives at that time – integrity, courage, resourcefulness, and unbounded patriotism. I wasn't one of his subordinates, but his name was a byword in the camps of the Palmah and we spoke of him with admiration…"

If that is the way he was seen by fighters who were not natural supporters of the IZL, you can imagine how the men he commanded felt about him.

Yitzhak Paglin, interview with the author, 1996

I remember a walk that we took together by the Yarkon, looking for lizards and snakes. We sat down in the shade of a tree (I reckon it was somewhere to the north of what is now the municipality of Tel Aviv) and we suddenly got into a bizarre conversation – what would we like to be if we had the choice. I said to him – "I want to be an artist." He said to me – "I want to be a commander." We were young then and didn't yet know what it meant to be a commander – but that was already his ambition.

I asked him, "Commander of what?"

"That depends on the time," he said. "To start with I want to be an underground commander, and if we get a state of our own, I want to be an army commander. No more and no less."

He was capable of taking on unlimited responsibility. Every time he chose or was allotted an assignment, he bore full responsibility for it, all the way to the end. Anyone who was with him knows that.

Before we joined the IZL we did a lot of strolling and talking together. He was a dreamer. He used to say, "We're going to get our independence, independence in a State of Israel." It was such a distant dream then. "I'll do whatever it takes to achieve that," he said.

And I used to ask him, "But Amihai, what happens after that? What do you want to do, apart from getting independence? What do you want to do afterwards?"

And he would reply, "Afterwards, when we have our independence, my job will be to defend it, to make sure it lasts."

David Danon, funeral oration, 1978

What impressed me most of all was the fact that he didn't know what fear was. We all did our best, but I, for example, always needed to overcome physical fear when putting myself in danger. For him, this hardly existed. It's a special kind of phenomenon, one I'd never encountered before. A youth ready for anything, an idealist, and a patriot – not your typical underground fighter. A man without hesitation, without doubts, undeterred and fearless, an individualist, not a compromiser, fighting jealously for the things he believed in. He wasn't an easy man to cooperate with; a figure like that, a naturally gifted leader, can't be treated just like anyone. Jobs and assignments had to conform to his own criteria – and that didn't make life easy.

Eliyahu Lankin,
recorded interview, 1978, Jabotinsky Archives

He was a genius in the way that he planned operations. A slogan summing up Gidi's approach would be something like: if you want to defeat the enemy then get in first – if only by a microsecond. That's the kind of man he was.

I'll focus on the operations that Gidi planned, prepared, and in some cases personally commanded. I'd say the "flagship" operations in Gidi's time, from a historical perspective too, were the bombing of the King David Hotel, the Acre prison break, and the hanging of the sergeants.

The King David Hotel episode effectively began the countdown to British withdrawal from the country.

The second operation, the Acre prison raid, was a carefully coordinated attack by commando forces, backed up by meticulous intelligence, the location of weak spots, the "soft underbelly" where the wall could be breached, exploitation of the soldiers' combat experience, and the inspired use of camouflage and disguise – all this was characteristic of Gidi's approach. He did not lead the raid in person but it was his operation, which he planned and for which he took full responsibility.

The last straw as far as the British were concerned was the hanging of the sergeants. It was a tough decision to make – and implementing it was a nightmare – but it served its purpose. As a direct result, no more IZL or Lehi fighters went to the gallows in this land.

Elizabeth Monroe, a British historian and Oxford professor, quotes from a cable sent by the British minister for war to the GOC Middle East two days after the hanging of the sergeants: preparations were to be made for the evacuation of British troops from Palestine and their transfer to camps in Egypt.

One needs only to look at the scale of the three actions cited above – all of them planned by Gidi, and for which he took responsibility as operations officer – to appreciate the importance of Gidi's role in the removal of British power from Eretz Israel.

Yitzhak Avinoam, interview with the author, 1996

Between Shraga Ellis (Haim Toyte) and Amihai Paglin there were ties of friendship that led to fruitful cooperation from the first day of their acquaintance. Shraga still clearly remembers, as if it were yesterday, the first time they met:

It was Eitan Livni's idea. This was the period following the split from Avraham Stern, and like many others I decided to take a short break from IZL activities, for the first time since joining up in 1938.

Then one fine summer day in 1943, Eitan Livni contacted me. "It's time you came back to full-time service in the Irgun," he said. "I'm sending a young fellow along to discuss it with you. He's someone you ought to meet anyway. I'm sure you'll hit it off." At that time I already had my own shop for welding and plumbing supplies; I was beginning to make money, and acquiring a taste for it… I wasn't overjoyed at the thought of returning to underground activities, and at the ripe old age of 21 I reckoned I was a bit long in the tooth for that kind of thing. But Eitan insisted and I didn't want to spoil the friendly relationship that we'd developed over the years. "Okay," I said, "send the guy along and we'll see…"

When he appeared, he needed no introduction. I'd never seen him before but I knew this was the man: tall, dark eyes, wearing shorts and biblical-style sandals. He looked around briefly and waited patiently by the door while I negotiated with one of my customers. Seeing him standing there leaning casually – a characteristic posture, as I discovered later – I couldn't help comparing him with Garibaldi, the hero of Italy's liberation war. (A film about him was showing in a Tel Aviv movie theater at the time, and his portrait was a familiar sight on posters around town.)

When I'd concluded my business, he said to me with a faint smile, "You must be Shraga."

"Yes," I replied, "and you're definitely Garibaldi…"

"Not yet," he said, and we both burst out laughing.

At that moment I understood for the first time the concept of chemistry in human relationships.

Once, when I was going through a hard time, I came and poured out my heart to him. He listened to me patiently and when I had finished he gave me a long look, and what he said to me, in that quiet voice of his, still echoes in my ears and will be with me for years to come, "Haim," he said, "we're all alive by a miracle. I'm not a fatalist in the absolute sense of the word, but I believe that what has to happen is almost impossible to prevent. This is our life and this is the destiny that we have chosen of our own free will. So take it easy, and just keep on going along the course you've set for yourself. That's all we can do, keep going towards the objective we have set ourselves. Beyond that – what has to happen, will happen anyway."

With these words, spoken in a calm and relaxed tone, Amihai Paglin effectively expressed the whole of his life's philosophy, the guiding principle behind all his actions, from the dawn of his youth and throughout his turbulent career, his audacious operations and the unremitting war he waged against the British between the years 1944 and 1948 – advancing resolutely towards the objective, without fear and without hesitation – until the cruel hand of fate caught up with him in 1978, the disastrous road accident in which he lost his life, together with his wife Tzipora, his constant and loyal companion from the underground days to the tragic end.

Shraga Ellis, recorded interview with the author, 1996

TZIPORA

"She was capable of loving him without limit, as he was. She knew his courage, understood the circumstances of his childhood, and how they had shaped him as a man. She admired him to the last day. She followed him, even into uncharted territory, and her hand was constantly in his," said their comrade-in-arms, neighbor, and close friend, Shmuel Tamir, in his funeral oration for Tzipora and Amihai. He added:

Tzipora, who was also capable of disagreeing with him, of taking him to task with her profound wisdom and her delicate wit, did this over the years with love that was infinite, in all conditions and unconditionally. She experienced with him all the achievements, all the heartaches, was with him in times of joy and times of dejection – at home, in the factory, in night actions, in attacks on airfields – until their final moment.

I remember, when it was my job to train her in broadcasting on "Voice of Fighting Zion." A charming, attractive girl, very keen to learn, to get it right so she could inspire our people in the underground, the whole of Israel.

Tzipora, who went into action and never faltered – one girl, among scores of young men – that was Tzipora, who gave Gidi the things most precious to him of all: family and children.

They are together now, Amihai and Tzipora, as they were in life and as they will remain in our hearts. And when their story is told, one of the great legends of Israel, the tale of Gidi will be entwined with the tale of Tzipora, who was with him to the end of the road.[1]

Describing Tzipora – wife, friend, mother, woman, who stood always at Gidi's side, not behind him, in total partnership, on fine days and rainy days – her close friend from teenage years on, Devora Nehushtan, says:

Tzipora, or Tzipi or Tzipa as we used to call her affectionately, was a very special person. Anyone who took the trouble to look beyond her glasses saw clear blue eyes, and a little smile at the corners of her mouth. She was soft-spoken, elegant, and restrained. There was a pleasant air about her and she had a refined, endearing sense of humor.

The first impression was one of fragility, but this was misleading. She was forged from solid material, an exceptional combination of steel and silk: gentle on the outside, strong-minded within.

Where did this strength of mind come from? First of all, from the family that she belonged to. The history of the Perl family of Safed is strewn with a number of jewels. Her mother was a descendant of the Baal Shem Tov, one of those descendants who immigrated to this country. This is one of the roots. Another strand in the Perl family derives from the founders of Mahanaim, the Galilean settlement. The other branch of the family settled in Safed in the first half of the last century. It's no wonder that these deep roots in Jewish tradition, combined with Zionist nationalism, produced the new generation whom we came to know so well in the days of our active service in Betar and the IZL.

The Perl family was like an institution in Safed, a well-known open house. The Herzliya Hotel served as a haven for underground activists, as well as accommodating official guests now and then. And talking of hospitality, most of the leaders of the IZL stayed there at one time or another – including the boss himself, Menahem Begin!

I got to know Tzipora in Tel Aviv in the 1940s, when she was still a pupil at the Herzliya High School. She was a Betarist; it had been in

---

1. Funeral oration by Shmuel Tamir, 1978.

her blood since Safed days. Afterwards – inevitably – she was active in the IZL, doing the full range of activities demanded of her, from making explosives to reconnaissance, from surveillance to administering first aid. She was in combat too.... She took part in the blowing up of planes at Kastina, together with Mitzi Tau. They were both there.

Later, through her connections with Amihai, she got to know a lot about what was going on. She kept masses of information stored up inside.... There were times when she clashed with the leadership, but she tended to be reticent. There was nothing arrogant about her. When people know a lot they feel flattered, they become conceited. There was no hint of this with Tzipora. She was and always remained modest; what she knew and what she heard she kept deep down, showing nothing on her face.

Tzipora's parties at 4 Reines Street in Tel Aviv were something special. We all loved going to them, and even gatecrashers were made welcome.

And there were hard times too, and she had the fortitude to get through them, with head held high and spirit unbroken. When Amihai was arrested on *Altalena* day (he was arrested but escaped), she didn't know what had become of him; for some time she didn't even know if he was alive or dead. The atmosphere was tense, especially in his parents' house where the fate of Neriel, his burial place unknown, still cast a dark shadow. For the benefit of the parents, Tzipora did her best to hide her concern, and put on a display of optimism....

I'll conclude with the last conversation I had with her, not long before the day of the tragedy. In the Aryeh Ben-Eliezer conference center there was going to be a lecture on the role of women in the underground. I'd been asked to invite some female veterans of the IZL, who would contribute accounts of their experiences and privations on active service. I phoned Tzipora. I felt with every fiber of my being that her participation, her revelations of that period in her life, would provide an excellent example for the young generation. I asked her, pleaded with her, "Tzipora my dear, please, please come." But she refused to be exposed like that, she didn't feel comfortable talking about herself. It just wasn't her way. Her modesty and her need for privacy were stronger than my powers of persuasion.

That was Tzipora, and that's how we shall all remember her – wise, pleasant, a truly noble lady.[2]

"From the moment we met her we called her Tzipa, and this affectionate nickname stuck to her till the end," Eitan Livni says of her. "She was a girl-warrior who turned into a woman of valor and everything it says in that Psalm is true of her; in the middle it goes, 'Her husband is known in the gates,' and it ends, 'And praise her deeds in the gates.' Perhaps her deeds haven't been praised as much as they deserve." And he goes on to say:

Tzipora was a native of Safed, and she came from a hotbed of IZL activists, as Devora Nehushtan has already pointed out. Both her brothers – Shmuel and Daniel – were commanders in the "Ma'amad." When the revolt began most of our people in Safed were rounded up in the first wave of arrests, including her brothers.

Safed was no longer serving as a consolidated branch, and what else did we have in Galilee besides Safed?

And then we turned to Tzipa, one of the activists in the Tel Aviv combat unit, and asked her to go back to Safed and reorganize the branch there. This was the only branch of the Irgun Zvai Leumi ever to be headed by a woman – that woman being Tzipa. And from nothing, it began to flourish again. These were tough times; the "Saison" was in progress. And she recruited boys and girls of 15 and 16. She kept the flame alive and when the siege of Safed came during the War of Liberation, those youngsters recruited by Tzipora played a vital role.

Her mission completed, she returned to active service in Tel Aviv. The number of those chosen to take part in operations was limited and selective. Everyone wanted a piece of the action. She exploited the patronage that she enjoyed in a positive way and participated in a relatively high number of operations, some of them at the side of her future husband, none other than Gidi.

War and dangers united them. To our sorrow, bitter fate also struck them down together.

---

2. Zvi Lavi's interview with Devora Nehushtan, 1978; cassette in the author's possession.

FOREVER AMIHAI

Sabbath Day, January 28, 1978. Blue skies and gentle spring sunshine.

Amihai has just returned from a visit to the USA and the whole family is setting out to visit the daughter, Galia, in Haifa. The party includes Neri and his girlfriend.

On the way back they pass Usafiyya. Gidi knows a good restaurant there. They stop off for a while and then resume their journey. At the Zikhron-Faradis intersection there is an argument between Neri and Amihai – which route are they to take, the old or the new?

They decide in favor of the coast road. Neri takes the wheel, his girlfriend beside him. The parents – Tzipora and Amihai – relax in the back. The road is smooth and traffic sparse. A small sedan appears on the horizon. Hardly worth a second glance.

Suddenly it happens. The oncoming vehicle veers from its lane and is racing towards them, head on. Neri tries frantically to swing the wheel to the left – but it's too late. A dull thud – and then silence.

Neri woke up in the hospital in Hadera. Beside him lay his father, his face bandaged.

"What happened?" he asked.

"An accident," Amihai murmured.

"Who was driving?"

"You were!"

It was all a blur. He remembered nothing.

Close by lay his girlfriend, with a cracked vertebra.

He felt as if his head would explode. Amihai had suffered injuries to the eye, and the hand – besides internal injuries. Before he could ask about his mother, Neri lost consciousness again.

Tzipora had already breathed her last.

For 30 days Amihai fought for his life in the hospital in Tel Hashomer. Just when it seemed he was finally recovering, a tiny blood clot defeated him.

Gidi, who had emerged unscathed from scores of battles, was laid low by a minuscule embolism to the brain. He died on Sabbath Eve, February 28, 1978 – exactly a month after the accident.

"We'd planned a party for him, a 'liberation party' we called it," David Danon recalls sadly:

> When he came out of hospital, we were all going to sing together. What were we going to sing? Something from the underground days maybe – a bit of nostalgia!
>
> Then, as I was driving along, I heard a familiar sound on the car radio – and my heart skipped a beat: "Live Forever, Amihai" – a song by Yaron London. We all knew the song, and it was an obvious choice. I practiced the guitar accompaniment and the moment Amihai walked in the door, we would sing a rousing chorus of "Live Forever, Amihai."
>
> It didn't work out that way.[1]

---

1. Author's interview with Professor David Danon, August 5, 1996.

SOURCES

GENERAL

1. *Testimonies and Documents* preserved in various archives: Beit Jabotinsky Archives; Haganah Historical Archives; Yad Tabenkin Archives; Beit Gidi Museum; IDF Museum; Jabotinsky Museum – as detailed in the notes to individual chapters.

2. *Documents from the British* CID located in the Haganah Historical Archives, Jabotinsky Archives, and the British Public Record Office (PRO), as detailed in the notes to individual chapters.

3. Recorded interviews with the author:
Bezalel Amitzur – 1997
Moshe Arens – 1991
Yitzhak Avinoam – 1996
Zvi Barzel (Cactus) – 1997, 1999
Aharon Ben-Ami – 1997
Aharon Cohen – 1997
Professor David Danon – 1996
Yehoshua Diamant (Amos) – 1997
Shraga Ellis (Haim Toyte) – 1996
Nicho Garman – 1996
Galia Giladi (Paglin) – 1997
Yosef Haddad (Yoska Altalena) – 1997
Shlomo Lev-Ami – 1996
Shimon Levi (Gad) – 1997
Yuval Meiri–1997

Yosef Nahmias – 1997
Colonel (Res.) Yehuda Naot (Globman) – 1997
Azriel Nevo – 1996
Uzi Ornan – 1997
Amihai Paglin (Gidi) – 1969
Neriel Paglin – 1996
Yitzhak Paglin – 1996
Zvi Pooni (Yuval) – 1997
Miriam Perl – 1997
Shmuel Perl – 1997
Isaac Raviv – 1997
Aharon Sadovnik – 1998
Aharon Schechter – 1997
Yitzhak Schulman (Shaika) – 1997
Eliyah Schwartz – 1997
Yitzhak Shamir – 1997
Nahum Slonim – 1996
Shula Slonim – 1997
Eliyahu Spector – 1997
Elimelech Spiegel – 1997
Ruth Tamir – 1997
David Tehori (Kister) – 1999 (an oral interview, not taped)
Raphael Vardi – 1997
Baruch Weiner (Konous) – 1996–1997
Col. Yosef Yariv – 1997
Pesah Zissin – 1997

4. Series of recorded interviews with Zvi Lavi in 1978 with comrades-in-arms and family members of Amihai Paglin (Gidi).

5. Radio Programs
"Ari be-soger" [Caged lion], Galei Zahal
"Kadei ha-halav she-ra'amu" [Milk churns that roared], Kol Israel – channel one, June 20, 1969

For "The Fateful Train"
Statement by Baruch Weiner (Konous) – March 1, 1977, Jabotinsky Archives
Lecture at memorial evening for Gidi – March 11, 1993, Jabotinsky Archives
Interview by Y. Amarami with Konous – March 1, 1977, Jabotinsky Archives
Author's interview with Konous – Aug. 4, 1996
Author's interview with Aharon Schechter – Feb. 17, 1997
Author's interview with Yuval Meiri – Jan. 5, 1997

Statement by Zvi Pooni (Yuval, Uri) – Jan. 5, 1997, Jabotinsky Archives
Author's interview with Zvi Pooni – 1997
Y. Ophir's interview with Shraga Ellis (Haim Toyte) – Aug. 12, 1957, Jabotinsky Archives
Recorded statement by David Abramowitz (Ben-Zev) – Jabotinsky Archives
Statement by Menachem Binder, Ben-Dor (Yosef) – IDF Archives
Review of "The Weapons Train" – Jabotinsky Archives
Recorded statement by Yitzhak Schulman (Shaika) – Jabotinsky Archives
Author's interview with Yitzhak Schulman (Shaika) – March 22, 1997
Diary of Eliyahu Schwartz – April 18, 1947 (photocopy of the diary in possession of the
     author)
Author's interview with Eliyahu Schwartz – September 7, 1997
Author's interview with Yosef Haddad (Yoske Altalena) – July 21, 1997
Memoirs of Yoska Altalena – *Yediot Aharonot*, April 21, 1957
Author's interview with Aharon Cohen (Aharale) – July 21, 1997; September 7, 1997
Author's interview with Zvi Barzel (Cactus) – June 8, 1997
Author's interview with Yehoshua Diamant (Amos) – September 16, 1997
Author's interview with Shimon Levi (Gad) – September 16, 1997
Statement by Eliezer Zemler (Jackson) – recorded reel, Jabotinsky Archives
Menahem Begin, *The Revolt* [Hebrew], pp. 429–30
Author's interview with Neriel Paglin – 1996

For "How It Began"
David Niv, *Ma'arakhot ha-Irgun ha-Tzeva'i ha-Le'umi 1944–1946* [The battles of the Irgun
     Zvai Leumi] [Hebrew]
Eitan Livni, *Ha-Ma'amad*, p. 159
Eliezer Pedahzur (Gad), *Night in the Underground* [Hebrew]
Yehoshua Ophir, *The IZL in Petah Tikva* [Hebrew], pp. 186–88

For "The Raid on the Tel Nof Camp"
Dov Goldstein's interview with Amihai Paglin – *Ma'ariv*, September 29, 1972
E. Pedahzur (Gad), *Seventeen in a Jeep* [Hebrew]
Author's interview with Baruch Weiner (Konous), 1999

For "The Battle for Jaffa"
Begin, Menahem, *The Revolt*
Ben-Ami, Aharon (Avishai), "Flight of the Shell," *Jaffa Album* [Hebrew], Jabotinsky
     Archives
Ben-Yakir, Eliezer (Shaul), "The Battle for Jaffa," Jabotinsky Archives
Elazar, David, "Liberation of Jaffa in 1948" [Hebrew], Jabotinsky Archives
Goldstein, Zev (Yoel), account, *Jaffa Album* [Hebrew], Jabotinsky Archives
Gur-Arye, Zvi, account, *Jaffa Album* [Hebrew], Jabotinsky Archives
Katz, Eli, account (April 25, 1957), *Jaffa Album* [Hebrew], Jabotinsky Archives

Lazar, Haim, *Conquest of Jaffa* [Hebrew]

Malitzki, Menachem, "Wall-to-Wall War" [Hebrew], *Makor Rishon*, Fifty Years to the Capture of Jaffa (1988)

Olitzky, Yosef, *Mi-me'ora'ot le-milhamah* [From riots to war]

Paglin, Amihai (Gidi), interview with Shlomo Lev-Ami (January 27, 1970), Institute for Contemporary Jewry, Documentation Division, Hebrew University of Jerusalem

Paglin, Amihai (Gidi), "Tactics in Taking Jaffa," *Herut* (April 19, 1949)

Paglin, Amihai (Gidi), Jaffa Operation, testimony by Zvi Shimshi (September 13, 1957), Jabotinsky Archives

Recanati, David, account by Zvi Shimshi (July 7, 1957), *Jaffa Album* [Hebrew], Jabotinsky Archives

Schertzer, Abba (Gundar Michael), testimony by Zvi Shimshi (March 19, 1957), *Jaffa Album* [Hebrew], Jabotinsky Archives

Shabtai, Nadiv (Ahituv), account (July 7, 1957), *Jaffa Album* [Hebrew], Jabotinsky Archives

Shani, Aharon, in recorded interview, Jabotinsky Archives

Sudit, Eliezer (Kabtzan), Fighting in Jaffa, personal journal, Jabotinsky Archives

"Thirtieth Anniversary of the Liberation of Jaffa," *Jaffa Album* [Hebrew], Jabotinsky Archives

Weiner, Baruch (Konous), account about the armor in the battles for Jaffa, *Jaffa Album* [Hebrew], Jabotinsky Archives

Wilenchuk, Yitzhak, account (April 25, 1957), *Jaffa Album* [Hebrew], Jabotinsky Archives

SELECT BIBLIOGRAPHY

ENGLISH

Begin, Menahem. *The Revolt*. London: W.H. Allen, 1951 (quotations are from the New York: Nash, 1977 edition).

Bethell, Nicholas. *The Palestine Triangle: The Struggle between the British, the Jews and the Arabs, 1935–48*. London: Andre Deutsch, 1979.

Bell, J. Bowyer. *Terror Out of Zion: Irgun Zvai Leumi, LEHI, and the Palestine underground, 1929–1949*. New York: St. Martin's, 1977.

Charters, David A. *The British Army and Jewish Insurgency in Palestine, 1945–47*. London: Macmillan Press in association with King's College, 1989.

Clarke, Thurston. *By Blood and Fire*. London: Hutchinson, 1981.

Cunningham, Alan. "Palestine: The Last Days of the Mandate." *International Affairs* 24, no. 4 (1948).

End of Empire (Palestine). London: Granada in association with Channel Four Television Co. and Granada Television, 1985.

Gal, Reuven. *A Portrait of the Israeli Soldier*. Westport, CT: Greenwood Press, 1986.

Gitlin, Jan. *The Conquest of Acre Fortress*. Tel Aviv: Hadar, 1962.

Hecht, Ben. *Perfidy*. New York: Messner, 1961.

Horne, Edward. *A Job Well Done*. Eastwood: Anchor Press, 1982.

Johnson, Paul. *A History of the Modern World: From 1917 to the 1980s*. London: Weidenfeld and Nicolson, 1983.

Katz, Samuel. *Days of Fire*. Garden City, NY: Doubleday, 1968.

Louis, Wm. Roger, and Robert W. Stookey, eds. *The End of the Palestine Mandate*. Austin: University of Texas Press, 1986.

Meinertzhagen, Colonel Richard. *Middle East Diary, 1917–1956*. London: Cresset Press, 1959.

Montgomery of Alamein, Sir Bernard Law. *The Memoirs of Field Marshal the Viscount Montgomery of Alamein*. New York: New American Library, 1959.

Silver, Eric. *Begin: A Biography*. London: Weidenfeld and Nicolson, 1984.

Wilson, R. Dare. *Cordon and Search: With 6th Airborne Division in Palestine*. Aldershot: Gale and Polden, 1949.

Zadka, Saul. *Blood in Zion: How the Jewish Guerrillas Drove the British Out of Palestine*. London: Brasseys, 1995.

HEBREW

Alfasi, Yitzhak. *Kol kinuyei ha-Etzel* [All the ephithets for Etzel]. Tel Aviv: Talpiyot, 1996.

Amitzur, Ilan. *Amerika, Britanyah ve-Eretz Yisrael* [America, Britain, and the Land of Israel]. Jerusalem: Yad Yitzhak Ben-Zvi, 1979.

Amrami, Yaakov (Yoel). *Ha-devarim gedolim hem me-itanu* [Things are bigger than we are]. Tel Aviv: Hadar, 1994.

Amrami, Yaakov, and Arye Melitz. *Divrei ha-yamim le-Milhemet ha-Shihrur* [History of the War of Independence]. Tel Aviv: Shelah, 1951.

Banai, Yaakov. *Hayalim almonim* [Unknown soldiers]. Tel Aviv: privately published, 1958.

Baranes, Hayya. *Olei ha-gardom* [Martyrs of the gallows]. Jerusalem: ha-Midrashah ha-leumit, 1978.

Ben-Gurion, David. *Likrat ketz ha-Mandat* [Toward the end of the Mandate]. Tel Aviv: Am Oved, 1993.

Cathedra 15 (1980).

Cohen, Geulah. *Mifgash histori: Mefakdei ha-Haganah, ha-Etzel, ve-ha-Lehi mi-saviv le-shulhan meruba* [A historical meeting: Commanders of the Haganah, Etzel, and Lehi around a square table]. Tel Aviv: Hotsa'at Yair, 1986.

Dror, S. *Neshek Briti: Le-mahsanei Etzel* [British weapons: To the Etzel storehouses]. Sifriat ha-Mered, vol. 3. Tel Aviv: Hadar, 1975.

Elam, Yigal. *Ha-Haganah: Ha-derekh ha-Tziyyonit el ha-ko'ah* [The Haganah: The Zionist way to power]. Tel Aviv: Zmora Bitan, 1979.

Eldad (Scheib), Israel. *Ma'aser rishon* [First tithe]. Tel Aviv: Hotza'at Hug Vatikei Lehi, 1963.

———. *Potzatznu metosim Britiyim* [We blew up British planes]. Sifriat ha-Mered, vol. 1. Tel Aviv: Hadar, 1975.

———. *Mi-nesharim kali me-arayot gaveru* [Swifter than eagles, braver than lions]. Sifriat ha-Mered, vol. 1. Tel Aviv: Hadar, 1975.

Eshel, Aryeh. *Shevirat ha-gardomim* [Defeating the gallows]. Tel Aviv: Zmora Bitan, 1990.

Evron, Yosef. *Magen ve-Romah* [Shield and spear]. Tel Aviv: Ministry of Defense, 1992.

Gilad, Haim. *Be-tsel ha-gardom: Sipurei shel mefaked be-Etzel* [In the shadow of the gallows: The story of an Etzel commander]. Tel Aviv: Israel Defense Ministry, 1983.

Gitlin, Jan. *Peritzat Mivtzar Akko*. Published in English as *The Conquest of Acre Fortress*. Tel Aviv: Hadar, 1962.

Golani, Yardena. *Ha-mitos shel Deir-Yassin* [The myth of Deir-Yassin]. Sifriat ha-Mered, vol. 7. Tel Aviv: Hadar, 1976.

Hacohen, David. *Et le-saper* [Time to tell]. Tel Aviv: Am Oved, 1974. Published in English as *Time to Tell: An Israeli Life, 1898–1984*. New York: Cornwall Books, 1985.

Hoffman, Bruce. *Iyyunim be-mahtarot u-ve-meri: Kishalon ha-estrategiyyah ha-tzeva'it ha-Britit be-Eretz Yisrael 1939–1947* [*The failure of British military strategy in Palestine 1939–1947*]. Ramat Gan: Bar-Ilan University, 1983.

Hovav, Meir. *Gal: Deyokan shel lohem* [Gal: Portrait of a fighter]. Tel Aviv: Association for the Dissemination of National Awareness, 1990.

Kanaan, Haviv. *Gardomim be-Netanya* [Gallows in Netanya]. Tel Aviv: Hadar, 1976.

Kister, Yosef. *Ha-Irgun ha-Tzeva'i ha-Le'umi 1931–1948* [The IZL 1931–1948]. Tel Aviv: Association for the Etzel Museum, 1998.

Lapan, Asa. *Ha-Sh"Y – Sherut ha-Yedi'ot* [The Sh-Y – the Intelligence Office]. Tel Aviv: Ministry of Defense, 1997.

Lapidot, Yehuda. *Be-lahav ha-mered* [In the flame of the rebellion]. Tel Aviv: Ministry of Defense, 1996.

Lazar (Lita'i), Haim. *Kibbush Yafo* [Conquest of Jaffa]. Tel Aviv: Shelah, 1951.

———. *Mivtzar Akko* [Acre Fortress]. Tel Aviv: Shelah, 1953.

Lev-Ami, Shlomo. *Ba-ma'avak u-va-mered* [In the struggle and in the rebellion]. Tel Aviv: Ministry of Defense, 1978.

Levy, Moshe (Yariv). *Mivtza he-havit ha-me'ofefet* [The operation of the flying churn]. Sifriat ha-Mered, vol. 13. Tel Aviv: Hadar, 1979.

Livni, Eitan. *Ha-Ma'amad* [The Stand (internal name for Etzel)]. Tel Aviv: Idanim, 1987.

Melitz, Arye. *Ve-kakh hithil ha-mered* [And this is how the rebellion began]. Sifriat ha-Mered, vol. 1. Tel Aviv: Hadar, 1975.

Naor, Mordecai, ed. *Leksikon koah ha-magen ha-Haganah* [Lexicon of the Haganah defense force]. Tel Aviv: Ministry of Defense, 1992.

Nedava, Yosef. *Darko shel lohem Ivri: Sipur hayav shel Yosef Simhon* [Way of a Hebrew fighter: The life story of Yosef Simhon]. Jerusalem: Merhav, 1965.

———. *Mi geresh et ha-Britim mi-Eretz Yisrael* [Who drove the British out of Palestine]. Tel Aviv: Association for the Dissemination of National Awareness, 1988.

———. *Sefer olei ha-gardom* [Martyrs of the gallows]. Tel Aviv: Shelah, 1952 (reprinted 1966, 1974).

Niv, David. *Ma'arakhot ha-Irgun ha-Tzeva'i ha-Le'umi 1944–1946* [Battles of the IZL 1944–1946]. Part 5, *The Rebellion (1946–47)*. Tel Aviv: Hadar, 1976.

———. *Ma'arakhot ha-Irgun ha-Tzeva'ii ha-Le'umi* [Battles of the IZL]. Part 6, *Open War (1947–48)*. Tel Aviv: Hadar, 1980.

Olitzky, Yosef. *Mi-me'ora'ot le-milhamah* [From riots to war]. Tel Aviv: Mifkedet Haga Tel Aviv, 1951.

Ophir, Yehoshua. *Ha-Irgun ha-Tzeva'i ha-Le'umi Petah Tikva* [The IZL Petah Tikva]. Kfar Saba: Intermedia, 1995.

Pedahzur, Eliezer (Gad). *Shiva-asar ba-jip* [Seventeen in the jeep]. Sifriat ha-Mered, vol. 2. Tel Aviv: Hadar, 1975.

———. *Layla ba-mahteret* [Night in the underground]. Sifriat ha-Mered, vol. 4. Tel Aviv: Hadar, 1975.

Shai, Avraham. *Kadei ha-halav she-ra'amu* [The milk churns that roared]. Sifriat ha-Mered, vol. 10. Tel Aviv: Hadar, 1977.

Shavit, Yaakov. *Maʾavak mered meri* [Struggle, revolution, rebellion]. Jerusalem: Shazar, 1987.

Shomron-Eli, David. *Guyasnu le-khol ha-hayyim* [We were drafted for life]. Tel Aviv: Yair, 1997.

Shmulewitz, Matti. *Be-yamim adumim* [On red days]. Tel Aviv: Ministry of Defense, 1978.

Slutzky, Yehuda. *Sefer toledot ha-Haganah* [History of the Haganah]. Vol. 3, *From Struggle to War*, part 2. Tel Aviv: Am Oved, 1972.

Yaakobi, Shlomo. *Hofshi!* [Free!]. Kiryat Ono: H. Yaakobi Hafakot, 1997.

Yellin-Mor, Natan. *Lohamei herut Yisrael* [Israel freedom fighters]. Jerusalem: Shakmona, 1975.

ORGANISATION OF THE IRGUN ZVAI LEUMI

1.   The Irgun Zvai Leumi is organised in three groups which are:

    1)   The Fighting Group, known as HOG with an estimated strength of 400 of whom 250 are in Tel Aviv and surrounding area, 150 in Jerusalem area and 100 in Haifa and Northern Palestine.

    2)   The Propaganda Group, known as HOTAM, the largest group with an estimated strength of 4,000 persons of all ages from 15 to 60 years and engaged in the writing, preparation and dissemination of propaganda and the collection of funds.

    3)   The Intelligence Group, organised in an internal security section and an external espionage section; the strength of this Group is estimated at about 500.

2.   The Fighting Group (HOG), as its name implies, carries out armed activities and appears to include a large element of trained ex-soldiers of the Palestinian units, a percentage of ex-soldiers of the Polish army, a number of ex-auxiliary Police and immigrants from Europe who may have had experience of irregular warfare. A number of recent recruits have been deserters from the Hagana.

3.   The Group's fighting qualities are not considered to be good and it has depended to date for its success upon daring, intimidation, surprise and weak opposition.

4.   The High Command of the IZL is located at Tel Aviv; plans for sabotage and other armed activities are made by District Commanders in the areas and submitted to the High Command for approval.

5.   The Fighting Group is organised in three districts, based on Tel Aviv, Jerusalem and Haifa and in each District the Groups are sub-divided into Combat Groups, believed to number approximately 15 men each. These groups do not operate in the area in which they live and move out of their respective areas when an operation is to take place in order to avoid being involved in subsequent Police and Military operations.

6.   A proportion of members of the Fighting Groups are employed on paid full time duties, salary being at the rate of £ 30 per month with expenses allowed up to a further £ 30 per month.

7.   Arms are said to be in short supply at present and difficulty has been experienced recently in financing the purchase of further arms. Air-raid shelters and basements have been used for storage of arms and explosives. Limpet mines similar in type

2/

Appendix E – Appendix I to CID Report, "Organisation of the Irgun Zvai Leumi"

slan for distribution to foreign correspondents; copies are handed over in the Eden Hotel.

The reason for frequent acts of terrorism in Jerusalem is that all Government buildings are centred there.

The Military Court Jerusalem is a likely target and has already been looked over.

The Area Commander I.L. Jerusalem is a well dressed, smart looking man, 2? years of age, thick set, 5' 8" or 9", who is well educated and speaks fluent Arabic.

When two barrels of high explosive were placed on a ... vehicle in Nassabi Street, Haifa, in June last, a British police sergeant entered a grocer's shop in the building next to that from which the explosives were taken. The barrels had been kept in an air raid shelter.

I.L. will pay compensation to Jews who have cars lost or damaged or sustain any damage due to IZL activities.

Desertification is definitely in charge of the Stern Group. Freidman Yellin is a suspect. The strength of the Stern Group throughout Palestine is not more than five hundred. The Group contains a high percentage of highly educated persons and their propaganda is of a higher standard than the IZL.

IZL would cease activities if Government allowed 100,000 Jews to enter Palestine. They would resume activities against the land restrictions immediately the immigrants had arrived. The Stern Group would probably do likewise but it not they would be dealt with by IZL or Haganah or both.

IZL and Stern Group are weak in Haifa because the Histadruth is strong. Haifa is an industrial town whilst Tel Aviv and Jerusalem are business towns.

IZL are sure that Government cannot suppress terrorism and state that there is no answer to terror except terror.

The Haganah are well disciplined and trained but disagree generally with the present policy of inactivity. Most new recruits to IZL and Stern are from Haganah sources. The strength of the IZL is estimated at 5,000.

The deputy commander of IZL in Jerusalem lives in a bungalow in Agabha Street, which is between the houses of Pishin and Gronsky. He is about 5' 8" well dressed, good looking, 2? years of age, probably Palestinian, well educated, believed to be an ex-Army officer, medium build with dark brown hair and is sometimes accompanied by a small white fox terrier.

Appendix D – Report No. 3, Reinhold's Statement of IZL History, Objectives, and Relationships to Other Underground Groups

Early in 1946 IZL decided to sabotage British
Embassies and Consulates wherever possible.   France,
Italy and U.S.A. were considered easiest and Egypt
and Syria were considered as possible targets. IZL
members have definitely left Palestine to organize
groups and a group stronger than the Irgun has already
been formed in Italy.   A group has already been
formed in France, it is not so strong as the Italian
group.   Attempts to carry out acts of sabotage in
U.K. will definitely be attempted.

The man in command of Combat Groups in Jerusalem
until 22.7.46 was known as "Shimon."   He is at present
in charge of Combat Groups in Rehovot area.   5' 9" or
10", medium build, thin smooth black hair, sun-tanned
complexion, looks like a Sephardic Jew, 30 years of
age.

Rennik has a sister residing at Shderot No. 3,
Beth Galin.

It is doubtful if Begin ever existed.   Old
timers have never seen him.

The IZL have come to the conclusion that the
only method to attack the C.M.L. Haifa which will
be successful, is by the use of gliders or ballons.
Glider pilots are available.

Countrywide attacks on railways are carried out
for their nuisance value.

The IZL recently purchased a large quantity of
dynamite from Arabs.   The melignite was mixed with
sand and three heavy charges placed under bridges in
the Haifa District failed to explode.

A man known as "Shimon" sabotaged the pipes outside
the C.M.L. when other acts of sabotage were carried out
on 8th September, 194 .   This man led the attacks on
the Haifa banks and is now under arrest.   He is a
Bulgarian with blond, curly, wavy hair, 5' 5", medium
build.   He was accompanied by a man named "Khallak"
who has since been arrested.

IZL arms and explosives are conveyed from town
to town wrapped in rags and tied to the chassis of
lorries and cars.   IZL are short of arms owing to
shortage of money.   All big merchants contribute to
IZL funds.   The Hagana could stop it - they could
stop everything.   IZL monthly running expenses are
£4,000.   This includes salaries, care of prisoners,
rents etc.   Attack on the Hablus bank was expected
to yield £ 100,000 but yielded only £ 5,000. Result
was considered disappointing. Arabs supplied the
information that the £ 100,000 was there.

The Stern Group have plenty of arms and explosives
and plenty of money.

All IZL and Stern Group propaganda is printed in
Tel Aviv and distributed mostly by messengers the majority
of whom are men. Special communiques are typed in Jeru-

Appendix D – Report No. 3, Reinhold's Statement of IZL History,
Objectives, and Relationships to Other Underground Groups

-3-

The limpets are for use with AFV's and Armoured Cars.

I.Z.L. believe that Arabs have been officially issued with PIATS by the British Army and they are endeavouring to obtain some. They also have 1,000 PIATS collected together either in Egypt or Italy but have not yet succeeded in arranging their removal to Palestine.

The largest training centre in Jerusalem, at Givat Shaul, was recently closed down.

The main explosive stores are in Tel Aviv or in the vicinity. Explosives are also held in districts.

The attempt by the I.Z.L. to sabotage a warship on 20th June last was frustrated by the Haganah. (Full details will follow in due course).

When the Railway was sabotaged in the Zichron area, three or four members arrived and put up in an hotel in Zichron as "convalescents".

Future targets:-

1) Central Prison, Jerusalem.
2) Unknown.

Arrangements to attack the Central Prison, Jerusalem, were planned a long time ago but lack of money prevented the attack being carried out. The release of certain prisoners there is vital to the I.Z.L.

Regarding No.2, plans are in process of being drawn up.

For the past two weeks, strengths of military and police forces at the Schneller, Allenby Barracks, Police Depot St. Andrew's Hostel, and all camps within one hour from Jerusalem, have been surveyed.

To carry out attack No. 2, the I.Z.L. hope to hold Jerusalem for two hours.

It is not certain whether acts 1 and 2 will be carried out simultaneously.

Appendix c – Report No. 2, October 28, 1946, Reinhold's
Statement of the IZL's Organization and Procedures

006 125

-2-

The monthly salary for a full time member of
the I.Z.L. is LP.30 with an average of an additional LP.30
expenses. Reznik pays the salaries and expenses. The
number of full time members of the I.Z.L. is not large.

Contact is made twice daily with I.Z.L. prisoners
in Central Prison , Jerusalem, and they are kept up to date.

Arms are available in large quantities from Arab
and British military sources. Shortage of funds only prevent their purchase at the present.

Foreign newspaper correspondents in Jerusalem
are contacted openly and requested to publish terrorist
acts as widely as possible.

The I.Z.L. and Stern Group are not subsidised by
any foreign power.

Reznik arranges blank Identity Cards which bear
correct dates and numbers, which indicates inside information and probably assistance from the Issuing Office.

The I.Z.L. are convinced that they will shortly
be chased by the Haganah and they are forming groups for
counter-action.

Haganah are collecting all available information
and are chiefly active in Haifa.

No Fighting Group member of the I.Z.L. is supposed
to know more than 6 or 7 other persons. All are known by
nick-names. They are verbally informed when and where to
attend meetings. Jerusalem meetings are usually held in the
rooms of Zev and Reznik. Code words and signs with newspapers
and books are used when meeting on the streets. No member
waits at a rendezvous more than five minutes. Important
members receive messages through Post Office boxes. Reznik
has a private Post Office Box which is the principal one in
Jerusalem.

The description of a Jew who has now taken up a
full job with the I.Z.L. is as follows:

Height 5'6" - 5'7"; very powerful build; a very
good boxer; 30-32 years of age; not very well
educated; Sephardic Jew; formerly worked in the
Survey Department in Jerusalem in a minor position,
and may still be so employed.

The leader for Northern Palestine lives on the roof
of No.36 Herzl Street, Haifa. He is known as Eliezer. 5'9"
in height, blonde, stronger than medium build, 26 or 27 years
of age, Rumanian or Hungarian nationality. He has a full
time job.

The son of Dr. Repnor in Jerusalem is definitely
I.Z.L. and probably a member of the Fighting Group.

I.Z.L. are now manufacturing limpet bombs, similar
to W.D. issue except that cardboard will be used instead of
bakelite. Magnets in manual telephones and in possession
of the Telephone Department, will be acquired for these limpets.

*Appendix C – Report No. 2, October 28, 1946, Reinhold's
Statement of the IZL's Organization and Procedures*

Report No.2   **29.10.46.**

The I.Z.L. is organised in three sections
as follows:

    1) Fighting Group (HOG)
    2) Propaganda Group (HOTAM)
    3) Intelligence Group.

      (a) Internal (observing movements of members).
      (b) Outside - for collection of material from
          enemy sources.

The strength of Group 1 in Jerusalem is 150.

Group 2 is by far the strongest and numbers are
being increased by persons now coming from the middle and
upper classes.

All three groups have increased in strength during
recent months.

Fighting Group considered not very good regarding
knowledge of military operations. Most of their successes
have been achieved through the following reasons:-

    1) Daring
    2) Surprise
    3) Weakness displayed by the defenders, among
       Police and Military.

Acts of sabotage are very well planned but before
being put into operation they must be approved by the Commander in Tel Aviv.

Contact is made between Jerusalem and Tel Aviv
daily by hand. Messages are in code - which is frequently
changed - and Reznik holds the codes.

Only the person making the plan other than Reznik
and the Commander, are aware of the time and place acts are
to be carried out.

Two hours usually before the act is due to take
place messengers warn members of the Fighting Group who muster
at an assembly point where they are briefed and issued with
arms. Persons who bring the arms are not seen and are not
aware of what is taking place. When the act has been completed persons wait on the route of retreat and take over
the arms.

Immediately preceding a terrorist act all members
of the I.Z.L. known to the Police are removed from the towns
concerned.

The I.Z.L. is not now co-operating with the Stern
Group. The Stern Group do not wish to co-operate, but the
I.Z.L. do in order to avoid bloodshed as far as possible.

The I.Z.L. are now in extreme financial difficulties
which is seriously handicapping their plans. They have a
large sum of money in U.S.A. but are unable to obtain same.
Money must be obtained immediately for which they will probably take bigger risks.

*Appendix C – Report No. 2, October 28, 1946, Reinhold's
Statement of the IZL's Organization and Procedures*

-4-

JERUSALEM   Surgeon who stands by in actions is Dr. Hepner Bezalal St. opposite Beth Hanna Olot.   Cars used in Jerusalem 4 seater Opel black either 5602 or 6502 was in Tel Aviv yesterday.

Tel Aviv cars one six seater light blue No.7062 but believed to have been sold last week was licenced. Another black car six seater not licenced No.60 or 80 something still in their possession.   The man who drives the Jerusalem car is very important.   Description 586 cms stocky build mechanic, wears blue overalls. 23-24.

Chief storekeeper of arms in Palestine lives in Tel Aviv, address unknown but name ex-Lt. Kaplan of Jewish Brigade (3rd btn) 5' 10", blonde, big blonde moustache, English appearance - 28.

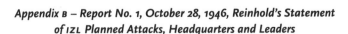

Appendix B – Report No. 1, October 28, 1946, Reinhold's Statement of IZL Planned Attacks, Headquarters and Leaders

-3-

there. He is not so very important but the room is
used for weekly group commanders meetings. This man
participated in the attack on the Haifa junction box
attack. Description 5' 8" or 9" - Sephardic Jew, black
hair and curly - age 24 or 25, medium build.

A religious Jew with curls and a girl were
arrested in Givat Shaul about a month ago. They were
both released but both were members of the fighting
command.

The girl lives in King George Street house beside bus station 5a (the first station coming from Jaffa
Street). The man took part in the attack on the train
near Ras El Ain when all passengers were taken off.

In Jerusalem there is a shirt factory called
"Hanna" Mahne Yehuda Quarter - first street on right of
Jaffa Street behind market. This factory which is only
a shop is used as a post No.3 by the IZL. The letter may
be found on the right hand side as you enter behind a
shelf. No.3 box receives letters addressed to Gideon.
I don't know where are post office boxes 1 and 2.

Tel Aviv. Dizengoff Street 146 basement used as tactical
headquarters. Always occupied by at least 3 but usually
occupied by 7 or 8 immediately after an action. An important man who used to live there has now moved - he
comes from Safad. There are 3 people living there now.

Another important place is in Yehuda Levy Street
or it may be the Mikveh Street in the Post Office side of
the Railway - in the street leading to the Citrus building.
The house is called passage "Goldin" it has entrances in
2 streets and several escape routes. A very important
member lives in this place with his parents who are very
rich. 5' 10" black wavy hair, thin, 26-27 years of age,
nice type of man. This man is the most important man I
know - all plans made in the country must be vetted by him.
I don't know his name. I know him as 'Gideon'.

HAIFA is the smallest place Hahalutz Street 48, entrance
to room by staircase leading around the house. Occupied by
a girl from Safad named Kallach.

PETAH TIQVA Man in charge is ex-sergeant major Cohen, M.M.
and several other medals formerly in Commandos in Abyssinia
and Western Desert - a very brave man. I think he is well-
known but I can point put where he lives on the map. I know
that arms were drawn from the Talmudic School there. I can
point the place out on a map. Petah Tiqva is the main
training centre.

NAHARIA A man known as Micki is in charge. He lives in
the north. Take the first turning on the right past the
cinema - go to the end - turn left and he lives in the
first or second house on the left-hand side. 5' 7", stocky
build, nearly bald, 35 or 37, rides bicycle. Hungarian I
think.

SAFAD Samuel Perl is believed to be the commander. It
is not a hard fact, but I guess it is true.

*Appendix B – Report No. 1, October 28, 1946, Reinhold's Statement
of IZL Planned Attacks, Headquarters and Leaders*

-2-

immediately the safety pin is removed. The chemical ignitor is usually timed for 30 minutes, but if not exact, it can go off earlier or later - we have had cases where a charge timed for 30 minutes went off in 3 to 4 hours. I emphasize that if the drum is moved it will explode immediately. The drum at the Haifa Railway Station was all explosives used during recent weeks were of the same type. Instructions have been given that warnings must be given in advance to the occupants of the buildings. It is possible that now I have disappeared, the plans may be changed. I don't know who is taking charge of the attacks 2 and 3, but I imagine that "Gideon" will take charge of one. I don't know his name, but he lives in Mahne Yehuda Quarter, in Agrippa Street at the corner near the Waller hospital. He is a Sephardice Jew. I guess he can be recognised by the cashier or the manager of the Nablus Bank, he was in charge of the attack there. He is about 24/25 years of age - 5'7" dark, medium build, wavy hair, clean shaven, no special marks. Speaks fluent Arabic. Attack on the Railway Station is to be under the command of a German Jew named "Yanai". Further particulars unknown. All I can say about arms is that in Jerusalem Givat Shaoul Quarter contains 2 or more arms caches. (I will draw a plan as the streets have no name).

Headquarters of the I.Z.L.

I have to draw a plan of the Kyriath Shmuel quarter. It is in the vicinity of a building which I am not sure is still occupied by the military or not. They have vacated it about 2 weeks ago. It is directly opposite - and it may have been vacated 3 weeks ago. This building now appears to be closed and shuttered. Personnel moving into this building in Police uniform can easily watch the I.Z.L. Headquarters. I suggest that this building is occupied at the earliest possible moment. I don't know the name of the military building but it has stories - it is a villa. The IZL Headquarters has 3 stories. The Headquarters is in a basement - there are 2 parts - one is a flat which is occupied by an old German couple. IZL place consists of one room only. The old Germans are innocent.

The IZL place is occupied by one man permanently and sometimes 2 - by night only. The permanent man is named Reznik - formerly in the Jewish Brigade - he is from Haifa. He might have a false identity card. Height 5' 6" thin black smooth hair more than thirty maybe 32 clean shaven usually wears a grey woollen pullover fastened with buttons down the front. There is a second bed which may be used by any important member and at present the second man is probably the area commander as this place is not in the curfew area. I don't know his name but his nickname is "Avinoam" Reznik is the secretary to the area commander. Description of the area commander 5' 9" broad well dressed not good looking but good eyes and smart looking clean shaven and is from a well known family - name not known. He has been in Jerusalem for more than a year. The IZL place is used for meetings of higher ranks mostly between the hours of 4 pm and 7 pm. There is another place, it is a room in Mihor Baruch Quarter Yohanan Hasandelar Street, the last house on the right side - there are no numbers - the street is a cul de sac - it has a dead end. I will draw a plan. First room on left side of yard. A man named "Zev" lives

Appendix B – Report No. 1, October 28, 1946, Reinhold's Statement of IZL Planned Attacks, Headquarters and Leaders

Report No. 1   28.10.46.

I will commence with three attacks which are
planned to take place this week - they will probably
take place on Tuesday or Wednesday, I would have
known definitely except for the curfew last night.

1st Target   Jerusalem Railway Station.

The attack will take place at 7 a.m. 11 a.m.
or 3 p.m. facilitated by passengers trying to board the
train. 7 men will draw up in a car coming from German
Colony facing Montefiore quarters. 2 men and a woman
will alight armed with pistols take possession of
station building, followed by 2 men carrying 3 suitcases
with explosives which will be placed in the booking
office. 2 other men will remain with the car - one
armed with a Sten gun and the other with a pistol - they
will cover the retreat of the others and possibly engage
guards stationed on the balcony of the Government Printing Press. Car will be kept running. Retreat via
Montefiore quarters (I mean the old one) where arms will
be taken by people awaiting attackers.

2nd Target.   The times of attacks 2 and 3 will coincide
                    with attack No. 1.

2 cars or I should say one car and a small lorry
of the delivery van type will be stolen in the usual manner 2 hours before the attack. The car will distribute
people covering the retreat whose position will be 2 Sten
guns road leading to Damascus Gate. 2 Sten Guns road
leading down to Mamillah. People will have Mills grenades
and "69" grenades. The latter do no damage but make a
loud noise. One will carry three people who will enter
building and hold up clerks and any members of the public
present, followed by 2 others carrying a drum which will
be placed in the central hall above the staircase. I
mean to say that they will mount the steps. The engine of
the car will be kept running with the driver carrying a
Sten Gun, and a girl for first aid purposes. No plan has
been made for the retreat and the dispersal of attackers
is to be made individually and on their own initiative -
mingling with any members of the public if possible.
They will endeavour to retain possession of their arms,
but will throw them away if necessary.

3rd Target.   Fingerprint Department C.I.D.

I am unable to give you any particulars of
this attack, but it will take place at the same time
and place as Nos 1 and 2.

These attacks would have already been carried
out except for elections. The drum will be placed in
the municipality and the cases to be placed in the railway
station will be initiated immediately chemically and will
blow up if moved. The latter is put into operation

Appendix B – Report No. 1, October 28, 1946, Reinhold's Statement
of IZL Planned Attacks, Headquarters and Leaders

40206/PS

C.I.D. HEADQUARTERS
JERUSALEM.

TOP SECRET

December, 1946.

Assistant Inspector General
Criminal Investigation Dept.

On 18th September, 1946 District C.I.D.
Haifa reported that information had been received
that ▮▮▮▮▮▮▮▮▮▮▮▮ an expert in the use of
explosives had led the attack on the King David
Hotel in July of this year.

2. Enquiries instituted by C.I.D. Headquarters resulted in the following particulars
concerning ▮▮▮▮▮▮ being obtained.

3. He was born in Berlin in 1916, entered
Palestine in 1934, joined the Palestine Police,
resigned in 1942 and enlisted in H.M. Forces;
he was discharged in May, 1946 and obtained
employment in the NAAFI. He gave his address
as 91 Herzl Street, Haifa but was not traced at
that address nor at addresses in Tel Aviv and
Jerusalem where he was known to have previously
resided.

4. His description was obtained and circulated
to all Districts and on 26th October, 1946 he was
traced and arrested at Haifa by District C.I.D.

5. Under interrogation by A.S.P., C.I.D.
Haifa he made a statement in the course of which
he provided information regarding the organisation,
activities and certain active members of the Irgun
Zvai Leumi.

6. At Appendix I is a summary of information
based on that provided by subject regarding the
organisation of IZL; at Appendix II is a summary
of information regarding activities and targets
planned by IZL; at Appendix III is a summary of
information regarding persons named by subject
as active members of IZL and at appendix IV is
a list of IZL meeting-places etc. given by subject.

(J. O'Sullivan)
Assistant Superintendent of Police
C.I.D.

Appendix A – Cover Page, CID Report on Heinrich Reinhold, December 6, 1946

APPENDIX

The CID Report on
Heinrich Reinhold (Yanai)
and the IZL

to those used by the W.D. but with cardboard in
place of bakelite are being manufactured with a
view to use against A.F.Vs etc and magnets from
manual telephone sets are being acquired for the
purpose.   The IZL has acquired 1,000 Piat guns in
either Egypt or Italy and is endeavouring to bring
them to Palestine.   The main explosive stores are
in Tel Aviv but other stores are maintained in the
Districts.   Arms and explosives are transported
concealed in rags etc. and are tied to the chassis
of motor vehicles.

8.   Training is carried out in open country, in
colonies and in the towns.   The principle training
area is in Petah Tiqva;   the principle training area
for Jerusalem was in Givat Shaul but this has now
been changed.

9.   Security is good and plans for operations
are made by the local commander with the cooperation
only of his second-in-command of secretary;   the
completed plan is then submitted to the Commander in
Tel Aviv;   contact is made daily between Jerusalem
and Tel Aviv. and probably elsewhere, by a messenger
who delivers coded messages.   Regular contact is
also maintained with the leaders in Central Prison,
Jerusalem.

10.   When a plan is approved messengers are sent
warning members of the fighting Group concerned.
usually two hours before the operation is to commence,
to muster at one assembly point. sometimes a school
or park, where they are briefed and issued with arms.

11.   A route of retreat is included in the plan and
after the operation a party awaits the return of the
attackers on the route to relieve them of their arms.

12.   No member of the fighting Group normally knows
more than six other members and all are known to each
other by aliases.   Members are informed verbally of
places and times of meetings.   Newspapers and books
are used as signals for street meetings and no member
waits at a RV more than five minutes.   Commanders
receive messages through Post Office boxes.

13.   Early this year the IZL decided to sabotage
British Embassies and Consulates abroad, particularly
in France, Italy, America, Egypt and Syria and members
of the IZL left Palestine to organise groups.   A
strong group has already been raised in Italy and
another in France.   Plans have also been made to carry
out sabotage in the United Kingdom and an attempt will
definitely be made to do so.

14.   There is a shortage of funds at present although
there is a large sum of money available in America but
it has not been possible to acquire this and desperate
efforts will be made to obtain funds by violence in
the near future.   All large merchants contribute. not
necessarily voluntarily. to IZL.   Expenses are approximately £ 4,000 per month.   IZL is not financed by any
foreign power.   Compensation is paid to Jews who suffer
injury or damage due to IZL activity.

....3/

Appendix E – Appendix I to CID Report, "Organisation of the Irgun Zvai Leumi"

15.   All IZL propaganda publications are printed
in Tel Aviv and distributed by messengers, most of
whom are men.   Special "communiques" are typed in
Jerusalem for distribution to foreign correspondents
who receive them at the Eden Hotel and are requested
to give them wide publicity.

16.   The Hagana is collecting information regarding
the IZL and the latter is convinced that it will be
attacked by the Hagana in the near future and is forming groups for counter-action.

17.   The IZL would temporarily cease terrorist
activity if the Government permitted 100,000 Jews
to enter Palestine but would resume activity against
the land restrictions immediately the immigrants
had arrived and Hagana and LHI would probably do
likewise.

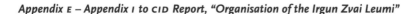

Appendix E – Appendix I to CID Report, "Organisation of the Irgun Zvai Leumi"

40206/PS   APPENDIX II

LIST OF TARGETS PLANNED BY IZL
FOR SABOTAGE

1. Jerusalem Municipality offices.

2. Finger Print Department, C.I.D. Headquarters.

3. Central Prison, Jerusalem with a view to
   release of prisoners.

4. Military Offices, Schneller Building, Jerusalem.

5. Allenby Barracks, Jerusalem.

6. Police Depot, Mount Scopus.

7. St. Andrew's Hostel, Jerusalem.

8. All Military Camps.

9. C.R.L. Haifa, glider-borne attack contemplated.

10. Palestine Railways, after close of citrus
    season.

11. The Military Court, Jerusalem.

Appendix F – Appendix II to CID Report, "List of Targets Planned by IZL for Sabotage"

40206/PS   APPENDIX III

MEMBERS OF IZL ARRESTED AND SOUGHT
AS RESULT OF INFORMATION PROVIDED.

---

1. Daniel AZULAI.   Took part in attack on Jerusalem
   Railway Station on 30th October, 1946 and was
   wounded in an encounter with Police immediately
   afterwards and subsequently arrested in Yemin
   Moshe Quarter. 2 grenades and a gelignite bomb
   found near the scene, were believed to have been
   abandoned by him.   Now in custody awaiting
   trial by Military Court.

2. Masoud BUTON. Description was given by informant
   on 29th October, 1946 as person who had recently
   joined IZL for full time activity.   Took part
   in Jerusalem Railway Station on 30th October,
   1946 and was arrested by military when endeavouring to
   escape.   Now in custody awaiting trial by Military
   Court.   (41112/PS)

3. Edwin CHOMER.   Identical with person described by
   informant as deputy-commander of IZL in Jerusalem.
   Description obtained and circulated. Now believed
   in Egypt. / Placed an Special List.
                              (41319/PS)

4. Mina COHEN.   Identical with a person described by
   informant as an active member of IZL who had taken part
   in armed attack on train at Ras el Ain.   Now
   detained under D(E)R 111 at Bethlehem.
                              (38173/PS)

5. Naftali Zvi COHEN.   Identical with a person described
   by informant as an active member of IZL who had taken part
   in armed attack on train at Ras el Ain.   Now detained
   under D(E)R 111 at Latrun.
                              (41158/PS)

6. Ex-Sgt.Maj. COHEN, described by informant as leader
   of the IZL in Petah Tiqva. Description obtained
   and circulated; not yet traced.
                              (28798/PS)

7. Meir FEINSTEIN, took part in attack on Jerusalem
   Railway Station on 30th October, 1946 and was
   wounded in an encounter with Police immediately
   afterwards and subsequently arrested in the Yemen
   Moshe Quarter and was found to be in possession
   of 6 rounds of .45 ammunition.   Now in custody
   awaiting trial by Military Court.
                              (41553/PS)

*Appendix G – Appendix III to CID Report, "Members of IZL
Arrested and Sought as Result of Information Provided"*

- 6 -

8. Nehamia FISHBEIN, arrested at 146 Disengoff Street,
   Tel Aviv described by informant as an IZL
   Headquarters and where a quantity of IZL documents were seized by Police. Believed to be
   an important member of IZL. Now detained
   under D(E)R 111. (41084/PS)

                   well-known
9. Ernst HEPNER, /doctor, a Revisionist politician,
   anti-British; reported by informant to stand by
   during terrorist attacks and provide secret treatment
   for wounded terrorists. He was arrested after
   Jerusalem Railway Station incident on 30th October,
   1946 and his attitude, and that of his advocate,
   left no doubt as to his knowledge of the reasons
   for his arrest. He has since been released to
   supervision under D(E)R 110.
                        (41175/PS)

10. Menachem HEPNER, son of Dr. Hepner; described by
    informant as member of Fighting Group of IZL.
    Arrested and now detained under D(E)R 111.
                   (30322/PS).

11. Moshe HOROWITZ, took part in attack on Jerusalem
    Railway Station on 30th October, 1946. was shot
    by military when endeavouring to escape custody
    and when searched was found to be in possession
    of a gelignite bomb. Now in custody awaiting
    trial by Military Court.
                   41089/PS)

12. Shlomo KALLACH, identical with a person of same
    surname reported by informant to be active member
    of IZL and to have recently left an IZL Head-
    quarters in Tel Aviv. Arrested at 48 Hechalutz
    Street, Haifa where informant had reported an
    IZL Headquarters was located. Now detained
    under D(E)R 111. Identified by informant as one
    of the leaders of the attack on Ottoman Bank,
    Jaffa in which two persons were murdered.
                   (41052/PS)

13. Sarah KALLACH, arrested in company of Shlomo KALLACH
    and found in possession of incriminating documents.
    Now detained under D(E)R 111.
                   (41057/PS)

14. Ex-Lieut. KAPLAN-PAJLWSKI, described by informant
    as chief armourer of IZL in Palestine. Partic-
    ulars and description obtained and circulated;
    has absconded from address in Tel Aviv and is now
    reported to be in Safad.
                   (41112/PS)

15. Yehuda KATZ, now remanded in custody following attack
    on Ottoman Bank, Jaffa, and charged with murder,
    identified by informant as leader of attack.
                   (40504/PS)

                                          1...7/

Appendix G – Appendix III to CID Report, "Members of IZL
Arrested and Sought as Result of Information Provided"

16. Moshe LEVANI, described by informant under alias "Micki" as leader of IZL in Nahariya. Has absconded from previous address and now believed to be in Benjamina. Placed on Top Grade Wanted List. (41148/PS)

17. Pina LEVY, answers description of woman known to have taken part in series of IZL outrages, believed to be woman who deposited explosives at Jerusalem Railway Station on 30th October, 1946. Arrested immediately after that incident when assisting Meir FEINSTEIN to escape. Now detained under D(E)R 111. (41047/PS)

18. Rivka MEDALION, found in same room as Sarah and Shlomo KALACH at 48 Hechalutz Street, Haifa; her handbag was found to contain IZL literature. C.I.D. Haifa subsequently received confirmation from an A2 source that subject was a member of IZL. She was arrested and is now detained under D(E)R 111 at Bethlehem. (41050/PS)

19. Itzhak MENACHEM, occupant of room at Yochanan Hasandler Street, Jerusalem which was reported to be an IZL headquarters, answers description of "Zev" described by informant as active member of IZL and at time of arrest, 4 a.m., appeared to be about to leave house. Now detained under D(E)R 111. (41160/PS)

20. Shmuel NOVACKI, arrested at 146 Dizengoff Street, Tel Aviv, described by informant as an IZL Headquarters and where a quantity of IZL documents were seized by Police. Believed to be an important member of IZL. Now detained under D(E)R 111. (41083/PS)

21. Shmuel PERL, a suspected member of IZL since 1942 and a supervisee under D(E)R 110 now reported by informant to be leader of IZL in Safad. Arrested and detained under D(E)R 111 at Latrun. (25201/PS)

22. Haim REZNIK, described by informant as secretary to IZL commander in Jerusalem, very important. Description and photograph obtained and circulated. Has absconded from previous address in Jerusalem. (41,054/PS)

23. Itzak TEPLITSKY, occupant of room at 36 Herzl Street, Haifa, described by informant as an IZL Headquarters. Search of premises in presence of Teplitsky revealed quantity of IZL documents; believed to be leader of IZL in Northern Palestine. Now detained under D(E)R 111. (41069/PS)

Appendix G – Appendix III to CID Report, "Members of IZL Arrested and Sought as Result of Information Provided"

40206/PS   APPENDIX IV

LIST OF IZL HEADQUARTERS AND
MEETING PLACES

1. House in Kiriat Shmuel, Jerusalem, basement used
   as residence by a leader and as a meeting place.
   Raided by Police, occupant absconded, documents
   seized.

2. House at Yochanan Hasandler Street, Jerusalem, room
   used as residence by a leader and as a meeting
   place. Raided by Police, suspect arrested.

3. "Hanna" Shirt factory, Mahne Yehuda Quarter, Jerusalem used as accommodation address by leaders.
   Under Police observation.

4. Room at 146 Dizengoff Street, Tel Aviv, headquarters
   of IZL, occupied by three men. Raided by Police,
   3 suspects arrested.

5. House at Golden Lane, Tel Aviv occupied by very
   important leader. Raided by Police, suspect
   not traced, now under observation.

6. Room at 48 Hechaluts Street, Haifa, occupied by
   2 important leaders. Raided by Police, 3 suspects
   arrested.

7. Talmudic School, Petah Tiqva, arms distribution
   centre. Raided by Police, no result.

8. Room at 36 Herzl Street, Haifa occupied by important
   leader. Raided by Police, 2 suspects arrested.

9. Arms dump at Givat Shaul. Raided by Police, large
   quantity of arms and ammunition seized. 1 suspect
   arrested.

Appendix H – Appendix IV to CID Report, "List of IZL Headquarters and Meeting Places"

INDEX